THE CAMBRIDGE COMPANION TO
LIBERALISM

The political philosophy of liberalism was first formulated during the Enlightenment in response to the growth of the modern nation-state and its authority and power over the individuals living within its boundaries. Liberalism is now the dominant ideology in the Western world, but it covers a broad swathe of different (and sometimes rival) ideas and traditions and its essential features can be hard to define. *The Cambridge Companion to Liberalism* offers a rich and accessible exploration of liberalism as a body of political thought. It includes chapters on the historical development of liberalism, its normative foundations, and its core philosophical concepts, as well as a survey of liberal approaches and responses to a range of important topics including freedom, equality, toleration, religion, and nationalism. The volume will be valuable for students and scholars in political philosophy, political theory, and the history of political thought.

STEVEN WALL is Professor of Philosophy at the University of Arizona. He has published widely on topics in contemporary political philosophy. He is the author of *Liberalism, Perfectionism and Restraint* (1998), co-editor (with George Klosko) of *Perfectionism and Neutrality: Essays in Liberal Theory* (2003) and (with David Sobel) of *Reasons for Action* (2009).

Continued at the back of the book

The Cambridge Companion to
LIBERALISM

Edited by

Steven Wall
University of Arizona

CAMBRIDGE
UNIVERSITY PRESS

CAMBRIDGE
UNIVERSITY PRESS

University Printing House, Cambridge CB2 8BS, United Kingdom

One Liberty Plaza, 20th Floor, New York, NY 10006, USA

477 Williamstown Road, Port Melbourne, VIC 3207, Australia

314-321, 3rd Floor, Plot 3, Splendor Forum, Jasola District Centre, New Delhi - 110025, India

79 Anson Road, #06-04/06, Singapore 079906

Cambridge University Press is part of the University of Cambridge.

It furthers the University's mission by disseminating knowledge in the pursuit of education, learning and research at the highest international levels of excellence.

www.cambridge.org
Information on this title: www.cambridge.org/9781107439412

First published 2015

A catalogue record for this publication is available from the British Library

ISBN 978-1-107-08007-2 Hardback
ISBN 978-1-107-43941-2 Paperback

CONTENTS

v

CONTRIBUTORS

RICHARD ARNESON is Distinguished Professor of Philosophy at the University of California at San Diego, where he has taught since 1973, and a sometime Visiting Research Professor at the University of Arizona. He has published widely in ethics and political philosophy.

MARK E. BUTTON is Associate Professor in the Department of Political Science at the University of Utah. His primary field of research is political theory, focusing on the history of political thought, ethics, and deliberative democracy. He is the author of *Contract, Culture, and Citizenship: Transformative Liberalism from Hobbes to Rawls* (2008).

THOMAS CHRISTIANO is Professor of Philosophy and Law at the University of Arizona, where he is co-director of the Center for Law and Philosophy. He is the author of two books in democratic theory: *The Rule of the Many* (1996) and *The Constitution of Equality* (2008).

JOHN CHRISTMAN is Professor of Philosophy, Political Science, and Women's Studies at Penn State University. He is the author of *The Politics of Persons: Individual Autonomy and Socio-Historical Selves* (2011), and has published widely on issues related to autonomy, liberty, and political philosophy.

ANDREW JASON COHEN is Associate Professor of Philosophy at Georgia State University, where he is also a faculty affiliate of the Jean Bear Blumenfeld Center for Ethics. He is the author of *Toleration* (2014).

PHILIP COOK is Lecturer in the School of Social and Political Science at the University of Edinburgh. He is a co-editor of *Res*

Publica. His research is primarily on contractualism, with particular interest in the moral and political status of children.

GERALD F. GAUS is the James E. Rogers Professor of Philosophy at the University of Arizona, where he directs the Program in Philosophy, Politics, Economics and Law. He is the author of *Justificatory Liberalism* (1996) and *The Order of Public Reason* (2011).

JEREMY JENNINGS is Professor of Political Theory at King's College London. He was a founding editor of the *European Journal of Political Theory*, and he is the author of *Revolution and the Republic: A History of Political Thought in France* (2011).

PAUL KELLY is Professor of Political Theory at The London School of Economics. He is the author of *Utilitarianism and Distributive Justice* (1990), *Multiculturalism Reconsidered* (2003), and *Liberalism* (2004). He is a past editor of *Political Studies* and *Utilitas*.

FRANK LOVETT is Associate Professor in the Department of Political Science at Washington University in Saint Louis. His primary research concerns the role of freedom and domination in developing theories of justice, equality, and the rule of law. He is the author of *A General Theory of Domination and Justice* (2010).

ALAN RYAN is the former warden of New College, Oxford. He has taught political theory at Oxford and Princeton since 1969. He is the author of *The Philosophy of John Stuart Mill* (1970), *John Dewey and the High Tide of American Liberalism* (1995), the *The Making of Modern Liberalism* (2012), and *On Politics* (2012).

JOHN SKORUPSKI is Professor of Moral Philosophy at the University of St. Andrews. He is the author of *Ethical Explorations* (1999) and *The Domain of Reasons* (2010).

JOHN TOMASI teaches political philosophy at Brown University, where he is the founder and director of the Political Theory Project. He is the author of *Liberalism Beyond Justice* (2001) and *Free Market Fairness* (2012).

JEPPE VON PLATZ is Assistant Professor in the Department of Philosophy at Suffolk University.

STEVEN WALL is Professor of Philosophy at the University of Arizona, where he is also a member of the Center for the Philosophy of Freedom. He is the author of *Liberalism, Perfectionism and Restraint* (1998) and co-editor of *Perfectionism and Neutrality: Essays in Liberal Theory* (2003).

DANIEL WEINSTOCK is the James McGill Professor in the Faculty of Law at McGill University. He has written extensively on a wide range of issues in political philosophy, including democratic theory, multiculturalism, and global justice.

NICHOLAS WOLTERSTORFF has taught at Yale since 1989. He was Noah Porter Professor of Philosophical Theology until 2002. He is the author of *Reason Within the Bounds of Religion* (1988) and *Justice: Rights and Wrongs* (2010) and co-author (with Robert Audi) of *Religion in the Public Square: The Place of Religious Convictions in Political Debate* (1996).

LINDA M.G. ZERILLI is the Charles E. Merriam Distinguished Service Professor of Political Science at the University of Chicago, where she is Faculty Director of the Center for the Study of Gender and Sexuality. She is the author of *Signifying Woman: Culture and Chaos in Rousseau, Burke, and Mill* (1994) and *Feminism and the Abyss of Freedom* (2005).

ACKNOWLEDGMENTS

This volume has taken a number of years to bring to completion. Thanks first are due to the contributors for their chapters and for their patience. Chandran Kukathas began this project as a co-editor, but was unable to complete it with me. His help at the initial stages, in selecting topics and contributors, was invaluable. David Schmidtz and the Center for the Philosophy of Freedom at the University of Arizona provided financial support for the project, for which I am grateful. Finally, I thank Hilary Gaskin for inviting me to undertake this volume and for her guidance and help in moving it forward.

Introduction

Liberalism resists easy description. Whether it refers to a political ideology or to a political philosophy, it covers a broad swathe of ideas. The swathe of ideas it covers is so broad, in fact, that efforts to identify its essential and distinctive features almost always come off as hopelessly narrow. For example, in the 1980s it was fashionable for political theorists to propose that liberals, unlike conservatives and radicals, are committed to the idea that the state should be neutral between contested conceptions of the good life.[1] However, this proposal in one fell swoop excludes Mill, Tocqueville, Hobhouse, Green, and many other influential members of the liberal camp. Rather than identifying a single unifying commitment, others have sought, more promisingly, to pick out family resemblance characteristics to zone in on the target.[2] But once again, the exercise looks ill-fated. True, the more characteristics that are picked out, the less restrictive the resulting characterization of liberalism becomes, but, at the same time, the broadened characterization makes it harder to view liberalism as a distinctive tradition of thought, one that differs in deep and informative ways from rival political traditions such as conservatism or republicanism. It might be advisable, then, to speak of multiple liberal political traditions rather than a single political tradition of liberalism. Or perhaps liberalism should be understood as a single political tradition, but one that is not very unified, encompassing a variety of rival strands of thought. What can be said with confidence is that liberalism is a label that attaches both to a history of a fairly diverse set of political movements, and to the ideas and arguments associated with those movements, and to an ongoing research program in contemporary political philosophy.

This volume introduces readers both to this history and to this research program. It certainly does not purport to be comprehensive.

Any volume of this size on a topic as expansive as liberalism must be selective. The historical periods and topics discussed here reflect the predilections and interests of the editor.[3] In selecting topics and contributors, I hope to convey the diversity and vitality of liberalism, but also to bring into view some of its blind spots.

FREEDOM AND PROGRESS

Liberal political movements and the thinkers who have supported those movements have engaged in a wide variety of political causes. As one commentator has put it, "the history of liberalism is a history of opposition to assorted tyrannies."[4] Liberals have fought against religious persecution in favor of toleration, against caste hierarchy and privilege in favor of meritocracy and social mobility, against arbitrary rule in favor of the rule of the law, and against totalitarian regimes in favor of limited government. These and other political causes have aimed to secure the freedom of individuals to lead their lives on their own terms and in free association with others as well as to expand the scope of those entitled to this freedom. Can we say, accordingly, that a strong commitment to individual freedom is at least a minimal unifying commitment of liberal political thought and liberal political philosophy?

Perhaps we can. Liberals do characteristically champion the cause of freedom. And it is certainly true that liberals very much tend to embrace individualism in the sense that they hold that the claims of individual persons, as opposed to social collectivities, are morally primary. But if this commitment to individual freedom is indeed a unifying feature of liberalism, then it is neither straightforward nor very informative. If we are told only that someone is strongly committed to individual freedom, we do not know too much about his politics. This is to be expected. Like other political and moral concepts, freedom is a contested ideal. It can be characterized in manifold ways, and liberal political thinkers have disagreed, often quite sharply, over how it is best understood. To take some important examples: Liberals have debated whether liberty is best construed in terms of rights and negative freedoms, or instead as a positive ideal of autonomy requiring access to a wide range of options. They have disagreed over the relationship, if any, between living in a free state and being a free individual. And while some liberals have held that freedom is valuable as such, many have insisted that it is only a set of important or basic freedoms that really matter.

Furthermore, even if all liberals are strongly committed to individual freedom on some understanding of that protean value, very few liberal thinkers have thought that liberty is the only political value. Other values, such as equality or democracy or community, have also been associated with liberalism; and different liberal thinkers have disagreed over both the significance of these other values and their relationship to individual freedom. Not surprisingly, these differences continue to be reflected in contemporary philosophical work on liberalism. It is not uncommon, for example, for critics to charge that in venerating individual freedom liberals ignore or give insufficient weight to other concerns. Thus, socialist critics of liberalism hold that liberals too easily sacrifice equality to liberty, and communitarian critics have long objected that the common good is neglected in a liberal society. Liberal writers respond either by asserting the primacy of individual freedom over these rival values or by contending that the values do not really conflict, but are complementary.

Finally, liberal political thinkers disagree over which institutions best advance the values that they share. Almost all liberals embrace constitutional government. They contend that governments, including democratic governments, can become tyrannical and that limits on government are necessary to secure the freedom of individual people. In addition, almost all liberals affirm the institutions that make possible free speech and free inquiry, at least concerning subjects that are, in Locke's words, of "maximal concernment" to the individual. Beyond these commitments there is little agreement on institutions, however. Within the tradition, or traditions, of liberalism, we get different answers to these questions, for example: Does democratic government, and the associated idea of majority rule, safeguard or threaten individual liberty? Is the capitalist market an essential component of a free society, or does it allow the rich to dominate the poor, thereby undermining their freedom? And is a freedom-promoting political order one that centralizes power so that local tyrannies can be disrupted or one that decentralizes power so that the bureaucratic state does not absorb into itself all space for experimentation and free association?

Different answers to these questions will seem more or less plausible in different times and places. The liberal commitment to individual freedom cannot on its own provide much guidance in answering them. Of much greater importance are the threats to individual freedom that the liberal perceives and responds to; and since these threats come from different quarters, it is no real wonder that liberal thinkers have supported different institutional arrangements to combat them.

The liberal commitment to individual freedom, however, is related to another commitment that many have taken to be central to liberalism, one that does help to distinguish it from some other political traditions of thought, particularly earlier traditions of political thought. This is the commitment to human progress. While there are anticipations of liberal ideas in ancient and medieval political thought, liberalism is widely, and correctly, viewed as a modern development. It is the offspring of the Enlightenment, and it bears the marks of its birth. Enlightenment thinkers very much believed in human progress, and it is characteristic of liberal Enlightenment thinkers to believe that freedom and progress go together.

How exactly might freedom of the individual and the progress of the species go together in the mind of the liberal? Various answers to this question can be given. In a perceptive essay on the nature of liberalism, Jeremy Waldron provides a particularly insightful one. "The Enlightenment," Waldron observes, "was characterized by a burgeoning confidence in the human ability to make sense of the world, to grasp its regularities and fundamental principles, to predict its future, and to manipulate its powers for the benefit of mankind."[5] This optimism, in turn, had a political dimension.

Society should be a transparent order, in the sense that its workings and principles should be well known and available for public apprehension and scrutiny. People should know and understand the reasons for the basic distribution of wealth, power, authority, and freedom. Society should not be shrouded in mystery, and its workings should not have to depend on mythology, mystification, or a "noble lie."

In short, if human beings can grasp the rational order in the world as the Enlightenment promised, then this order can be explained to them. The limits on their freedom need be neither arbitrary nor inexplicable. Once this thought is granted and gains currency, then each individual, as a rational agent, is in a position to demand that the restrictions on his freedom be justified to him.

In retrospect, the Enlightenment confidence in human reason can look quaint. It was often excessive. But it took different forms, and some expressions of this confidence were more plausible than others. A major divide within liberalism is reflected in the differences between the Scottish and French wings of the Enlightenment. The French, and to a lesser extent the Germans, tended to be rationalistic, stressing the power of the human mind to design a rational political and social order, whereas the Scots tended to emphasize the limits of human reason and the need to learn from experience.[6] Still, the Scots, like the French, remained optimistic about the prospect that human beings would use new scientific advances, including advances in economic and political science, to improve their political and social lives. Hayek, the steadfast critic of constructivist rationalism and twentieth-century heir to the Scottish Enlightenment tradition, was himself a firm believer in progress, albeit a cautious one. As he saw matters, human beings have used advances in knowledge to improve their societies, and they can be expected to continue to do so in the future. However, to make progress they must use the knowledge they can acquire "not to shape the results as the craftsman shapes his handiwork, but rather to cultivate a growth by providing the appropriate environment, in the manner in which a gardener does for his plants."[7]

Not infrequently, critics of liberalism on both the left and the right seize on this commitment to progress and the universalism that goes with it. Liberals, the critics charge, misrepresent the particular as universal. They present their ideals as rationally mandatory, ideals to which all of humankind must aspire.[8] In reality, however, liberalism is merely the "official ideology of the western world."[9] In pressing this objection, the critics are heirs to an important and powerful anti- or Counter-Enlightenment current (or currents) of thought.[10] The anti-universalist criticism concerns the status of liberal values and ideals. In thinking about it, it is fair to ask, could not one accept wholesale the Counter-Enlightenment critique of liberal universalism and yet remain steadfastly committed to liberal politics? Many examples suggest an affirmative answer, of which Richard Rorty's "postmodernist bourgeois liberalism" is perhaps the best known. But possibility and plausibility are not the same. On inspection, it may turn out that liberal politics must presuppose some commitment to universalism – some commitment to truth in politics – in order to make good sense of the demand that the distribution of power and freedom in a society should not be shrouded in mythology, mystification, or lies.[11]

The relationship between liberalism and the Enlightenment commitment to progress is, of course, more complex than these brief remarks suggest. Like Tocqueville, some liberals are not particularly sanguine about the future. Others, as indicated, are skeptical of universal claims. The view ventured here concerns general tendencies of thought within liberalism. The suggestion is that these tendencies are significant enough to make it plausible to associate liberalism with them. More often than not, critics of human progress and of the possibility of universal values are critics of liberalism.

THEORY AND PRACTICE

Philosophers typically characterize liberalism in terms of certain ideals and values, such as freedom or equal concern or toleration, but liberalism does not refer only to these ideas. It has a history in practice, one that is enacted by liberal political movements and by liberal political societies. This volume does not attempt to trace this history. As mentioned, it is very selective, focusing on only a few historical developments.

The relationship between liberalism as a theory of politics and liberalism as it has been enacted in practice is complex and contested. There is very often a gap between liberal ideals and liberal practice. And this raises the interesting issue of whether liberalism should be identified with its ideals or with its practice. To take an example, it is sometimes said of liberalism in America that, with respect to race, it has repeatedly failed to live up to its own ideals. In tension with this claim, it is also often said that American liberalism itself is defective, that it contains internal contradictions, and that these contradictions are exposed by its treatment of race. Or to take another example, consider the status of women in liberal societies. Feminist critics sometimes reject liberalism because, as they see it, liberal societies have failed to bring about equality between the sexes. Others claim that this failure is merely a failure of these societies, not any failure of liberalism as such.

No resolution of this issue can be defended here. However, two observations are in order. First, as a general matter, it is a mistake to reject liberalism because of defects or failures associated with one of its contingent manifestations. The defects and failures of a particular liberal society often tell us more about that society than about liberalism. Second, if it is a characteristic, even if not an essential, feature of liberal societies that they generate certain maladies, then it becomes more plausible to view this feature as a defect of liberalism. If every attempt, or almost every attempt, to put some ideal into practice results in disaster, then the defensive response that this merely reveals a failure of the societies, but no failure in the ideal, will ring hollow.

To illustrate this second observation, it is helpful to consider briefly the relationship between liberalism, on the one hand, and private property and commercial society, on the other. (This relationship is surveyed by Jeremy Jennings in his contribution to this volume.) As indicated earlier, liberal thinkers have had very different views about the desirability of modern capitalism. The divide between classical liberalism and the modern liberalism that emerged in the middle of the nineteenth century and blossomed in the twentieth century pivots on this very issue. The classical liberals viewed the economic liberties associated with private property and contract as essential components of what Adam Smith termed "the natural system of liberty," whereas the modern liberals viewed capitalism, particularly laissez-faire capitalism, with great suspicion, seeing it as a threat to, not an institutional realization of, individual freedom. Still, modern liberals, while distrustful of capitalism, were not inclined to reject it outright. They did not recommend that we abandon the market and replace it with centralized economic planning, for example.

The modern liberals, like the classical liberals, accepted the legitimacy of private property, including private property in productive assets, and they were not, in general, hostile to commerce. Moreover, and more to the point at hand, liberal societies have always been commercial societies. And commerce and the institutions that facilitate it, such as private property, free trade, and the free movement of people, often have been thought to generate social pathologies. Commercial societies, we have been told, produce "possessive individualists" who erode valuable community and who lack a concern for the public good. These societies also generate high levels of material inequality. These are familiar complaints. Our present concern is not to evaluate their truth, but to consider their implications for an assessment of liberalism. If the complaints were true, would this show a defect in liberalism or merely a defect in liberal practice? To think about this question, consider a character we might call the *pure liberal*. The pure liberal holds that liberalism is not committed to any social and political practices at all. Any institutional structure may fail to serve liberal values, and the structures that the liberal should support depend solely on how well they serve liberal values in this or that circumstance. The pure liberal may come to reject all of the institutions typically associated with liberal practice. If constitutional government, democracy, or markets generate social pathologies, then these institutions may need to be reformed. Thus, the pure liberal could come to reject liberal institutions because of his or her commitment to liberal values. (To be sure, the pure liberal may believe that the values that liberal institutions serve are more important than the social pathologies they generate. If so, then he or she will have to acknowledge that liberal institutions come at a price; and, to that extent at least, the critics of liberalism are right.) We can think of John Stuart Mill as a paradigm pure liberal. He took an experimentalist approach to institutional design, assessing institutions in terms of their propensity to advance the interests of "man understood as a progressive being." Markets and private property in time may need to be replaced with some form of socialism. Democratic government may need to be supplemented in various ways so that the "instructed classes" have sufficient influence on public affairs. And colonialism and imperialism may have their place in advancing the cause of human progress and freedom.

In contrast to the pure liberal, most liberals have believed that certain institutions, such as the market or constitutional democracy, are not merely instruments for advancing liberal values, but integral components of the liberal ideal. For them, the study of liberal practice – the study of how the institutions and practices associated with liberal politics actually function – is crucial to an assessment of liberalism. If markets do indeed generate too much material inequality, then this is a strike against liberalism. If commercial societies characteristically erode community and encourage destructive self-seeking in social life, then this too is a strike against the view. Retreating from liberal institutions to liberal ideals is not an option for those who define liberalism, in part, in terms of its institutions.

It remains open to liberals of this unpure kind to contend that the social maladies associated with liberal institutions result from nonideal circumstances. The problem, they can argue, is not with the institutions as such, but rather with the conditions under which the institutions operate. However, this maneuver comes at a steep price, especially if the imagined ideal conditions are far removed from actual conditions. The liberal now may have to concede that liberal institutions do not work well in the world as we know it.

These reflections on the relationship between theory and practice in liberalism underscore the significance of liberalism's history to its contemporary claim to acceptance as a normative theory of politics. A study of its practice, as revealed in various historical moments, may also help us to distinguish between institutions and practices that are not integral to liberalism, but were appropriate for a given time and place, and those institutions that have a stronger claim to be part and parcel of the liberal ideal.

FOUNDATIONS

I have been emphasizing the diversity of liberal political thought and practice. Debates in contemporary political philosophy over the best understanding or best conception of liberalism reflect this diversity. Rival liberal theories build on different normative foundations. The difference in foundations, in turn, is reflected in different understandings of the nature of liberalism. The claim that the essence of liberalism is the commitment to state neutrality with respect to conceptions of the good life, while not plausible as a general characterization of liberalism, is much more plausible as a characterization of some important strands of liberalism, for example.

At the cost of some distortion in the service of theoretical tidiness, one can distinguish three broad approaches to providing normative foundations for liberal politics. These are, respectively, natural rights, social contract, and consequentialist approaches. In the early modern period in which liberalism first emerged, the appeal to natural rights was the dominant approach. Natural rights were taken to provide the rational grounding for a political order that secured individual liberties against absolutist rule. Thinkers like Grotius and Locke employed the state of nature construct to articulate the pre-political rights and duties of individuals. These rights and duties, in turn, were understood to place strong limits on the authority of political rulers.

To contemporary ears, the notion of natural rights can sound rather suspect. "[T]he truth is plain: there are no such rights, and belief in them is one with belief in witches and in unicorns."[12] For Grotius and Locke, the natural law, from which natural rights and duties could be derived, had a lawmaker. Take that lawmaker away, the thought goes, and there is no natural law. The foundation of natural rights collapses in a disenchanted world.

Despite its currency, this quick refutation of natural rights liberalism is hardly persuasive. Philosophers who defend a natural rights approach to politics do not need theological premises. An appeal to natural law can be construed as an appeal to the objectivity of morality. Anyone who is not committed to some version of relativism or subjectivism about morals can pursue the natural rights approach to justifying liberalism. And indeed Locke himself, as scholars have pointed out, often appealed to secular considerations in justifying the natural law. His defense of natural law and natural rights, while incomplete, was overdetermined.[13]

The most influential contemporary statement of natural rights liberalism is Robert Nozick's *Anarchy, State, and Utopia*. This book opens with a ringing sentence. "Individuals have rights, and there are things no person or group may do to them (without violating their rights)." As critics noted, Nozick did not provide a moral basis for the rights he assumed. He sought to make progress at the superstructural level, while leaving work on the foundations for another time. But Nozick's practice in this regard is pretty unexceptional. Much work in deontological ethics proceeds in exactly the same manner, first proposing general principles about rights and entitlements and then proceeding to work out their implications. Commentators on natural rights theories often forget that argumentative support for rights claims can take different forms. It does not have to proceed in foundationalist mode, drawing inferences from normative bedrock. The natural rights approach to defending liberalism needs both the superstructural argumentation of the sort that Nozick provided and the deeper work that connects rights to their underlying moral basis. Since both of these enterprises are respectable enterprises in contemporary philosophy, natural rights liberalism remains a viable and important approach to defending liberalism.

Social contract theory emerged in lockstep with natural rights liberalism. The device of the state of nature, or some variant of it, is fundamental to social contract theory. And natural rights liberals, as mentioned, employed this device to articulate the content of natural rights. However, there is a fundamental difference between the social contract and natural rights approaches to grounding liberalism, one that comes into clear view only in contemporary versions of social contract theory. To explain: On the natural rights picture, the social contract is a contract between individuals, who are taken to have pre-political rights, and their rulers.[14] Rulers are entrusted with authority to safeguard the natural rights of those individuals. By contrast, contemporary social contract theorists employ the device of the social contract to fix the content of the rights. Put differently, for the natural rights liberal, rights are not constructed by a social contract. Political authority, not principles of right, is the object of agreement in the contract. But for the contemporary social contract theorist, rights and entitlements fall out of the contract. The object of agreement in the contract is a set of principles of justice, which in turn fix the claims and entitlements of citizens.

Contemporary social contract theorists, unlike natural rights liberals, are thus constructivists about justice and rights. The theorists divide into two broad camps: contractarian and contractualist. Contractarians present the social contract as an agreement between rationally self-interested bargainers. In doing so, they follow Hobbes. The rights and entitlements of citizens are fixed by the principles of justice that self-interested bargainers would converge on. Prominent contemporary contractarians include David Gauthier and James Buchanan. Contractualists, by contrast, present the social contract as an agreement between morally motivated contractors. In doing so, they follow Kant. The rights and entitlements of citizens are fixed by principles that no one, with the appropriate moral motivation, could reasonably reject. Prominent contemporary contractualists include T. M. Scanlon and Brian Barry.

The most famous contemporary social contract liberal is, of course, John Rawls. Rawls's approach to the social contract straddles the divide between contractarianism and contractualism. In line with contractarianism, the parties to his original position are mutually disinterested. But, in line with contractualism, the design of the original position reflects moral assumptions. Rawls viewed the social contract as a heuristic. It is, he said, "a device of representation," one that "models what we regard (here and now) as reasonable restrictions on reasons that may be used in arguing for principles of justice to regulate the basic structure" of a society. As these remarks suggest, there is an intimate link between the social contract approach to justifying liberalism and the ideal of publicity. This ideal is expressed in Rawls's own account of public reason. Inspired by Rawls's work, discussions of public reason and public justification, as several chapters in this volume attest, have come to play a large role in contemporary philosophical discussions of liberalism. Proponents of social contract theory, and the attendant notion of public reason, often advertise it as a fitting response to the deep pluralism of modern democratic societies. They insist that if fully reasonable citizens fundamentally disagree over the nature of the human good or the meaning of life, then these issues must be bracketed in order to construct a shared account of public reason. In response, critics of liberal public reason frequently object that the shared public reason constructed by social contract theorists is not genuinely impartial. By effect, if not by design, it favors some conceptions of the good life over others.

The merits of this critique cannot be assessed here, but it can be said that social contract theory does not provide the only possible response to the deep pluralism of modern societies. Different responses have been developed by other liberal writers. Some writers contend that toleration, not public reason, is the key liberal idea. Rather than seeking to construct a shared account of public reason for large and diverse modern states, these writers propose a different model, one that seeks to break these states down by decentralizing political power. This model allows different groups of people to live under different rules and arrangements in different territories. The model remains liberal by ensuring that individuals have a right to exit from any arrangement to which they are subject. The result is a tolerant framework, even if different groups aggressively promote their own way of life within the boundaries created by the framework.[15]

This toleration-centered model of liberalism is congruent with natural rights liberalism, since the right to exit can be construed as a fundamental natural right. A different response to the pluralism of modern societies invokes the value of personal autonomy. Discussing it brings us to the third, and more consequentialist, approach to defending liberalism. This consequentialist approach has it roots in nineteenth-century England, where liberalism and utilitarianism were deeply intertwined. Jeremy Bentham and James Mill, as well as other Philosophic Radicals, proposed and defended liberal reforms by appeal to a utilitarian calculus of pleasure and pain. Liberalism was defended on the grounds that it was the political view that, if institutionalized, would increase aggregate welfare, where welfare was understood in hedonic terms. The marriage of liberalism and utilitarianism is a fragile one, however. Utilitarian political morality is aggregative, and it values individual liberty only insofar as it promotes welfare. For these reasons, utilitarianism came to be seen by many as an anti-liberal doctrine, one that, in Rawls's memorable words, fails to take seriously "the separateness of persons."

A secure consequentialist defense of liberalism must move beyond simple utilitarianism. John Stuart Mill, in his efforts to improve upon Bentham's view, took a decisive step in this direction. An essential element of human welfare, he argued, is individuality. Individuality involves both personal autonomy and self-development. For Mill human welfare thus has a perfectionist dimension. We live well only if we freely develop our talents and human powers. By building individuality into an account of human welfare, Mill forged a tight link between utilitarian political morality and individual liberty. To promote welfare, political and social institutions must secure the freedom that is necessary for the expression of individuality.

It is likely, however, that an adequate consequentialist defense of liberalism must go much further than Mill went in breaking with utilitarianism. For even if Mill's view about human welfare is accepted, his account of political morality remains aggregative. In principle, the liberty of some may be sacrificed for the common good of the society. In itself, this is not objectionable, but the worry is that the utilitarian underpinning of Mill's liberalism will sanction restrictions on individual liberty that no liberal could accept. Mill thought that he could ground his commitment to liberty by appealing only to the Principle of Utility, so long as that principle was properly understood. But most commentators have reached the conclusion that his project had to fail. The circle cannot be squared. Liberalism and utilitarianism are contingent allies, at best.

Utilitarians, and consequentialists generally, have tended to favor doctrines of maximization. Applied to politics, an institution, practice, or policy is right if and only if it maximizes aggregate value or expected aggregate value. Doctrines of maximization, in turn, tend to assume that the value of different alternatives (and the consequences or expected consequences of adopting those alternatives) are fully rationally comparable. The combination of the doctrine of maximization and the strong assumption of value comparability yield the aggregative character of the resulting view of political morality, and it is this aggregative character that looks to be incompatible with the strong liberal commitment to individual freedom. Might there be a defense of liberalism, then, that is consequentialist insofar as it holds that political institutions should be judged in terms of their promotion of human well-being, but anti-consequentialist insofar as it rejects the doctrine of maximization and the strong assumption of value comparability? This possibility is realized in the perfectionist liberalism of Joseph Raz.[16] Like Mill, Raz holds that freedom is an important aspect of human well-being.[17] But, unlike Mill, he makes a clean break with the value monism of the utilitarian tradition. Affirming the doctrine of value pluralism, and emphasizing the presence of widespread and significant incommensurabilities in our understanding of the value of the different options made available to us by our social forms and conventions, Raz articulated a version of consequentialist political morality[18] that was free of the aggregative character that seemed to be in fundamental tension with liberalism. He thus showed how liberalism could be put on a firm foundation with no mention of natural rights or a social contract.

In surveying these different foundations for liberalism, I have wanted to underscore the simple fact that there is not a canonical understanding of liberalism in contemporary political philosophy. Political philosophers and theorists reach liberal political conclusions from many different starting points, and how they understand the nature of liberalism – what is fundamental to it and what is of merely derivative significance – is shaped by their starting points. The diversity of approaches to liberalism's foundations thus complicates the discussion of how liberalism relates to topics such as religion, democracy, multiculturalism, or nationalism. Contributors to this volume have wrestled with this complication, often opting to focus on certain strands of liberal thought rather than seeking to provide a comprehensive guide to how liberals have addressed the topic in question.

CHALLENGES

Liberalism is not without its detractors. I have already mentioned the Counter-Enlightenment critique of liberalism. This is a searching critique, but it is often very unclear what alternative to liberal politics these critics have in mind. Less radical critics of liberalism seek to retrieve values or ideals that liberalism, or so the critics charge, has downplayed or obscured. The communitarian critique of liberalism that raged in the 1980s often took this form. The liberal concern with individual rights, it was said, foreclosed the possibility of genuine community. Liberals celebrated individualism at the expense of civic virtue and a shared common good. But it soon emerged that the communitarian critique was not as sharp-edged as it first seemed. Many communitarian writers made it plain that they sought to combine communitarian concerns with liberal values. They proposed a liberal communitarianism rather than a rejection of liberalism.[19]

The same may be said of the more recent revival of republican or neo-Roman political thought. Republican writers charge that liberalism has an impoverished view of individual liberty, one that construes it in terms of noninterference. They propose an alternative view of freedom, one that has been dubbed "freedom as nondomination,"[20] and they claim that liberal writers have failed to appreciate how being subject to arbitrary power, as opposed to being interfered with in various ways, can curtail individual freedom. The republican critique looks powerful when Hobbes and Bentham are taken to be the representatives of the liberal view, but if Locke, Mill, Hayek, or Raz are counted as liberals, as surely they must, then the divide between the republican and liberal view of freedom looks much less sharp. Contemporary republicans propose not so much a rejection of liberalism, but a republican form of liberalism.[21]

Feminism presents a rather more complicated challenge to liberalism. As Linda M. G. Zerilli observes in her contribution to this volume, "feminism and liberalism have a complex and fraught history." Many feminists celebrate liberalism and view the struggle to achieve gender equality as a natural extension of liberal ideals of freedom and equality. But many others view liberalism with suspicion. Liberal writers have often stressed the importance of draw-ing a distinction between the public and private spheres of life, with the family then assigned to the private sphere. Feminists charge that this distinction hides from view forms of power and inequality that women experience on a daily bias. Only by supplanting the liberal public/private distinction can feminism achieve its goals.[22] A still more fundamental feminist critique of liberalism takes aim at the liberal ideal of freedom. As I have explained, liberals understand freedom in various ways, but most believe that individuals should be left free to make their own choices and decisions about how to lead their lives, so long as they respect the rights of others to do the same. Drawing on insights from Marxism and critical theory, some femi-nists maintain that liberalism does not have the resources to combat forms of oppression that are in part self-imposed. Male oppression may induce forms of delusion and false consciousness that both limit the freedom of women and can be expected to perdure even under well-functioning liberal institutions.

There is no chapter in this volume on socialism, and this omission requires brief comment. For most of the twentieth century, social-ism, and especially Marxist socialism, represented the major alter-native to liberal politics. The political thought of Popper and Hayek, and to a lesser extent Berlin, is animated by the felt need to respond to the socialist challenge. But socialism challenged liberalism primarily by challenging its institutions, both political and economic. Socialist ideals were not in fundamental tension with liberal ideals, or at least liberal ideals as these were understood by modern social democratic liberals. The collapse of socialism as a viable institutional alternative to liberalism thus robbed socialism of much of its critical edge. The most acute socialist critics of liberalism have reconceived them-selves as radical liberals, liberals who press for a more thoroughgoing egalitarianism than the mainstream view.[23]

Contemporary republican, feminist, and socialist critics of liberal-ism present themselves as offering a more radical critique of existing institutions than the liberal is comfortable with, often by invoking ideals, such as freedom and equality, that liberals themselves accept. But liberalism is also challenged by defenders of tradition and estab-lished practice. Critiquing the ideological style of politics, in which liberal writers engage and the pure liberal mentioned above exempli-fies, the conservative critic views liberal ideology as an impoverished abridgement from traditional practice. The mark of the liberal, as well as his republican, feminist, and socialist critics, is to substitute abstract and inflexible political ideals – a rule book conception of politics – for the fluid and adaptable understanding of political experience that comes from a mastery of the traditions of behavior that have given rise to those ideals.[24] This kind of conservative thus seeks to defend political practice, including the political practice of liberal societies, from the abstract philosophical systems of men and women of principle. But another kind of conservative critic engages directly with the philosophical presuppositions of liberal political thought. As John Skorupski explains in the concluding chapter of this volume, there is a form of conservatism "that sees continuity, community, tradition and hierarchy as organic elements of a good society, and gives broad philosophical grounds for doing so." This conservative critic may or may not support liberal politics in practice, but he challenges the key tenets of philosophical liberalism – its commitment to individualism, its belief in the equal self-governing capacity of human beings, and its optimism with regard to the consequences of free thought and discussion. As a philosophical critic, this conservative presents a far more radical challenge to liberalism than the republican, feminist, and socialist views surveyed here.

NOTES

1. Dworkin, "Liberalism"; Ackerman, *Social Justice in the Liberal State*.
2. Gray, *Liberalism*.
3. As noted in the Acknowledgments, Chandran Kukathas assisted me in selecting topics and authors for the volume.
4. Ryan, "Liberalism," p. 28.
5. Waldron, "Theoretical Foundations of Liberalism," p. 43.
6. See Hayek, "The Errors of Constructivism."
7. Hayek, "The Pretence of Knowledge," p. 34.
8. See MacIntyre, *After Virtue*.
9. Scruton, *The Meaning of Conservatism*, p. 192.
10. See Berlin, "The Counter-Enlightenment."
11. For a subtle exploration of this point, see Williams, *Truth and Truthfulness*, esp. ch. 9.
12. MacIntyre, *After Virtue*, p. 69.
13. See Simmons, *The Lockean Theory of Rights*, chs. 1 and 2.

14. Hobbes and Rousseau construe the social contract as one in which individuals transfer all, or nearly all, their pre-political liberties to the sovereign. By so doing, they advance nonliberal versions of social contract theory.

15. See Kukathas, *The Liberal Archipelago* and Otsuka, *Libertarianism Without Inequality*, ch. 5.

16. Raz, *The Morality of Freedom*.

17. Two qualifications are in order. (1) Personal autonomy, for Raz, is not the same ideal as Mill's individuality, although both ideals are intended to explain the value of individual liberty. (2) Raz holds that personal autonomy is an important aspect of well-being, not for humans generally, but for those who live in modern societies.

18. Since Raz's perfectionist liberalism rejects many of the assumptions associated with consequentialism, it might be better described as consequentialist in an attenuated sense only. (See Raz, *The Morality of Freedom*, p. 266.) Still, unlike natural rights and social contract defenses of liberalism, Raz's liberalism is concerned primarily with the promotion of human well-being.

19. Taylor, "Cross-Purposes."

20. Pettit, *Republicanism*.

21. Dagger, *Civic Virtues* and Pettit, *On the People's Terms*.

22. The public/private divide has been given a range of different formulations in liberal political thought, and some of these formulations are less vulnerable to feminist critique than others. For a good discussion of this issue, see Kymlicka, *Contemporary Political Philosophy*, pp. 247–62.

23. Cohen, *If You're an Egalitarian, How Come You're so Rich?*

24. Oakeshott, "Rationalism in Politics."

I   Historical perspectives

1 American liberalism from colonialism to the Civil War and beyond

With the benefit of hindsight, American liberalism can be understood as the story – at turns both epic and tragic – of a culturally diverse set of peoples striving to reconcile liberty with political authority under dynamic socio-historical conditions. But what liberty means precisely, which groups have an equal claim to the full panoply of human freedoms, and to what degree personal liberty depends upon or is imperiled by social and political institutions have been among the most contentious philosophical questions and enduring practical challenges for the incorporation and adaptation of liberal political philosophy in America. Balancing personal liberty with political union, and balancing political liberty with multidimensional pluralism remain the "unfinished work" of a nation "dedicated to the proposition that all men [sic] are created equal"[1] because that proposition and the commitment to test it in practice come up against a variety of complex internal-political questions as well as powerful opposing social currents that seek to contain or reverse the universalist aspirations of liberal egalitarianism.

American liberalism can also be understood as the cultural and political process of constituting Americans as liberals, of fashioning them – both discursively and juridically – as a people who are identifiable as a people by their attachments to the "self-evident truths" of the equal natural rights of all persons. While this process of self-definition is very much ongoing today, the "consensus" historiography that had once made it possible to simply equate a mature political liberalism with the "American Way of Life" has undergone significant challenges over the last half-century or more. Whereas earlier scholars[2] had conceived American national identity as inextricably (and at times irrationally) bound to a dogmatic liberalism from its point of origin – in the famous words of Tocqueville, Americans were "born equal" and thus did not, like their European counterparts, have to fight to become so – a more recent group of scholars have emphasized the importance of a variety of countervailing traditions operating within the formation of the American republic, including deeply illiberal ones like nativism, racism, and sexism.[3] These scholars have joined an already extensive group of historians who have highlighted the contributions of alternative (but not necessarily incompatible) philosophical discourses to Lockean liberalism within American political history, including Calvinism, radical Whiggism, civic republicanism, and Scottish moral sense philosophy.[4] While a growing number of scholars no longer view liberalism as the exclusive ideological core of American history or national identity, the very idea of American liberalism still excites interpretive battles among historians and contemporary political pundits alike. For their part, historians continue to debate the intellectual sources considered most responsible for shaping the origins and direction of American political development, with liberalism as one dominant strand within this complex history,[5] while writers both within and outside of the academy continue to contest the meaning, value, and propriety of a "liberalism" associated (since the Progressive and New Deal eras) with an activist state committed to various kinds of social and political reform.

One of the consequences of this interpretive diversity is that a considerable amount of confusion exists about the precise meaning and core intellectual and political priorities of American liberalism. Since liberalism in America has never been a singular or fixed ideology but a diverse family of ideas and practices, some of this confusion is both understandable and appropriate to the subject. In America liberalism has been a dissident's creed for individual rights against the trepidations of political power (including democratic majorities), and it has served as a public philosophy to mobilize social and political power in pursuit of greater equality and social justice. In a figure like Lincoln, both of these features of liberalism are joined together in evanescent union, albeit with enormous difficulty and intrinsic limitations. One of the additional consequences of this intellectual diversity is that American liberalism – as both an historical phenomenon and a contemporary political philosophy – has generated a plethora of critics who have variously charged it with, on the one hand, inflating the significance of individual reason and personal rights over the values of tradition, community, and public duty[6] and, on the other hand, failing to take individual rights of property seriously enough (a prominent critique from the political right), and underestimating the ethical and political significance of cultural pluralism and socioeconomic disparities (a prominent critique from the political left).[7]

Still, for all of its protean characteristics across a range of different historical contexts and in relation to a diversity of intellectual progenitors, liberalism in America (as elsewhere) has come to stand for something relatively stable: the freedom of individuals understood as rights-bearing persons with morally equal and "unalienable" claims to "life, liberty, and the pursuit of happiness." In accordance with this view, legitimate governments are conceived as the artificial creations of human beings and arise out of the consent of the governed in order "to secure these rights" for all (Declaration of Independence). It is therefore the right and the duty of free people to "alter or to abolish" those governments that fail to secure or actively undermine the equal pursuit of these specific ends, especially the natural right to property.[8] If these are the core premises of liberalism in America (with their obvious debts to the political philosophy of John Locke), then the American variant of liberalism is unique – if it is at all – not simply because it has jostled alongside a variety of alternative philosophical idioms, but rather because American liberalism contained within its origins and historical unfolding the very antithesis of its core commitment to the equal liberty of man: chattel slavery based on race. Just as there is no United States without the forced removal and destruction of native peoples, the Constitutional legitimation of slavery (until 1865), and the exclusion of women from full civic membership (until 1920), there is no American liberalism without the persistent endeavor to define and redefine the meaning and practical scope of liberalism in the face of its numerous internal contradictions and outright disavowals.

With this basic thesis in mind, this chapter highlights four important stages within the historical formation of American liberalism. The first section provides a brief discussion of the colonial origins of the American republic, focusing on the meaning of liberty in this period and on the struggle for one of the central moral values of liberalism: religious toleration. Despite popular mythic constructions to the contrary, the Puritans in America were not liberals, but in many ways American liberalism took shape within and against the

religious and political backdrop that Puritan communities established in the seventeenth century. The next two sections of this
chapter turn to the revolutionary period and the Constitutional founding (respectively) where classical liberal ideals of natural rights
and free consent are utilized, first, to resist intrusive, capricious,
and unaccountable political power in the form of the British
Government (1763–76), and then (after a twelve-year experiment
with de-centralized political authority under the Articles of
Confederation), liberal principles of private rights (especially in property) are enlisted to create and defend a powerful federal government
(1787–89). The core meaning of liberty and its proper institutional
safeguards are the subject of fierce debate during the late eighteenth
century, but out of these battles one of America's greatest contributions to the history of liberalism is made in the pages of the *Federalist
Papers*. The final section provides a discussion of the relationship
between liberalism and racism/sexism in the nineteenth century as
both the denial of liberalism's moral and political premises and the
cultural and political context out of which the pursuit of a "new birth
of freedom" (Lincoln) repeatedly takes shape in American politics –
most dramatically in the period leading up to the Civil War, but also
in the post-reconstruction and civil rights era.

PRE-LIBERAL BEGINNINGS

If the ancient *polis* was a "moral community of men permanently
united as a people by a common way of life,"[9] then the Puritans in
America had more in common with ancient republicanism (or medieval corporatism) than they did with modern liberalism. The dissenting English Puritans who migrated to North America in the
seventeenth century placed the "care of the public" over the interests
of all "particular estates" and subordinated both the community and
the individual to the fulfillment of a divinely appointed mission to
purify the Christian commonwealth on earth.[10] These were communities, in places like Massachusetts Bay and New Haven, that
were "knit together" as one body through "the bond of love" for the
elect among them, and thus trucked neither religious diversity from
"false churches" (e.g., Quakers and Baptists) nor internal dissent from
so-called "antinomians" (e.g., Anne Hutchison and Roger Williams).
In the New England colonies of the seventeenth century, liberty

meant the freedom to be a godly Christian after the manner carefully defined and strictly regulated by civil and ecclesiastical laws. This was not natural liberty but "civil or federal liberty," as John Winthrop put it, "a liberty to that only which is good, just and honest." Far from being opposed to social hierarchy or political authority, "this liberty is maintained and exercised in a way of subjection to authority."[11] As a consequence of this conception of the substantive meaning of liberty and given the high stakes of fulfilling their "special commission" with God, religious toleration was not on the ethical horizon of American Puritanism. As Nathaniel Ward explained (casting his glance back across the Atlantic to a decadent England): "He that is willing to tolerate any religion, or discrepant religion, besides his own, unless it be in matters merely indifferent, either doubts of his own, or is not sincere in it."[12]

The primacy of social and religious cohesion over personal liberty meant that Puritanism shaped the development of liberal thinking in America by placing serious obstacles in the way of the meaningful exercise of freedom of conscience and toleration for religious diversity.[13] Yet Puritanism also had a positive influence on the development of liberal constitutionalism in America by enacting compacts and covenants that tied governmental authority to a principle of popular sovereignty through frequent elections and by enumerating the specific "liberties, immunities, and privileges" that free men held against both civil and church authorities.[14] The individualist dimensions of Protestant Christianity combined with congregationalist commitments to church government meant that the Northern colonies became laboratories for early experiments in voluntarist forms of collective self-governance rooted in the consent of the governed.[15] The covenant and compacts in accordance with which various settlements and cities were established and regulated throughout the seventeenth century were neither fully liberal nor democratic, but these compacts established a tradition of written constitutional forms generated through the consent (or rather the oaths) of the governed that would be a model for later political architects – especially for figures like John Adams during the revolutionary period in the eighteenth century.[16] While the historical narrative of a Puritan "declension" into individual yeoman farmers and self-interested economic actors during the demographic and economic transformations of the mid-eighteenth century captures part of the background story to

American liberalism,[17] the echoes of Puritanism reverberate within American politics any time the question arises as to how much commonality and shared moral unity is necessary or sufficient to secure social and political order with personal liberty.

LIBERTY AND AUTHORITY: FROM COLONIALISM TO REVOLUTION

Liberalism was one of the intellectual and cultural *products* of the revolutionary and Constitutional periods of American history, not an autonomous philosophical cause of those events. Neither liberalism nor civic republicanism were articulated as discrete or coherent political programs in 1776 or 1787; nor were these intellectual traditions (as we now think of them) understood as mutually antagonistic.[18] Instead, recognizable features of what scholars now identify as constitutive elements of a liberal political outlook on the relationship between the individual and society filtered into the writings, speeches, and sermons of this period alongside many other diverse philosophical idioms and traditions as various social actors sought to address two very practical questions with enormous social and political implications: how to justify resisting and ultimately dissolving pre-existing political authority among a people proud of their English Constitutional heritage and British identity, and how to establish new and more legitimate forms of political organization amid the diversity, passions, and conflicting political and economic interests that a newly independent America both embodied and energized.

To address the first question, we need to turn to the voluminous literature that was generated during the 1760s and 1770s in response to British imperial reforms in the economic governance of the colonies. Yet, even before the passage of revenue-raising measures like the Sugar Act (1764), the Stamp Act (1765), and the series of militaristic Coercive (or "Intolerable") Acts (1774), important philosophical groundwork was being laid within Puritan congregations that seemed to anticipate up-coming events. Jonathan Mayhew (1720–66) is particularly significant in this context because he combined widely accepted Christian beliefs in the divine source of all "higher powers" (Romans 13) with a Lockean commitment to the idea that the people must take responsibility as the ultimate judges of the justice and reasonableness of the exercise of political power.[19] Mayhew's sermon

"Concerning Unlimited Submission and Non-Resistance to the Higher Powers" (1750) looked back to the execution of Charles I one hundred years earlier and argued that, so far from being a sin, active resistance to habitually unjust rulers is consistent with the apostle's injunctions of subjection to power because the essential end of all civil government is the good of society. The failure to withdraw political allegiance and to resist unjust rulers is equal to joining civil authorities in "promoting slavery and misery" which, Mayhew reasoned, is contrary to the will of God.

Mayhew's reference to slavery was a theme that would be picked up and repeated numerous times in various pamphlets, broadsides, and sermons during the crisis years of the 1760s and 1770s. James Otis, John Adams, John Dickinson, and Thomas Jefferson all spoke to the idea that the rights to which the freemen in the colonies were entitled in virtue of the common law, the English Constitution, and the higher laws "of God and nature" meant little if these rights depended upon the mercy of others. They reasoned that where property (in the form of taxation) can be taken without consent, a basic liberty has been removed contrary to the "natural, inherent, and inseperable" rights of men, and under these circumstances individuals are reduced to a condition of slavery and subject to the arbitrary despotic rule of others.[20] From imperial writs of assistance, to duties on colonial imports and exports, to various restrictions on free trade, Jefferson discerned a "series of oppressions" that plainly proved "a deliberate, systematical plan of reducing [the inhabitants of British America] to slavery."[21] While it was rare for American colonists to consider how the scorn they placed on the inferior and dependent status of the political "slave" might reflect upon the condition of actual slaves in America,[22] this language pointed to the complex set of ideas about freedom that motivated American colonial resistance while also serving to designate the abject "other" to a budding revolutionary social consciousness. During the revolutionary and early founding period, there is no single or exclusive conception of freedom that dominates: it means personal liberty against government interference in relation to personal and economic pursuits (like trade), but it also carries a distinctly political meaning in the sense of participating in one's own self-governance.[23] Contrary to the recent tendency to distinguish republican freedom as concerned with collective non-domination and liberal freedom as restricted to "negative" rights of noninterference,[24] Americans in the revolutionary period combined these concerns into an account of freedom that ultimately stressed the importance of political self-determination[25] within the constraints set by a higher law theory of natural rights.

During the early stages of colonial resistance, the language of individual rights is initially articulated with reference to the common law and English tradition with as much frequency as the defense of rights as an expression of a philosophical belief in human nature as such. For example, as late as October 1774 the First Continental Congress asserted that the rights of English colonists in North America derive from the combined sources of "the immutable laws of nature, the principles of the English constitution, and [their] several charters or compacts." But as colonial resistance mounted with each new tax, mercantilist protection, and coercive act of the Crown and Parliament, the political rhetoric of dissenting Americans grew more recognizably liberal as it grew more radical. As Joyce Appleby has put it, "the American Revolution developed its revolutionary character not by redeeming the rights of Englishmen, but by denying English sovereignty and the conceptual order which tied liberty to the English constitution."[26] In this context, Thomas Paine's wildly popular contributions in The Crisis and Common Sense, with their unmerciful attacks on hereditary rule and rousing belief in the self-governing capabilities of masculine patriots, along with Jefferson's universal egalitarian language of natural rights, were critical in the process of galvanizing armed resistance in defense of both popular sovereignty and divinely bestowed rights to the pursuit of happiness.

If figures like Paine and Jefferson were merely conveying "the common sense" of the American mind on the question of Independence (as Jefferson would later claim), then Lockean principles of natural right, social contract, consent, and justified rebellion had seeped rather deeply into American consciousness by the summer of 1776.[27] Nonetheless, the presence of Tories loyal to the Crown, slaves rebelling from their masters, and women pleading for incorporation within the structures of political representation remind us that American liberalism lacked neither domestic philosophical opposition nor serious internal (logical) contradictions from its revolutionary point of origin.[28]

LIBERTY AND AUTHORITY: FROM
REVOLUTION TO UNION

The American Revolution was a colonial war fought not for liberalism but for independence and republican (popular) self-rule within the plural United States. It is frequently forgotten (or insufficiently considered) that the immediate effect of the Revolution – in political-constitutional terms – was a decentralized league of political confederation that treated each of the thirteen rebelling states like independent nation-states rather than equals within a collective political whole. The Articles of Confederation were fashioned by delegates from the thirteen states in 1777 (ratified in 1781) more as a "league of friendship" than a national government and explicitly affirmed that "each state retains its sovereignty, freedom, and independence." In the context of a purposely weak Continental Congress (with no executive branch, no judiciary, and no power to regulate commerce or collect taxes), real political power was located in the states and further dispersed throughout the legislatures of the various states. During this period (1776–87), constitution writing (and alteration) became a significant national pastime. Undergirding all of these state experiments in republican governance was the idea that personal freedom and the preservation of natural rights required the adoption of written frames of laws crafted and ratified by the men subject to them.[29] The newly independent states also gave careful attention to the framework of legislatures and sought to ensure the effective political participation of most white men in their own governance through frequent elections, limited terms of office, and by enlarging the size of representative assemblies and expanding suffrage. The Continental Congress and the thirteen states operated with a "delegate" model of representation that emphasized close lines of communication and accountability between officials and citizens as a means of preserving political freedom and securing social trust.[30]

The above points are important to establish as a means of appreciating the significant transformations that the eventual adoption of the new US Constitution (1788) would have on the nature of American liberalism. While Americans embodied the Lockean view that human liberty presupposed the existence of a known and shared legal order to provide reciprocal securities for the pursuit of diverse human interests, they also learned through repeated trial and error that established political powers posed significant threats to life, liberty, and the individual pursuit of economic prosperity. These lessons in the capriciousness and injustice of political power – whether in the form of colonial administrators, or later, with state legislatures under the Articles of Confederation – did as much to inform the political thinking of figures like Madison, Hamilton, and Wilson as did the political science they gleaned from Montesquieu, Blackstone, and Hume. In this context, Madison's recounting of the numerous "vices" of the Articles of Confederation raised a profound problem for all liberal republicans because it compelled them to ask whether "the fundamental principle of republican Government, that the majority who rule in such Governments, are the safest Guardians both of public Good and private rights?"[31] The turn to a more liberal political outlook on the relationship between the individual and the state is in part the product of taking this question seriously and seeking institutional remedies for the "mortal diseases" of republican rule. As Madison would argue in the *Federalist Papers* (1787), the aim of the new Constitution was to "combine the requisite stability and energy in government with the inviolable attention due to liberty and to the republican form."[32]

The institutional configuration most conducive to the preservation of personal liberty within the establishment of effective general governance is the central question at issue in the ratification debates that surround the proposed Constitution of 1787. The difference between Federalists and Anti-Federalists was not one between liberalism and republicanism but was rather a difference in the ways that the representatives of these opposing views on the proposed Constitution sought to balance republicanism and liberal principles within the organization of political power. In pushing for decentralized nodes of political power in the states and for closing the space between the government and the governed (as well as blurring the demographic characteristics between rulers and ruled), the Anti-Federalists sought to maximize local republican rule within liberal natural rights constraints. By contrast, the Federalists sought to maximize personal rights and the advantages of a commercial society within a republican frame stretched over an extended sphere incorporating a diversity of contending interests and opposing moral values.

Anti-Federalists like "Brutus" and the "Federal Farmer" saw the destruction of liberty behind every article of the Constitution that appeared to create a consolidated republic over a confederated one (taxation power, necessary and proper clause; supremacy clause, etc.) because they and other "Anti-Federalists" held a conception of freedom that was more oriented to an ideal of popular sovereignty and collective self-rule than was true of the Federalists. There was general agreement between the friends and opponents of the Constitution that an extended republic had to have a federal political form, but as the center of political authority shifted away from the more culturally homogenous social conditions within the states, the Anti-Federalists feared a general decline in the confidence and trust of the people in a distant and unrepresentative (i.e., aristocratic) government. The anticipated consequence of this more consolidated union, operated by a much smaller number of elite men, was that the federal government would have to rely upon "an armed force to execute the laws at the point of the bayonet – a government of all others the most to be dreaded."[33] (The suppression of the Whiskey Rebellion of 1794 would vindicate some of these fears.)

The Federalists and Anti-Federalists were united in their fear of tyranny – and in this restricted sense they participated in a shared English opposition ideology concerned with the encroachment and corruption of power – but far more significant was the fact that they each saw tyranny coming from very different sources. Whereas the Anti-Federalists saw tyranny arising from a distant and unrepresentative aristocratic few compelled to rely upon force to execute laws among a heterogeneous group of states, the Federalists saw tyranny arising from democratic energies mobilized from below by demagogues bent on economic leveling. The American Revolution had been a revolution in favor of liberty; what was needed now, according to the Federalists, was a "revolution in favor of government."[34] As Hamilton put it in the first of the *Federalist Papers*: "the vigor of government is essential to the security of liberty" and a "dangerous ambition more often lurks behind the specious mask of zeal for the rights of the people than under the forbidding appearance of zeal for the firmness and efficiency of government." For Hamilton the task of accepting these new truths would be fulfilled through an enlightened estimation of America's long-term interests in security and economic prosperity and from a candid account of human nature that stressed the passionate, short-sighted, and acquisitive features of human motivation as the "true springs of human conduct."[35]

One of the primary challenges for the Federalists was to simultaneously restrain majority passions in order to secure individual rights while remaining "strictly republican." As the Puritans had also found, social environments that are conducive to liberty also give rise to factions and pluralism, and for Madison and Hamilton the question was how to control some of the worst effects of factionalism – especially the erosion of private rights and the loss of trust in public administration – and to make personal freedom (the absence of interference) safe amid the plural sources that inevitably divide society into different and opposing interests and parties (sources like religion, unequal property, political opinions, etc.).[36] In adapting republican governance rooted in the sovereignty of the people to an extensive sphere constituted by polyglot and factious beings of acquisitive passions, the Federalists latched onto liberal institutional remedies (representation, circumscribed and separated governmental powers, checks and balances, etc.) for republican ills and shortcomings (popular parties and demagogues, elite corruption, lack of civic virtue, absence of a shared faith, etc.). These were "liberal" remedies insofar as they originated in and did not stray from a conception of individuals as equally entitled to liberty but also equally prone to pursue self-interest to the detriment of both the rights of others and the "aggregate public good." However, these liberal mechanisms were not offered as an alternative to but rather as a means of perfecting republican governance, even as they also insulated government from collective political participation.[37] According to Madison, the elected representatives of the American republic ("guardians ... selected by the people themselves") would be better able to discern the aggregate public good than the people themselves.[38] It is noteworthy that Madison did not ignore the importance of virtue – among rulers and ruled alike – for securing a government dedicated to the public good,[39] although it must also be conceded (consistent with the liberalism of "Publius") that very little was done to actively cultivate the virtues upon which republican governance was still thought to depend.[40]

In sum, the Federalists confronted the difficult challenge of supplying a national government with the requisite powers to coordinate the workings of an extensive commercial republic while sustaining the liberal commitment to a limited government of laws. One of the ironies of American liberal constitutionalism is that the most important set of constraints on governmental power in the eyes of most Americans – the Bill of Rights – was secured by those who lost the argument about the proper institutional setting for securing freedom within American politics (the Anti-Federalists), and those rights were adopted in large measure to safeguard the powers of states and localities, not to advance a national project of liberal individualism.[41] The frequent recurrence of anti-federalist ideology (from Jacksonian era democracy to contemporary conservative jurisprudence) alongside the gradual development of a liberal, individual rights frame of reference on the Bill of Rights (post-Civil War) strongly suggests that the contested question of the proper political framework for the preservation of freedom will long endure within American politics.

UNION, LIBERTY, AND DIFFERENCE: THE SECOND AMERICAN REVOLUTION

Almost immediately after the ratification of the US Constitution, significant cleavages arose among the Federalists about (among other things) the proper role of government in the economy and the wider society.[42] These divisions (on questions of debt, the national bank, and manufacturing) helped to spur the formation of the political party system and consolidated the basic ideological fault lines within American politics, even when political parties (like the Progressives) sought to surmount the party system altogether.[43] However, the fiercest battles in American history would be waged over the more fundamental question of who is included in the category of citizen.

In this context, the history of American liberalism must also be understood as the story of peoples (slaves, free blacks, native tribes, and women) – at best relegated to the margins of political society, and at worst turned into the human instruments of white male domination – tapping into their shared social agency to challenge their exclusion, exploitation, and humiliation in "the land of the free." In almost every instance of nineteenth-century social reform and civil rights politics, from David Walker's "Appeal to the Colored Citizens of the World" (1830), to Elizabeth Cady Stanton and the "Seneca Falls Declaration" (1848), to Frederick Douglass's speech concerning "The Meaning of July Fourth for the Negro" (1852), these actors militated for political and economic inclusion by utilizing the liberatory political ideals (and Christian moral beliefs) that had previously inspired America's revolutionary struggle against recalcitrant political power. For example, Douglass drew upon the patriotism and just pride that surrounded the commemoration ceremonies of the signing of the Declaration of Independence to exclaim that, "The existence of slavery in this country brands your republicanism as a sham, your humanity as a base pretense, and your Christianity as a lie."[44] The Seneca Falls Declaration that called for women's "sacred right to the elective franchise" was carefully crafted to mirror the Declaration of Independence in both substance and style: effectively undermining while correcting the false universalism of American liberalism. To be sure, there were significant conflicts internal to reform movements like abolition, as testified by the distance between William Lloyd Garrison's public burning of the Constitution as a "compact with the devil," and Douglass's championing of the Constitution as a "glorious liberty document." While united in the aspiration for equal freedom and human dignity, oppositional politics in nineteenth-century America did not follow a singular liberal script but moved between commitments to non-violent "moral suasion" (Angela Grimke, Lucretia Mott), complete disengagement from a corrupt political order (Garrison, Thoreau), to violent armed struggle against slave holders (Nat Turner, John Brown).

That liberalism in America has flourished with racial, ethnic, and gender hierarchies for most of its history is not simply a contradiction between high moral principles and everyday social practice; it also highlights the existence of powerful opposing commitments to sustaining white male superiority in multiple spheres of life (political, economic, domestic). "Inegalitarian ascriptive ideologies" that have simultaneously animated liberal politics while undermining the philosophical (logical) coherence of American liberalism include such things as biblical and scientific justifications for slavery and the removal of Native peoples, legal doctrines of female coverture, and principles like "republican motherhood."[45] These sets of beliefs in the natural inequality of people based on race, ethnicity, and gender were undergirded and further energized by prevailing economic relations and reasoned legal decisions. For example, broad economic reliance on slavery between Northern manufacturing interests and

Southern planters, Congressional decisions like the Kansas–Nebraska Act (1854), and Supreme Court rulings like *Dred Scott v. Sanford* (1857) all drew upon and further mobilized beliefs in innate black inferiority. In this setting, the constitutional theory of John Calhoun is also significant because it offers a defense of liberty that is presented as an improvement on the work of the Federalists in securing minority rights against the trepidations of democratic majorities (through mechanisms like nullification and concurrent majorities), while simultaneously providing even greater legal protections to the dominance of the white planter class in the South (although Calhoun does not explicitly name the institution of slavery).[46] Calhoun's arguments about a compacted federal union composed by the free participation of sovereign independent republics reveals (among other things) that the ideal of a liberal national union did not pass from the arguments and institutional arrangements of the Constitutional period into the culture of American society as Madison and Hamilton had hoped;[47] instead, the Civil War would become the event to make the theory of a liberal union practical.[48]

At the start of the Civil War, Abraham Lincoln posed a question to a special session of Congress that had also vexed James Madison prior to the Constitutional Convention in Philadelphia: "Is there, in all republics, this inherent, and fatal weakness? Must a government, of necessity, be too *strong* for the liberties of its own people, or too *weak* to maintain its own existence?"[49] In answering this question by means of coercive military force, Lincoln established the priority of the Union for the preservation of personal and political liberty while extending and more fully completing the liberatory promise of the American Revolution. Yet until he issued the meticulously crafted Emancipation Proclamation, Lincoln had long made it clear that while he opposed slavery as a "monstrous injustice," this did not mean interfering with the institution of slavery in the states where it existed, nor did it mean "contending for the establishment of political and social equality between the whites and blacks."[50] Until the last years of the war, racial differences constrained the practical scope of Lincoln's liberalism, but in consistently working to prevent the extension of slavery into new territories, he pushed for the equal liberty of all persons, irrespective of race, to reap the rewards of their free labor as a primary condition for recognizing their shared humanity.[51] Lincoln's free labor ideology mixed

Lockean themes about the natural rights of persons to the fruits of their own work together with a set of economic and moral beliefs about the broader conditions for national economic prosperity and personal independence.[52]

In "fully and fairly" conceding the institution of slavery where it existed (inclusive of the 1850 Fugitive Slave Act) but checking its "cancerous" growth westward and treating it as a moral wrong, Lincoln adopted an intricately balanced position that simultaneously alienated many in both the South and the North (receiving less than 40 percent of the popular vote in 1860). Yet Lincoln understood this stance as one consistent with a respect for the Constitution and the primacy of the Union along with the guiding natural rights philosophy of the Declaration of Independence, "the sheet anchor of American republicanism." Lincoln could be legalistic and pragmatic about chattel slavery in ways that incensed abolitionists in the North, but he also exhibited a firm belief in the idea that American politics has a moral dimension that can neither be sacrificed to economic interests nor reduced to the votes of democratic majorities.[53] The moral core of politics for Lincoln was essentially liberal and included the rights of life, liberty, and the pursuit of happiness, and the free consent of people in their own governance.

Judith Shklar has rightly argued that "until the Civil War amendments America was neither a liberal nor a democratic country, whatever its citizens might have believed."[54] Yet, with greater historical sensitivity to the reliance of American liberalism on the "racial contract"[55] and the "gender contract,"[56] and mindful of the string of broken promises that constituted postbellum reconstruction, we could also argue that America was neither a liberal nor a democratic country until the passage of the Civil Rights Act (1964) and the Voting Rights Act (1965), although it always had in place both the principles and the institutions to become a liberal democratic republic well before these more recent dates.

CONCLUSION

Liberalism in America was formed with great difficulty over several centuries of profound moral and political conflict. The construction of American liberalism took place against the persistent backdrop of its forceful rejection in the form of religious establishments, imperial and colonial hierarchies, and racial, ethnic, class, and gendered exclusions. To put the liberty of individuals and the pluralism of human associations first – as a philosophical conviction and an organizing political commitment – is something both historically rare and ethically more demanding than is often realized – even for the founders of the liberal tradition in American politics. The history of American liberalism provides multiple chapters for the confirmation of this baleful observation. Hence, for every properly canonized epic hero of American liberalism – John Adams, Thomas Jefferson, James Madison, and Abraham Lincoln – there are tragic heroes who still largely remain outside the dominant narrative frame of American liberalism – Angela Grimke, David Walker, Frederick Douglass, and W. E. B. Du Bois (to name only a few).

Across nearly all ideological and denominational lines, Americans revere their "founding fathers," but they remain uncertain about what to do with those immanent critics of American political history who have urged the republic to "rise up and live out the true meaning of its creed" (Martin Luther King, Jr.). Thus, if Americans have gradually come to accept a broad "liberal consensus" – granting reciprocal freedoms to all citizens, tolerating reasonable group differences, and providing for a limited state authorized and accountable to the people – this "consensus" has always been less wide and less deep, at almost every stage of the republic, than most Americans, past or present, might otherwise care to admit. For the questions of who is a citizen, what makes for legitimate group difference, and how much of a role the state should play in the society and the economy were quandaries that vexed Americans at the founding of the republic, and continue to define the basic contours of American politics to this day. But if American liberalism stands for anything that can be shared within and across these interminable differences, it is to sustain the liberal tradition as one of the primary conditions for coordinating these conflicts in a manner that can do justice to the freedom, rights, and equal dignity of all persons.

NOTES

1. Lincoln, "Address at Gettysburg," p. 295.
2. Myrdal, *An American Dilemma*; Hartz, *The Liberal Tradition in America*; and Hofstadter, *The American Political Tradition*.

3. See Shklar, *American Citizenship*; Smith, *Civic Ideals*; Poole, *The Pursuit of Equality in American History*; Morone, *Hellfire Nation*. While differing in both aim and purpose, this more recent scholarship was preceded by important historical work like Du Bois's *The Suppression of the African Slave Trade to the United States of America 1638–1870*. See also Morgan, *American Freedom, American Slavery*.

4. See Bailyn, *The Ideological Origins of the American Revolution*; Wood, *The Creation of the American Republic, 1776–1787*; Pocock, *The Machiavellian Moment*; May, *The Enlightenment in America*; White, *The Philosophy of the American Revolution*. Several excellent review essays have been written about this extensive literature. See, in particular, Shalpole, "Toward a Republican Synthesis" and Gibson, "Ancients, Moderns and Americans."

5. For reassertions of the centrality of liberalism in American political history, see Diggins, *The Lost Soul of American Politics*; Zuckert, *Natural Rights and the New Republicanism*; Zuckert, *The Natural Rights Republic*; Greenstone, *The Lincoln Persuasion*; and Huyler, *Locke in America*.

6. See Sandel, *Democracy's Discontent*.

7. See Young, *Reconsidering American Liberalism*.

8. See Nedelsky, *Private Property and the Limits of American Constitutionalism*.

9. Rahe, *Republics: Ancient and Modern*, p. 31.

10. See Winthrop, "A Model of Christian Charity" [1630], in *Puritan Political Ideas*, pp. 75–93. Some of the most influential studies of American Puritanism include Miller, *Errand into the Wilderness* and Bercovitch, *The American Jeremiad*.

11. Winthrop, "The Journal of John Winthrop," in *Puritan Political Ideas*, pp. 138–39.

12. Ward, *The Simple Cobbler of Aggawam* [1646], in *The Puritans in America*, p. 181.

13. As Ward argued (*ibid.*, p. 182), "Conscience is free only to the extent that it is free from error."

14. See, in particular, Ward, "The Massachusetts Body of Liberties, December 1641."

15. Tocqueville celebrated this dimension of American Puritanism: "A democracy more perfect than antiquity had dared to dream of started in full size and panoply from the midst of an ancient feudal society" (*Democracy in America*, trans. Reeve, vol. 1, p. 35).

16. Especially noteworthy here is Penn's *Frame of Government for Pennsylvania* and the *Charter of Privileges*.

17. See Bushman, *From Puritan to Yankee*. For a different account that places Puritan declension within the seventeenth century, see Miller, *The New England Mind*.
18. Writing as "Novanglus," John Adams explained that the "revolution principles" in America were the principles of "Aristotle and Plato, of Livy and Cicero, and Sidney, Harrington, and Locke," in *The Revolutionary Writings of John Adams*, p. 152. Thomas Jefferson had a very similar list: see his Letter to Henry Lee, May 8, 1825. For the argument that republicanism in the late eighteenth and early nineteenth century is a species of liberalism in America, see Ericson, *The Shaping of American Liberalism*; Greenstone, *The Lincoln Persuasion*; see also Banning, "Jeffersonian Ideology Revisited."
19. The Congregationalist minister John Wise, responding to the earlier tax policy of Governor Andros, provides another important example of American Puritanism drawing on Lockean themes of natural reason and personal judgment in matters affecting the individual pursuit of happiness. See Wise, "A Vindication of New England Churches." To be sure, Locke is not an exclusive source for these ministers, as Mayhew also draws extensively from Bishop Benjamin Hoadly; see Bailyn, *Ideological Origins of the American Revolution*, ch. 2.
20. See Otis, "Rights of the British Colonies Asserted and Proved." For related language see Hopkins, "The Rights of the Colonies Examined"; Adams, "A Dissertation on the Canon and Feudal Law," in *Revolutionary Writings*; Dickinson, "Letters from a Farmer in Pennsylvania"; and Jefferson, "A Summary View of the Rights of British America."
21. Jefferson, "A Summary View of the Rights of British America," p. 9.
22. Some notable exceptions include: Benjamin Rush, "An Address to the Inhabitants of the British Settlements in America Upon Slave-Keeping" [1773], and Nathaniel Niles, "Two Discourses on Liberty" [1774], in Hyneman and Lutz (eds.), *American Political Writings During the Founding Era, 1760–1805*, vol. 1. See also Bailyn, *Ideological Origins of the American Revolution*, ch. 6.
23. See also Ketcham, *Framed for Posterity*, ch. 6.
24. See Pettit, *Republicanism*.
25. See Wood, *The Radicalism of the American Revolution*.
26. Appleby, *Liberalism and Republicanism in the Historical Imagination*, p. 185. For Appleby this deliverance from an attachment to English Constitutional history also amounted to liberation from the strictures of classical republicanism and the adoption of liberal belief in "a natural harmony of benignly striving individuals."
27. On these points see Breen, *American Insurgents, American Patriots*, ch. 9.

28. For an example of loyalist political writing that does not concede Locke to the revolutionaries, see Galloway, "Candid Examination of the Mutual Claims of Great Britain and the Colonies" (1775); on slave resistance during the revolution, see Nash, *Race and Revolution* and Frey, *Water from Rock;* for an early call for a modest kind of gender equity during the Revolution, see Abigail Adams, Letter to John Adams, March 1776.

29. "The Virgina Declaration of Rights" (1776), the Constitution of Massachusetts (1780), and Adams's "Thoughts on Government" (1776) all played a formative role.

30. On all of these points, see Wood, *Creation of the American Republic,* ch. 5; Kramnick, "Editor's Introduction" to *The Federalist Papers,* ed. Rossiter.

31. See Madison, "Vices of the Political System of the United States" (April 1787), in *James Madison: Writings,* p. 75. See also Madison's "Letter to Thomas Jefferson," October 24, 1787; and *Federalist Papers,* no. 14.

32. *Federalist Papers,* no. 37, p. 226.

33. "Brutus" Essay I, October 18, 1787; and "Federal Farmer" Letters, October 8 and 9, 1787, in *The Anti-Federalist Papers and the Constitutional Convention Debates,* ed. Ketcham, pp. 270–80 and 257–69 respectively. More broadly, see Storing, *What the Anti-Federalists Were For* and Sinopoli, *The Foundations of American Citizenship.* "Publius's" response to these specific concerns can be found in *Federalist Papers,* nos. 27 and 34.

34. From the pro-Constitution newspaper the *Pennsylvania Packet* (September 1787), cited in Kramnick, "Editor's Introduction" to *The Federalist Papers.*

35. See *Federalist Papers,* nos. 6, 9, 10, 15, 55.

36. See *Federalist Papers,* no. 10.

37. See *Federalist Papers,* nos. 49, 63.

38. See *Federalist Papers,* nos. 55, 57, 63. See also Gibson, "Impartial Representation and the Extended Republic" and Kalyvas and Katznelson, *Liberal Beginnings,* ch. 4.

39. See Vetterli and Bryner, *In Search of the Republic.*

40. See Berkowitz, *Virtue and the Making of Modern Liberalism.*

41. See Amar, "The Bill of Rights as a Constitution"; Ketcham, *Framed for Posterity,* ch. 10; Smith, *Civic Ideals,* pp. 134–35.

42. See Elkins and McKitrick, *The Age of Federalism,* ch. 7.

43. This is the insight behind the observation (frequently repeated) that the Progressives employed "Hamiltonian means for Jeffersonian ends." See Mowry, *Theodore Roosevelt and the Progressive Movement,* p. 145.

44. Douglass, "The Meaning of July Fourth for the Negro," p. 203.

45. See Smith, *Civic Ideals* and "'One United People.'"
46. See Calhoun, *Union and Liberty*.
47. In this context Madison's reactions to the idea of nullification and the wider "compact" theory of the Constitution that it served is illuminating. See his Letter to Edward Everett, August 28, 1830.
48. On this point see Foner, *Politics and Ideology in the Age of the Civil War* and McPherson, *Abraham Lincoln and the Second American Revolution*.
49. Lincoln, "Message to Congress in Special Session," July 4, 1861.
50. Lincoln, "Speech on the Kansas-Nebraska Act at Peoria, Illinois," (1854); and "First Lincoln-Douglas Debate" (1858).
51. Free labor also had its share of critics in America, from the social radical Orestes A. Brownson, to the paternalistic defender of slavery for all poor people, George Fitzhugh. See Brownson, *Selected Writings* and Schlesinger, Jr., *Orestes A. Brownson*; Fitzhugh, *Cannibals All!*
52. See Foner, *Free Soil, Free Labor, Free Men: The Ideology of the Republican Party before the Civil War*.
53. On the Kansas–Nebraska Act, Lincoln argued: "I object to it because it assumes that there can be a moral right in the enslaving of one man by another. I object to it as a dangerous dalliance for a free people – a sad evidence that, feeling prosperity we forget right – that liberty, as a principle, we have ceased to revere." "Speech on the Kansas-Nebraska Act," p. 72. See also Greenstone, *The Lincoln Persuasion*, ch. 1.
54. Shklar, *Redeeming American Political Thought*, p. 92.
55. Mills, *The Racial Contract*.
56. Pateman, *The Sexual Contract*.

2 Liberalism and the morality of commercial society

The Sermon on the Mount, beginning with the Beatitudes and containing Christ's injunction that we consider the lilies of the field for "they toil not, neither do they spin," can be seen as an abridgement of Christian teaching on matters relating to money and economic activity in general.

However, if Christ enjoined his followers to give up their possessions and counseled that the rich might find it difficult to enter the Kingdom of Heaven, the early church quickly reconciled itself to the economic realities of a fallen world. Later scholastic writers, most notably Thomas Aquinas, not only argued that private property was not opposed to natural law – it was, Aquinas argued, "an addition to it, devised by human reason" – but also that trade was part of "the necessary business of life" and, as such, was neither "vicious" nor "contrary to virtue." Nevertheless, the profit motive was to be tempered by the requirement that the activity of selling and buying must be at the just price. Charging interest on money was "unnatural" and therefore sinful. So, too, the Christian remained under the duty of charity. "Whatever a man has in superabundance," Aquinas wrote, "is owed, of natural right, to the poor for their sustenance."

This is not the occasion to examine the controversial thesis advanced by Max Weber linking Protestantism – and specifically Calvinism – with the spirit of capitalism and what he termed "the development of a rational bourgeois economic life."[1] For the most part, the Protestant view remained that wealth should be used for the good of society and should not be pursued as an end in itself. Nonetheless, as Weber recognized, for all its asceticism the Protestant ethic turned the marketplace into a location for possible salvation. If work was a religious duty, economic success was a sign of God's favor.

42

By the time, therefore, that Dr. Johnson voiced the opinion in 1760 that there were few ways in which a man could be more harmlessly employed than in money-making, he was one among many participating in what amounted to the rehabilitation of our earthly passions and interests.[2] When, for example, in *The Wealth of Nations* Adam Smith suggested that we should not trust to the benevolence of the butcher, the brewer, and the baker but to their self-love, he was only generalizing a by-now familiar argument that we should take human beings as they are rather than as they might be – what David Hume, in his essay *Of Commerce*, referred to as "the common bent of mankind" – and that there was much of public benefit to be gained from commercial activity regardless of the motives that produced it.

Where the *Private Vices, Public Benefits* argument usually associated with Bernard Mandeville has its origin is open to discussion. E. J. Hundert locates its unlikely source in seventeenth-century French debates over the role of grace and redemption in the interpretation of Saint Augustine.[3] Duncan Kelly has similarly argued that for Jansenists such as Pierre Nicole, "public virtue could . . . be manufactured through the wise regulation of private selfishness."[4] Hence, according to Nicole, a society founded on self-love could operate just as well as one driven by charity.

In the pages of Mandeville's *The Fable of the Bees*, however, the argument that avarice was necessary to the well-being of society was advanced to undermine the belief in personal rectitude as the source of public good and thereby to characterize the maxims of Christianity as a combination of hypocrisy and self-deception. Vices, according to Mandeville, were "inseparable from great and potent Societies." It was vanity and envy, rather than self-denial and frugality, which drove economic activity forward and kept trade alive. As our wants were boundless, the pursuit and enjoyment of luxury were coterminous with the existence of society.[5]

Adam Smith, no less than David Hume, shared the Enlightenment's distaste for religion and for religious fanaticism.[6] He, too, challenged those Christian (and also Stoic) moralists who believed that wealth and virtue were incompatible. Yet, for Smith, in contrast to Mandeville, all was not self-love. "How selfish soever man may be supposed," Smith wrote in the very opening sentence of *The Theory of Moral Sentiments*, "there are evidently some principles in his nature, which interest him in the fortune of others, and render their happiness necessary to him."[7]

If Smith's starting point was that society was held together by utility "without any mutual love and affection" and that we had a natural propensity to place our own interests before those of others, he also believed that nature had "endowed" man not only "with a desire of being approved of, but with a desire of being what ought to be approved of." Our natural sense of sympathy, of "fellow feeling," he believed, inclined us to cultivate our moral sentiments. If our duty to care for others was not universal – "to what purpose," he wrote, "should we trouble ourselves about the world in the moon" – we could, if we followed the guidance of "the inhabitant of the breast, the man within" come to transcend the partiality of our own passions. For Smith, then, the cardinal virtues were prudence, benevolence, justice and self-command.[8]

For all Smith's appreciation of the benefits afforded by the "pleasures of wealth" and "the industry of mankind," therefore, he preserved a concern for the moral dangers of commerce. "The disposition to admire, and almost worship, the rich . . . and neglect persons of poor and mean condition," Smith wrote as late as 1790, is "the great and most universal cause of the corruption of our moral sentiments."[9]

Moreover, Smith's praise of the "frugal man" as a "public benefactor" brought with it a preference not just for parsimony but also for productive labor and productive expenditure over needless and wasteful private consumption. "A man grows rich," Smith wrote, "by employing a multitude of manufacturers. He grows poor by maintaining a multitude of menial servants."[10] Admittedly, Smith's strictures on this subject did not match those found throughout the writings of Jean-Jacques Rousseau, but there can be no doubt as to Smith's disapproval of both private and public prodigality. It was this in part that explained his eagerness to limit the activities of government. Sovereigns and their ministers, Smith believed, were prone to behave like the "greatest spendthrifts." The broader point was that governments were neither best-placed nor well-suited to promote virtue among their citizens.

The same preference for production over consumption, and especially the productive use of capital, emerged as a key feature of what we would now see as liberal or classical political economy in France. A seminal influence here was Anne-Robert Jacques Turgot. As the title of Turgot's *Reflections on the Production and*

Distribution of Wealth (1766) suggests, his major preoccupation (like that of many of his contemporaries) was the analysis of the production, distribution, and circulation of wealth in society.

In brief, Turgot postulated that the activity of exchange arose from differences in the productive capacities of land holdings and from the multiplicity of human needs. "The intelligence, industry, and, above all, the thrift of some, and the contrasting indolence, inactivity and improvidence of others," Turgot wrote, is the "most powerful cause of inequality." The consequent unequal distribution of land had given rise to two kinds of income: the subsistence wages of the worker and the surplus or rent derived by the landowner. Here was the point of transition to a commercial society, for, as Turgot next observed, there was another way of becoming rich: "living on the interest received from money lent."

To advance this argument Turgot needed to address the origin of money, exchange, and the division of labor, but he did so in order to prove that the accumulation of capital – "movable wealth" – was the "indispensable preliminary" to the creation of wealth more generally throughout society. Crucially, the practice of advancing capital was extended beyond agriculture to industrial and business enterprises, and this was done by those prepared to accept the risks and the effort involved. Thus, with the advent of capital, society found itself divided into two distinct groups: "that of the entrepreneur manufacturer . . . in possession of capital, which they make profitable by means of their advances to make work possible; and the second group composed of artisans, who have no wealth except their hands, who advance nothing except their daily labour, and whose profit is only their wage."

To this division, Turgot then added a third group: merchants. Their indispensable function was to facilitate commercial exchanges between producers and consumers, to match abundance to scarcity, to send goods from "where they are cheap to where they are dear." However, Turgot's point was that the accumulation and circulation of capital was central to the production of wealth. It was this, he wrote, that "animates all the work of society, which maintains the activity and life of the body politic, and which there is good reason to compare with the circulation of the blood in the animal body." Without it, society would sink into "the deepest distress and destitution."

A similar set of arguments can be found in the writings of later leading French liberal political economists. If, for example, Jean-Baptiste Say disagreed with Adam Smith, it was because the latter, in his opinion, had placed the virtue of frugality above that of industriousness when they should have been given equal importance. The primary function of production, according to Say, was to satisfy our fundamental needs rather than to provide fleeting sensual pleasures. The same sentiments are found in Destutt de Tracy's *A Treatise on Political Economy*, first published in 1817.

Breaking with the physiocratic orthodoxy of the eighteenth century, he argued that all those who labored and therefore who belonged to the "laborious class," be they manufacturers or merchants, were producers of utility and, therefore, of riches and wealth. "Industrious men," Destutt de Tracy wrote, "are commonly frugal and too often not very rich." Government, by contrast, was "the greatest of consumers," and its expenditure, even when necessary, was unproductive. An even stronger statement of this position can be found in the doctrine of "industrialism" formulated by Charles Dunoyer and Charles Comte in the 1820s.[11] As the above suggests, one object of liberal scorn was the economically "sterile" aristocracy. If the road to wealth was through the accumulation of productive capital, the key figure in this process was the industrial entrepreneur rather than the powdered aristocrat.

One fascinating aspect of these discussions of frugality and prodigality was the continued discussion of the merits or otherwise of luxury. This was one of the great intellectual debates of the eighteenth century,[12] and it continued well into the nineteenth century. One of Adam Smith's central insights was that the division of labor would produce "universal opulence" and a "general plenty" throughout the different ranks of society. On this view – as developed in Italy by Antonio Genovesi, for example[13] – a "moderate luxury" was required if a nation was to leave a savage state. Nevertheless, if later liberal writers abandoned the traditional anti-luxury remedy of sumptuary laws, it did not stop them trying to discipline consumption or to moralize commerce. Bourgeois (and especially *parvenu*) ostentation replaced the effete luxury of the aristocracy as the object of disquiet and disproval. If this attitude changed, it did so only at the end of the nineteenth century and only then because, in the hands of men such as Paul Beaulieu-Leroy, luxury was no longer characterized in terms of opulence but as the pursuit of personal comfort. Seen thus, luxury did not waste human and natural resources and was not the monopoly of a narrow and privileged elite.

These themes were particularly evident in the writings of French liberals. Like their British counterparts, liberals in France were not slow to praise the greater wealth, gentler mores, and new political freedoms they increasingly associated with an emerging commercial society. Montesquieu might be better described as a proto-liberal rather than a liberal, but his *The Spirit of the Laws* indicates that he was in no doubt that commerce "cures destructive prejudices" and that the spirit of moderation and "exact justice" it engendered helped produce the mixed government under which liberty could flourish. Montesquieu, as much as David Hume, blamed the fall of Rome not on too much wealth – as had been conventionally the case – but on too much military conquest and bad government. Montesquieu (like many a later liberal) also believed that "the natural effect of commerce was to lead to peace." As he observed, "two nations that trade with each other become reciprocally dependent; if one has an interest in buying, the other has an interest in selling, and all unions are founded on reciprocal needs."[14]

In the early part of the nineteenth century, we find very similar sentiments in the work of Benjamin Constant. Commerce, Constant declared in his famous speech contrasting the liberty of the ancients with that of the moderns, "inspires in men a vivid love of individual independence. Commerce supplies their needs, satisfies their desires, without the intervention of the authorities."[15]

As for Alexis de Tocqueville, we get a clear glimpse of his view of the character of commercial society in one of the earliest letters he wrote from America in June 1831. Here he asked his close friend Ernest de Chabrol to imagine a society lacking roots, memories, common ideas, and national character. What bound such a society together? Tocqueville's answer was self-interest, and, moreover, a self-interest that displayed itself openly and was never bashful. The Americans, Tocqueville told Chabrol, "put one in mind of merchants who have convened as a nation just to do business. And the more one delves into the national character of Americans, the clearer it seems that they seek the value of all things of this world in the answer to only one question: 'How much money will it fetch?'" America, he continued, was not the place to look for the "ancient traditions of honour and virtue bred into various of our old European societies." Nevertheless, in America there were none of the vices attending idle wealth. Habits were regular. Morals were pure. Not just this but, as Tocqueville confirmed, in America "private interest never runs contrary to the general interest."[16] It was these first impressions that were to inform so much of the content of *Democracy in America*.

This picture of a positive appreciation of the combined moral and economic benefits of commercial society is confirmed if we look at the positions endorsed by liberal political economists in this period. If the study of economics emerged relatively slowly as a distinct field of inquiry in France, it did so fully formed in its commitment to free-market assumptions. By the mid-eighteenth century, for example, Vincent de Gournay had clearly established the principle that "in the case of unrestrained commerce" it was "impossible for the individual interest not to concur with the general interest." From this followed the key maxim that "every man ought best to be left at liberty to do what he likes."[17]

These sentiments were given even clearer expression in Constant's later *Commentary on the Work of Filangieri* (a work not yet in English translation). There, in Constant's critique of the doctrines of eighteenth-century mercantilism, we read not only that we have entered the "epoch of commerce" but also that "the functions of government are negative: it should repress evil and leave the good to act of itself." The very last sentence of the book reads: "With regard to ideas, education, and industry, the motto of government must be: *laissez faire et laissez passer.*"

Indeed, writers such as Pellegrino Rossi, Jean-Gustave Courcelle-Seneuil, and Gustave de Molinari were referred to as the laissez-faire *ultras*. Adolphe Blanqui (brother of the famous revolutionary agitator) opposed legislation on maximum working hours and minimum wages and argued that it was not the government's responsibility to help workers in either old age or sickness. Frédéric Bastiat developed a theory of "economic harmonies" resting upon a conception of a self-regulating market that denied that the interests of labor and capital were opposed. If Bastiat characterized the innumerable forms of government intervention as "legal plunder," he also refuted the pessimistic conclusions of the so-called "iron law of wages": the wealth accruing to the workers, he believed, would not decline but increase in both percentage terms and total amount. In sum, the liberal school held to an optimistic conception of commercial society, where man was guided by self-interest; the individual pursuit of profit was not in contradiction with the general interest; and competition eliminated the possibility of the exploitation of the consumer. The widely held belief was that emulation of British industrial expansion demanded as little regulation by the state as possible.

However, if we return to our most well-known protagonists, it would be a mistake to imagine that the liberalism of Montesquieu, Constant, and Tocqueville was grounded solely upon a belief in the virtues of an interest-driven world and the market.

To begin with Montesquieu, he believed that the good citizen was motivated not by the pursuit of self-interest but by a sense of honour. Second, Montesquieu made a distinction between commerce "ordinarily founded upon luxury" and commerce "more often founded on economy." Under the former there was the danger that an "excess of wealth" would so predominate that individual citizens, isolated from one another, would place the satisfaction of physical comforts before the claims of liberty, thus opening up the possibility of a new form of despotism.

Moreover, if Montesquieu saw that religion could be used by the despot to induce passivity in his subjects, he also saw that the Christian religion played a crucial role in preserving morality and maintaining the stability of society. "He who has no religion," Montesquieu wrote, "is that terrible animal who feels his liberty only when it claws and devours."

With regard to Constant, two points stand out. First, Constant's concern was that, in our pursuit of private pleasures and our particular interests, we might abandon our active participation in public life, and to our great cost. We had to learn to combine ancient and modern liberty. Second, far from presenting a liberalism that was a rationalization of materialistic egoism, Constant believed that the seed of individual autonomy and self-cultivation was a religious sentiment.[18] The latter argument was fully developed in Constant's *On Religion* (another major work yet to be translated). Here Constant distinguished two broad moral systems. The first posited personal well-being as our goal and self-interest as our guide. Under its influence, people had been driven within themselves, always consumed by a narrow egoism. In these circumstances, liberty could be no more enjoyed than it could be established or preserved. The second imagined that we could be motivated by a sense of self-abnegation and personal sacrifice. It was this alone that made us worthy of our freedom and this alone that drew upon the inner religious sentiment. For Constant then, as Helena Rosenblatt has commented, "liberal societies needed a robust religious life in order to survive and prosper."[19]

As for Tocqueville, there are several points worthy of mention. The first is that Tocqueville was deeply influenced by Catholic social theory. Recent scholarship has shown that he learned much in particular from the Christian political economy of Alban de Villeneuve-Bargemont, for whom the science of economics was as much about "moral riches" as it was about "material riches."[20] In a letter to one of his closest friends from 1834, for example, Tocqueville wrote as follows: "Although political economy today strikes me as materialistic in all its efforts, I would like ... to emphasise the more immaterial aspects of this science; I would like it to bring in ideas and morality as elements of prosperity and happiness."[21] The second is that Tocqueville came increasingly to see the dangers of the connection between the individualism characteristic of the democratic citizen and the love of material pleasures. It was the latter, Tocqueville believed, that would foster the "individual servitude" he associated with a new despotism where each nation would be reduced "to being nothing more than a herd of timid and industrial animals of which government is the shepherd." If America was to avoid this fate it would be precisely because the strength of religious belief turned the souls of Americans toward immaterial pleasures and a taste for the infinite. In this way would Americans come to appreciate what Tocqueville termed "interest well understood."

I would also suggest that the religious impulse remained a vital ingredient in British liberalism well into the nineteenth century. If any book established the paradigm that, for liberalism, the individual is essentially the proprietor of his own person and capacities and therefore that human society consisted only of series of market relations, it was C. B. Macpherson's *The Political Theory of Possessive Individualism*. "Society," Macpherson wrote, speaking of Hobbes and Locke, "becomes a lot of free equal individuals related to each other as proprietors of their own capacities and of what they have acquired by their exercise."[22] However, no sooner was this thesis advanced in 1962 than a body of scholarship – beginning with John

Dunn's study of John Locke – showed how deeply the earliest formulations of liberal doctrine were impregnated with religious preoccu-
pations. Recent work on Locke by both John Marshall and Jeremy
Waldron confirms this point.[23] Within the liberal frame of mind, the
resolutely non-theological deductions from human nature of Thomas
Hobbes were the exception, rather than the rule. That this remained
so long after Locke is confirmed by Thomas Babington Macaulay's
later criticisms of the "false principles" that informed James Mill's
Essay on Government. "What proposition," Macaulay wrote, "is
there respecting human nature which is absolutely and universally
true? We know of only one: and that is not only true, but identical;
that men always act out of self-interest ... But, in fact, when
explained, it means only that men, if they can, will do as they
choose."[24]

The Manchester School associated with Richard Cobden and John
Bright would be a good example of the close association of religious
conviction and liberal thinking. No group of people was more representative of British liberal opinion at this time than these ardent
defenders of free trade and a minimal state. Yet, for Cobden, free
trade was the International Law of the Almighty. Believing, like
Locke, that the mission of man in this world was to possess the
earth and subdue it and that the first great law of humanity was
that of labor, in 1843 he argued that the Corn Laws would not bring
prosperity to either agriculture or industry precisely because they
interfered with "the wisdom of Divine Providence."[25] Cobden's
close associate, Sir Louis Mallet – with whom he worked on the
negotiations leading up to the Anglo-French trade treaty of 1860 –
had no hesitation in affirming that Cobden believed in "the perfect
harmony of moral and economical laws, and that, in proportion as
these are recognised, understood, and obeyed by nations, will be their
advance in all that constitutes civilisation."[26]

If this was liberalism clothed in the language of religious dissent
and non-conformity, the British Idealists – Green, Bosanquet,
Bradley, and their many associates – gave it a decidedly Anglican
flavour. As is well known, British Idealism imported its philosophy
from Germany but, in rejecting the individualism of the age and what
T. H. Green saw as an ethically unsatisfactory hedonism, it also
sought to rescue and restore what were regarded as the essential
principles of Christianity. From this unorthodox perspective,

therefore, religion was seen as being integral to human self-realization. To quote David Boucher, for the British Idealists "the test of a morally worthwhile existence" was "the extent to which the individual attempts to do God's work in the world by achieving his or her own potential and contributing to the common good."[27] In this way, the moral ethos of Christianity was to inform the duties of a full and active citizenship, thereby opening up the route to the development of a "new liberalism," one that would subordinate economics to morality and ultimately lay the intellectual foundations of the welfare state in the United Kingdom.

As we have seen, many of the principal theorists of liberalism – certainly up to the end of the nineteenth century – did not divorce their thoughts on commercial society from broader ethical concerns. For many, economic justice and the precepts of Christian morality went hand in hand. We misunderstand their writings if we fail to take their views on religion seriously.

Yet liberals also took exception to the remnants of theological power still exercising clerical influence in European society. Following in the footsteps of Diderot, Helvétius, d'Holbach, and Condorcet, liberals not only insisted upon freedom of thought and expression but also sought to ground ethics upon what they perceived as the solid and irrefutable principle of utility. In France, this aspiration was given its clearest expression in the doctrine of *Idéologie* developed by Destutt de Tracy, Pierre Cabanis, and others during the years of the French Revolution and the First Empire. In Britain that honor fell to Bentham and his many admirers.

As conceived by Destutt de Tracy, "ideology" was "the science of thought." Upon the achievements of this new and unique discipline, he believed, rested the possibility of all human advance. At a minimum this entailed an almost limitless enthusiasm for conceptual reform and the belief that an essentially scientific epistemology could found morality upon rational principles. Here, then, was a distinctively secular version of liberalism, and it was one that gave equal weight to the constraints imposed by religion upon individual liberty as it did to those arising from arbitrary government in its various forms. It also gave primacy to economics over politics – the chief purpose of society, Destutt de Tracy held, was to satisfy our material needs – and presumed that the perfection of our social, economic, and political institutions should be directed toward the attainment of *le bonheur social*.

Politics, wrote Destutt de Tracy, was "the science of human happiness." Specifically, Destutt de Tracy's scientific study of our mental faculties provided a description of the individual self as a collection of desires, and from this followed an equation of freedom with the satisfaction of those desires. If, in political terms, this entailed a support of representative government, it also demanded a society resting upon the solid foundations of private property and the removal of artificial barriers to trade and industry. On this view, it was no part of the functions of government to reduce inequality. The solution to poverty lay in private philanthropy and the provision of education. Exploitation existed only to the extent that idle landowners – *les oisifs* – lived off the economic surplus provided by their rents.

Ultimately, in Destutt de Tracy's opinion, we were all united by "our common interests as proprietors and consumers," and everyone stood to benefit from an expanding economy, even if some benefited more than others.[28]

Of one thing we can be sure: the followers of Jeremy Bentham – the sect of so-called Philosophic Radicals – ardently wished to turn political economy into a secular science. The heart of that science was the Benthamite maxim that the interests of society as a whole could only be understood as the sum total of the interests of those individuals who made up that society. It was in the hands of these men that, in the coinages of Thomas Carlyle, classical political economy became the "dismal science" and our relationships with others ones determined by the "cash nexus" alone. This was only one of many literary portrayals of the hard-heartedness and spiritual impoverishment associated with the tradition of classical political economy. What was undoubtedly the case was that liberal political economists increasingly came, rather gloomily, to focus their attention on the problems of over-population, unemployment, the laboring poor, and the economic crises associated with the business cycle.[29]

That John Stuart Mill, like his father, was an irreligious man cannot be doubted. Indeed, the full extent of Mill's antipathy to religion only became fully apparent to a broader public after his death. For all that, no one can deny that Mill – like Wilhelm von Humboldt[30] – was concerned with "the internal culture of the individual" and that he regarded this as one of "the prime necessities of human well-being." If, following the "crisis" in his "mental history," he still regarded Bentham as "the great questioner of things established," he also saw that Bentham was "a systematic and accurately logical half-man" and that his philosophy was appropriate only to the "merely *business* part of the social arrangements." Man, Mill wrote, was "never recognized by him as a being capable of pursuing spiritual perfection as an end."[31]

With this in mind, not only did Mill set about a major revision of the utilitarian creed – "better to be a human dissatisfied than a pig satisfied," he famously wrote – but he also concluded that "the most serious danger to the future prospects of mankind" was to be found in the "unbalanced influence" of the "commercial spirit."

Required therefore was "the salutary check" provided by "an agricultural class, a leisured class, and a learned class."[32] It was this concern about the deleterious impact of the prevalence of the commercial spirit that explained the appeal for Mill of both the Coleridgean institution of a clerisy – in effect, a secular national church – and Auguste Comte's concept of a *pouvoir spirituel* as a necessary alternative to "the ascendancy of mere wealth."

More intriguing still were Mill's reflections, in his *Principles of Political Economy*, on what, following David Ricardo, he called "the stationary state" where both the accumulation of capital and industrial progress would cease. "I cannot," Mill wrote, "regard the stationary state of capital and wealth with the unaffected aversion so generally manifested towards it by political economists of the old school." "I confess," he continued, "I am not charmed with the ideal of life held out by those who think that the normal state of human beings is that of struggling to get on ... the best state for human nature is that in which, while no one is poor, no one desires to be richer."[33] It was but a short step from this to Mill's conclusion that what mattered most was not the creation of wealth but its better and fairer distribution.

The scientism that underpinned Mill's utilitarianism did, however, bear other fruit. One can see how by looking at a figure such as Herbert Spencer. Spencer's liberal anti-statism was rooted in the dissenting traditions of Britain's northern industrial cities, but when he came to formulate his comprehensive "Synthetic Philosophy" he was content to consign the ultimate questions of religious belief to the realm of what he termed the "Unknowable." If this conveniently allowed him to deny charges of atheism, it also meant that he could ground an evolutionary ethics on the evidence provided by the knowable universe. "As well," Spencer wrote in his *Social Statics*, "might we seek to light a fire with ice, feed cattle with stones, hang our hats on cobwebs, or otherwise disregard the physical laws of the world, as go contrary to its equally imperative ethical laws." And what those ethical laws told Spencer was that government should in no way attempt to interfere with the pursuit of gratification by individuals subject to what he termed the law of equal freedom – least of all by intervention in the workings of the economy. As Spencer announced, "The ultimate result of shielding men from the effects of their folly is to fill the world with fools." What mattered was "the survival of the fittest."[34] In short, anything beyond the minimal regulation of economic activity was immoral.

A second – perhaps more congenial – form of evolutionary ethics was developed by L. T. Hobhouse. This effectively amounted to preserving the rational kernel of the philosophy of British Idealism and removing any explicit reference to its Christian underpinnings, producing, as Hobhouse saw it, a combination of the utilitarianism of J. S. Mill and the ethical idealism of Green. At bottom, Hobhouse believed, humans were not moved by ideas or by principles but by "impulse feeling."

Man, he wrote, was "a would-be rational animal." However, although "cruel and anarchic struggle" was the law of the organic world, there was, Hobhouse believed, "a principle making for harmony in a world of discord." One could refer to this principle as God, Hobhouse observed, but it served little purpose to do so. It was more accurate to say that the "ethical life" was the "flower of the evolutionary process" and that it was through this process that individuals would come progressively to recognize their mutual involvement in the rational and common good. Moreover, it was on these grounds – rather than out of any religious considerations – that Hobhouse came to recommend a greater degree of state intervention in the economy.[35]

It was perhaps no accident that liberalism went into crisis at the beginning of the twentieth century. Certainly both Celestin Bouglé in France and J. A. Hobson in Britain spoke of such a crisis. If liberals continued to defend private property and free trade, a growing awareness of the failings of capitalism found them increasingly aligned with the rise of collectivism. As Donald Winch has observed, for Alfred Marshall, Professor of Political Economy at the University of Cambridge, "there were no grounds for believing that the outputs and prices generated under a system of competitive markets represented a position of 'maximum satisfaction.'"[36] Marshall's student, John Maynard Keynes, took this argument a step further in the interwar years. "The world," Keynes wrote, "is not so governed from above that private and social interest always coincide ... It is not a correct deduction from the principles of economics that enlightened self-interest always operates in the public interest."[37] Accordingly, it was the allotted task of government not only to pursue countercyclical policies but also to direct economic forces in the interests of social justice.

What followed is a complicated story but when, at a theoretical level, the period of liberal decline came to end – the Lippmann Colloquium in Paris in 1938 is often identified as the point of renewal – it was in the guise of a neo-liberalism that postulated a spontaneous order of self-regulating markets. For supporters of the Austrian School associated with Ludwig von Mises and Friedrich von Hayek, the advantages of a market economy based upon private property and limited government were threefold: it was best placed to cope with conditions of imperfect knowledge; it allowed for experimental evolution; and it provided protection against the abuse of (political or economic) power by a selfish minority. The alternative, as the title of one of Hayek's most famous books declared, was the road to serfdom.

This is not a version of liberalism that has had or has much, if any, recourse to questions of ethics, and to religious ethics in particular. Evolutionary rationality was to be our guide. Nevertheless, those who gathered at the inaugural meeting of the Mont Pèlerin Society in 1947 were in no doubt about their purpose. The mission statement written by Lionel Robbins equated the defense of the free market with a defense of "the central values of civilization."[38]

Of course, for all the ostensible dominance of neo-liberalism over recent years this has not been a paradigm immune from criticism. Censure has focused upon the charge of market failure – unregulated markets, it is claimed, do not operate efficiently nor do they guarantee equilibrium – and that markets undermine the morality (or social capital) required for the market itself to function. More fundamentally, the growth of income inequality has prompted the charge that the vision of a free-market economy embraced by classical liberals cannot meet the requirements of social justice.[39] Most obviously, this is a view articulated by John Rawls in A Theory of Justice, and it is one that has attained near-hegemonic support among political philosophers. Resolutely non-utilitarian in approach, Rawls here develops a set of principles to demonstrate that, in a situation where basic liberties can be exercised, economic advantages must be so arranged as to ensure the greatest benefit to the least advantaged members of society. From this there can be developed an argument in support of income redistribution and the welfare state.

There has, then, by no means been a single, settled liberal perspective on the morality of commercial society. Religious and secular perspectives have jostled for pole position, and liberals have never quite been able to agree whether human beings were motivated primarily by self-interest or not. Nor have they been of the same mind about whether an unregulated economy would operate with optimal efficiency and therefore maximize utility. Not everyone has embraced the prospect of greater wealth associated with the activity of commerce with unreserved enthusiasm. At bottom, however, liberals of whatever persuasion have believed that a commercial society based upon some form of market economy and the institution of private property was most likely to protect the freedom of the individual and enhance his or her well-being. In comparison with their agreement about this fundamental truth, their disagreements about how the defects or abuses of a commercial society might be remedied are minor matters.

NOTES

1. Weber, The Protestant Ethic and the Spirit of Capitalism, p. 117.
2. Hirschman, The Passions and the Interests.
3. Hundert, The Enlightenment's Fable. See also Force, Self-Interest Before Adam Smith.
4. Kelly, The Propriety of Liberty, p. 25.
5. Mandeville, The Fable of the Bees or Private Vices, Publick Benefits.
6. See Phillipson, Adam Smith.
7. Smith, The Theory of Moral Sentiments, p. 9.

58   JEREMY JENNINGS

8. See Hanley, *Adam Smith and the Character of Virtue* and Forman-Barzilai, *Adam Smith and the Circles of Sympathy.*
9. Smith, *The Theory of Moral Sentiments*, p. 61. See Winch, *Riches and Poverty*, pp. 57–89.
10. Smith, *An Inquiry into the Nature and Causes of the Wealth of Nations*, p. 330.
11. See Dunoyer, "Notice historique sur l'industrialisme," pp. 173–99.
12. See Hont, "The Early Enlightenment Debate on Commerce and Luxury," pp. 379–442.
13. See Bellamy, "'Da Metafisico a Mercatante,'" pp. 277–99.
14. Montesquieu, *The Spirit of the Laws*, p. 338.
15. Constant, *Political Writings*, p. 315.
16. Tocqueville, *Letters from America*, pp. 66–69.
17. See Turgot, "In Praise of Gournay", pp. 448–76.
18. See Garston, "Religion and the Case Against Ancient Liberty," pp. 1–30.
19. Rosenblatt, "On the Need for a Protestant Reformation," p. 121. See also Rosenblatt, *Liberal Values.*
20. Drolet, *Tocqueville, Democracy and Social Reform* and Swedberg, *Tocqueville's Political Economy.*
21. Quoted in Jaume, *Tocqueville*, p. 175.
22. Macpherson, *The Political Theory of Possessive Individualism*, p. 3.
23. Marshall, *John Locke* and Waldron, *God, Locke and Equality.*
24. Macaulay, *Miscellaneous Writings and Speeches*, p. 180.
25. Cobden, *Speeches on Questions of Public Policy*, p. 35.
26. Mallet (ed.), *The Political Writings of Richard Cobden*, p. xxxvi.
27. Boucher (ed.), *The British Idealists*, p. x.
28. Destutt de Tracy, *A Treatise on Political Economy.* See Head, *Ideology and Social Science* and Welch, *Liberty and Utility.*
29. See Winch, *Riches and Poverty.*
30. See von Humboldt, *The Limits of State Action.*
31. Mill, "Bentham," pp. 77–121.
32. Mill, "De Tocqueville on Democracy in America (Vol. 1)," p. 264.
33. Mill, *Principles of Political Economy*, pp. 111–17.
34. See Greenleaf, *The British Political Tradition*, pp. 48–82.
35. See Hobhouse, *Liberalism; Social Evolution and Political Theory;* and *The Rational Good.*
36. Winch, *Wealth and Life*, p. 241.
37. See Parsons, "Politics and Markets," p. 49.
38. See Wapshott, *Keynes Hayek*, pp. 213–14.
39. See Pennington, *Robust Political Economy.*

3 Liberalism 1900–1940

This chapter is anything but comprehensive. It consists of three short vignettes and a very short coda with some introductory observations to illuminate the history and to raise conceptual questions that bedevil any attempt to describe the essence of liberalism. My first vignette is of the "new liberalism" of L. T. Hobhouse, and my second of its transatlantic cousin, the liberalism of Herbert Croly and John Dewey; my third is of the inability of European liberalism to counter the totalitarian threat of the period from 1918 to 1940; I end with a brief note on liberalism in the post-1945 and post-1989 world. In discussing liberalism in the United States, I deal briefly with the "Hartz thesis," Louis Hartz's claim that an "irrational Lockianism" is so much the political air that all Americans breathe that they are no more aware of it than fish of the water in which they swim.[1] When "liberal," or the "L-word," as the first President Bush dismissively put it, has become a term of abuse in American politics, and American politicians compete to display their social, economic, and political conservatism, it is hard to share Hartz's belief that there is no room on the American ideological spectrum for a true conservatism. Nonetheless, there is more than a grain of truth in his insistence that opinion in the United States is distinguished by a unanimous belief in the sanctity of property and a conviction that economic success is a touchstone of individual worth. It is not only in political style that American conservatives are disciples of Tom Paine rather than Edmund Burke. Religion is another matter, but although Evangelical Christian conservatives revile the skeptical Paine, they have no truck with a Burkean defense of prejudice.

Ball and Bellamy (eds.), *The Cambridge History of Twentieth-Century Political Thought* usefully expands on much that I discuss briefly here, and I have referred below to appropriate chapters in that work.

There are striking differences between the meaning of the word "liberal" in an early twenty-first-century American context and "liberal" in a late nineteenth-century British context; but there are also striking differences between British and European conceptions of liberalism, to say nothing of differences between these and ideas about liberalism current in Latin America, Asia, and Africa. The profession of liberal values by British colonial administrators had limited success in fostering enthusiasm for those values in former African colonies. Liberal values fared better elsewhere; they "took" in North America, the "White Commonwealth" (exception made for apartheid South Africa), and, more surprisingly, India, though not Pakistan. Much the same could be said of the mixed success of French colonization in attempting to establish French Enlightenment and republican values, and of American attempts to inculcate American political values in formerly Spanish America. Of course, colonial and neo-colonial practice in Africa, Asia, and Latin America was always more likely to foster some form of ultra-nationalism than any kind of liberalism. The analysis of the conditions under which a political ideology will "take" is beyond the aspirations of this chapter, though it is very relevant to the vexed question of why liberal democracy fell on hard times in interwar Europe, as well as why liberalism took root when and where it did.

Here I rely on familiar ideas about the strains of urbanization and industrialization, the lingering effects of feudalism, the resentments caused by defeat in war or the failure to gain from apparent victory, the effects of a militaristic nationalism, and the "backwash" of the nineteenth-century colonialism that accustomed Europeans to treating other races as less than fully human and poisoned ethnic relations in Europe.[2] Since much of south and central Europe emerged from World War I suffering the effects of many or all of these, the failure of liberalism to "take" was overdetermined. That may suggest that there was a substantial pressure to establish liberal democracy which failed; the truth is that many aspects of liberalism had little appeal either to a mass audience or to most elites. Like all generalizations, this must be taken with a pinch of salt; if "economic liberalism" is equated with a belief in the virtues of free trade and a market economy, many European economists were economic liberals. They were also attached to the ideal of the rule of law, the virtues of uncorrupt administration, and governmental accountability in some form.

How far this extended to a belief in democracy as a means of achieving accountability is another matter. They were often socially conservative, and had little time for egalitarianism in any form beyond equality before the law; they were culturally and often politically thorough-going elitists. One representative example is Joseph Schumpeter, inventor of what has become known as the "elite theory of democracy."[3] Some turned to fascism out of disgust with the corruption of parliamentary politics. Most did not; they remained liberals, but socially and politically conservative liberals, as Ortega y Gasset did, to take a once prominent example.[4]

I rely here, as elsewhere, on a simple analytical scheme;[5] this characterizes different periods of liberalism and different forms of liberalism, negatively by what were perceived as the most salient threats to freedom, and positively by the way liberal thinkers imagine a free individual thinking and behaving. On this view, the analysis of liberty should distinguish between external and internal conditions that diminish freedom; external threats to liberty include both physical coercion and social pressure intended to deter us from some course of action or to make some course of action compulsory, such as imprisonment and physical restraint, boycotts or "shunning," and more ordinary forms of moral reproach. How far "nudging" is to be seen as a limitation on freedom is an open question on which opinion divides very sharply.[6] Limitations on our liberty may be both external and self-imposed; if we tell our friends to drag us out of the bar if we are getting into a fight, we restrict our own liberty, in order to stay out of jail and preserve our longer-term freedom. Internal threats are harder to characterize, but include "overmastering" emotions or addictions that render their possessor incapable of acting on their own best judgment, as well as "undermining" conditions that disable the agent's judgment. The distinction between these is not sharp: overpowering emotions make it impossible to assess a situation clearly.

This way of thinking about freedom implies that freedom as a positive attribute is a matter of being one's own master, or autonomous; characteristically, the external reduction of liberty means that someone else is one's master, either generally, or with respect to some particular part of one's behavior, and the internal aspect is a matter of what disables one from directing one's own behavior even in the absence of external coercion.[7] This implies that the "two concepts" made famous by Isaiah Berlin are not two concepts but divergent theories; the negative libertarian thinks that almost always a man is his own master if he is not subjected to control by others, while positive libertarians emphasize internal impediments. There may be an interplay between these aspects inasmuch as an obvious way of controlling someone else's behavior is by playing on irrational fears and anxieties; holding a gun to someone's head plays on entirely rational fears, while much political advertising plays on irrational fears in order to manipulate the victims' behavior in the desired direction. Paradigmatically, the slave is at the opposite end of the spectrum from the free man, his status defined by the existence of an owner who is the master of his entire person. The paradoxical insistence by Stoic writers that a slave might nonetheless be free, because it was possible for him to become so much the master of his own reactions that nothing external could really harm him, is an exaggeration of the well-taken point that the victim of compulsive or otherwise uncontrollable reactions is non-autonomous, a "slave to his passions." The problem with the Stoic view is that even if the slave exercises a genuinely free choice between available options, his options are so few that they hardly merit the label of options.

Problems arise when we qualify "liberal" with any of a range of adjectives, although we surely must be ready to do so. A "political" liberal may be a cultural conservative and an economic socialist; the sociologist Daniel Bell characterized himself in just such terms.[8] It is easy to imagine someone who is a sexual liberal and a fiscal conservative, a believer in same-sex marriage and a balanced budget, for instance. The converse is equally easy to imagine. The intensity of the so-called culture wars in American politics since the 1960s may tempt us to believe that matters of personal conduct are central to disputes between liberals and others, and that deep philosophical and metaphysical convictions are invariably at stake. This is far from true. A liberal who thinks that liberalism is essentially a political doctrine may think that it is none of the political theorist's business what individuals do with their liberty; the theorist's business is to give a coherent and cogent account of legitimate state action, and what individuals do outside those limits is their business and nobody else's. It may show poor taste to spend one's abundant leisure slumped on the couch watching football games and eating junk food; but the couch potato is no less free, though he may well be less healthy, than his self-improving neighbor. There is much to be said for the view that even a less austerely "political" liberalism is not obliged to pronounce on all aspects of life. Other than in the sense of taking a relaxed view of directorial licence, it would be odd to propose a liberal theory of operatic performance, even if liberals think that people should be able to compose, stage, and attend operas unimpeded. There might, to be sure, be operas that carried liberal political messages, as did some of Verdi's, and there might be profoundly illiberal regimes that imposed a party line on composers, as did Stalin's Russia, just as there might be legal or social constraints on how innovative an opera production was allowed to be. It does not follow that a liberalism that takes no view of the pros and cons of particular operas is incomplete.

Here, I ignore the "culture wars" that have been a prominent feature of arguments between self-described conservatives and their opponents in the United States. Nonetheless, it is obvious that in a somewhat different sense of "culture," cultural conditions friendly to liberalism are crucial to whether liberalism "takes." This is not self-contradictory, although it points to a large problem. Many liberals, Karl Popper among them, think that liberalism – what he called the "Open Society" – is profoundly unnatural.[9] Human beings, on this view, are naturally inclined to seek intellectual and emotional comfort; they are conservative, creatures of habit, respectful of authority. They are more naturally tribal than members of an open society. Not all liberals have thought this; the more optimistic members of the Enlightenment thought that once men were liberated from the reign of kings and priests they would govern themselves by the light of reason. John Stuart Mill gives the impression of thinking both things at once: that once we have experienced the pleasures of rational self-government, we will not sacrifice them for any amount of comfort and security *and* that most of mankind are all too willing to hand over responsibility for their lives to someone else or to society at large. What assumptions about human nature a liberal must make is a difficult question. Among recent writers, John Rawls distinguished between a "metaphysical" and a "political" view of the self; we may prescind from holding any "deep" theory of human nature, so long as human beings are capable of living in a society which respects human rights and refuses to impose by whatever coercive means it may be one moral, religious, or philosophically based conception of the good life on its members.[10] Rawls's critics, including Michael Sandel and Charles Taylor, doubt that the distinction between a political and a metaphysical conception of the self will hold up.[11] Even the most sympathetic reader must think that if critics are right that even a cautiously "political" liberalism conflicts with the religious and cultural convictions of much of mankind, loyalty to a liberal political order cannot be taken for granted.[12]

These observations are intended to cast some light on the so-called new liberalism of the late nineteenth and early twentieth centuries. Its novelty consisted in its insistence that we could enhance individual liberty by collective action to reduce inequalities of opportunity. The "let-alone" liberties of speech and conscience were fundamental and sacred, but even in a broadly democratic society there were more threats to liberty than "the friar, the gibbet and the stake" evoked by Hume.[13] Unregulated economic power was one such threat. The New Deal, which was largely an exercise in extempore adaptation to an ill-understood political and economic crisis and dismissed by John Dewey as "messing about," defies analysis as the implementation of a political theory, but its success ensured that "liberal" in post-New Deal American terminology came to mean an enthusiasm for governmental action directed toward protecting the "Four Freedoms" of which Franklin D. Roosevelt spoke in 1940.[14] Herbert Hoover resented the way in which he had been cast as a conservative, maintaining that he was an old-fashioned liberal devoted to "rugged individualism."[15] Only after 1945 did he concede that he was defending a lost cause, but subsequent events have done little to reduce the terminological confusion inherent in a situation where conservatives set out to conserve a liberal – a nineteenth-century liberal – political and economic order. Because that order disappeared many years ago, it lends American conservatism the appearance of a radical reaction.[16]

On the view taken here, what determines whether policies are liberal is not a matter of what social and economic measures they involve but of what their purpose is. A social policy such as the provision of unemployment or medical benefits paid for by compulsory national insurance can be defended on many grounds; one would be simple humanitarianism, the relief of the misery of the sick or unemployed, another might be political prudence, with governments fearing uprisings from the unemployed or the families of the sick unless they were given adequate relief. Bismarck's introduction of pensions and unemployment benefits was an attempt to steal the clothes of the socialists and essentially conservative; years later, the imperialist Leo Amery argued for the creation of a British welfare state on the grounds that it would create healthy young people to serve their country in war. For the welfare state to be a liberal undertaking, it must be justified by some conception of freedom, as in Roosevelt's "Four Freedoms," with "freedom from want" as one of those freedoms. More generally a central feature of a liberal defense of collective action must be a focus on individual liberty rather than on a collective goal such as national glory or on social cohesion as an end in itself. How far Herbert Croly and John Dewey emerge as unequivocal liberals by these standards is a topic for discussion in due course.

HOBHOUSE AND NEW LIBERALISM

L. T. Hobhouse is regarded as the standard bearer of "new liberalism." In terms of his influence on other thinkers, this is fair enough, but he was riding a wave that carried many of his contemporaries with him. Hobhouse's *Liberalism*, published in 1911, was both a history of British liberalism and a manifesto of the new liberalism; it is an extremely shrewd piece of work, but many of Hobhouse's views were shared by the Fabians, who began as anti-socialist liberals, became "lib-lab," and in due course became less than liberal Fabian socialists. On the other side, more conservative thinkers such as Bernard Bosanquet, an intellectual pillar of the Charity Organization Society and an enemy of the welfare state, had more fondness than Hobhouse for the state, understood in a Hegelian fashion not as a collection of officials but as the institutionalized social, legal, and political ethos of a society; in practice, however, Bosanquet's vision of the functions of the state was animated by the idea that it should foster individual autonomy and a capacity for self-help in individuals who needed assistance to attain that condition. He offers the interesting spectacle of a thinker deriving economically individualist and anti-welfare state policy prescriptions from collectivist premises. Nonetheless, the fact that he was at odds with the defenders of the liberal welfare state did not mean they were at odds over the terms in which it was to be justified or condemned.

Where new liberals diverged from John Stuart Mill, who was himself more friendly to state intervention in the economy than many new liberals, was partly a matter of metaphysics rather than public policy, partly the result of the new liberals having a greater sense of the extent to which individuals were the creatures of their environment, and mostly the result of changes in that environment itself. One of the oddities of Mill's *On Liberty* is that it depicts the average inhabitant of Victorian England as an almost helpless slave to public opinion and social convention, but pays little attention to imagining social arrangements that might sustain those individuals who strike out to think for themselves and help them set up such "experiments in living" as they might choose to pursue. This was partly a matter of Mill's rhetorical mode, which was marked by a fondness for violent antitheses, some of them softened on reflection, and partly because Mill put a good deal of faith in heroic individuals whom he credited with first instituting everything worth having in human existence.[17] Moreover, while Mill as a good utilitarian well understood the ways in which government action, especially legislative action, might help people to realize their goals as they could not otherwise do, he focused on the ways in which we take our moral and political cues from our environment on a case-by-case basis – when discussing the disabling impact of social convention on women's education, for instance, or the temptations to mendacity implicit in conventional employment relations.

The way in which metaphysical disagreements fed into disagreements about policy was not simple, but in essence the new liberals thought of themselves as holists and their predecessors as atomists. It is tempting to draw a line between individualist and "communitarian" liberals, but caution is needed. All liberals were individualists, and none denied the importance of community. None thought that Thomas Hobbes's methodological injunction to consider men as if new sprung from the ground like mushrooms was the way to proceed, even if they were methodological individualists in the sense in which Karl Popper and Friedrich Hayek subsequently used that expression. All agreed that human beings grow up in communities, cannot survive in isolation, and are in innumerable ways dependent on one another both physically and psychologically. The two obvious ways in which the contrast between the metaphysical or methodological presuppositions of old and new liberalism emerge are, first, that writers from T. H. Green onwards insisted that a happy life was not made up of a series of happy moments, but was to be judged a success or failure as a unity; and second, that society is not best understood as resting on an implicit contract between independent individuals but as an organism. Hobhouse greatly admired Mill, but tended to praise him for working his way toward an organic view of society that he never quite embraced.[18] The question is not whether new liberals thought the development of individuals as rational, autonomous, and public-spirited persons was the central aim of liberalism, but *how* they conceived of the process, philosophically and in policy terms.

There is a narrow line between exaggerating the differences between old and new liberalism and blurring them, but the crucial contrast is less to be looked for in the philosophical disagreements that separated the empiricist Mill from the lapsed Idealist and evolutionary sociologist Hobhouse than in the transformation of the economic and political landscape between 1860 and 1914. In 1860, only one in seven adult males possessed the vote; trade unions were in their infancy; the Whigs had not yet adopted the label of the Liberal Party. The scramble for Africa had yet to break loose, and neither Germany – not yet united by Prussian *force majeure* – nor the United States had become the formidable economic competitors they were soon to be.

Britain achieved universal adult suffrage only in 1928, when voting rights for men and women became identical; but women got the vote on less favorable terms in 1918, and adult male suffrage was all but a reality after 1884. Trade unions had become powerful national institutions, as was revealed when the Taff Vale decision of 1901 that threatened their financial viability by allowing employers to sue for loss of profits due to strike action was overturned by parliament in the Trade Disputes Act of 1906. Confidence in the ability of a free-market capitalist economy to meet the needs of all members of the community was at a low ebb, however, at the time Hobhouse was writing. At the same time, liberal critics of British imperialism such as J. A. Hobson, with whom Hobhouse substantially agreed, blamed the existence of the empire for the maldistribution of purchasing power that they, in turn, blamed for inadequate domestic demand and persistent unemployment. There were liberal imperialists, among whom Bertrand Russell was very briefly one, but most new liberals had their doubts about the imperial project confirmed by the Boer War.

The other thing that separated new liberals from Mill was their acute anxiety about "the social problem," an ill-defined phenomenon but certainly embracing drunkenness, irresponsibility, and a lack of ambition among the working class. Temperance movements were a feature of Victorian society, and a very visible dividing line between Mill and his new liberal successors was his antipathy to temperance campaigns; nobody was more savage than Mill in condemning men who came home from the pub drunk and angry, and in a mood to beat their domestic partners and children. Mill would have had them jailed for long periods, but for assault, not drinking, although he thought drunkenness an aggravating factor in the case of a second offense. His new liberal successors thought that a man addicted to the bottle could hardly be said to be a free agent; protecting him from the temptation of cheap booze was, in Green's formulation, "hindering a hindrance to the good life." This was not "forcing him to be free," which no new liberal believed to be possible, but forcing his enslavers, or seducers, to stop undermining his capacity for free choice. Before turning to the transatlantic version of these ideas, it is worth noticing what happens to the idea of rights in this perspective. It is a commonplace that liberalism is "about" rights; the American Declaration of Independence justifies the colonists' rebellion on the grounds that it is their last and only resort in defending the natural rights that the British government is trampling on. Modern liberal theories are overwhelmingly theories of rights.

New liberalism was not hostile to talk of rights, but it was sensitive to the fact that their ontological and epistemological status was not what it had seemed to Jefferson in 1776. Hegel had written at length about rights, both rights of the person and rights of property, but deplored talk of "natural" rights.[19] New liberalism inherited his readiness to talk about rights and his doubts about their naturalness. A later age, thinking essentially of rights *against* state interference in certain sacrosanct areas of life, found some of the new liberal formulations hard to swallow; the thought that claiming a right was claiming to be the agent of the infinite good seemed to make rights conditional on being the right sort of person, whereas most of us think rights are possessions held against the world, inviolable, or to be overridden only *in extremis*.

What the new liberal view of rights more usefully achieved, perhaps, was a coherent view of the interconnection of rights and duties.

A well-known volume, *Property: Its Rights and Duties*, published in 1913,[20] caught the argument neatly; the thought that individual property owners were essentially performing a public or social function did not mean that private property was less important than previously thought. It did mean that *personal* property was an essential aspect of individuality, while the ownership of vast landed estates or vast industrial undertakings was not. Property that gave its owners economic power over others was held in trust, and its regulation was not an infringement of the rights of ownership but a reflection of their social nature.

Striking the right balance in the creation and implementation of public policy was not easy. An emphasis on the reciprocal character of rights and duties led naturally to an insistence that persons looking to be supported from public funds should show themselves willing and able to contribute to those public resources by working conscientiously to the best of their abilities.

The question was what to do about those who either could not or would not do so, the hopelessly inept, or the "work-shy." The most extreme suggestion came from Beveridge, best known later for the 1942 report that launched the post-1945 British welfare state; adopting the suggestion common to St. Paul and Lenin that "he who does not work, neither shall he eat," in 1906 he toyed with the idea of work camps in the countryside, the exclusion of the inept and/or work-shy from family life, and "rapid starvation."[21] Liberalism, whether old or new, was vulnerable to the complaint that liberal values and liberal social arrangements suited those who by nature or nurture – socialization – accepted them as a guide to individual conduct and social policy, but had nothing beyond coercion or hand-wringing to offer to anyone who did not, or would not, or perhaps could not, accept them. It is an embarrassment to liberals in the twenty-first century that such measures as the compulsory sterilization of the mentally feeble were put on the statute book at least as often by liberal reformers as by conservatives. Such measures were consistent with the rule of law, the protection of free speech, and other bedrock requirements of political liberalism; in the twenty-first century, they would be thought to violate the respect for intimate personal relations enshrined in such documents as the European Convention on Human Rights.

HERBERT CROLY AND JOHN DEWEY

On the other side of the Atlantic, the liberalism of Croly and Dewey is undeniably a form of "new liberalism," if we give an affirmative answer to the question whether either Croly or Dewey was a liberal at all. Croly's most famous book, *The Promise of American Life*, was dedicated to the defense of what Croly called "new nationalism," an expression Theodore Roosevelt made his own, and on the basis of which he campaigned for the presidency in 1912.[22] The value most often appealed to in the book, however, is "democracy," although in the next book he wrote, *Progressive Democracy* of 1914, he appealed to a new, post-laissez-faire liberalism.[23] It is plausible that he had previously thought that "liberalism" too readily evoked "old," laissez-faire liberalism, and had simply changed his mind. Dewey more often appealed to "democracy" as the fundamental value of the modern, and especially the modern American world, than to liberty or freedom. The book that Dewey regarded as providing the most complete account of "my philosophy such as it is" was *Democracy and Education*, written in 1916. Not until *Individualism Old and New* and *Liberalism and Social Action* in the early 1930s did he put forward a view of the politics appropriate to Depression-era America that was self-consciously and avowedly liberal.[24] Horace Kallen, writing in a collection of essays celebrating Dewey's ninetieth birthday in 1949, admitted that he thought that William James was a more consistent and convincing defender of an unabashed liberal individualism than was Dewey.[25] James, after all, had dedicated *Pragmatism* to Mill, "whom I like to fancy our leader." The explanation of Dewey's doubts about old-fashioned individualism is not hard to find. Like his British contemporaries, Dewey looked for the restoration of social harmony; he greatly admired T. H. Green, even though he thought that Green's belief in a Universal Self came dangerously close to the sort of "apart thinking" that Dewey deplored in Kant, whose contrast between the noumenal and the empirical self replicated the division between a judgmental God and sinful man that Dewey had found "lacerating" in the Congregationalism of his pious mother. Later in life, Dewey responded irritably to critics who said that he had never really rejected the Hegelianism that he had embraced in his early years; that it had left a "permanent residue" he never denied, but the residue was confined to his belief in a loosely organicist conception of society.[26] What he rejected and never again hankered after was the "Absolute." The quest for certainty had been abandoned, and the notion that there was some fixed destination to which the cunning of reason, manifest destiny, or the hand of God would lead mankind was firmly rejected; "growth" was Dewey's key concept, but growth toward what was something on which he refused to pontificate.

In intention at least, *The Promise of American Life* was less philosophical and more practically minded than most of Dewey's work; unless Dewey was advocating some immediate action, such as a vote against allowing sectarian instruction in public schools or rallying support for anti-communist candidates for posts in the teachers' union, his natural mode was to search for underlying principles. Croly was doing two things above all. The first was reminding his fellow Americans that it was up to them to redeem the promise that America held out. It was not going to be redeemed by divine intervention; there was nothing manifest about the destiny of America; and the assumption that Americans were uniquely blessed by providence and would be transported into the promised land without any effort on their part was the surest way to ensure that the promise remained unfulfilled. As to why the notably energetic American needed reminding of any of this, Croly offered rather little explanation. It is not hard to construct one, however, and it takes us back to the thought that "old" liberalism had taken the blessings of absolute property rights and laissez-faire too much for granted, and that the changed world of modern industry and the great industrial and financial trusts demanded something quite other than being left alone to regulate itself.

The second thing that Croly did, then, was to advocate what he called "new nationalism." This was the policy of pursuing Jeffersonian goals by Hamiltonian means. The idea is one that we can safely assume would have been rejected on the spot by both Jefferson and Hamilton, whose detestation of each other was complete. Nonetheless, it makes considerable sense. To see why, we must take a short detour through Louis Hartz's *Liberal Tradition in America*.[27] Hartz's thesis, which was greeted with incredulity in 1955 when the book was published but has provoked readers ever since, was that America was, so to speak, doomed to be liberal – in a very particular sense. Like many writers, Tocqueville among them, Hartz emphasized the importance of the peculiar history of America.

It had never been a feudal society; it lacked a real aristocracy, and therefore lacked a social class with the historical memories of European aristocracies. By the same token, its religious establishments had been feeble, and at a national level were explicitly outlawed by the Constitution. There were no religious tests for national office, and soon there were none for public office at a local level.

This meant, on Hartz's view, that America was a liberal society *ab initio*. This was not the absurd claim that the Puritans of seventeenth-century New England had been enthusiasts for religious laissez-faire or seized of the virtues of cultural pluralism; they hanged Quakers and witches and had a very clear sense of what our duties to God and man involved and of the legitimacy of enforcing them. It was the oddly phrased but not unpersuasive view that America was built on a foundation of irrational Lockianism (Hartz's spelling): that is, the essence of an individual was his capacity to acquire property and dispose of it at his own will; the essence of government the preservation of the social and economic conditions that would allow individuals to acquire property. It was "irrational" inasmuch as the rights of property were unchallenged and unchallengeable. So all-pervasive was the belief that personhood and ownership stood and fell together that Americans hardly knew they believed it, save when it was challenged.

There could be no genuine conservatism in a society that had not fought its way out of feudalism; socialism was equally unthinkable. In the absence of a true aristocracy, there were no barriers to social mobility; Lincoln's famous speech rejecting the "mudsill" theory of the inevitability and necessity of an underclass whose toil supported everything valuable in society became the American creed. Any man might work for another for a time, become a self-employed farmer or shopkeeper and, if he prospered by his efforts, finally employ others. The ideal was not solidarity as a European proletariat understood it, but individual prosperity. What one did with that prosperity was debatable, but the assumption that a decent member of the community would use his resources to keep the community in good heart was universally entertained. This was the society where, said Mill, there was none but a middle class; it was not a middle class "between" an upper and a lower class, but a monolithic petit bourgeoisie. The fact that 90 percent of Americans today describe themselves as middle class suggests the power of "Lockianism." The absence of a proletariat meant that there was no clientele for the socialist appeal that made so much more sense in Europe. Add to that the fact that white adult male suffrage was almost universal by the 1830s, while in Europe it was a far-off radical aspiration, and the contrast was complete. Marx put the demand for universal suffrage at the head of the socialists' demands because he thought the proletariat would demand what the bourgeoisie could not give them, and socialism would follow. In America, voters demanded what it was easy for governments to provide: easy access to land and no barriers to making money.

In what sense a country could be said to be "liberal" while 4 million of the 30 million Americans on the eve of the Civil War were enslaved Negroes is a large question. That slavery was an anomaly was widely, but far from universally, felt. Two notable defenders of slavery, Calhoun and George Fitzhugh, took the line, familiar from Aristotle onwards, that if a society was to have a leisured class, and anything resembling a true civilization, let alone the possibility of pursuing liberal values for those who were able to lead the life of an autonomous and civilized being, there must be a laboring class who were – in Marxian terms – exploited.[28] They must produce the resources that their superiors used, receiving a bare subsistence in return. Whether it was the laboring class of the Northern states, exploited by capitalist employers or slaves in the Southern states, whom the defenders of slavery claimed were exploited less severely than their northern counterparts, made little difference.

The implausibility of this conclusion needs no demonstration. Slaves tried to escape to the Northern states where they were likely to find social exclusion and a hostile welcome from the white workers with whom they were in competition. Workers in the northern states did not offer themselves for slavery or indentured servitude in the Southern states. In any case, the Civil War settled the matter. Badly as the black population would be treated after Reconstruction, nobody could own another human being. The Lockean principle that nobody is born to be the property of another was built into the Constitution by the Thirteenth Amendment, even if the sanctity of property in other human beings remained in the Constitution of the state of Kentucky as late as the 1890s.

Croly and Dewey were writing in the aftermath of the great burst of economic expansion that followed the Civil War. The most obvious feature of that expansion was the rise of the great trusts; aided by a complaisant Supreme Court that gave corporations – fictitious persons – all the rights of natural persons, industrial, railroad, and financial conglomerates could wield an economic power that single individuals could not, other than the single individuals at the helm of the conglomerates. Their ability to influence the political system was obvious enough, as well. It was said that nobody could obtain high political office without a *nihil obstat* from Jay Gould; as for the petroleum interests in Pennsylvania, they were said to have done everything with the state legislature but refine it. Dewey was unreservedly hostile to big business; both Democrats and Republicans he dismissed as "bag carriers for business." Croly's outlook was more interesting.

He had been brought up a Comtean Positivist, and although he lost his faith in Positivism without acquiring a more conventional faith in its stead, he retained enough of Comte's outlook to understand that the rise of the trusts was not accidental. Like his British contemporaries and Dewey, too, he thought that a wholly unorganized laissez-faire capitalism was an impossibility in the twentieth century. When railroads were tying together a vast continent and offering opportunities for greatly increased productivity, one could hardly operate as if nothing had changed from the era of the small yeoman farmer.

The "promise" of American life was a promise that individuals could achieve self-realization, a decent standard of living, find interesting work, and give an unfeigned loyalty to the political system that promoted individual self-realization. The danger posed by big business was that it would block individual advancement; the benefits of America's astonishing industrial advance were in danger of being monopolized by the already rich and well-connected and well-organized. The American promise was not *narrowly* economic; like many of his European and American contemporaries, and like Matthew Arnold thirty years earlier, Croly feared that one casualty of the race for riches would be civilized existence itself. If the rich lived in bloated luxury and the ordinary man lived in mean surroundings, the promise of a democratic culture would remain unfulfilled. Croly himself was an architectural critic and a very competent architect.

In *The Promise of American Life*, the political creed he advanced was "new nationalism." Its other name was democracy. When he

wrote *Progressive Democracy* in 1914, it was liberalism. The difference was essentially verbal. Previously "liberalism" would have
suggested "old liberalism," or the liberalism of Victorian Britain. By
1914, the regulatory state was no longer a novelty; American cities
had become used to owning natural monopolies such as streetcar
lines and, where they did not own the utility companies themselves,
to setting rates for utilities such as water, gas, and electicity. This
was part of the movement that was sometimes called "gas and water
socialism," but which was "socialist" only to the extent that it often
involved public ownership, and in many respects was liberal in its
aim of preventing firms from benefiting too much from natural
monopolies, and recreating a more nearly level playing field between
consumers and suppliers. Croly's concern, however, was with the
blocking of opportunity for the individual, so that his interest in
making the national interest prevail over the particular interest of
the owners of an enterprise was in a broad sense liberal, at least
inasmuch as preserving the American promise was a "Jeffersonian"
project. *Progressive Democracy* was unabashed about characterizing
Croly's stance as liberal. Readers a century later may well wince at a
good deal of *Progressive Democracy*, not because of Croly's views,
but because Croly's strictures on the American tendency to engage
in mindless worship of the Constitution, and the Supreme Court's
tendency to protect the property interests of corporations against the
interests of their employees and the wider society remain as pertinent
today as in 1914.

LIBERALISM DEFEATED

Britain and the United States shared many ideological attachments,
but it is always worth keeping American exceptionalism in mind.
Britain had an aristocracy as the United States did not, and an organized labor movement with a political party avowedly committed to
promoting the interests of workers by hand and brain by the public
ownership of the means of production, distribution, and exchange.
They seem more similar than they were for the usual reason; they
were more different from other countries other than members of the
white commonwealth. Of course, that claim itself has to be taken
with a pinch of salt. The French Third Republic was a liberal political
creation; until Mussolini destroyed parliamentary government in

1924, Italy was a liberal parliamentary monarchy, in narrowly legal terms a constitutional monarchy not wholly unlike Britain.[29] The authority of the German and the Austro-Hungarian emperors was vastly greater than that of the British head of state; they were essentially authoritarian regimes, whose national identity depended on a mystique of military glory – better founded in the case of Prussia than in the case of Austria – and a tradition of opposition to the liberal and republican regimes of Britain and France that was inevitably political and military but in the twentieth century became cultural. Thomas Mann's defense of the German side in World War I is not exactly typical, because Mann was a literary genius and a fearless writer; but the idea that there was a distinctive German *kultur* that it was the duty of Germans to protect and, if necessary, to die for in war was widely shared.

The case of France is more illuminating than any, since France is as much the fountainhead of modern liberalism as Britain or the United States, and Tocqueville and Constant certainly rank with Mill as defenders of individual liberty. Yet, French writers also contributed more than any others to the theory of fascism, whether to "blood and soil" nationalism, to the craze for ethnic purity and an attendant anti-Semitism, to the cult of leadership, or to a general anti-rationalism. Sorel, Barrès, and Maurras were sophisticated thinkers and had a substantial if often indirect influence; it is a well-known irony of history that both Lenin and Mussolini wished to erect a monument to Sorel. There are perhaps three aspects of French politics that explain the ambivalence of the French toward liberalism. The first is that it was never clear whether the French Revolution had been a "success." As late as 1980, it was a bold rhetorical move for François Furet to declare that the Revolution was definitely over; many of his readers believed it was unfinished business.[30] What was unfinished was debatable, but among the arguable topics was the place of the Catholic Church in modern politics, and the extent of the loyalty that the church could be expected to feel toward a republic that was ostentatiously "lay." The church had, after all, spent much of the nineteenth and twentieth centuries denouncing liberalism. By 1989, thirty years had elapsed since Charles de Gaulle had pre-empted a military coup that would have run a grave risk of civil war and would certainly have prolonged the agony of Algerian independence; but de Gaulle had not emulated Napoleon III or General Mahon. He had built a stable democratic republic and had defused the hostility of many Catholics toward the republican state. The debate between the enthusiasts for government by a man on a white horse and the defenders of slow and messy parliamentary government had been won by the latter with the aid of the former. Finally, perhaps, the French intoxication with the concept of revolution had come to an end; the second centenary of 1789 coincided all too neatly with the end of communist rule in Eastern Europe, the fall of the Berlin Wall echoing the fall of the Bastille.

Furet was an unequivocal liberal and admirer of Tocqueville. Nonetheless, a second aspect of French ambivalence about liberalism is that liberty was for a long time not primarily associated with English notions of laissez-faire in economics and negative liberty protected by the rule of law as the central political value. Liberty was rather, as Benjamin Constant observed, understood in terms of republican government and the sovereignty of the people. Constant's essay on the liberty of the ancients and the moderns was written 140 years before Isaiah Berlin's *Two Concepts of Liberty*, but makes the essential point more sharply than Berlin's lecture did. It is not a conceptual confusion to call a share of the sovereignty "liberty," as did the popular republics of the ancient world, but it is a mistake to overlook the danger that "the people" collectively will tyrannize over "the people" individually.[31] We want Socrates' right to free speech protected against even an impeccably constituted Athenian dikastery. To the extent that the French left was republican, populist, and democratic, it was not friendly to liberalism in the sense here at issue, the "liberty of the moderns." Attach those sentiments to an ethnic nationalism, and one may have a wonderful instrument for exporting the principles of the revolution on the points of the bayonets of Napoleon's soldiers, but not a wholly reliable support of liberalism.

The third aspect was, of course, the French attachment to the idea of revolution; this was not always, and in the twentieth century very rarely, the "bourgeois" French Revolution of 1789–94, but to something less tangible and readily taken over by the French Communist party in its Leninist guise and rhetorically available to bourgeois-hating philosophers such as Jean-Paul Sartre, who had an attachment to the idea of politics as violence that one would have thought more at home in the work of Carl Schmitt than a dissident Marxist. The idea has always been that the Revolution is unfinished business; indeed, one thought is that the Revolution must be unfinished business, a process that is more nearly Nietzschean in its emphasis on a continuous process of "overcoming" than Marxian in its emphasis on achieving the final breakthrough to a wholly rational society free from exploitation and oppression of all sorts. The "anti-bourgeois" aspect of such a political vision is obvious enough; whatever one might imagine as the world vision of the European bourgeoisie, "permanent revolution" is not it. The gales of creative destruction celebrated in the *Communist Manifesto* and given their name by Joseph Schumpeter a century later were acceptable only if confined to the means of production; the sanctity of property, stable, cheap, and predictable government, and no military adventures were more to the bourgeois taste.

The wilder reaches of the revolutionary tradition were not all that there was, of course. The liberal tradition that runs from Montesquieu to Aron by way of Constant, Guizot, Tocqueville, and Halévy suffered eclipse as a result of World War I and the attraction of Marxism on the one hand and violent nationalism on the other. Another variety of French liberalism of the early twentieth century was of great importance. This was offered by Emile Durkheim.[32] Like much of Durkheim's work it defies simple summary, but for Durkheim the crux was a distinction between two forms of individualism. What one might, for simplicity's sake, describe as "bad" individualism is what Tocqueville described as *individualisme*, a form of separation from the rest of society, and a kind of social and moral isolation; it is not exactly the individualism of rational economic man, whose horizons are bounded only by the pursuit of his own self-interest. That individualism is also a "bad" individualism, since it undermines the moral solidarity that gives coherence to a society; in Durkheim's view the essence of society, what gives it its "thing-like" quality is its normative character. Liberalism, in Durkheim's analysis, is defined by what one might call "good" individualism, an individualism of the kind explained and defended by Immanuel Kant. This was not selfish or self-centered individualism but the individualism of persons who thought of themselves as called to make the most of themselves, to take responsibility for their lives and ideas. What Kant saw as the imperatives of the noumenal self,

Durkheim saw as imperatives addressed to individuals by the society in which they lived. Then, as was true of other new liberals, he was faced with the question of whether society did indeed display the kind of moral coherence that his view implied that it should. The answer too often was that it did not, and that bad individualism eroded both our commitment to the ideals implicit in modern liberal society and the capacity of the society to operate according to those ideals.

Durkheim's proposed remedies relied heavily on turning occupational associations into something more than devices for advancing the narrowly economic interests of their members. This was another aspect of what in many ways was the common theme of liberals who were not willing to follow revolutionary socialist proposals for the abolition of private property in the means of production and its replacement by common ownership; the thought was that some intermediate form of ownership and organization would retain the virtues of private ownership in the usual sense, focusing on the incentive it provided to individuals to be self-supporting, hard-working, and generally self-respecting members of society but allowing society a larger role in regulating work, industry, and the marketplace, preferably by giving secondary associations a large role in economic life. The chaos of the war of all against all that free enterprise could too easily represent or the tyranny of a central dictatorship that socialism could too easily represent could both be avoided.[33]

None of this came to pass, of course. Whatever marked European society between 1900 and 1945, it was not the triumph of a modestly corporatist liberalism. The very possibility of a genuinely liberal but corporatist state is often denied, usually because the states that proudly represented themselves as corporate states were Fascist states, Italy first among them. Instead of giving secondary associations a free and expansive role, the state employed them as a means of enforcing its will on their members. From the point of view of a liberal, the villain of the piece was nationalism, and fascism of whatever variety was, above all, an ultra-nationalist movement.[34] The appeal of nationalism in post-1918 Europe hardly needs elaborate explanation. In the nineteenth century liberalism and nationalism had often been allies for good reason; the multi-national and multi-ethnic empires against which movements for national independence had been directed were generally speaking authoritarian and repressive. Moreover, anyone who imagined a future in which the rule of law was observed, property was not subject to arbitrary expropriation, and a widely diffused prosperity could be looked for had to imagine a competent nation-state providing the necessary legal and institutional framework. That it must be a *nation*-state was not an implication of the quest for a liberal society, but it certainly must be a state, which is to say an organization able to make law and enforce it by coercive means. Once traditional forms of legitimacy had been undermined, the obvious basis of support was national identity. Mill and Acton thought a liberal state required a strong sense of national cohesion, and plausibly so. The problem was, and is, that exactly what constitutes a nation is indeterminate, and national identity is all too likely to match conventional national borders very inexactly. Liberalism has difficulty providing a satisfactory answer to the question of what makes a person a member of one nation rather than another, because liberalism treats states as convenient forms of organization; a national "myth" which separates insiders from outsiders, and "us" from "them," is not intrinsic to liberalism, although there can be and are nations whose myth is that they are "empires of liberty." At all events, where illiberal nationalism confronted liberalism in interwar Europe, liberalism was the loser. As was said earlier, this should not be taken to mean that nationalism overcame strong liberal resistance in countries such as Hungary, Roumania, or Yugoslavia, although Czechoslovakia was another matter. The crucial state, of course, was Germany, since the truncated Austrian Republic, all that remained of the Austro-Hungarian Empire, was torn between right-wing conservative parties and social democratic and communist parties which were ineffective, but threatening enough to make their conservative opponents ready to resort to violence in putting down their socialist enemies. Once the Nazis had come to power, it was only a matter of time before Hitler launched the *Anschluss* or takeover of Austria, the destruction of parliamentary government, and the imprisonment of many politicians, conservatives among them. The political disasters that befell Germany herself are hardly to be tackled briefly, especially when the roots of those disasters lie in the failure of the 1848 revolutions to replace Prussian autocracy with a constitutional parliamentary republic.

The question that underlies every discussion of German political history is whether it was simply impossible that a liberal democracy could have been successfully established in Germany, either before or after World War I. Neither a positive nor a negative answer is satisfactory; to suppose that Germany was doomed to produce Hitler and to follow him into catastrophe surely underestimates the ability of both politicians and the population at large to bring about rational and undestructive political outcomes, while the thought that Germany might, for all we know, have turned into a parliamentary liberal democracy much like France or Britain, but for a few difficulties, runs into the problem that the list is a very long one and the weight to be given to different items impossibly hard to specify. They are commonly summed up as the problem of "belatedness," which is more nearly a gesture toward the fact that Germany did not follow the path of Britain and France into the modern world than any sort of explanation of that fact. At all events, on the eve of World War I, Germany was more nearly an autocracy than a parliamentary democracy, even though the Reichstag was a representative assembly elected on a wide manhood franchise.

The fatal event was the war. Although Germany was very nearly starved into defeat and for long periods had much the better of the conflict on the battlefield, defeat was intolerable. The legitimacy of the German Reich rested on the myth of military invulnerability, together with a national sense that Germany had never been accorded the respect due to a major power by Britain and France. The Weimar Republic faced an uphill struggle to establish itself.

Economically, the postwar settlement imposed excessive burdens on the German economy; like many of the defeated countries, Germany suffered appalling inflation that wiped out the savings of many of the middle classes and gave the impression that a parliamentary democracy could not govern successfully. Above all, too large a segment of the population believed that the country's defeat in the war had been a "stab in the back," and looked for revenge against an ill-assorted set of enemies, among whom Bolsheviks, speculators, and Jews were prominent. It is hard to see who might have prevented the Nazi rise to power; a notionally demilitarized Germany could not readily call out troops to crush Nazi street fighters, and in any event, ex-soldiers and young men spoiling for a fight were readily found among the Nazi and Communist fighters but hardly among enthusiasts for liberal political institutions.

POSTSCRIPT

World War II was an unequivocal defeat for Nazism and Fascism. It was a very equivocal victory for liberalism. Of the Allies, Russia was a tyranny, Nationalist China a military autocracy. Among uninvolved European states, Spain and Portugal were semi-fascist dictatorships. The liberalism of Western European countries and the United States was thereafter put under considerable pressure both by the Cold War, and by the strains of decolonization. On the other hand, the growth of an international human rights culture, slow and imperfect as it has been, has provided pressure of a broadly liberal kind embodied most impressively in the European Convention on Human Rights and the institutions created to give the convention greater purchase on the behavior of those governments that subscribed to it. Intellectually, the liberalism that became something like the common sense of political philosophers in the anglophone world is continuous with the "new" liberalism described above. As a consensus, it has provoked many reactions to left and right, both from thinkers who wished to defend some variety of socialism or some form of conservatism, and from thinkers who wanted to think in wholly different ways from what they saw as anglophone orthodoxy. All that is beyond the scope of this chapter.

NOTES

1. Hartz, *The Liberal Tradition in America*, pp. 5–14.
2. Mazower, *Dark Continent*; Arendt, *The Origins of Totalitarianism*.
3. Medearis, *Joseph A. Schumpeter*; Schumpeter, *Capitalism, Socialism and Democracy*, ch. 22.
4. Gasset, *The Revolt of the Masses*; Bellamy, "The Advent of the Masses and the Making of the Modern Theory of Democracy," in Ball and Bellamy, *Cambridge History*, pp. 70–103.
5. Ryan, "Liberalism", pp. 15–44.
6. Thaler and Sunstein, *Nudge*.
7. Contra Berlin, "Two Concepts of Liberty."
8. Bell, *The Cultural Contradictions of Capitalism*.
9. Popper, *The Open Society and Its Enemies*, pp. 55ff.

10. Rawls, *Political Liberalism.*
11. Sandel, *Liberalism and the Limits of Justice.*
12. Nussbaum, *Political Emotions.*
13. Hume, *Political Essays*, p. 219.
14. Roosevelt, "State of the Union Address to Congress," January 6, 1941.
15. Indeed the term was one that he popularized, notably in a presidential campaign speech at Madison Square Garden, October 23, 1928.
16. Robin, *The Reactionary Mind;* Hartz, *Liberal Tradition.*
17. Mill, *Liberty and the Subjection of Women*, p. 76.
18. Hobhouse, *Liberalism*, p. 125.
19. Hegel, *Elements of the Philosophy of Right*, pp. 275ff.
20. Gore and Hobhouse (eds.), *Property: Its Rights and Duties.*
21. Bellamy, *Liberalism and Modern Society*, p. 55.
22. Croly, *The Promise of American Life;* Forcey, *Crossroads of Liberalism.*
23. Croly, *Progressive Democracy.*
24. Dewey, "Individualism Old and New"; Dewey, "Liberalism and Social Action."
25. Kallen, "Dewey and Pragmatism"; Kallen, "Individuality, Individualism, and John Dewey."
26. Dewey, "From Absolutism to Experimentalism," p. 154.
27. Hartz, *Liberal Tradition*, ch 1.
28. Calhoun, "Slavery a Positive Good," Speech to the US Senate, February 1837; Fitzhugh, *Cannibals All!*
29. Bellamy, *Liberalism and Modern Society*, chs. 2–3.
30. Furet, "The French Revolution Is Over," pp. 1–79.
31. Constant, "The Liberty of the Ancients Compared with that of the Moderns," in *Political Writings*, pp. 309–28.
32. Bellamy, *Liberalism and Modern Society*, ch. 2.
33. Durkheim, *Professional Ethics and Civic Morals.*
34. Ball and Bellamy (eds.), *History of Twentieth Century Political Thought*, chs. 4–6.

II Normative foundations

4 Liberalism, contractarianism, and the problem of exclusion

INTRODUCTION

For liberal contractarians, moral and political principles are justified if agreeable to persons as free and equals.[1] But for critics of liberal contractarianism, this justification does not apply to all those who should be treated as free and equal, but only to those capable of agreement. Some will be unable to agree because they lack the understanding or ability to make agreements. Others have so little to offer that there is no benefit to contracting with them. So if the justification of liberal political morality rests on agreement, it is not justified to those such as children or people with many different kinds of disability who lack the full capacities to form rational voluntary agreements. Such excluded may be treated kindly under contractarian politics, but they are not treated as fellow free and equals.

Although the problem of exclusion is one among a number of fundamental objections to contractarianism, it is particularly important. The problem of exclusion derives from the centrality of agreement in contractarianism. Agreement represents the ideal that principles of political morality must be acceptable to each individual. Agreement is taken to demarcate contractarianism from other approaches to liberal political morality, notably utilitarianism. Understanding why contractarianism suffers from the problem of exclusion helps up understand the distinctive character of contractarianism and the importance of agreement in particular. But need exclusion be problematic? I suggest contractarianism need not be objectionably exclusive. I first consider why agreement is important in contractarianism, and then introduce the main versions of contemporary contractarianism and their different understandings of agreement. I discuss how agreement results in exclusion in each, and distinguish two kinds of response to the problem of exclusion: differential inclusion and permissive inclusion. Differential inclusion is unsuccessful because it offers those not fully capable of agreement unequal status. Permissive inclusion may either make the circumstances of agreement more open, or characterize the capacities required for inclusion more permissively. I advocate the latter as the most promising response to the problem of exclusion. I outline a more inclusive contractualism based on the capacity to share goals. We participate in relationships of sharing with a wide range of people, including children and people with different kinds of disabilities, not all of whom are fully capable of rational voluntary agreement. These relationships of sharing form the basis of relational duties that fit contractualist circumstances of agreement. We can therefore include as equals all those with whom we share goals in the relevant way in a contractualist justification of moral and political principles.

WHY AGREEMENT?

What lies at the heart of the exclusion objection? For contractarians, agreement represents an important aspect of our practical relations with each other: Individuals are capable of choosing constraints on their interactions with others and, when chosen freely, these constraints are justified. Principles are not chosen because they are justified; they are justified because chosen.[2] Historical contractarians considered how agreement might represent consent, and how consent may justify the constraints of political authority. These arguments suffered badly at the hands of utilitarians, however.[3] Freely chosen agreement to the power and authority of governments is conspicuously absent from ordinary political life. But each person's interest in their lives going well is conspicuously pervasive. For utilitarians, political authority is justified if it makes people's lives go better. Utilitarianism as public philosophy complemented liberal commitments to skepticism of political authority and the importance of treating people as rational and free to pursue that which makes their lives go well.[4] The justification of laws and political morality through hypothetical agreement receded as utilitarianism offered a rational and determinate method to manage society and promote its greater well-being.

Though utilitarianism complements many liberal commitments, it jars with others. As free responsible adults, we are no doubt entitled to make choices and sacrifices between our preferences for our own greater benefit. But utilitarianism suggests society as a whole should be governed like this. So the question changes from which interests of mine should I sacrifice for my greater well-being, to whose interests should be sacrificed for society's greater well-being?[5] This classical utilitarian view, that social policies are right and institutions just if the aggregate of well-being is maximized, may threaten the stable order of society. It asks an individual not just to sacrifice one of their lesser interests for one of their greater; it asks one individual to sacrifice his or her interests for the greater interests of others. It imposes a burden that it is rational to reject out of self-interest, or reasonable to reject because unfair.

So though utilitarianism gives liberals a clear method for making policies, it may affront liberal convictions that political authority be acceptable to each person. Acceptability to each person must then be a hallmark of a liberal order for it to be stable and legitimate.[6] It seems natural that social rules may be acceptable if we are confident each person is bearing a fair share of the burdens they entail. If we can be confident that no rules will be enforced on us unfairly, and that each will share in maintaining these rules, we may hope that social life will be stable because agreeable.

Though welcome, actual agreement is not required for rules to be agreeable. The notion of agreement is hypothetical; it represents the practical relations with which we are concerned. It represents each individual's entitlement to refuse to accept a policy or principle that would treat them unfairly. For example, I might rightly refuse to accept a rule if it imposed on me a cost without benefit; or I might refuse obedience to a law enforced on me while others went free to ignore it. Although historical contractarians may have emphasized agreement as representing consent, today's contractarians emphasize agreement as representing the inviolable worth of each person. Agreement represents what is impermissible in a liberal society: the enforcement of any law or principle that is unacceptable to anyone, on good grounds. Agreement's representation of the inviolability of persons demarcates contractarianism from consequentialism in liberalism.

Agreements differ in views of the circumstances of agreement, the characteristics of those agreeing, the process of agreement, the subject matter of agreement, and the outcomes of the agreement. Contractarians disagree about whether agreements should represent simply our prudential interests in dealing with others; or also our moral commitments toward others. All agree, though, that representing the inviolability of individuals in contracts secures the justifiability and hence stability of liberal society better than utilitarianism. But if preserving the inviolability of individuals depends on agreement, what about those incapable of agreeing? Does contractarianism merely swap the unacceptable burdens of aggregation for some for the unacceptable exclusion of others?

AGREEING BECAUSE IT IS FAIR AND JUST

Rawls turns to agreement to justify principles for the just government of society's most fundamental institutions. Utilitarianism fails to recognize the importance of the claims of justice of each person taken separately, but agreement does. Rawls takes agreement to concern the justice of social institutions because social life is characterized by a moderate scarcity of resources between persons roughly equal in mind and might, who see the merits of cooperation.[7] Though cooperation is appealing, it is difficult because people have differing plans for their lives that may lead to conflicting claims over the scarce resources. These circumstances, combined with a limited generosity toward others, raise the problem of dealing justly with individuals' claims. Individuals will be concerned that their entitlements are addressed fairly by those institutions that have the most pervasive and coercive effect on their lives.[8] If the most basic rules are fair to all, they should be regarded as agreeable to each. And if justice prevails, stability follows.

For Rawls, individuals' most important interests are to be able to develop their powers to understand and be motivated by the demands of justice (an effective sense of justice); and to be able to choose, follow, and revise if necessary how one's life should go (a capacity to form and revise a conception of the good).[9] Having an interest in pursuing our good life while living justly with others motivates us to seek a justification that is mutually agreeable. We are motivated to find an agreement that we and others feel will provide a shared basis for the promotion of our common interest in an effective sense of justice and pursuit of a conception of the good. We do not know what terms might be mutually acceptable, as we have no special insight into what justice might be independently of what we agree it to be.

Contractarians typically agree that requirements of freedom and equality are not knowable directly through perception or a special kind of reasoning. They must be decided upon using a procedure that ensures the outcomes will be clear and specific, and will conform to our prior general commitments about what freedom and equality entail. There will be no way to judge whether the outcomes of a procedure fit perfectly with what freedom, equality, or justice requires, because this depends purely on what comes out of the procedure. While we don't know the content of an agreement in advance, we can be clear and sure, however, about the condition under which we must agree. If we are able to represent these commitments in the conditions under which we seek agreement, we can be confident that the agreement is justifiable because just.[10]

The circumstances of the agreement, Rawls's original position, are constrained by his view of the practical nature of persons and the implications of this for our claims on each other. The constraints on the original position represent fairness.[11] The content of the agreement is constructed through the idea of representative individuals considering what principles would best enable them to fulfil their highest-order interests. To eliminate partiality for their own particular view of the good life, Rawls denies these representatives knowledge of their personal life-plans and information about their individuality that may naturally affect decisions about what goods are most advantageous to them.[12] Representative individuals choosing with attitudes of mutual indifference to each other (no envy or self-sacrifice), choosing rationally and self-interestedly in these fair conditions, would be assured to choose principles that are fair.

On Rawls's contractarian view, individuals have good reason to agree to the principles constructed in the original position. Everyone, including those whose lives are less advantaged than others, will see that the content of the agreement represents their moral commitments to a fair social order. They will also see that their chances to pursue their plans for a good life are as advantageous as possible, even to the extent that greater advantages for some are allowed only if they benefit those least advantaged.[13] The principles of justice can be shown to be agreeable from a common or shared point of view, irrespective of an individual's particular commitments and goals (the point of view of the representatives in the original position). These principles can also be shown as agreeable and preferable to others because they are consonant with each individual's natural desire to live alongside others justly. Given our common desire that justice be effective in regulating our lives with others, Rawls argues that we will each endorse these principles because they create the social conditions for justice to be effective in our lives.[14]

While the principles of justice as fairness may be more acceptable than alternatives, individuals may find that they conflict with their plans for a good life. So though justified from a common, or shared, point of view, they may not have sufficient priority in individuals' everyday lives to make the agreement stable. Rawls initially sought to show that the constrained choice of the original position would also be the choice of individuals who know about themselves and their plans for their lives. The principles would be agreeable to an extent that individuals would defer to them finally, and so the agreement would be stable. Individuals would accept them, even knowing about conflicts with their more particular goals and commitments, because it could be demonstrated that living under principles of justice is also good for them. So principles of justice would be agreeable, and stable, because congruent with our good.[15]

Rawls later came to see that arguments for the congruence of justice and a person's good could not ensure stability, because it involves people regarding a life of freedom and equality as the most important good.[16] In a free society individuals are able to adopt and pursue lives with different priorities, such as the religious who value obedience and self-negation most highly. Reasonable people, committed to living together under institutions that are just, may decide autonomy is not of ultimate value. In these circumstances of reasonable pluralism, Rawls argues that we could still demonstrate that the two principles of justice would be chosen over others from the point of view of individuals' general and shared interests, as expressed in the original position.[17] But when considering how the principles would be acceptable from each person's particular point of view, we have to recognize that the agreement is limited in scope to political life.[18] Thus, Rawls turns from demonstrating the agreeability of the principles from a point of view that encompasses people's values and beliefs comprehensively, to one that appeals to their values and beliefs as citizens of a democratic polity. Citizens of a well-ordered society will regard themselves and others as entitled to be treated as free and equal in the most central matters of politics. They will be able to form a consensus among citizens acting in good faith toward each other as free and equal fellow citizens, and who are mindful of the limitations and restrictions on appeals they can make to their personal plans and commitments in justification of political authority.[19]

Limiting the reasons and justification to those political standards shared by all does not make the justification weaker or merely a pragmatic compromise. Whilst society may be composed of a plurality of reasonable views of the good life, it also contains within it a shared tradition of regarding its citizens as free and equal. The ideal of living together with other citizens justly will have its own independent value: a political value. However, the reasons people find to support it will be consonant with their personal views of the good life. While persons will find different reasons for supporting this political view of society, each will find that to be regarded as a citizen who is free and equal and entitled to respect as such (and to regard others as such too) is good for them as citizens. Given the special moral and practical importance of living in a just polity, citizens will also see this as part of what it is to lead a good life as an individual. So, Rawls came to see that the principles of justice, chosen by persons from a common point of view, must not rely on an appeal to only those views of the good life that value being free and autonomous throughout one's life. Even those who value religious obedience most highly, if committed to living alongside other citizens under a just and legitimate regime, would find the experience of mutual respect and flourishing as citizens to be part of what it means to lead a good life.[20]

However, is it necessary to show, as does Rawls, that principles are agreeable because they appeal both to our prudential rationality and to our reasonable moral commitments? What if our interests and commitments conflict? Which is authoritative? Within the contractarian tradition we find some who argue that common prudential interests alone can lead us to adopt constraints on our behavior that are agreeable and represent what we mean when we speak of justice and fairness. Others argue that moral reasons are sufficient in themselves to justify agreement on moral or political principles. Thus, from Rawls's combination of rational and reasonable considerations, contractarians divide into two camps. The first camp seeks to derive principles for cooperation from prudence alone, while the second camp seeks to derive these principles from our moral commitments to the freedom and equality of all.

AGREEING BECAUSE IT IS TO OUR MUTUAL ADVANTAGE

If all our interactions with others were like transactions in a perfect market, where all individuals acting purely from self-interest would make everyone as well-off as they could be, we would have no use for rules of cooperation. Morality and justice would be unnecessary; harmony and satisfaction would be optimum. But Gauthier agrees with Rawls that we find ourselves in circumstances of moderate scarcity, limited benevolence, and yet with the potential to benefit mutually from cooperation.[21] Is it possible to explain that rules of cooperation are rational and so can be adopted voluntarily, or do rules of cooperation require a threat of coercion to ensure obedience?

Gauthier argues that it would be rational to reject utilitarianism as a basis for designing cooperative social institutions or principles for cooperating with others. Utilitarianism may mean some receive unearned benefits, and others incur uncompensated costs, in order to maximize utility. This would create free-riders and parasites.[22] Utilitarianism may also regard individuals' endowments (their property and factors they may use in market activity) as subject to redistribution to maximize utility. However, this would affect individuals' freedom in work and exchange, and would treat the distribution of factor endowments as arbitrary and not a matter of rightful entitlement.[23] It would be rational for individuals not to comply with such rules, and this would threaten the stability of society. Such rules would need to be coercively enforced, and so utilitarianism fails to explain or justify stable voluntary cooperation between individuals.

Gauthier's alternative is contractarian. Moral and political constraints agreeable to all are justified and hence stable. Justice is rational; free riding and parasitism irrational.[24] For Gauthier, we find something valuable if it contributes to fulfilling our preferences. Gauthier denies that there is a universal or objective list of preferences common to all. We prefer different things for different reasons. But there is a common and objective structure to preferences and our pursuit of them. If our preferences are settled and organized, it is rational for us to pursue that which we expect to fulfill our preferences most fully.[25] When faced with dealing with others, we have to take into account that others are also motivated to maximize their expected utility. This seems a recipe for conflict, as we each try to bargain to obtain the most we can. We also seem faced with the challenge that while cooperation may sometimes be beneficial, at other times cheating may be less costly and more beneficial than cooperating. If we come to doubt the trustworthiness of others to keep agreements and cooperate faithfully, society may descend into the paradox where it is rational for each of us to distrust the other and choose options we know will make us worse off, rather than risking trust and mutually benefiting.[26] However, Gauthier argues that given the instability and the disbenefit of forgoing opportunities to cooperate, it is rational to constrain our reasons to maximize in each interaction. So we would adopt a strategy in dealing with others of seeking agreement to mutually constrain our maximizing reasons in order to gain from the expected benefits of opportunities to cooperate. However, it would only be rational to agree to constraints on our maximizing reason if we had some warranted assurance that others were similarly motivated. If we have sufficient reason to accept that others adopt the strategy of voluntarily constraining their maximization of expected utility, then cooperation and its benefits will flourish.[27] But though we are now willing to constrain our reasons to maximize the fulfillment of our preferences, we still wish to fulfill them as fully as possible whilst interacting with others. So, Gauthier argues, it is rational to adopt a strategy where we make the smallest concession to others to obtain the greatest fulfillment of our preferences: minimax relative concession.[28] Yet for each to accept the outcomes of such a bargain voluntarily, each would need to be assured that the relative bargaining advantage was roughly equal, that no one had acquired property or technology or advantage at the expense of others: Gauthier's Lockean proviso on the conditions for agreement.[29] If the initial conditions of bargaining allowed predation by the strong over the weak, agreements may be struck where the weak accept from desperation and not advantage. Bargains lacking mutual advantage would rely on coercion and threats to be enforced because we could hardly be assured of the voluntary assent of the weak who receive no benefit. Such agreements are unstable and costly, and therefore we could expect them to be of less value to us over time than agreements between more equally situated cooperators agreeing voluntarily to constrain their choices and actions for mutual advantage.

By constructing morality and justice through the agreement of rational, self-interested persons, Gauthier's contractarianism aims to justify the authority of principles on the basis of our capacity to decide freely when it is in our best interest to constrain our behavior according to principles agreed with others. Whilst we may see the value of constraining our reasons to maximize our expected utility, Gauthier emphasizes that all agreements must lead positively to the pursuit of our self-interest. This provides a bulwark against legitimizing any relationship where someone becomes merely an instrument for someone else's pleasure or satisfaction. Exploitation, oppression, and false consciousness about one's preferences due to deceit are illegitimate and unjustified on this contractarian view.[30]

An implication of Gauthier's contractarianism is that others are of value to us only insofar as we benefit from interacting with them. That others have only instrumental value denies what is, for many of us, a fundamental liberal principle: Individuals have intrinsic value and are entitled to equal respect. Most liberals who endorse such a commitment would accept that it is permissible to bargain and agree constraints on maximizing one's interests, and that this may explain the morality of a certain set of personal relationships. But they would contest that the whole of our moral interactions can be reduced to this. For Gauthier, rational self-interest justifies the constraints on our private and public lives with others. Even if such bargains can be struck and found stable; even if these bargains resemble our moral intuitions about justified political authority; and even if they protect people from harmful subjugation; for many it neglects an important aspect of the value of living together on moral terms. For many of us, we are called to live on terms mutually agreeable because we regard it as wrong to live under rules which some reject for good reason. It is not wrong simply because of any harm which follows from such rules. It is also wrong at a more fundamental level.

AGREEING FROM MUTUAL RECOGNITION

Many contractarians reject Gauthier's attempt to derive agreement on rules of cooperation from prudential rationality. Purely self-regarding agreements about morality or justice would be unstable: at some point free riding may be the most rational choice for an individual.[31] Rather than appeal solely to prudence, we should appeal directly to the motivation to agree on terms which treat all as free and equal. As the agreement is between those motivated to agree on moral terms, we need not steal away facts about ourselves in order to decide the content of principles of justice or rightness. We need not model constrained prudence; we can count on those motivated by moral concerns to constrain their prudential interests. Principles of justice or morality are agreeable because they fit our will to be just.

Once prudential reciprocity is eliminated from the motive to agree, principles governing our relationship with others should represent our motivation to live together on terms no reasonable person has good reason to reject.

Basing agreement on moral rather than prudential reasoning and motivation represents a distinct form of contractarianism: what Scanlon describes as contractualism. Scanlon argues that if persons are motivated to live together on such terms, then this commitment will give content and also constrain the reasons they give and evaluate from others in justification. In other words, reasonable people will seek to agree terms that cannot be reasonably rejected because of their interest and commitment to living in unity with others similarly motivated.[32] The value of living this life of mutual recognition will have a special importance in their relations with others, and take priority over other values which may seem to conflict.[33] Scanlon argues that this motivation is based on the good reasons that count in favor of living a life of mutual recognition with others.[34] We are creatures whose attitudes such as beliefs, intentions, and preferences are sensitive to our judgments about considerations in favor of or against things. When we judge that there are good reasons in favor of an action or belief, we normally come to hold those beliefs, or try to act on those reasons. We need no other mechanism such as a desire to propel us. Those things for which considerations count in favor, we regard as good and of value. This does not mean that we always want to promote that thing: having more friends is not necessarily better than having a smaller number who are sensitive to what friendship requires from us. But reasons counting in favor of something are sufficient to motivate and to confer value. If we recognize that persons are creatures whose attitudes are sensitive and responsive to their judgments about reasons, we have good reason to recognize this as a fundamental quality that should shape the conditions under which we live with others. If, as also seems natural, we see good reason to live alongside others, then we have good reason to want such a social life to be one we find mutually acceptable. All those motivated by this commitment to respect each person's freedom and equality share an ideal of social life as unified by the value of mutual recognition. The value of mutual recognition expresses each person's entitlement to accept or reject principles governing social life. To accept this value and allow it to order the claims we make and responses we give to others is what it means to be reasonable.[35] Reasonableness is an idea with moral content: the morality of right and wrong in dealing with others who share a motivation to respect each other's freedom and equality.

Principles governing our relations with others are acceptable if they cannot be rejected by anyone motivated by the value of mutual recognition. The principles must be acceptable, or not rejectable, to each person considered individually. Individuals may draw on a plurality of considerations that affect them personally, and these considerations will alter and adjust dynamically according to the context or issue at hand. Thus, reasonable rejection is deliberately left unspecified concretely. But individuals may only give reasons that affect them; they may not reject a principle for reasons that are to do with the common good or considerations independent of a person-affecting reason.[36] This prevents utilitarian arguments and fortifies the value of mutual recognition as the equal recognition of each person individually.

While Scanlon has concentrated mostly on the morality of personal relationships with others, his contractualism bears on liberal political thinking in important ways. If we conceive of an agreement about right and wrong as characterized by the reasonable personal reasons of individuals, then utilitarianism is unjustified. Utilitarian justifications will include those considerations that concern the aggregate of individuals, and whilst individuals can be assured that their interests will be counted, their importance will be weighed against the aggregate. Individuals have good reason, from their point of view, to insist that their interests should not be considered according to their weighting relative to the sum of positive utility; their interests should be counted on their own merits.[37]

Contractualism also challenges the utilitarian view that justification of political authority should be decided by weighing the relative satisfaction of preference produced by different policies. Different people will have different considerations that will be relevant to judging a principle. It will be normal and reasonable to offer considerations of personal well-being and preference satisfaction, but well-being will not be a single measure or master-value when deciding if a principle should be rejected.[38] The procedure of considering personal reasons and evaluating their reasonableness also reflects the importance of publicity and transparency in agreement. Publicity and transparency promise to make agreements more stable, but they also express the importance of agreements being accessible to each person as free and equal.[39]

More positively, contractualism offers liberals a perspective on what matters about justice. For some liberals, justice is primarily a matter of the justifiability of a distribution of some good. Liberal egalitarians differ about which good should be distributed and according to which principle; however, many share a concern that justice is a question of distribution. But contractualism looks primarily to whether individuals stand in relations of mutual recognition and respect to each other. A person who has so little money that it makes their life hard, anxious, and vulnerable suffers a distributive injustice, whereas people with plenty may suffer social stigma. These people too suffer an injustice: a relational injustice. Contractualism explains what is wrong about this relational injustice, and thus gives liberals a broader and more pluralistic view of what we owe to others as a matter of justice.[40]

This Scanlonian view appeals to the substance of our commitment to live with others on reasonable terms, acceptable to each individually. Scanlon accepts explicitly that living with others unified by a commitment to mutual recognition is assumed, or at least aspired to. There is no deeper or prior feature of human nature or reason from which we can derive or argue for this commitment. We may have good reasons to hope that it is common among those with whom we share lives. However, we also have reasons to be skeptical that we can explain or even persuasively justify the presence and forcefulness of this commitment in people's lives. For some this is appropriately modest and sufficient: We should not need an explanation of the dispositions and ideals of morality in order to give it a special importance and priority in our lives. But for many this is inadequate.

For contractualists, underlying all that we call wrong in our relations with others is a common thread of failure to respect another's reasonable rejection of that which wronged them. It vindicates this view of the morality of right and wrong by appealing to our commitment to living alongside others on reasonable terms, characterized by the value of living together in a unity of mutual recognition. When faced with deciding whether a rule is reasonably rejectable, we have to draw on our considered substantive views about what reasonableness entails. However, it seems circular to consider something wrong because reasonably rejectable if we reject it due to considerations about reasonableness which have moral content. Not only is the account of wrongness accused of circularity, but the basis of our considerations of right and wrong is held to be assumed, and not explained fundamentally either. Can contractualism explain the fundamental basis for our moral relations with others and avoid circularity?[41]

Southwood argues all normally developed adults share the capacities to reason together deliberatively. If we imagine people who are able to deliberate perfectly about the rules governing their lives together, their deliberations will result in agreement about what morality means for us. The ideal of perfect deliberation explains the fundamental basis for the form of the rules we agree should govern our relations with each other. It includes constraints such as considering the interests of all those affected by the decision, responding appropriately to the reasons provided by others, and reflection and adaptation in light of deliberation.[42] These formal procedural constraints on deliberation do not involve concrete moral commitments. To deliberate discursively and reflectively with others is primarily a question of the style of reasoning and not an ostensibly moral matter. However, the constraints on ideal deliberation express the importance of our relations with each other. Ideal deliberation therefore provides normative practical constraints that help produce agreements that fit our ordinary understandings of morality while avoiding circularity. Reasonableness is therefore characterized by the formal constraints of the procedures of deliberation, rather than the substantive value of mutual recognition.[43] Southwood argues that contractualism can therefore explain the fundamental basis and normativity of morality by deriving it from our capacities as citizens of a community of deliberators.

Contractualism differs from contractarianism by basing the motivation and reasoning of agreement on reasonableness, and not only or also self-interest. If our prudential self-interest is not a fundamental motivation of agreement, then scarcity and limited benevolence are ephemeral as circumstances of justice. The circumstances of contractualism are a community of reasonable people motivated to find rules agreeable to each other. Thus in contractualism, parties are characterized according to the notion of reasonableness that motivates the agreement. Scanlon characterizes contractors according to the motivation and capacity to deliberate about the implications of governing relations with others according to the value of mutual recognition. Southwood characterizes contractors according to the more formal capacities of ideal deliberation.

AGREEING TO EXCLUDE

Contractarians typically object to utilitarianism's treatment of those with preferences the fulfillment of which would not contribute to greater overall well-being. Agreement is meant to protect each individual's interest and entitlement to live under only those rules which are acceptable to them, given others' acceptance also. However, if justification depends on agreement, those incapable of agreement are excluded.[44] This in itself is not necessarily a problem, unless numbered in the excluded are those whom we feel have moral standing. This is not a matter of untidiness or as yet incomplete extension to complex cases. The problem of exclusion is inescapable to contractarianism and contractualism. Agreement is the bulwark against utilitarianism. Contractarianism, contractualism, and consequentialism often overlap in ambition and concern. Agreement as the representation of acceptability to each divides contractarianism from utilitarianism. But saving individuals from the teeth of aggregation through justification as acceptability to each costs. What capacities are required to be counted among those qualified to contract? There are many we regard as having moral standing, toward whom we have moral concern, but who do not seem to possess the capacities required for reciprocal agreement. Is the cost of saving some individuals from aggregation to exclude others from our agreements?

Of course, contract theorists see that agreement implies exclusion: The scope of agreement may be narrower than the scope of our moral concern for others. We recall that agreement is understood hypothetically in contractarianism. Principles are not justified because of any actual agreement between persons. Agreement represents the notion that principles should be agreeable to each person and understood appropriately; if not they should not be enforced. The hypothetical agreement should represent and explain accurately the practical relations with which we are concerned. If there is a lack of fit between what a contract theory says and our deeply held convictions about morality, then one or the other must be at fault. Either we doubt the theory, or we doubt our convictions. Gauthier argues the latter.[45] Our moral convictions may not be entirely reliable. If the disabled, the poor, and the frail elderly cannot contribute to the collective surplus, it is not rational from a purely self-interested view to agree rules of cooperation with them. Cooperation is not possible as we would receive nothing in return for our labors. Such people are incapable of joining agreements about morality or justice, and so on contractarian terms they are not entitled to the standing and benefits derived from agreement. Gauthier's theory is often criticized for such seemingly morally offensive conclusions. We might protest offense, but the merest glance at our avoidance of the reality of global and domestic poverty and neglect of the condition of the severely disabled among us may vindicate Gauthier's honesty.[46]

The narrow inclusion of Gauthier's contractarianism may fit much of what we do and may explain that we do this because we regard morality as a contract for mutual advantage. Neverthless, many contractarians are dissatisfied. We can see two different ways of broadening the scope of agreement: differential inclusion and permissive inclusion. Differential inclusion maintains that relevant capacities are required to agree on principles of justice and morality. Those fully able to co-contract are jointly and equally subject to the agreement. Many contractarians wish to extend further the contractarian protection of individual interests and standing to those who do not share in the full capacities of those agreeing. The benefits of agreement are offered to them, but co-authorship is not.

We might provide differential inclusion in contracts of mutual advantage if we endorse our moral consideration for those such as children and the severely disabled, even if they are incapable of cooperation.[47] Anyone failing to grant them moral standing would be reprehensible to us, and we would choose not to cooperate with them. This threat of non-cooperation would provide reason to extend moral consideration and thus protection and benefit to those less capable. But an agreement which includes consideration for the incapable is not then strictly one of mutual advantage, as morality cannot now be explained purely in terms of rational self-interest.

If we turn instead to Rawlsian contracts motivated by both self-interest and fairness, we might more easily find scope for differential inclusion of those incapable of cooperation. Maintaining the difference between entitlements of cooperators and non-cooperators seems legitimate when selecting principles of distribution, as occurs in the *original position*.[48] But non-cooperators have interests and needs that merit moral consideration, and so parties may offer support through a social minimum they establish when deciding more concrete constitutional matters at stages of agreement later than the original position. Those incapable of cooperation are included because of their needs, not because of reciprocity, and this different inclusion denies them entitlements to distributive equality.

Southwood argues that those affected by the agreement but incapable of agreeing themselves should be included as in a broad sense of agreement. The interests of these people should feature directly, even if the people themselves do not. Representatives and trustees should act on their behalf in the agreement, maintaining that crucial contractualist commitment to the entitlement to reject principles from a personal point of view, even if that point of view is represented by other persons.[49] Southwood's broad inclusion differentiates those who are fully equals in democratic citizenship and so direct contractors, and those unequal due to lack of capacity who are indirect contractors.

In each of these cases, those suffering some kind of incapacity are included in agreement, but differently from those fully capable of agreement. Introducing moral constraints prior to an agreement of mutual advantage is ad hoc and renders it simply a more self-interested version of a moral contractualist agreement. However, even if we accept this cost to the explanatory economy of mutual advantage contractarianism, those included have very different standing from fully capable contactors. Their standing depends on others having consideration for them, and so their moral status is derivative, whereas the standing of the contractors is based on their own capacities.[50] Those capable contractors who have consideration must also possess a powerful altruism toward the incapable excluded in order to accept the costs to themselves of not cooperating with inconsiderate contractors. Relationships based on altruism are not reciprocal, and reciprocity of either advantage or recognition is important to contractarianism in general. Inclusion without reciprocity amounts to exclusion from contractarian agreement. It denies them the entitlement to object to a principle from their own interests, which is central to contractarianism. Thus, the substance and basis of the moral relationships between capable and incapable con-tractors is different from the relationships between co-contractors.

Incorporating non-cooperators on the basis purely of their needi-ness not only denies them relational advantages, such as the equality guaranteed by the difference principle, but also expresses an attitude that regards them as inferior, which is an objectionable relational harm. Southwood's account includes the interests of "atypical" per-sons directly in deliberative contractualism. However, this is the wrong kind of reason to include persons if we wish to express equal respect to others. We are in effect diluting contractualism with con-sequentialism as we take effects on people's interests as the morally important fact about them, rather the attitudes of respect we feel owed them in virtue of their equal standing as persons.[51] This creates a different kind of moral relationship between contractors and those incapable of contracting fully independently.

Differential inclusion is always justified by the variations in capacity that are taken to merit unequal moral standing. But an alternative approach to the problem of exclusion seeks to minimize the capacities required for inclusion in the agreement. This permis-sive approach to inclusion may be achieved by dropping a seemingly necessary condition to agreement. We might show that the require-ment that each contribute to receive benefits is unnecessary to be included in agreements of mutual advantage.[52] Non-cooperators can be included in agreement if we assume cooperation will involve each of us having periods when we are inactive and not contributing to the cooperative surplus and periods when we are productive and contri-buting. It is therefore rational to recognize that as we are sometimes either providers or recipients, we might receive a benefit without at the same time providing benefit in return. Thus, contribution is not a necessary condition to receive a benefit from those motivated by self-interest. But dropping the condition that contribution is necessary to receive benefit in agreements of mutual advantage threatens to make the scope of morality or justice infinitely open. Unrestricted inclu-sion seems as unattractive as narrowly restricted inclusion.

Alternatively, rather than dropping a necessary condition to the circumstances of the agreement in order to widen inclusion, we may understand the capacities for agreement more permissively. Children and many people with disabilities contribute to family life through their bonds of affection and reciprocal attachment, and this adds greatly to the quality of relational goods enjoyed by all the family.[53] If contractualism is motivated by a commitment to treat others with mutual recognition, and if we understand the participation of children and those with disabilities in important relational goods such as family life as involving forms of mutual recognition, then those lacking the full capacities for rational agreement can be included as equals in agreement.

A permissive understanding of the capacities for agreement seems the right kind of response to the problem of exclusion in contractarianism. Permissive inclusion focuses on including those with very different capacities as equals in full standing. It therefore fits accurately our moral convictions that such persons should be included as equals, and not merely accommodated retrospectively. However, this permissive view of inclusion must explain how significant relationships of mutual recognition can be present in the absence of capacities normally taken as necessary to agreement. We cannot merely observe the more permissive presence of cooperation as participation in relational goods without explaining its structure and moral significance in cases between people with widely different capacities.

Such an explanation may emerge from understanding how practices of sharing between people with very different capacities serve as the basis for the moral relationships with which contractualists are concerned.

AGREEMENT AS SHARING

How can we include those who do not have the capacities for agreement as characterized by rational, informed, voluntary acceptance of rules? Versions of differential inclusion tend to require a high level of cognitive and volitional capacities for agreement. But capacities necessary for agreement can be characterized permissively so that those who are incapable of fully rational informed voluntary agreement may yet be included because they are capable of sharing in relationships of mutual recognition.

If we look to our relationships with a broad range of people who are not fully agents, including children and many types of disabled people, we find rich bonds of sharing. If we look first at those with whom we share morally relevant relationship, and what that sharing involves, we find that in our sharing we are making agreements with many who are typically excluded from contractarian models of morality. Sharing is normatively significant, and we share with those who may not yet or ever meet our ideal of free, autonomous, rational contractors.

Sharing in plans and sharing intentions demands a lot from us intellectually. Perhaps most significantly, it requires knowledge of others and of propositions about their minds. It requires, for example, that I know that I intend to paint the house, that I know that you intend to paint the house, and that I know that we intend to paint the house together.[54] Clearly, children and many people with various cognitive or developmental disabilities will be unable to share plans and intentions in this way. But this kind of sharing is the result of a process of coming to know others and their minds. Sharing intentions is not something we bootstrap ourselves into doing when we become adults. If we examine how the capacities for sharing intentions develop, we find that they grow from a more fundamental practice of sharing that does not involve the full range of abilities required for sharing intentions. For example, while children and adults may not be able to share intentions, they can share goals.[55] Putting away the toys together can be a shared cooperative goal. Both the adult and the child can order their activities around the fact of sharing the goal: They may go about picking up different toys to put in the box; they may get out of each other's way waiting for their turn to put the toys in the box. This illustrates that sharing goals is common between a much wider range of people than merely those competent to share intentions and make explicit agreements. Children and those with developmental disabilities will share goals of various kinds with able adults. This requires cognitive and volitional capacities that distinguish those capable of sharing (such as children and people with a range of disabilities), from those incapable (such as those in a persistent vegetative state and many kinds of non-human animals).

Sharing, including sharing in goals, is normatively significant. It does not always create moral duties between sharers. We could share in performing an immoral act and be under no duty to the other to continue sharing. But sharing can create morally significant relationships.[56] If the goal is morally permissible, then the fact of sharing a goal creates expectations and relationships of reliance between the sharers. When others come to rely on us, and plan around that reliance, we incur obligations toward those with whom we are sharing. Explicit agreements or ostensible assurances about the shared goals are not required to form duties of performance and due consideration to other sharers. Even in cases of our relations with very young children or those disabled developmentally, we can be co-authors and co-subjects of our shared goals. This sharing provides a basis for relational duties of reliance and loss prevention more widely than only between those fully capable of rational voluntary agreement.

Those who share goals and intentions create constraints and duties that may be understood from a contractualist point of view. Thus, sharing will involve moral relations that are relevant to contractualism. By understanding the required capacities for agreement more permissively, namely those capacities necessary only for sharing goals, we can include those who have not developed the full range of capacities required for rational, voluntary, independent agreement. So children and those with learning disabilities have the capacity for sharing in relationships with others, but not the full set of capacities required for agreement.

Sharing in goals with children or disabled people can create relational duties, and can therefore require us to respect their entitlements in sharing, such as reliance and loss prevention. We as fully able adults are also required to mitigate our attitudes of blame and resentment if those with whom we share cause us loss or prove unreliable due to their limited capacities. So there is an appropriate asymmetry in how characterizing capacities for agreement permissively affects inclusion and responsibility. Children and people with various disabilities are able to form those relationships that are relevant from the point of view of contractualist agreement: practices of sharing which then create moral duties involving mutual recognition. It is therefore appropriate to attribute moral standing permissively to those with capacities for sharing in goals. But it is also appropriate to mitigate our judgments of substantive moral responsibility toward those with limited capacities and experience.[57]

Addressing the problem of exclusion by characterizing the capacities for agreement permissively according to the practice of sharing has several advantages for contractarianism. First, it provides the right kind of reason for inclusion. By lowering the bar of inclusion from capacities of fully rational voluntary agreement to capacities for sharing in goals, we include all those for whom we have moral concern in the scope of agreement. Agreement is understood more broadly but still with sufficient determinacy to exclude those incapable of ordering their mutual interaction by sharing goals. This is therefore permissively inclusive, but appropriately exclusive of those incapable of the practice of sharing goals. Second, this view of permissive inclusion through sharing is explanatorily accurate and fundamental. It does not rely on abstractions or hypotheses about contractors, but is derived from understanding accurately the practices of sharing in which we participate with a wide range of people. Similar to the structure of Southwood's deliberative contractualism, it offers a fundamental explanation because it does not appeal to substantive moral commitments to ground contractualist moral principles, but is derived from primarily non-moral capacities and practices (sharing) which in certain circumstances subsequently create moral relations of mutual recognition that then constitute the circumstances of contractualism. Finally, it is able to explain how we can both permissively include as equals persons with a wide range of capacities, and also recognize the appropriateness of different judgments of substantive responsibility in our agreements.

CONCLUSION

Agreement is fundamental to contractarianism, and the problem of exclusion is entailed by agreement. But contractarianism need not be objectionably exclusive. If we look closely at the real practice of sharing with others, we see that we are already in the right kind of relationships with those who may lack the full capacities for rational voluntary agreement. Including permissively in agreement all who are capable of sharing goals may help us respond to the exclusion objection to contractarianism and explain how everyone for whom we have moral concern can be included in an inclusive contractualist moral community.

NOTES

1. I use the term "contractarianism" as a general description for the family of views that characterize the justification of moral and political principles as a form of agreement. While I explain the difference between contractualism and contractarianism, and will use "contractualism"

when referring specifically to these views, I include contractualism in the broad category of contractarianism as appropriate when discussing the approach generally. I reserve the term contractualism for the views of Scanlon and Southwood, but do not mean to imply that Rawls's view could not legitimately be labeled contractualist. Typically contractarianism in its narrow sense is applied to views based on prudential rationality such as Gauthier's, and contractualism refers to views based on moral motivations such as Scanlon's. Rawls draws on both, and so either might be appropriate depending on the context. For different views on these distinctions, see Freeman, "The Burdens of Public Justification" and Darwall, "Introduction," in *Contractarianism/Contractualism*, pp. 1–8. Similarly, I use broad terms such as "moral and political principles" to describe the subject matter of agreement when discussing liberal contractarianism generally, and distinguish more specifically between agreements about justice or morality as appropriate when discussing the individual theories.

2. Pettit, "Can Contract Theory Ground Morality?" p. 79.
3. Famously, see Hume, "Of the Original Contract," pp. 164–81.
4. For an argument that this includes a utilitarian concern with distributive justice, see Kelly, *Utilitarianism and Distributive Justice*.
5. Rawls, *A Theory of Justice*, rev. edn., pp. 23–24.
6. For wider discussions of the importance of acceptability to each person in liberalism, see Hampton, "The Common Faith of Liberalism" and Waldron, "Theoretical Foundations of Liberalism."
7. Rawls, *A Theory of Justice*, rev. edn., pp. 109–22.
8. *Ibid.*, pp. 6–7.
9. *Ibid.*, pp. 131–32; Rawls, "Social Unity and Primary Good," pp. 359–87.
10. Rawls, *A Theory of Justice*, rev. edn., p. 75.
11. *Ibid.*, p. 17.
12. *Ibid.*, pp. 118–22.
13. *Ibid.*, p. 65.
14. *Ibid.*, pp. 130–39.
15. *Ibid.*, pp. 499–505.
16. Rawls, *Political Liberalism*, pp. xvii–xix and Weithman, *Why Political Liberalism?*, pp. 42–67.
17. Rawls, *Political Liberalism*, pp. 22–28.
18. *Ibid.*, pp. 11–15.
19. *Ibid.*, pp. 144–49.
20. *Ibid.*, pp. 201–11.
21. Gauthier, *Morals by Agreement*, p. 114.
22. *Ibid.*, p. 105.
23. *Ibid.*, p. 110.

24. *Ibid.*, p. 113.

25. *Ibid.*, ch. 2.

26. *Ibid.*, pp. 79–82.

27. Gauthier later argued that rational individuals would not seek agreement with others by constraining their maximizing reason. Rather, individuals would coordinate their actions with others in order to achieve Pareto-optimality (where individuals gain the most they can without making anyone else worse off). Gauthier argues that if we understand individuals forming agreements as mutually "agreed Pareto-optimizers," this allows us to explain voluntary cooperative behavior better than if we regard individuals as constrained maximizers. Gauthier, "Twenty-Five On," pp. 601–24 (part of a symposium on Gauthier's *Morals by Agreement*).

28. *Ibid.*, pp. 165–70.

29. *Ibid.*, ch. 7.

30. Hampton, "Two Faces of Contractarian Thought."

31. Barry, *Justice as Impartiality*, pp. 31–46.

32. Scanlon, *What We Owe to Each Other*, p. 153.

33. *Ibid.*, pp. 158–68.

34. *Ibid.*, p. 162.

35. *Ibid.*, pp. 191–97.

36. Ridge, "Saving Scanlon."

37. Scanlon, *What We Owe to Each Other*, pp. 229–41.

38. *Ibid.*, pp. 141–43.

39. Freeman, "The Burdens of Public Justification."

40. On the connection between contractualism and relational egalitarianism, see Anderson, "The Fundamental Disagreement Between Luck Egalitarians and Relational Egalitarians."

41. For a detailed discussion of varieties of these objections, see Southwood, *Contractualism and the Foundations of Morality*, pp. 61–84.

42. *Ibid.*, pp. 87–96.

43. *Ibid.*, pp. 128–35.

44. See, for example, Hooker, *Ideal Code, Real World*, pp. 66–71; Phillips, "Contractualism and Moral Status," pp. 183–204; Nussbaum, *Frontiers of Justice*.

45. See, for example, Gauthier, "Why Contractarianism?" pp. 15–30.

46. See Binmore, *Just Playing*, pp. 258–59, quoted in Vanderschraaf, "Justice as Mutual Advantage and the Vulnerable," p. 128.

47. Christopher Morris explores these ideas in Morris, "Moral Standing and Rational-Choice Contractarianism" and Morris, "Justice, Reasons, and Moral Standing."

48. Stark, "How to Include the Severely Disabled in a Contractarian Theory of Justice"; Stark, "Contractarianism and Cooperation."

49. Southwood, *Contractualism and the Foundations of Morality*, pp. 107–17.
50. *Ibid.*, pp. 49 and 169.
51. Southwood in fact regards this as a merit of his account, as it includes them as equals in one sense but ensures that they are not regarded as fully equal co-authors of an agreement. *Ibid.*, p. 170.
52. Vanderschraaf, "Justice as Mutual Advantage and the Vulnerable."
53. Hartley, "An Inclusive Contractualism"; Hartley, "Justice for the Disabled."
54. Bratman, "Shared Intention," pp. 97–113.
55. Butterfill, "Joint Action and Development," pp. 23–47.
56. Alonso, "Shared Intention, Reliance, and Interpersonal Obligations," pp. 444–75.
57. See Scanlon, *What We Owe to Each Other*, pp. 248–51 on the importance of the difference between substantive responsibility and responsibility as attributability.

5   Public reason liberalism

PUBLIC REASON LIBERALISM: PAST, PRESENT, AND FUTURE

The idea of public reason is almost always associated – sometimes exclusively – with John Rawls's political liberalism. Many, no doubt, believe that if there is such a creature as "public reason liberalism" it is a Rawlsian creation. This is an error. The social contract theories of Hobbes, Locke, Rousseau, and Kant all are based on the conviction that the main aim of political philosophy is to identify an agreed-upon public judgment or public reason that allows us to overcome the disunity and conflict that would characterize a condition in which each followed her own private judgment or reasoning about morality and justice. Captivated by their own concerns, however, political philosophers have, with very few exceptions, read the fundamental place of public reason out of the contract tradition.[1] Hobbes is typically viewed simply as a theorist of self-interest and a proto-game theorist, Locke as a natural rights proto-libertarian, Rousseau as essentially a radical democrat.[2] In the second section of this chapter focusing on Hobbes and Locke, I take some modest steps to reverse this misreading, pointing out how classical social contract theory was fundamentally and explicitly concerned with identifying a source of public reason.[3] Liberalism and public reason, I argue, arose together as interrelated responses to the modern problem of creating a stable social order in societies deeply divided by religious and moral

Versions of this essay were presented to audiences at California State University – Fullerton, McGill University, Ohio State University, and the University of Queensland. My thanks to participants for their comments and suggestions. I am especially grateful to Steve Wall for his valuable comments.

disagreements. The problem with which social contract theorists such as Hobbes and Locke were grappling is distinctively modern: In matters of religion and convictions about the ultimate value of life, morality and justice, the free exercise of human reason leads to disagreement. Their question – which is also the question of public reason liberalism – is whether a society faced with "intractable struggles" and "irreconcilable" conflicts of "absolute depth" can share a common social and political existence on terms that are acceptable to all.[4]

Seen in this light, Rawls's doctrine of public reason is – as he originally claimed of his theory of justice – a development of social contract theory.[5] In the third section I analyze the development of Rawls's thought in terms of the different conceptions of public reason on which different versions of his theory were built. I argue that while his account in *A Theory of Justice* relied on two traditional claims of liberal public reason that we find in the social contract tradition – what I call the *shared reasons* and *insulation* claims – his later versions manifest doubts about both. The final Rawlsian account is distinctive insofar as it seeks to provide a case for liberal public reason while taking seriously challenges to these two traditional claims.

The fourth section then considers what we are to make of the Rawlsian legacy. At the end of his career, Rawls made a number of innovations in public reason liberalism, but these were not, I believe, well worked out. In this section I present what I see as the way forward, embracing some of Rawls's most radical ideas and pressing even further along those lines. A truly diversity-based public reason liberalism offers a conception of public reason as an "overlapping consensus" in which the different reasons (and reasoning) of citizens converge on liberal principles, rules, and institutions. On this view both the shared reasons and insulation claims are either dropped or so weakened as to play but a secondary role in the account of public reason. The critical dispute in contemporary public reason liberalism is, I believe, between those who insist that the future of public reason liberalism is to develop a deeper understanding of what diverse citizens *share* and how this sharing can be insulated from their disagreements, and those who are convinced that a diversity of perspectives, reasoning, and values is itself the basis of a free and stable social and political order.

THE PROBLEM OF CONFLICTING PRIVATE
JUDGMENT AND THE CELESTIAL SOLUTION

Hobbes's recognition of the problem and his illiberal solution

Although in the orthodox, game-theoretical interpretation of Hobbes, his concern is simply the problem of conflict among essentially self-interested individuals, more careful interpretations have recently come to stress the root of conflict in differences in *judgment*.[6] In a crucial passage in Chapter V of *Leviathan*, in his initial discussion of reason, Hobbes writes:

> reason itself is always right reason, as well as arithmetic is a certain and infallible art, but no one man's reason, nor the reason of any one number of men, makes the certainty ... And therefore, as when there is a controversy in an account, the parties must by their own accord, set up, for right reason, the reason of some arbitrator, or judge, to whose sentence they will both stand, or their controversy must either come to blows, or be undecided, for want of a right reason constituted by nature, so is it also in all debates of what kind soever. And when men that think themselves wiser than all others, clamour and demand right reason for judge, yet seek no more, but that things should be determined, by no other men's reason but their own, it is ... intolerable in the society of men ... For they do nothing else, that will have every of their passions, as it comes to bear sway in them, to be taken for right reason, and that in their own controversies, bewraying their want of right reason, by the claim they lay to it.[7]

Because "all laws, written, and unwritten, have need of interpretation,"[8] when, as in the state of nature, we each rely on private judgment, we disagree about almost everything, including our application of the laws of nature.[9] Those who insist on employing their own reason to determine the requirements of the law of nature, asserting that their reason is right reason, prevent a peaceful social life, for they are essentially insisting that we remain in the state of nature.

Thus, as R. E. Ewin argues, for Hobbes a cooperative and peaceful social life requires "a public mark of right reason."[10] Each alienates his own right to private judgment on the condition that others do so, by settling on a sovereign, whose voice is the voice of public reason: "we are not every one," says Hobbes, "to make our own private reason, or conscience, but the public reason, that is, the reason of

God's supreme lieutenant, judge."[11] Hobbes thus proposes that disagreements in private reason (including disputes about the demands
of the laws of nature) are to be resolved by the sovereign, who is to
serve as the voice of public reason.[12] Thus the social contract:

a *commonwealth* is said to be *instituted*, when a *multitude* of men do agree,
and *covenant, every one, with every one,* that to whatsoever *man,* or *assembly of men,* shall be given by the major part, the *right* to *present* the person
of them all (that is to say, to be their *representative*) every one, as well he
that *voted for it,* as he that *voted against it,* shall *authorize* all the actions
and judgments, of that man, or assembly of men, in the same manner, as if
they were his own, to the end, to live peaceably amongst themselves, and be
protected against other men.[13]

The idea of accepting and authorizing *the judgment* of the sovereign
occurs repeatedly in *Leviathan.* It is important for Hobbes that
while the *will* concerns deliberation about action, *judgment* is "the
last opinion in the search of the truth."[14] Hobbes identifies public
reason with judgment of the sovereign, and so the sovereign provides
a public determination of the truth, for example, of a claim that a
miracle has occurred.[15] Certainly Hobbes thinks that "when it comes
to confession of that faith, *the private reason must submit to the
public.*"[16] Although the sovereign cannot directly command us to
believe a proposition, since belief is not under the control of the
will,[17] Hobbes appears to hold (i) the sovereign has authority to
declare public truths from which we are obligated not to dissent;
(ii) we can be obligated to publicly affirm these truths; and (iii) the
sovereign has authority to shape the environment in which opinions
are formed.[18]

Because he sees *all* private judgment as *potentially* a threat to the
social order, Hobbes's aim was to show that there is no limit on the
authority of the sovereign to determine disputes.[19] Hobbes endorses
the judgment of Cromwell and later the Tory Restoration parlia-
ments: the brief experiment in free private judgment during the first
years of the Commonwealth was an appalling threat to social order.[20]
Private judgment must be subservient to the public reason of the
sovereign.[21] Underlying this conservative response to rising diversity
of belief is the important insight that there is no neat way to insulate
the political from the religious: disputes about the former can always
lead to disputes about the latter.[22] Faced with the tendency of all

beliefs to become political, Hobbes puts the teaching of all doctrines under the authority of the sovereign. "For the actions of men proceed from their opinions; and in the well-governing of opinions, consisteth the well-governing of men's actions, in order to their peace, and concord."[23]

Hobbes thus seeks to show that *whatever* the sovereign proclaims to be public reason *is* public reason. No limits can be placed on the sovereign's authority: "he is judge of what is necessary for peace; and judge of doctrines: he is sole legislator; and supreme judge of controversies."[24] This "umpiring" or procedural solution to disagreement applies to *all* moral disputes. Remember, Hobbes starts out with disputes about the laws of nature – basic rules of ethical social conduct. His solution is to politicize all disputes about interpretations of these rules of social conduct by submitting them to the sovereign. If we closely follow Hobbes, it looks as if the political procedure will be determinative of all moral disputes about interpersonal conduct – having justified a judge or an umpire, we appear to have reason to appeal to it when we disagree about the dictates of the basic rules of ethical social conduct. Politics swallows up morality. Thus, Hobbes is scathing about the doctrine "That every *private* man is judge of good and evil actions." Admittedly, this "is true in the condition of mere nature, where there are no civil laws; and also under civil government, in such cases as are not determined by the law. But otherwise, it is manifest, that the measure of good and evil actions, is the civil law; and the judge the legislator, who is always representative of the commonwealth."[25] This is not to say that the sovereign's judgment determines the *truth* about the laws of nature and whether they have been violated: Hobbes is clear that the sovereign can err in interpreting the laws of nature.[26] It is to say, though, that according to the contract we no longer have the right to judge him to be wrong, or to act contrary to his judgment, for his is the public reason. In contrast, the sovereign *does* construct the truths of justice; justice is determined by the civil law, and there is no civil law without the sovereign making it so.[27]

Locke and the emergence of liberal public reason

Locke concurs with some fundamental points of the Hobbesian analysis. He concurs that diversity of private judgment about religion is a fundamental social fact that must be reconciled with the demands of social order; he also accepts the crux of Hobbes's analysis of the causes of disputes about the laws of nature and how they are to be resolved. In a passage that recalls Hobbes's complaint that, while the laws of nature are clear to all, we nevertheless disagree because we are "blinded by self-love," Locke holds that "though the Law of Nature be plain and intelligible to all rational Creatures; ... men being biassed by their Interest, as well as ignorant for want of studying it, are not apt to allow of it as a Law binding to them in the application of it to their particular Cases."[28] Peace and justice, Locke concludes, can only be secured by *"all private judgment of every particular Member being excluded,* [so that] the community comes to be Umpire[d] by settled standing Rules, indifferent, and the same to all Parties."[29] It is the task of government to serve as Umpire – the voice of public reason. Once again, the solution is essentially procedural and, once again, the political order becomes the interpreter of the moral rules regulating interpersonal actions.

Locke, however, insists that though we disagree deeply about religion, we share a common conception of civil interests.[30] "The commonwealth seems to me," says Locke, "to be a society of men constituted only for the procuring, preserving, and advancing their own civil interests. Civil interest I call life, liberty, health, and indolency of body; and the possession of outward things, such as money, lands, houses, furniture, and the like."[31] In contrast to Hobbes, Locke is clear that a demarcation between religious and civil disputes is both possible and necessary. "I esteem it above all things," Locke continues, "necessary to distinguish exactly the business of civil government from that of religion, and to settle the just bounds that lie between the one and the other. If this be not done, there can be no end put to the controversies that will be always arising between those that have, or at least pretend to have, on the one side, a concernment for the interest of men's souls, and, on the other side, a care of the commonwealth."[32] Throughout the "Letter on Toleration," Locke repeatedly invokes this fundamental distinction between the spheres of the civil and the religious. Because the civil has no authority over the spiritual, private judgment must rule in religious matters – not only in matters of belief, but in forms of worship generally. In controversies between churches about whose doctrine is true, "both sides [are] equal; nor is there any judge ... upon earth, by whose sentence it can be determined."[33] For the magistrate to seek to regulate such matters would be simply an exercise of private, not public, reason: "as the private judgment of any particular person, if erroneous, does not exempt him from the obligation of law, so the private judgment, as I may call it, of the magistrate, does not give him any new right of imposing laws upon his subjects, which neither was in the constitution of the government granted him, nor ever was in the power of the people to grant."[34]

Locke thus moves toward the quintessential liberal account of public reason based on three claims:

The Moral Disagreement Claim: when individuals reason about the require-ments of morality and justice (the law of nature), they disagree, so peaceful and cooperative social and political life requires that, within limits, they abandon their private judgment about morality and justice, submitting to the public reason of impartial law.[35]

The Shared Reasons Claim: the basis of civil society is our shared reasons to advance on our civil interests; the resolution of our moral disagreements is a fundamental shared civil and political interest.

The Insulation Claim: private judgment about religious matters can remain free and private. These deep and enduring conflicts do not infect, and in so doing unravel, our concurrence on the Moral Disagreement and Shared Reasons Claims.

As we saw, the Moral Disagreement Claim is also held by Hobbes; it is the heart of all public reason political philosophy. As such, all public reason accounts are fundamentally at odds with the picture of social life as one composed of fully autonomous moral agents, each independ-ently acting on the basis of all her own substantive judgment about the demands of justice. Such a condition *defines* the state of nature, where, as Kant put it, each claims "the right to do what *seems just and good to him*, entirely independently of the opinion of others."[36] Public law, then, allows us to avoid reliance on our own controversial private judgment about morality, rights, and our civil interests, acting instead on impartial considerations that all can endorse. As Rousseau put it, the law as pronounced by the sovereign is the "celestial voice" of "public reason."[37] But in contrast to Hobbes (and to some extent Rousseau),[38] for Locke public reason does not concern itself with religious matters; according to the Insulation Claim, those disagreements can continue unabated so long as religious belief does not infect a citizen's views about basic civil interests and the authority of the public adjudication of moral disputes.

Locke's case for toleration thus does not extend to Roman Catholics, for their conception of religious authority leads them to a conception of civil interests and public authority incompatible with that of other citizens (since the Pope claimed that excommunicated monarchs were not owed political obedience). "Liberal toleration" thus only applies to religious views that do not challenge the public authority of shared reasons about civil interests. Only if the private doctrine itself endorses the Insulation Claim is it to be tolerated. Yet, while Locke's exclusion of Catholics presupposes the Insulation Claim, his other famous exception to toleration – the atheist – calls it into question. Atheists are not to be tolerated because their lack of religious belief undermines our trust in their word: their lack of belief in the religious sphere spills over into a civil liability.[39] And this is because, as Locke says, morality is a concern of both spheres: "Moral actions belong therefore to the jurisdiction both of the outward and inward court: both of the magistrate and conscience."[40] As Locke notes, this gives rise to a "great danger, lest one of these jurisdictions intrench upon the other, and discord arise between the keeper of the public peace and the overseer of souls."[41] Locke assures us that this difficulty can be removed if we accept his account of the limits of these two spheres. But these limits suppose the Insulation Claim, the very claim that the bi-jurisdictional status of morality challenges. If the moral partakes both of the spiritual and the civil, given that a primary task of civil government is to adjudicate moral disputes (recall the Moral Disagreement Clam), it is puzzling how the Insulation Claim can be maintained.

RAWLSIAN PUBLIC REASON

Moral, not simply political, liberal constitutionalism

As we saw, both Hobbes and Locke embrace the Moral Disagreement Claim: our private judgments about morality systematically diverge, and so we require a procedure – law announced by the sovereign or government – to provide a public impartial mark of right reason. A worrisome consequence of this account of public reason is that politics becomes the ultimate arbiter of all moral disputes. In his first published paper – "Outline of a Decision Procedure for Ethics" – Rawls also sought a procedural resolution to the problems of conflicting moral claims. Like the social contract tradition, the point of departure is a clash of conflicting claims: Each advances claims that are self-authenticating in the sense that "(a) Every claim shall be considered, on first sight, as meriting satisfaction. (b) No claim shall be denied possible satisfaction without a reason."[42] The procedure is meant to show not simply what claims we see as reasonable, but what is a reasonable social ordering of conflicting claims.[43] The problem, then, is once again to provide an impartial, public ordering of claims based on divergent individual perspectives. And once again the solution is procedural: Rawls develops an account of impartial, competent, moral umpires, who develop public principles and rules to order the claims. Rawls's great departure from the social contract tradition is that this is not a political procedure, and these are not actual political umpires: our modeling of how the umpires would decide allows us to develop a theory of social ethics or social justice. Hobbes's and Locke's Moral Disagreement Claim thus becomes:

> *Rawls' Moral Disagreement Claim*: when individuals reason about their claims on each other, they disagree, so a cooperative and just social life requires that they abandon their private judgment about their claims and submit to the public reason of impartial justice.

It is crucial to realize that Rawls is not talking about mere conflict of interests, but what we see as our *claims* on others – what he would later call our "self-originating" or "self-authenticating" claims.[44] It is because Rawls is ultimately concerned with a social ordering of claims based on divergent individual reasoning that his theory of justice has such close ties to social contract public reason theories.

This may seen confusing: The social contract's distinction between private judgment about justice and public *legal* rules of justice makes perfect sense, but it may be unclear what the analogous distinction is in Rawls's theory. Many read Rawls's early and middle works as advancing a contractarian procedure that constructs the truths about morality; if so, he could not possibly be describing a conflict between private and public moral judgment. On these readings he is simply performing the traditional role of the moralist, telling us what our private judgments should be. It was not until the mid-1970s that Rawls explicitly recognized that this was not his project – that he was engaging in a distinctive form of moral inquiry, which was entirely consistent with each individual having her own view, based on her personal reasoning, about moral truth. In order to clarify this, Rawls needed to distinguish a distinct form of moral inquiry focused on social morality, or the social moral framework, from traditional moral philosophy understood as investigations into moral truth. In his important essays on "The Independence of Moral Theory" and "Kantian Constructivism in Moral Theory"[45] Rawls depicts a mode of moral inquiry that he calls "moral theory," which is not concerned with uncovering the "moral truth" but, rather, is a

search for reasonable grounds for reaching agreement rooted in our conception of ourselves and our relation to society ... The task is to articulate a public conception of justice that all can live with ... What justifies a conception of justice is not its being true to an order antecedent to and given to us, but its congruence with our deepest understanding of ourselves and our aspirations, and our realization that, given our history and the traditions embedded in our public life, it is the most reasonable doctrine for us. *We can find no better basic charter for our social world.*[46]

Moral theory thus understood is a search for what Rawls calls a "moral constitution."[47] Rawls never claims that this moral constitution supplants moral philosophy or religion understood as the search for moral truth; rather, it supplements them in the sense that it seeks to arrive at a shared moral framework all can live with in a social world where these understandings of moral truth clash.[48] The way in which Rawlsian moral theory is an analog of social contract political philosophy now becomes manifest – it is a search for a "constitution" (moral, not political) that allows public adjudication of diverse individual claims that arise from differing moral and valuational perspectives.

A theory of justice: a double shared strategy

A Theory of Justice defends public principles of liberal justice by extensive appeal to the shared reasons claim. The key to the enterprise is the "thin theory of the good," which allows us to identify "primary goods." As is well known, the parties in the original position choose the two principles of justice under a "veil of ignorance" – a range of information that is specific to their own and their society's identity is excluded from the choice situation. Requiring the parties to choose under such conditions helps ensure that their choice will be reasonable and not moved by bias;[49] the problem is that without information about what they consider good and their particular plans of life, they do not have a definite basis for choice. Rawls thus supposes that the parties have knowledge of some universal features of good lives, so they know what to aim at.[50] The primary point of part III of *Theory* is to present the "thin theory of the good" – structural and substantive features of all rational and good plans of life. However, for the first stage of the argument from the original position all that is required is, as it were, a part of the thin theory: that which specifies certain primary goods – things that rational individuals "whatever else they want, desire as prerequisites for carrying out their plans of life."[51] These are liberties, opportunity, wealth and income and the social bases of self-respect – analogs of Lockean civil interests.[52] This part of the derivation aims to show that the parties to the original position, because they share common interests, will select the two principles of justice.

Now it is often supposed that this *is* the entire argument from the original position, and once the parties have made their choice of the two principles their work is done and they can, as it were, fold up shop. Not so. "*Persons in the original position*," Rawls tells us, must consider whether a well-ordered society founded on justice as fairness will be more stable than alternative conceptions considered in the original position.[53] "Other things equal, persons in the original position will adopt the most stable scheme of principles."[54] There has been extensive debate as to whether Rawls's concern with stability was an error, or is somehow inappropriate in a theory of justice.[55] However, once we appreciate that Rawls's aim is to provide a public moral constitution that solves the modern problem of achieving a cooperative social life under conditions of moral disagreement, we see that the concern with stability is absolutely necessary (and so we have some confirmation that the public reason reading of the core Rawlsian project is on target; it makes central what Rawls saw as central). Recall the Hobbesian challenge to public reason liberalism: Disagreements based on private judgment will infect, and so undermine, any agreement we might have about civil interests, and so the liberal solution to the problem of disagreement fails. Once a liberal public reason account is based on an appeal to shared civil reasons, it must respond to the Hobbesian critique.

Locke's liberalism replies by asserting the Insulation Claim: Religious disagreements will not undermine the justification based on shared civil interests because the latter will not infect the former. Locke comes close to defining acceptable (what Rawls would call "reasonable") religious doctrines in terms of whether they endorse the Insulation Claim: Roman Catholicism is excluded because its religious claims are not insulated from the civil. Rawls presents a novel, and much deeper, defense of the Insulation Claim: We might think of it as a *double shared strategy*. We not only share a concern with primary goods and a devotion to a just cooperative order (the analog of Locke's civil interests), but also share large parts of our personal conceptions of the good life. To get a bit clearer about Rawls's strategy, let us characterize a person's overall concerns into three sets: A, shared reasons concerning justice; B, shared elements of the good; C, unshared goods and religious beliefs. Rawls's ultimate claim in *Theory* is that set B strongly endorses the conclusions based on set A, ensuring that any disagreements arising from our diverse values and concerns cannot lead a person to abandon the conclusions based on A. Rawls thus remedies Locke's failure to provide a systematic defense of the insulation claim: our sharing of set B serves as a sort of firewall, insulating the argument based on the shared set in A from the deep disagreements in C.

Part III of *Theory* advances two claims:[56] (i) given our sense of justice, we will become devoted to the principles of justice (based on set A) and so not be tempted to act on diverging private judgment[57] and, importantly, (ii) when individuals reason from the "self-interested" view, or the point of view of their own good narrowly defined (sets B and C above), they will affirm their sense of justice, and so the conclusions of (i). When considering their good narrowly defined (leaving out the good of acting justly), Rawls accepts that individuals may be tempted to injustice. This confronts a well-ordered society with what Rawls called the "hazards of the generalized prisoner's dilemma" – each sees the collective rationality of acting on the principles but is tempted to defect in her own case when recommended by her self-interested point of view.[58] To overcome this hazard, as Paul Weithman has recently argued, Rawls sought to show in *Theory* that in a well-ordered society justice as fairness constitutes a sort of Nash equilibrium: "Each member of the W[ell] O[rdered] S[ociety] judges, from within the thin theory of the good [i.e., set B above], that her balance of reasons tilts in favor of maintaining her desire to act from the principles of justice as a highest-order regulative desire in her rational plans, *when the plans of others are similarly regulated.*"[59] Acting justly would then be the best reply to others acting justly.[60] Thus, we might say, that the congruence of the practical reasoning based on sets A and B ensures that any discordant reasoning from set C will not overturn our devotion to the principles of justice.

While a great advance on previous defenses of the Insulation Claim, public reason liberals must have serious reservations about this congruence analysis: it surely underestimates the extent of our disagreements. Liberal justice is said to be stable because we share so much. Although we commenced with the modern problem of a society with deeply pluralistic perspectives, in the end we all share a conception of the good with both structural and substantive components. In the course of his stability analysis argument, Rawls makes the following strong claims about shared understandings of the good:

(i)   We share an understanding of the good as plans of life with a certain structure.[61]

(ii) We share a conception of our social nature as forming a community in which members "recognize the good of each as an element in the complete activity the whole of which is intended to give pleasure to all."[62]

(iii) We possess "natural sentiments of unity and fellow feeling."[63]

(iv) We aim at sincerity in our relations with others.[64]

(v)   We are attracted to plans that conform to the Aristotelian Principle – according to which "other things equal, humans enjoy the exercise of their realized capacities (their innate or trained abilities) and this enjoyment increases the more the capacity is realized, or the greater its complexity"[65] – as well as its "companion effect": "As we witness the exercise of well-trained abilities by others, these displays are enjoyed by us and arouse a desire that we should be able to do the same thing ourselves. We want to be like those persons who can exercise the abilities we find latent in our nature."[66]

(vi)   Individuals "have a desire to express their nature as free and equal moral persons." [67]

Political, not moral, liberal constitutionalism: the abandonment of the double shared strategy

As Rawls says, his move to the political was motivated by a search for a more adequate ground for stability in light of our "intractable struggles" and the fact that we witness "irreconcilable conflict" of "absolute depth" on a variety of moral and religious issues.[68] One aspect of this response is obvious but not sufficiently appreciated: he abandons his major innovation of resolving the conflict of private judgment through a moral, as well as a political, constitution. The "political" turn is actually a return to the strategy of early public reason liberalism, seeing the political as the sole sphere of public reason, and so once again politics becomes the arbiter of moral disagreement. This contraction in ambition is striking, and in many ways signals his pessimistic conclusion that his three-decade project (from the 1950s through the 1970s) failed.

In terms of our analysis in the previous subsection, we can understand political liberalism as abandoning the double shared strategy. Instead the three sets, *A*, *B*, and *C* (where we share the first two), political liberalism assumes that "citizens' overall views have two parts" – that which is shared and on which the public conception of justice is built, and that which is part of a person's comprehensive conception of the good.[69] Because the dropped set *B* can no longer serve as a firewall between the shared set *A* (on which he builds his liberal account) and the deep disagreements in set *C*, it is hard to see a plausible way to insulate the disagreements in *C* from infecting *A*.[70] Rawls's response is a fundamental breakthrough in public reason liberalism: instead of insulating *A* from *C*, he argues that in our contemporary world a wide array of set *C*s *support* the conclusions based on the shared set (*A*) in a variety of ways – *A* may be congruent with *C*, not conflict with *C* or, at a minimum, not conflict "too sharply with" *C*.[71] As long as set *C* does not too sharply conflict with *A*, the shared political conclusion based on set *A* will be stable. In this case there would be an "overlapping consensus" on the political principles derived from *A*.

Overlapping consensus may not have been available to Locke as a core claim of his public reason liberalism: It is plausible to suppose that a major change between the seventeenth and twenty-first centuries was what we might call the general liberalization of conceptions of the good in Western democracies. The basic tenets of liberalism, including freedom of speech and thought, representative institutions, wide scope for freedom of action and lifestyles, privacy and the market order, are very widely embraced and embedded in a wide variety of worldviews.[72] Yet, while we may suppose that there is such a convergence on these essential features of liberal democracy, it is doubtful that, when looking at the combined implications of the shared set A and each person's own set C, there is agreement on specific property rights, principles of distributive justice, or laws concerning abortion, health care or, say, gay marriage. And it is no mistake to bring set C into justificatory issues: Rawls explicitly tells us that the principles derived from the "pro tanto" argument based on set A alone are not "fully justified" until the beliefs and values of a person's set C are considered and confirm (or not conflict too much with) those principles.[73] Unless a citizen affirms the principles on the basis of both sets, the principles are not fully justified to him.

Civil public reasoning: the return to an Insulation Claim

Toward the end of his career, Rawls appeared to become pessimistic that, even restricting our reasoning to simply the shared set A, we could arrive at the sort of detailed principles of justice he defended in *Theory*. In the preface to the paperback edition of *Political Liberalism*, he stresses that reasonable pluralism and the burdens of judgment apply to the political conception as well:

> In addition to conflicting comprehensive doctrines, PL does recognize that in any actual political society a number of differing liberal political conceptions of justice compete with one another in society's political debate ... This leads to another aim of PL: saying how a well-ordered liberal society is to be formulated given not only reasonable pluralism [of comprehensive conceptions] but a family of reasonable liberal conceptions of justice.[74]

Rawls thus observes that the same considerations that show us that we inevitably will disagree about the good and religious matters "lead us to recognize that there are different and incompatible liberal political conceptions."[75]

Now because the fact of reasonable pluralism infects set A, we cannot suppose that reasoning on the basis of shared reasons will lead us all to the same conception of justice (and this includes Rawls's own two principles).[76] There is no uniquely reasonable way to organize and weigh the shared values of set A. Consequently, as the implications of the fact of reasonable pluralism for the political set becomes our main concern, what Rawls calls "the principle of liberal legitimacy" takes center stage. Even if a state does not act on the principles of justice we see as most reasonable, we can still see it as legitimately exercising political power if it can be reasonably justified based on shared values. The guidelines for this justification are given by what Rawls calls "the idea of public reason."[77] In justifying the coercive use of political power on matters of basic justice and constitutional essentials, citizens are to appeal only to conceptions of justice involving reasonable weightings of the shared set (A), along with methods of inquiry which are themselves part of the public culture (and so in A). Rawls is explicit that the content of public reason cannot be restricted to his two principles of justice. "Rather, its content – the principles, ideals, and standards that may be appealed to – are those of a family of reasonable political conceptions of justice."[78]

One more twist in our tale about the Insulation Claim: at this point Rawls resurrects it. After jettisoning it in the justification of his own principles of justice (where it is replaced by the idea of an overlapping consensus), in the public forum a moral duty of civility applies. In the original specification of this duty, we are to restrict our arguments to political reasons shared by all citizens, and so not employ considerations based on our comprehensive conceptions (set C) in matters of basic justice and constitutional essentials. Rawls later relaxes this, allowing reasons from set C to enter into public discourse so long as, "in due course," they can be supported with reasons from set A.[79] In essence, Rawls holds that citizens have a moral duty in public discourse about matters of basic justice to endorse the insulation of the divergent reasons in their sets C from the shared set A. After such a long search to show that conclusions based on our shared reasons will not be overturned by disagreements from our unshared reasons, it must be seen as disappointing to "show" this by asserting a moral duty that it be so.[80]

SORTING OUT RAWLS'S LEGACY

*The Rawlsian trajectory: the shrinking influence
of shared reasons and the evaporation of insulation*

A number of prominent and sophisticated philosophers essentially
endorse Rawls's political liberalism and see it as, overall, well justified and coherent.[81] It is, however, very hard not to see it as an
unfinished project; major changes became prominent only in sketchy
presentations rather late in the day, and it is hard to conclude that
their implications were fully worked out.[82] On the basis of the above
analysis, we can see that a major unresolved problem is the implication of allowing significant disagreement into set A – the freestanding
political argument. As late as the 1993 introduction to *Political
Liberalism* Rawls claimed that "the political conception is shared
by everyone while the reasonable doctrines are not" (we agree on set
A and its implications but not on C), while in the 1996 preface to the
paperback edition Rawls stresses that reasonable pluralism applies
to the political conception as well.[83] Now once we allow serious
disagreement within the set of "shared reasons," the core of the
shared reasons strategy begins to collapse. The point of Rawls's
"two set" strategy was to separate that on which we basically agree
from that to which reasonable pluralism applies, hopefully with the
result that a favored conception of liberal justice could be justified by
appeal to shared reasons. But once reasonable pluralism applies to
both sets, Rawls abandons this hope.

A powerful reason for Rawls's followers continuing to insist on the
two set strategy in the justification of political principles is, perhaps,
to forestall what we might call the *Nightmare*: unless we restrict the
range of reasons relevant to political justification to a small set, A
(and so exclude set C), perhaps no version of liberalism can be justified (more on this later).[84] So the suggestion is that we focus the
justification of liberal principles only on A, a set of shared liberal
commitments. Oddly, however, Rawls's insistence that political
principles are not "fully justified" until they are confirmed by a
citizen's comprehensive conception of the good (set C) shows that
focusing on set A as the initial justification cannot prevent the
Nightmare, for in the end set C has its say. Indeed, Rawls's strategy
increases the likelihood of the Nightmare. Rawls requires that the

full justification of liberal principles passes two tests: first a *pro tanto* justification on the basis of set *A* alone, and then a full justification on the basis of set *C*. Suppose that there are some citizens who reject the argument for liberalism based on *A*, but endorse liberal principles (constitutions, etc.) based on their *C*. For Rawls, because they have not affirmed liberalism on both sets it is not justified to them; if only one test – based on all of one's normative commitments – were required more, not fewer, citizens might endorse liberal principles.[85]

In *A Theory of Justice* the shared reasons requirement for justification made sense: the shared sets *A* (the considerations employed in the argument from the original position) and *B* (the rest of the shared thin theory of the good) were meant to overwhelm any residue disagreement from set *C* that might lead to unjust action. But once overlapping consensus replaces this picture and set *B* drops out, set *C* takes on justificatory relevance, while set *A* no longer even has determinate political implications. Now once it is admitted (i) that set *C* is of justificatory relevance and (ii) the political implications of set *A* are rather vague, insisting that considerations from *C* cannot be appealed to in political discourse (the duty of civility) looks under-motivated. Why should considerations of justificatory relevance be insulated from political discussion? It is revealing that Rawls's more orthodox followers justify this version of the insulation thesis on the grounds that it induces stability: Because stability requires insulation of the sets, we have a duty to insulate. Leaving aside for now its plausibility,[86] this claim reverses the order of justification: rather than (as in *Theory*) showing that liberal principles will be stable because they are insulated from controversial reasons based on comprehensive conceptions, it is now argued that because we seek stability, we must admit a moral duty to insulate public discussion from controversial reasons.

Retreating to liberalism as shared reasons

Perhaps it would be too strong to say that, at the end, Rawls's public reason liberalism was in disarray; but certainly fundamental puzzles are unresolved concerning the relative roles of shared reasons and those based on one's own comprehensive conception in justifying, and preserving, a liberal polity. To many of his followers, Rawls offered a deeply attractive theory of justice based on the shared reasons modeled in the original position (leave aside for now Rawls's worries that even within the shared reason phase of the argument disagreement may arise); the problem for them is that Rawls was unsuccessful in insulating this argument from broader conflicts. In particular, it is doubtful that the conclusions of the "freestanding argument from the original position" (based on set A) remain intact once deliberators consider their comprehensive conceptions of value (set C). The radical response by some neo-Rawlsians is to simply deny that set C could ever overturn the conclusions of set A. Thus, as Jonathan Quong sees it, to allow full justification (set C) as a check on the argument from the original position (set A) renders A's results hostage to "illiberal" values and unjust views.[87] For Quong the aim of political liberalism is to justify liberal principles to liberals; those who would reject arguments based on shared liberal values simply because they clashed with their deep metaphysical or religious commitments would simply show themselves not to be liberals. We thus seem back to our Lockean starting point: Liberals just *are* those who endorse the Insulation Claim, and liberalism is a doctrine for such people. Just as Locke excluded Roman Catholics from the justificatory public because they rejected the Insulation Claim, Quong deems "unreasonable" any who would question the conclusions of set A on the grounds of their C.[88] But this looks more like a doctrine of liberal reason than of public reason. Once again, endorsing the insulation thesis is a requirement for admission to full membership in the liberal community.

Liberalism without insulation

We are now, I think, in a better position to see the way forward for public reason liberalism. Rawls's later work shows us the deep implausibility at the heart of the shared reasons strategy: it supposed that while our reasoning about religion, morality, and metaphysics is deeply pluralistic, our reasoning about our moral and/or political constitution is homogenous. As Rawls came to appreciate, however, the very burdens of judgment that produce disagreement in the former leads to pluralism in the latter. If, somehow, we could plausibly claim that reasoning in one sphere was basically homogenous while in the other highly heterogeneous, it would be worthwhile seeking to build firewalls (as in *Theory*) to stop the diversity from contaminating that about which we agree. But once we abandon this implausible bifurcation of our normative reasoning, we are left wondering whether the attempt to insulate set A from the disagreement in set C is worth the effort. Moreover, Rawls shows us how we might proceed without insulation: the ideas of an overlapping consensus and full justification presuppose that set C, rather than being a danger to a justified liberal order, may be a resource to be drawn upon. Thus, the way forward: abandon the separation of sets A and C_i, where A is the set of all the relevant reasons members of the public share, while C_i concerns all the relevant justificatory reasons that member of the public i holds, but does not share with all others.[89] A moral or political constitution (or rule within such a constitution) is thus publicly justified if for all i who are members of the public, $\{A, C_i\}$ endorses it. We might call this public reason in the distributive sense; the reasoning is distributed over the entire public, each endorsing the constitution (or rule) on the basis of her own $\{A, C_i\}$ set.[90]

Waking up from the Nightmare

Rawls's followers reject this option partly because, I believe, they think it leads to the Nightmare. As Quong puts it, those with "unjust" and "illiberal" views would be able to veto liberal principles, either leaving us with a publicly justified illiberal constitution, or no justified constitution at all. In order to avoid this Nightmare, Quong and others make committed Rawlsian liberals the voice of public reason, in a way not so dissimilar to Hobbes, who made the sovereign the voice of public reason. If the total reason of everyone counts, then surely we will be able to justify nothing – or at least nothing recognizable as "liberal." The reason of liberals becomes the celestial voice.

Consider the worst Nightmare first: Nothing at all will be justified, because someone will exercise her veto for every proposal. Talk of "veto" can lead us astray; we are apt to think of haggling or bargaining, where a person has the right to say "no," and uses this to her strategic advantage. But our concern now is whether, given the reasons of the members of the public, there is any moral or political constitution that all members of the public have reason to endorse. To make the choice problem well formed, let us model it in terms of pairwise choices: confronted with options x and y, the person's reasons indicate either that x is better than y, y is better than x, or they are equal.[91] Now once we translate a "veto" into such a choice problem, a veto of constitution y[92] must mean that the person would choose to have no constitution at all rather than y. If, for example, she simply had reason to choose constitution x over y, this would not be a "veto" of y, but simply a ranking of an alternative constitution as superior.

Once we see what is constituted by a veto, we also see how, surprisingly, Hobbes helps us wake up from the Nightmare: A common system of moral and political rules is a tremendous good to all, for it is the very foundation of a cooperative and fruitful social life. A framework of social and political rules that all deem legitimate, and are willing to internalize (and so feel guilty when they violate them), and are devoted to maintaining is the *sine qua non* of our life together. To veto such a framework is to deem it so unjust or otherwise costly that one would rather forgo the tremendous benefits of a morally ordered social life than endorse and internalize such a constitution as normative. This certainly may happen, but it is not a decision that a serious person lightly makes. To be sure, there is a great deal of posturing in our philosophical discussions that one would veto all constitutions that do not conform to one's favored philosophical account, but the real question is whether one would really have reason to choose a sort of normative anarchy of social life in preference to it. That we all – even moral and political philosophers – teach our children the basic moral rules of our society rather suggests not.

The neo-Rawlsian Nightmare

Perhaps, then, the neo-Rawlsian Nightmare is that, unless our normative conclusions are confirmed by set A alone, public reason cannot be guaranteed to yield a truly liberal framework; as Quong suggests, the results of public justification are "held hostage" to those with illiberal views. Now we should distinguish two versions of this liberal Nightmare: that (i) the basic framework might be authoritarian or deeply hostile to individual liberty and (ii) the moral constitution will not conform to certain controversial accounts of liberalism, such as Rawls's two principles of justice. Now (i) seems implausible. Liberalism broadly construed simply *is* the historically generated solution to the problem of how people who deeply disagree about almost everything can share a system of social cooperation that all see as normative. The constitutions that really will be vetoed are those that build social order on the requirement that some renounce their most cherished convictions even as ideals in their own personal lives. While many of us might rank most highly social orders that express our ideals in public life, what is truly unacceptable are social and political orders that insist we abandon our deep ideals as the basis of our own existence.

In contrast (ii) is likely: There is no guarantee that comprehensive public reason – that which draws on each member of the public's total set of evaluative considerations – will endorse any specific controversial "theory of justice." What, I believe, is most likely is that a set of liberal constitutions will be deemed eligible by the public (each will be ranked by everyone as better than no constitution at all, though we will disagree about which is best). Notice that this is the conclusion at which Rawls himself arrived: a "family" of liberal arrangements are justified, but there is no uniquely publicly justified version.[93] This family, I suspect, is rather broader than Rawls or many of his followers would like. Perhaps one motivation for insisting on the primary justificatory importance of set *A* alone is to narrow the range of acceptable liberalisms to those that conform to a certain theory of distributive justice. But that is hardly compelling for those who do not already embrace that theory.

Once we accept that public reason can only identify a set or family of eligible constitutions, public reason liberalism is faced with an equilibrium selection problem. Since any eligible constitution is ranked as better than no constitution at all by all members of the public, any eligible constitution can provide the sort of Nash equilibrium Rawls sought. For any constitution in the eligible family, if everyone else is conforming to it, one's best response is also to conform; this is guaranteed by the fact that, given each member of the public's *entire set of relevant reasons* $\{A, C_i\}$, she ranks conformity to such a constitution as better than unilateral defection. The question for contemporary public reason liberals is how one of the many equilibria is to be selected.

THE FUTURE OF PUBLIC REASON LIBERALISM?

I have tried to show that the public reason project has been at the core of liberal theory. At least since Locke, it has been built on the Insulation Claim: We can insulate our deep and intractable disputes about religious convictions and personal ideals from agreement on shared civil interests. The highpoint of this "insulation" view of public reason was A Theory of Justice. Rawls's revolutionary later philosophy was to work toward a version of public reason liberalism that dropped the Insulation Claim and lessened the role of shared reasoning in public justification. Although some of his most important followers seek to move Rawls back closer to Theory, the way forward in the public reason project is to investigate how diverse reasoning can lead to publicly endorsable rules and constitutions.[94] My discussion has only skimmed the surface of the complexities and possibilities. Yet this much is clear: the future of public reason liberalism is not to develop a controversial ideological position that seeks to exclude large parts of our society as "unreasonable," but to press the bounds of inclusiveness as far as possible – and in doing so show that the deep strength of liberalism is its unique ability not only to accommodate, but also to draw upon, our deep diversity.

NOTES

1. An important exception is the wonderful appendix of Lawrence Solum's "Constructing an Ideal of Public Reason." See also Button, Contract, Culture and Citizenship.
2. And Kant? His complex political philosophy is most often ignored in the English-speaking world, though with the publication of Ripstein's Force and Freedom this may change.
3. For a much fuller account, see Turner and Gaus, The History of Public Reason in Political Philosophy.
4. Rawls, Political Liberalism, pp. xxvi, 4.
5. Rawls, A Theory of Justice, rev. edn., p. 10.
6. I develop this point more fully in "Hobbesian Contractarianism, Orthodox and Revisionist."
7. Hobbes, Leviathan, p. 23 (ch. 5, ¶3). Gauthier focuses on this passage in his fascinating essay on "Public Reason." I discuss his interpretation in my Contemporary Theories of Liberalism, ch. 3.

8. Hobbes, *Leviathan*, p. 180 (ch. 26, ¶21).
9. *Ibid.*
10. Ewin, *Virtue and Rights*, p. 67.
11. Hobbes, *Leviathan*, p. 300 (ch. 37, ¶13). This remark occurs in Hobbes's discussion of belief in miracles.
12. See Gauthier, "Public Reason."
13. Hobbes, *Leviathan*, p. 100 (ch. 18, ¶1). Italics in original.
14. *Ibid.*, p. 35 (ch. 7, ¶2).
15. *Ibid.*, p. 299 (ch. 37, ¶13), and in note 21 on this page in the Latin edition.
16. *Ibid.*, p. 300 (ch. 37, ¶13). Emphasis added.
17. *Ibid.*, p. 246 (ch. 32, ¶5); p. 300 (ch. 37, ¶13).
18. I have greatly benefited from discussions with Shane Courtland on this matter.
19. This, of course, leads right to the deep paradox at the heart of Hobbes's theory. A person employs his private reason to conclude that he must subject himself to public reason, seeing that his ends will be better served by such subjection. But private reason reserves the right to determine when this subjection is not valid – when subjection to public reason frustrates the basic aims that led the person to public reason in the first place. I consider this problem at length in *Contemporary Theories of Liberalism*, pp. 71ff.
20. Milton's defense of freedom of thought and speech in *Areopagitica* (1643) represented the sort of dangerous thinking to which Hobbes is reacting.
21. This is not to say that Hobbes recommends that the sovereign always seeks to control the religious beliefs of his subjects, but that he always has the authority to control their actions, and seek to influence the formation of their opinions, should they lead in directions that endanger the civil order. Hobbes criticized the priesthood for their desire to take away the use of people's natural reason by metaphysical charms and spells, claiming an authority to subject their followers' reason to their own (*Leviathan*, p. 487, [ch. 47, ¶20, Latin edn.]). Because salvation requires genuine belief, to subject one's beliefs to the reason of others is essentially to play a lottery with your soul – if the priest in right, you win, if not, you lose (*Leviathan*, p. 482 [ch. 47, ¶20]). Hobbes thus indicates that the best policy is generally to leave people's reasoning in their own hands; such a policy encourages, rather than undermines, natural reason. But none of this constitutes a claim to freedom of conscience: it is a criticism of the priesthood and their attack on reason.
22. Freedom of conscience resulted in a plethora of radical religious doctrines that sometimes led to radical political views. Sects such as the Quakers, the Shakers, the Ranters, and the Muggletonians arose. Among the most interesting of these sects were The Fifth Monarchy Men, who interpreted

Daniel's dream (Dan. 7) as indicating that there would be five great legitimate monarchies: the last of which would be that of Christ. They believed that the fourth monarchy, the Roman Empire, had been overturned by the Church of Rome, and so were awaiting the Reign of Christ. Consequently, on the basis of their reading of the Bible they denied the legitimacy of all states between the Roman Empire and the Reign of Christ (which, unfortunately for them, included the Commonwealth). The Fifth Monarchy Men brought home two great lessons. First, once freedom of thought was allowed, the proliferation of interpretations of the Bible would be endless: the hope that the priesthood of all believers would lead to consensus was an illusion. Second, the same freedom of thought that led people to conflicting religious beliefs could lead them to conflicting political convictions.

23. Hobbes, *Leviathan*, p. 113 (ch. 18, ¶9).

24. *Ibid.*, p. 128 (ch. 20, ¶3).

25. *Ibid.*, p. 212 (ch. 29, ¶6). I argue for a more absolutist interpretation of Hobbes – which sharply distinguishes him from Locke, in "Hobbes' Challenge to Public Reason Liberalism," pp. 155–77.

26. See, for example, Hobbes, *Leviathan*, p. 139 (ch. 21, ¶7).

27. *Ibid.*, p. 138 (ch. 21, ¶7). See Ewin, *Virtue and Rights*, p. 20. There is a deep complication raised by Hobbes's puzzling claim that the civil law and the law of nature contain each other. *Leviathan*, p. 174 (ch. 26, ¶8).

28. Locke, *Second Treatise of Government*, §124. Compare Hobbes, *Leviathan*, p. 180 (ch. 26, ¶20).

29. Locke, *Second Treatise of Government*, ed. Macpherson, §87. Emphasis added.

30. I argue for this interpretation more fully in "Hobbes' Challenge to Public Reason Liberalism."

31. Locke, "A Letter Concerning Toleration," p. 10.

32. *Ibid.*, pp. 9–10.

33. *Ibid.*, p. 19.

34. *Ibid.*, p. 43.

35. "To avoid this State of War (wherein there is no appeal but to Heaven, *and wherein every the least difference is apt to end, where there is no Authority to decide between the Contenders)* is one great *reason of Mens putting themselves into Society*, and quitting the State of Nature: for where there is an Authority, a Power on Earth, from which relief can be had by *appeal*, there the continuance of the State of War is excluded, and the controversy is decided by that Power" (Locke, *Second Treatise of Government*, ed. Macpherson, §21. First emphasis added; others original). I elsewhere consider the importance of Locke's claim that, because our disagreement is limited, the jurisdiction of the umpire is limited to

resolutions with a certain range, whereas for Hobbes there are no limits on the sovereign's competency; see Gaus, "Hobbes' Challenge to Public Reason Liberalism" and, more generally, Gaus, *Justificatory Liberalism*, part II.

36. Kant, *The Metaphysical Elements of Justice*, 2nd edn., p. 116 [§43]. Emphasis added.

37. Rousseau, *Discourse on Political Economy* in *The Social Contract and Discourses*, at pp. 256–57.

38. See Book IV, ch. 8 of *The Social Contract* in ibid.

39. Locke, "A Letter Concerning Toleration," p. 47.

40. *Ibid.*, p. 41.

41. *Ibid.*

42. Rawls, "Outline of a Decision Procedure for Ethics," p. 14.

43. Rawls, "Justice as Fairness," p. 59.

44. Rawls refers to the claims as "self-originating" in "Kantian Constructivism in Moral Theory," p. 334, and as "self-authenticating," in *Justice as Fairness: A Restatement*, p. 23.

45. Chapters 15 and 16, in *John Rawls: Collected Papers*.

46. Rawls, "Kantian Constructivism in Moral Theory," pp. 306–7. Emphasis added.

47. *Ibid.*, p. 326.

48. Although it can override them – when one's claim based on one's own perspective is inconsistent with an agreed upon way to socially order conflicting claims.

49. Rawls, *A Theory of Justice*, p. 392.

50. *Ibid.*, pp. 348–50.

51. *Ibid.*, p. 348.

52. *Ibid.*, p. 54.

53. *Ibid.*, p. 398. Emphasis added.

54. *Ibid.*

55. For a relentless criticism, see Barry, "John Rawls and the Search for Stability." See also Cohen's *Rescuing Justice and Equality*, pp. 327–30.

56. Rawls, *A Theory of Justice*, p. 397. I consider these matters in much more depth in "The Turn to a Political Liberalism."

57. Rawls, *A Theory of Justice*, §§71–75.

58. *Ibid.*, pp. 505, 435. This, of course, is precisely the Hobbesian problem.

59. Weithman, *Why Political Liberalism?*, p. 64. Emphasis added.

60. This would not assure stability on justice, for it shows only that acting justly is a possible equilibrium. Because of this we confront a sort of assurance game: we need to be assured that others will play the cooperative equilibrium (Weithman, *Why Political Liberalism?*, p. 49). Weithman (pp. 98, 157, 173) argues that a general recognition that "everyone else's

plans will be regulated by their sense of justice" would do the trick. I question this conclusion in "A Tale of Two Sets."

61. Rawls, *A Theory of Justice*, pp. 358–72.
62. *Ibid.*, p. 459.
63. *Ibid.*, p. 439.
64. *Ibid.*, pp. 499–500.
65. *Ibid.*, p. 374.
66. *Ibid.*, p. 376.
67. *Ibid.*, p. 462.
68. Rawls, *Political Liberalism*, pp. xxvi, 4.
69. *Ibid.*, p. 38; Weithman, *Why Political Liberalism?*, p. 333.
70. To say that set *B* is dropped is not to say that all the elements of *B* are dropped from the analysis. A particularly perplexing feature of the move to political liberalism is that many of the elements of set *B* (such as civic friendship) gravitate to set *A* (the shared public reasons), while others end up in *C* (most appeals to the Aristotelian Principle). To add to the complexity, the features undergo changes in their characterization as they move from set *B* to set *A*, becoming "political" ideas, and often seeming to be considerably less important values when considered as such. See my "The Turn to a Political Liberalism."
71. Rawls, *Political Liberalism*, pp. 11, 40, 140. One reason that they may now conflict (but not too much) with *A*, is that the set of values in *A* has been reinforced by some of the former elements of set *B* (see previous note); *A*, as it were, carries more values on its own and so can overcome modest conflict with *C*.
72. I defend a version of this claim in "The Role of Conservatism in Securing and Maintaining Just Moral Constitutions."
73. Rawls, *Political Liberalism*, pp. 386ff.
74. *Ibid.*, p. xlvii.
75. *Ibid.*, p. xlvii.
76. *Ibid.*, p. 219.
77. *Ibid.*, pp. 225–26, 243.
78. *Ibid.*, pp. l–li.
79. I consider these matters more carefully in "The Place of Religious Belief in Public Reason Liberalism." See *Political Liberalism*, Lecture vi and Part iv.
80. Not surprisingly, this duty has been trenchantly criticized by many faith-friendly liberals. This dispute is central to Vallier's *Liberal Politics and Public Faith*.
81. Perhaps the most prominent and subtle is Samuel Freeman. See his *Justice and the Social Contract*.
82. Burton Dreben thought that the 1996 paperback edition should be considered a second edition of *Political Liberalism*. See his "On Rawls on

Political Liberalism." For Rawls's views on the last set of changes, see *Political Liberalism*, pp. 438–39. By the end, "justice as fairness ... has a minor role."

83. Compare Rawls, *Political Liberalism*, pp. xix, xlvi.

84. It is important to stress that our concern here is shared reasons in the fundamental justification of the basic constitutional structure, not shared reasons in political discourse (see subsection on civil public reasoning). In regard to fundamental justification, public reason liberals may, of course, endorse the shared reasons claim on other grounds than that explored here, such as sincerity (see Quong, *Liberalism Without Perfection*, pp. 265ff.) or as a norm of respect in dialogue (see Larmore's *Patterns of Moral Complexity*, p. 53 and "Political Liberalism.")

85. Requiring only endorsement based on C weakly dominates requiring endorsement based on both A and C; it cannot do worse (in terms of the people to whom liberalism is justified) and can do better. See further my "On the Appropriate Mode of Justifying a Public Moral Constitution."

86. Weithman (*Why Political Liberalism?*, pp. 327ff.) has argued, following Rawls, that restricting political debate about basic justice and constitutional essentials to shared reasons induces stability by promoting mutual assurance that we are all just. I have questioned this analysis in "A Tale of Two Sets." For similar doubts, see Thrasher and Vallier, "The Fragility of Consensus."

87. Quong, *Liberalism Without Perfection*, pp. 167–69.

88. "Such people are not part of an ideal, well-ordered liberal society, and so obtaining their agreement is irrelevant to the project of liberal theory's internal coherence" (*ibid.*, p. 181).

89. The subscript C_i indicates that for each member of the public, C_i will be different. I am assuming that there may be a shared set A; if there is not, then all considerations that person i draws upon will be in C_i.

90. This is the approach I develop in *The Order of Public Reason*, especially Part II.

91. In *The Order of Public Reason* (pp. 303–10), I show that a considerably weaker condition will suffice; even if a person cannot rank x and y, we still can model a rational social choice situation.

92. From here on I shall simply talk of a "constitution," allowing that this could be applied to what Rawls called either a moral constitution or a political constitution. Or, we could focus instead (as I think we should) on specific rules within the constitution. See *The Order of Public Reason*, pp. 490–97. See also my "On the Appropriate Mode of Justifying a Public Moral Constitution."

93. Rawls, *Political Liberalism*, p. xlvi.

94. Fred D'Agostino has been a pioneer in analyzing diverse public reasoning; see his *Free Public Reason: Making it Up as We Go*. Especially important here are the works of younger scholars such as Kevin Vallier, John Thrasher, and Ryan Muldoon. See, for example, Vallier, "Consensus and Convergence in Public Reason"; Thrasher and Vallier, "The Fragility of Consensus"; and Muldoon et al., "Disagreement Behind the Veil of Ignorance."

6   Autonomy and liberalism: a troubled marriage?

In its various guises, liberalism rests on principles that place a central value on the capacity of citizens to govern their own lives in pursuit of what they take to be the good. Yet from both inside and outside the liberal camp, this coupling of principles of justice with the value of individual self-government has been questioned. Some liberals think that placing primary value on autonomy exemplifies an insufficiently pluralist account of justice since being self-governing in the way that trait is usually defined is not a central component of all reasonable value orientations.[1] Similarly, others who resist being labeled liberal also see the reliance of principles of justice on the value of autonomy as overly exclusionary, and/or an instance of the imposition of contestable (e.g., male, Western) values on otherwise marginalized and denigrated groups and cultures.[2]

To help illuminate, but not to pretend to settle, these trenchant debates, I will examine some powerful challenges to the linkage between autonomy and principles of justice, both those defended by self-described liberal thinkers and those who eschew that label. As we will see, the major sticking point in these discussions is whether a commitment to the value of autonomy is sufficiently compatible with the kind of pluralism or respect for difference that must come with liberal democratic orders. I will take a moment, then, in the first section, to discuss some of the various ways that resistance to the value of autonomy has been expressed, homing in specifically on those that rest on a commitment to pluralism. I then turn to autonomy and consider variations on that idea, and I will suggest how a plausible understanding of that notion may

I am grateful to Steven Wall for comments on an earlier draft of this chapter.

well avoid the critiques discussed, though seeing such an idea
as central to liberal principles of justice may well alter the view
we take of liberalism itself.

RESISTANCE TO AUTONOMY, LIBERAL AND OTHERWISE

The relation we will be considering between liberal (and other
pluralist) approaches to justice and autonomy is along the following
lines: The justification of the principles that underlie political
institutions and the dominant social practices[3] that go with them
are legitimate (in part) because the value of individual autonomy is
presupposed and promoted. This means that the commitment to
the value of autonomy orders the interests that citizens are said
to have, specifically in their pursuing values that they competently
and independently espouse as self-governing agents. By extension,
these interests will help specify the order of basic rights and liberties
that will be protected in a constitution.[4] An autonomy-based politics
will include a strong presumption against paternalism and
most types of legal moralism, though certain forms of perfectionist,
autonomy-based views will leave room for the state's promotion
of ideals.[5] Such a politics will also support educational and
social welfare policies, as well as economic arrangements, that secure
and support autonomy for its citizens. Further, on some views, a
commitment to self-government at the individual level links with
a commitment to self-government at the collective level as
well, so that democratic institutions and practices will be constitutive of the just society, and not merely an instrumental device for
aggregating preferences.[6]

The vortex of the critical discussion of the relation between
liberalism and autonomy will be located in the former's commitment
to pluralism in conceptions of value, culture, and identity. Liberals
of all stripes as well as more radical theorists claim that crucial to
a just social order is a fundamental commitment to accepting,
if not celebrating, *difference* in the social and cultural landscape
of that society. The worry that is most trenchant in this setting
is whether valuing autonomy is, in effect, taking sides in a competition among value frameworks rather than providing a neutral
mechanism to adjudicate those very social confrontations.

The idea of autonomy motivating these critiques, generally speaking, refers to an independent individual whose social attachments are all voluntarily chosen and controlled and whose status as a self-governing person makes no reference to those current or historical social attachments. The crux of the objection raised against seeing autonomy in this sense as a fundamental political value is that it marks out a parochial conception of a flourishing life rather than a universal human value. John Gray puts the point this way: "if autonomy is construed ... as a relatively closed concept [as one that prizes substantive independence and individual self-determination], autonomous choice will be compatible only with a fairly narrowly defined range of ways of life." A politics built on the value of autonomy in this closed sense cannot help but be exclusionary in a way that is in conflict with true liberal pluralism.[7]

An additional powerful line of critique waged against autonomy-based politics (and any version of liberalism that is committed to this) rests on the assumption that autonomy is a notoriously *individualist* virtue. The autonomous "man" is self-made and on his own, an individualist and often of the rugged kind. Feminist theorists have been most powerful in voicing opposition to this ideal of the citizen. For the characteristic of independence, coupled with a voluntarist understanding of social connections, is a trait prominent in the self-conceptions of privileged males who traditionally assume social relations that are typified by public interactions with relative strangers governed by contractual arrangements. In contrast are women and others who (again, traditionally) take on roles marked by close connections with others, mutual (and sometimes asymmetrical) dependence relations, and life outside of the public sphere. Viewing autonomy in this hyper-individualist sense as a core political value clearly has exclusionary and inegalitarian ramifications in the way citizens' interests will be represented and promoted.

Further, critical discussion of the relation between liberalism and autonomy has become especially intense regarding issues of culture and identity, as theorists grapple with the balance between respecting the self-determination rights of cultural groups and safeguarding the enjoyment of liberal rights for all individuals, including members of such groups whose traditions may not prize individual self-determination. The liberal commitment to pluralism, and tolerance and inclusiveness along with it, conflicts with the insistence that all such groups must incorporate the virtue of individual self-government in order to receive social protection and support.[8]

The tension point in these considerations is the commitment to pluralism that runs through liberalism as well as its more radical cousins in democratic theory.[9] The most general version of the opposition to autonomy, then, is that valuing autonomy as the basic characteristic of citizens to be protected and promoted is in conflict with pluralism so understood. As William Galston puts it: "the decision to throw state power behind the promotion of individual autonomy can undermine the lives of individuals and groups that do not and cannot organize their affairs in accordance with that principle without undermining the deepest sources of their identity."[10]

Extending this line of critique, Charles Larmore argues that reason cannot function the way it does in autonomy-based liberal views like Rawls's (even in his political liberalism); these views make the mistake of assuming that value commitments must be self-chosen to be obligatory for people.[11] Autonomy understood as self-determination in this way cannot be viewed as an uncontroversial value, in particular since it conflicts with various moral doctrines espoused by reasonable people who see values as binding independent of choice. More generally, Larmore argues, reason itself must be understood to function as a means of tracking both truth (in epistemology) and value (in ethics); so it cannot be seen as the *source* of such truth. Therefore, autonomy understood as the use of reason to determine values for ourselves, values which are grounded in that very reflective acceptance, is a wrongheaded idea, or at least it is a controversial one and so cannot serve to support an allegedly neutral political framework.

A fundamental assumption in this diagnosis is the idea that self-legislation must involve the exerise of a kind of *choice*, a decision to take on a law for ourselves or not, and reason is the faculty that singularly guides that choice. As we will see, however, such a voluntarist account of self-legislation is not the only way to capture that idea, as it ignores the way that reasons can support *accepting* a value or principle that has independent support for me. Reason validates the value for *me*, though my reasons for accepting the value as mine may well lie in considerations having to do with the value apart from my acceptance of it.

We can extract from these critiques, in fact, three aspects of autonomy that represent the focal point of these controversies, namely the dimension of *choice* (over one's values and circumstances), the issue of the *source* of the values that form one's basic moral orientation (and whether autonomy alone can be such a validating source), and the level of *control* over one's character and circumstances that autonomy presupposes. What this means, more generally, is that the concept of autonomy must be examined more carefully to ask whether these elements must take the shape that is assumed for them in the critical accounts we are considering. Let us, then, turn to that task.

AUTONOMY: THE PROTEAN CONCEPT

The concept of autonomy has been discussed widely, and a full survey is not feasible here.[12] However, some important distinctions are relevant. For example, autonomy can refer either to individual choices or to the person as a whole. In discussing autonomy as a concept relevant to political philosophy, it likely is the latter sense that we have in mind, or at best autonomy as it relates to the basic value commitments of the person.[13] Second, autonomy can be seen as an all-or-nothing quality or as a scalar notion. The former is most apt when speaking of the characteristic of citizens that grounds their basic rights and status as having equal standing before the law. These political privileges cannot be seen along a sliding scale. But insofar as autonomy is an aim of social institutions, such as educational and social welfare policies, seeing the concept as measured in degrees may be more apt.[14]

The idea of autonomy in the liberal tradition, especially that branch of it influenced by Mill, is one which is equated with *individuality* – being oneself in opposition to dominant social trends, traditions, and reigning power structures. However, this assumption gives rise to the question of whether that trait must actually be seen in an entirely individualist manner, rather than as a feature of social relations. Correspondingly, writers on autonomy disagree about whether being self-governing implies that one is committed to particular values or whether autonomy is value-neutral. These are related controversies, since many of the theories that claim autonomy is a product of social relations include requirements of value commitment as well, for example those who argue that that self-government requires having self-respect, and being treated with respect.[15]

However it is defined, the notion of autonomy should help capture the force of moral and social norms linked to people's status as independent beings, such as the limits placed on paternalism, the grounds of respect and recognition, and why other autonomous agents are included equally in social deliberations over issues that affect them (which extends to one's status as a citizen). In other words, while autonomy may not be the only marker of a citizen with full political status, it will largely direct our practices of including some and not others (in the same manner) in collective decisions. Children, for example, or those in a permanently debilitated condition that prevents self-government will not represent themselves in social deliberation in the way that mature, autonomous agents will. The model of autonomy in question should help illuminate why this is so.

A prominent approach to autonomy is the view that self-government requires that one's first order motives be such that one can reflectively endorse, identify with, or accept them without alienation.[16] Critical self-reflection, on these views, is the fulcrum upon which authenticity rests, and requirements of open options and non-coercion are seen as contingently related to a person's ability to identify with her motives, given her situation. Others have also added reference to the diachronic or historical dimensions of these reflections, claiming that self-acceptance of this sort must take place in light of one's own personal history.[17]

However, in saying that we critically accept our motives given our condition, are we saying that we *control* those motives and conditions? While saying yes is intuitively attractive as an aspect of self-government, it would seem to be too strong, since most of our life situation, even that which structures central aspects of our identity and values, is not under our control. The number of ways that events and other structural factors in our social world shape our values and priorities is endless, and a few examples will make the case: Consider how our parents' personalities and choices about where and how to live shape the range and priorities of the values we are able to pursue. Further, one's body, sexuality, physical capabilities, demeanor, as well as the rich social meanings that all those factors carry, shape one's perspective on how one's life should go, and for most people most of the time (or all people in some ways), these are unchosen and unrevisable. All such factors both facilitate and also structure (and in many ways limit) the networks of options and the values that rank them in making our way through life.[18]

This raises one of the most difficult problems in specifying conditions of autonomy for finite, socially located, embodied beings, namely distinguishing the aspects of our social situatedness that undermine self-government from those that are compatible with it. A mugger threatening me with a gun structures my choice situation in ways that undercut my ability to see my choice (to hand over money to her) as my own, given that structured situation. In normal cases, however, my choices are limited by my physicality, the contingencies of my birth, and countless other unchosen and unchangeable aspects of my condition, but my inability to escape from such contingencies does not cast any shadow on the reflective acceptance of my actual choices.

Raz writes, for example, that the "ideal of personal autonomy is the vision of people controlling, to some degree, their own destiny, fashioning it through successive decisions throughout their lives."[19] However, one can have a kind of *monitoring* control over the central aspects of one's life, such as the ongoing relation to a loved one, without having that relation be the result of "successive decisions." If one glides through a happy life on a kind of auto-pilot, accepting with glee the good fortune of having relationships with people one loves, even ones that were not fully and consciously chosen but were happened into, so to speak, one can be said to be leading a fulfilling life. What one has, however, is a kind of monitoring control in the sense that, were things to begin to go wrong – the person betrays you or drifts away or turns out to be unlovable after all – one can release oneself from one's connection, albeit with great pain and effort perhaps and only over time. This is a kind of control that should be contrasted with the model of freely choosing a pursuit or relation because one judges it to be valuable before entering into it. Or so I would claim.

As I mentioned, a prominent approach to autonomy at the psychological level requires that one be able to critically reflect on one's lower-order motives and values (and presumably other aspects of one's person relevant to action and choice). But then we must ask, what must the result of that reflection be for me to retain my self-governing status? For example, for my motives to be authentically mine, must the result of my critical reflection on them be that I wholeheartedly *identify* with them or, at the other extreme, simply that I prefer to have them move me to action?[20] The requirement I would defend is reflective self-*acceptance* without alienation. What is meant by this is that we are able to accept our motives in light of our social situation, our histories, and their relation to the value orientation that makes us who we are, practically speaking – our practical identities, in Christine Korsgaard's phrase.[21]

Alienation in this sense means that, given one's history and circumstances, one cannot view one's principles and values as reasons that are one's *own*. This is a stronger reaction than merely judging them as deficient, all told, since various kinds of ambivalence may attach to many aspects of our lives in some ways without undercutting our ability to lead our own lives (none of us are perfect). This idea of alienation echoes what David Velleman describes as the inability to see the actions that flow from one's character as *intelligible*, given one's self-conception (one's practical identity in my sense).[22]

So to be autonomous is to pursue ends which are grasped competently and deemed to be acceptable as one's own as part of a diachronic life narrative). These two components refer to competency conditions and authenticity conditions for autonomy.[23] This implies, however, that autonomy need not assume the general ability to extricate ourselves from the normative structure of our social space, as long as we are not alienated from those structures. Now some may worry that this seriously weakens the conditions of self-control at the heart of self-government, as it allows a person to be entirely passive regarding her core motivations, and perhaps to fall victim to the "oppressive lethargy of choicelessness," as Chimamanda Ngozi Adichie puts it.[24] A view of autonomy that attempts to avoid the overly demanding requirement that we have chosen or are always able to choose to be the way we are must explain how a person who passively accepts her values and lot in life, albeit reflectively and competently, still bears the marks of agency central to autonomy. A related worry, which we will face in the final section, is why we should think that procedural autonomy in this sense commands the equal respect required of democratic practices.

One answer to this challenge is to point out the way that critical self-acceptance without alienation (authenticity) reflects the perspective of one's practical *identity* – it is simply who one *is* as an agent. So even passive acceptance of my motivational structure by way of critical self-appraisal is a way of grasping my self-concept, echoing Luther: "Here I stand, I can do no other." So insofar as one has reason to respect agents, and the reflective expression of one's practical identity expresses who one is as an agent, then autonomy in the procedural sense should still serve to support these normative strictures.

As we noted, this relates to the question of whether the concept of autonomy should include reference to certain value commitments or remain "content neutral" in that regard. For example, is it plausible to say that a person is self-governing regarding her acceptance of her first-order motives if those emanate from self-denigration, or subservience? If not, that would imply that a motive of self-respect is constitutive of autonomy. Others have gone further and argued that recognition *from others* of a level of respect and acknowledgment of one's "normative authority" is required for autonomy.[25]

In both cases, the defender of the content-neutral approach (or what I would prefer to call "widely content invariant") can reply by claiming that these requirements are contingently required for but not constitutive of autonomy, in that they are required because of the psychological necessity of valuing oneself to some degree in order to adequately and reflectively accept one's motives and values. Saying this protects the idea that autonomy *itself* is not tied to any particular set of values except contingently, the way being a competent agent is related to having adequate nutrition. This marks the distinction between a relatively substantive account of autonomy and a proceduralist (or internalist) one.[26]

However, this leaves open the question of what kind and degree of critical self-reflection is truly needed to secure autonomy. For recall Larmore's worry that autonomy involves an implausible understanding of the role of reason in the determination of our basic principles and commitments. In the proceduralist model what matters is being able to ascertain a level of self-acceptance that undergirds authenticity. This means that one must be sensitized to the self-alienation that would undercut that state. Alienation involves resistance and disaffection from one's motives, given one's history and circumstance, so self-reflection must enable one to realize that one is alienated in this sense. How this works psychologically is complex, but suffice it to say here that the self-examination involved in the process does not require a disembodied, groundless judgment that so worried Larmore and other critics. That is, one must be able to consider reasons that one has for one's lower-order judgments, the connections these reasons have to one's identity, and the implications of those values for one's future and for interaction with others.[27]

The question of value invariance in our understanding of autonomy relates to the issue of autonomy and pluralism directly. If we think that being autonomous means leading only a life of independence, self-sufficiency, social mobility, and/or the pursuit of objectively valuable ends, then valuing autonomy will sit uncomfortably with the commitment to pluralism that liberal and other democratic theories demand. However, if we understand autonomy in the more minimal, proceduralist manner alluded to here, these implications fail to arise. That is, if a person can be said to be a competent decision maker and reflectively accept her lot in life (in light of the various factors we have mentioned), but still lead a life of subservience and self-denigration (to a degree not incompatible with practical competence itself), then we should still label her autonomous. And ways of life that include roles for some members of this sort would not be denigrated by a politics that prized autonomy. At least they would not be so denigrated by virtue of the commitment to *autonomy* – there certainly might be many other grounds upon which to criticize them (for example, that they undercut the full dignity of some of their participants), but that is a different charge.[28]

It should be added that this procedural account of autonomy will, as far as possible, be an all-or-nothing affair, in that those who meet the procedural conditions relative to their basic value commitments (along with other competence conditions) will count as autonomous; and having this trait will be widely invariant across whatever value commitments people happen to have, as long as those commitments are not themselves undercutting of self-government in other ways. This leaves open the possibility, however, that an alternative notion of autonomy as substantive independence, as having the capacity for ongoing reflective decision making about one's life and commitments, might be a personal or even social ideal in some settings. It may also be seen as a matter of degree. My claim here, however, is that such a substantive, scalar notion should not be understood to function in the basic justification of principles of democratic justice in the way autonomy does in my view. I will return to this point below.

In broad outline, then, the view of autonomy proposed here requires competent self-acceptance without alienation given the current and historical social conditions that structure one's character, identity, and values. Alienation from those conditions is marked by cognitive and affective resistance to the choices one is forced to make, such that one is unable to reflexively value one's capacities to pursue projects and make judgments about what is worthwhile. The critical self-reflection involved in such social self-acceptance need not extend to a perspective outside of one's self-defining value frame, but it does require that one consider the depth of one's commitments and their effect on others in light of the possible option to alter one's circumstance. Such reflection, however, does not presuppose or require that one valorize change per se, or see oneself apart from the social and affective connections that structure one's self-conception. One must be competent, however, in this ability to self-reflect and reflect on one's circumstance.

This is clearly a psychologically nuanced model of autonomy, and it relies on fine-grained descriptions of a person's psyche that cannot feasibly function in the arbitration of public policy decisions, but it nevertheless can serve as a model and source for such guidelines. This will require the use of various kinds of proxies that model the more nuanced trait but which can serve as a measure of autonomy for political purposes. This reflects the point that the idea of self-government operative in political principles is a *model* of the person not a description. However, the model must be able to function as a representation that organizes citizens' interests and perspective in a way that they, as actual persons, can support.[29]

To further consider this understanding of autonomy, let us return to debates in political philosophy over whether self-government can function as a fundamental value in a political regime that values inclusion and pluralism. The particular arena where these questions have been most poignantly raised of late concerns the social acceptance of cultural forms that seem to eschew the liberal values of individual independence and critical self-reflection and what accommodation or recognition should be afforded to them in a liberal democratic regime.

AUTONOMY AND CULTURE

The general form of opposition to autonomy-based politics is this: Liberal democratic politics should support pluralism of value schemes at both the individual and cultural level; however, some ways of life, ones included in the scope of that pluralism, do not value autonomy, so giving primacy to autonomy expresses denigration toward those ways of life. The interesting question to raise, as we have seen, is whether the notion of autonomy that best motivates the directive to afford individual self-government fundamental status in democratic forms is the same as that which is eschewed by the cultures in question. And if so, whether that means that these cultures are consistent with democratic values after all.[30]

One important line of argument put forward by liberals about strong cultural identities is that the protection of a right to *exit* – the right to extract oneself from associations and commitments – is fundamental in the protection of individuals in just societies, and this right must take precedence over any call for the protection of cultural groups.[31] Although some pluralists insist that even protecting the right to exit is itself culturally parochial,[32] this right is widely seen as a general limitation on whatever claims might be made for the recognition or protection of identity groups in a just society. That is, group interests can be identified and given special weight, but only if membership in such groups is in some way voluntary and the right to disavow such connections is somehow protected.[33]

However, while for some social identities the idea that one can (and should be given the right to) separate from them is crucial, for others it is not only unimportant but also virtually incoherent: the idea that we should be able to "exit" a social grouping that defines us, such as being a minority group member or a woman (indeed, regarding most ascriptive identities), will appear absurd for many people. In addition, which factor among the multiple aspects of our identity becomes prominent may often be pressed upon us by external treatment or social location. A person insisting on the centrality of her (say) ethnic identity to her self-concept may be a direct response to a denigrating social environment vis-à-vis that identity. Moreover, political structures which *encourage* questioning all commitments and an openness to revising them (as well as the geographical and symbolic mobility that this involves) will skew the priorities of political institutions from the point of view of those who have no need to make such changes and, moreover, are harmed, in a unique way, when openness to change is a social priority.

This brings us back to the issue of self-control and choice in the model of autonomy operative in this context. Insofar as autonomy is the dominant political value which shapes social policy regarding the (limits to the) protection of cultures that do not prize choice and mobility, and autonomy is defined as having the ability to extricate oneself from social surroundings, then valorizing autonomy results in policies which will disadvantage those cultures. However, in the proceduralist approach to autonomy sketched earlier, what is important is not that one has *chosen* one's values or one's social condition; nor is it always important that one can control that condition or exit readily from it. It is merely required for autonomy that one be able to alter one's condition *were one to be alienated from it.*

The scope of the counterfactual here is crucial. For there is an important difference between the sentences "were one to be disaffected from one's social group one has feasible exit options" and "one already has functioning exit options because one may become disaffected from one's social group." The first does not imply that one always has on hand resources that facilitate "exit" from one's condition, only that they become available in the event one becomes disaffected. This is consistent with there being mechanisms that kick in when people's alienation from their social group arises. What is important about that formulation is that it does not require the *promotion* of always-available routes of escape, or the valorization of powers of change and choice. And it is these social values that traditional cultures often object to as being inimical to their own emphasis on loyalty and devotion to tradition.

To put the contrast differently, for some the existence of an option is *costly*, either because it is a reminder that one might or ought to consider escaping from one's condition or because such options represent the, at times, false and perhaps insulting assumption that one's connections are voluntary, since for many they are not experienced in this way. However, this is different from having the ability to *create* an option to exit if one comes to need it. Social resources and practices can facilitate this capacity to create options if needed, but their availability or use need not be touted as a predominant social resource.

This may appear an ephemeral distinction, but it has concrete policy implications. For insofar as people are defined by their social connections and are not alienated from those conditions (and other aspects of their autonomy are secured), there is no need to direct social resources (such as social welfare and educational practices) toward encouraging them to reconsider the option to alter their life situation. Moreover, for such individuals the protection of their autonomy entails supporting the social forms that structure their identity rather than their ongoing ability to leave. Of course, for those who *do* experience alienation and disaffection from their cultural connections, protections and support must be mobilized to help them facilitate that change, but that comes after the breakdown of autonomy, not before. The nature and number of options one faces, and their relevance to one's autonomy, depends entirely on the character of one's self-defining commitments.[34]

The procedural account does not require, then, substantive independence from social connections, and insofar as non-alienation requires that one is able to flourish within a stable set of such connections, then autonomy requires supporting them. Now in fashioning such a thin conception of self-governing agency, it must be noted that even if it successfully facilitates a defense against prominent critiques of autonomy-based politics, its adoption could be thought to undercut the very power that autonomy brings to strategies of justifying liberal democratic institutions. The value-invariance of proceduralist autonomy implies that the autonomous person may or may not pursue valuable ends, objectively speaking, as long as the ends pursued do not debilitate autonomy-related competences themselves. Moreover, the view of autonomy as competent self-acceptance, as opposed to independent self-creation and control, may rob that trait of its most obvious appeal as a personal ideal. Why, then, should we build a political view on the value of autonomy in this minimal sense?

What is left to show, then, is that a proceduralist account of autonomy may still be used as part of a scheme that helps establish the legitimacy of (liberal) democracy. While I cannot lay out such a strategy in any detail here, I will close with a brief sketch of how it might proceed (and has done so in others' work). However, doing this will show, in fact, that the liberalism that is being justified by such a view will be one that is fundamentally tied to the operation of democratic practices, much more so than is typically acknowledged by liberal thinkers.

CONCLUSION: SELF-GOVERNMENT AND DEMOCRATIC LEGITIMACY

One indirect way to support the attraction of autonomy-based politics is to note the many ways in which those who deny the crucial importance of autonomy in justifying political practices and institutions nevertheless put forward replacement positions that are themselves reliant on what amounts to the value of self-government, at least when that latter idea is seen in the proceduralist and socially structured manner outlined here.[35] John Gray, for example, eschews any brand of liberalism more demanding than a Hobbesean modus vivendi (hence autonomy-based politics), but in doing so he embraces a position drawn from George Santayana supporting a politics that accepts all ideals that meet two important conditions, one of which is "that these ideals be radically sincere and adequate to the actual nature and capacities of the creatures that accept them."[36] But this condition comes quite close to requiring that all competing values be held with "radical" sincerity and which are adequate to the social situation of those persons. Any plausible account of autonomy, and in particular the one outlined here, would surely attempt to express just such a requirement.

Similarly, Iris Young rejects the liberal approach to justice and all of the central components that come with it.[37] In place of this view, she promotes a politics centered on the elimination of "oppression" and "domination." Domination is defined as "institutional conditions which inhibit or prevent people from participating in determining their actions or the conditions of their actions."[38] But clearly, any plausible account of autonomy will come very close to this idea, namely the ability to "participate" in the determination of their actions and their structuring conditions, or at least to accept those conditions without alienation or to be able to change them if alienated. Domination can easily be seen, then, as the systematic denial of autonomy.[39]

More generally, however, the question at issue is why basic political principles (and the institutions and practices shaped by them) should rest on the value of individual autonomy when that idea is not understood in terms that relate directly to valued aims. The pluralism that forms part of the autonomy-based politics envisioned here requires that people's status as equal citizens whose interests are represented in the institutional arrangements and social practices of a society is not dependent on their commitment to objectively determined values.

Consider, in this light, Raz's claim that although the concept of autonomy does not presuppose having any particular values on the part of the self-governing person, the *value* of autonomy does. Only if autonomous persons pursue valuable ends is it worthwhile for them to be autonomous, and hence worthwhile for the state to protect and promote their autonomy. In this way, he argues, autonomy-respecting state institutions can and should promote valuable ideals.[40] He is then able to claim that "[s]ince autonomy is morally valuable there is reason for everyone to make himself and everyone else autonomous."[41]

However, this argument rests on the idea that autonomy is valuable only in the pursuit of objectively valuable ends, and this assumption is rejected in the proceduralist view adopted here. Consider devotees of religious views that one knows are unfounded. (This must be the case of at least some world religions since they are incompatible with each other, so they cannot all be correct.) Do we want to say that the autonomy with which persons pursue those religions is not valuable because of this mistake? Or that it is less valuable than those others who happen to pursue the correct worldview (religious or not)? This seems implausible.

More generally, the thin conception of autonomy will be part of a set of political principles that reject the perfectionism implicit in views such as Raz's. Specifically, the conditions of legitimacy of political institutions espoused here do not include reference to objectively determined values or the complementary idea that "political authorities should take an active role in creating and maintaining social conditions that best enable their subjects to lead valuable and worthwhile lives."[42] The path taken by these theorists is to claim that autonomy is among the values that constitute human well-being and so it is among the values the state ought to protect and promote. The autonomy-based politics defended here, in contrast, would rule out reference to the promotion of human well-being (in this sense) in the basic constitutional design of its central institutions and in the social practices promoted in civil society.

Of course, democratic societies may enact various provisions that do promote a particular perfectionist conception of good lives. If stable majorities enact such provisions, and they do not in effect deny the basic ability of any citizens to enjoy minimal procedural autonomy (such as those who would be alienated in such societies), then nothing I have said here rules this out. But notice that the justification of such a provision, say in the educational policies of a state or province, is based on the legitimacy of the procedures that produced it and not on the objective validity of that conception of human flourishing. That is a crucial distinction that separates proceduralists and perfectionists in politics.

Now the proceduralist account of autonomy here described will be thought to be too thin to ground the legitimacy of democratic institutions built upon it. That is, the mere claim that another person is autonomous (in this sense) will not successfully justify institutions that ask me to restrict the pursuit of what I take to be valuable, just because that other person sincerely, competently, and reflectively presents herself as the person she is, despite engaging in what I take to be (and what may well in fact be) a morally flawed way of life. Why should you or I relate to this person (and all her fellow travelers with whom you have similar differences) in a way that affords her/them equal status in the determination of your own life prospects?

A possible answer, which can only be gestured at here, is that respect for autonomy in this sense is part of a broader political vision which is itself justified, specifically a pluralist democratic one.[43] Defenders of autonomy-based conceptions of legitimacy must claim that social structures which shape the lives and opportunities of citizens – what we could call restrictive social structures, including but not limited to political institutions – are legitimate only if the they involve the represented interests of all autonomous citizens and that those interests are fairly represented in those processes.[44] The claim that processes which produce restrictive social structures must be *fair* makes room for any number of argumentative strategies justifying democratic institutions. These may rest on a fundamental commitment to equality, or more particularly to equal respect, or to public reason, or to reciprocity among citizens, or to the interpersonal nature of reason and communication.[45] Further, one might claim that these values are justified based on comprehensive philosophical argument or that they merely are dominant in the political sociology of the age.[46] In any case, such a position includes a fundamental reference to the autonomy of those whose lives and prospects are structured by the institutions and practices that such processes give rise to.

What this picture shows, however, is that democracy is an *inherent* part of the conditions of political legitimacy of which autonomy is central. Individual self-government and collective self-government are two sides of the same coin.[47] Democratic processes – fair procedures for the generation and critical reappraisal of dominant social structures – are not merely additional mechanisms to aggregate public sentiment in the promotion of the public good, but rather function as constitutive elements of a constitutional structure that expresses the value of citizen autonomy (while perhaps also advancing the public good).[48]

For that reason, the politics that emerges from an attention to autonomy is liberal only in the sense of a liberal *democracy*, so that those pictures of liberalism that do not include such a basic role for democratic procedures will not sit happily with the view of autonomy sketched here. As with any marriage, for the partnership to work between autonomy and liberalism, both have to adapt. What I've suggested here is that for autonomy to be compatible with the deep pluralism required by liberalism, it should be seen in the proceduralist sense I sketched.

Liberalism also cannot retain the overly individualistic guise it traditionally has worn but rather must be seen as part of a broader order of collective self-government. Hence, both partners must change to keep the relationship intact, and the glue that does this work for them is democracy.

NOTES

1. See, for example, Larmore, *The Autonomy of Morality*; Galston, *Liberal Pluralism* and Gray, *Post-Liberalism*.
2. See, for example, Young, *Justice and the Politics of Difference* and Connolly, *The Ethos of Pluralization*. Although the primary focus of

this chapter will be liberalism, many views that reject that label but are committed to broad pluralism and diversity, and who reject autonomy as a fundamental value because of this commitment, will be subject to many of the reflections expressed here.

3. The phrase "dominant social practices" is meant to refer to those non-institutional (non-legally enforced) practices that are supported by significant social pressures, such that resistance or non-conformity with them involves sanctions similar in severity to those of legal penalties. Norms of civic cooperation, use of dominant languages in public discourse, tolerance of social difference, general participation in democratic activities, and so on are examples. The inclusion (albeit loosely) of this category is to avoid prejudging the question of whether questions of political philosophy arise only in relation to the state (and public legal institutions). Non-state practices do as much if not more in some realms to shape social opportunities and ways of life as do legal structures. For discussion, see Young, *Justice and the Politics of Difference*.

4. This is the role that reference to autonomy plays in Rawls's view, namely that the moral powers connected to autonomy ground the higher order interests citizens have (are represented as having) in pursuing reasonable comprehensive goods within the bounds of justice. See *Political Liberalism*, pp. 74f.

5. See, for example, Raz, *The Morality of Freedom* and Wall, *Liberalism, Perfectionism and Restraint*. For prominent defenses of this view, see Sher, *Beyond Neutrality* and Hurka, *Perfectionism*. For a general discussion of perfectionism, see Wall, "Perfectionism in Politics."

6. This approach is most prominently developed, for example, in Habermas, *Between Facts and Norms* and Cohen, "Deliberation and Democratic Legitimacy."

7. Gray, *Post-Liberalism*, p. 227; as Gray puts it, such a view "underestimates the variety of human nature" (*ibid.*).

8. See Taylor, *Multiculturalism and the "Politics of Recognition"*; Kymlicka, *Liberalism, Community and Culture*; Benhabib, *The Claims of Culture*.

9. In the latter camp are those agonistic democratic theorists who see the commitment to liberal rights and principles as themselves a contentious stance that ignores its own shaky foundations. Characteristic of this view is the work of Connolly, *The Ethos of Pluralization*. See also Mouffe, *The Democratic Paradox*. For a general discussion of liberalism, see, for example, Gaus and Courtland, "Liberalism" and Christman, *Social and Political Philosophy*, ch. 4.

10. Galston, *Liberal Pluralism*, p. 21.

11. See Larmore, *The Autonomy of Morality*, ch. 5.
12. For an overview of the concept, see Christman, "Autonomy in Moral and Political Philosophy" and Buss, "Personal Autonomy."
13. For a parallel distinction, see Meyers, *Self, Society and Personal Choice*, pp. 48–49.
14. For treatments of the notion that connect it specifically to education, see Gutmann, *Democratic Education*; Cuypers, *Moral Responsibility, Authenticity, and Education*; and Brighouse, *School Choice and Social Justice*, pp. 65–111.
15. This connects to the so-called relational approach to autonomy. For discussion, see the essays in Mackenzie and Stoljar, *Relational Autonomy*; Oshana, *Personal Autonomy in Society*; and Anderson and Honneth, "Autonomy, Vulnerability, Recognition, and Justice."
16. See, for example, Dworkin, *The Theory and Practice of Autonomy* and Frankfurt, "Freedom of the Will and the Concept of the Person."
17. For example, Mele, *Autonomous Agents* and Christman, *The Politics of Persons*, ch. 7. For general discussion, see Christman, "Autonomy in Moral and Political Philosophy."
18. Many philosophical and political traditions stress these structural features of embodiment and social existence. See, for example, Young, "Throwing Like a Girl."
19. Raz, *The Morality of Freedom*, p. 369.
20. These two disjuncts mark views that Frankfurt has held over the course of his thinking about freedom/autonomy. See "Freedom of the Will and the Concept of the Person" and "The Faintest Passion."
21. Korsgaard, *The Sources of Normativity*. Frankfurt echoes this idea when he claims that autonomous self-acceptance must be in light of our deepest *cares*. See Frankfurt, "The Faintest Passion".
22. See Velleman, *How We Get Along*, pp. 13f., though I would want to avoid the narrowly cognitive connotations of the idea of intelligibility.
23. For discussion, see Christman, "Autonomy in Moral and Political Philosophy" and Buss, "Personal Autonomy."
24. The phrase is from the novel *Americanah* by Chimamanda Ngozi Adichie. For the worry in question, see Bratman, *Faces of Intention*, pp. 185–206.
25. See, for example, the works cited in n. 15 above.
26. Some have argued that views that contain minimal value requirements for the psychological reasons I mentioned should be called "weakly substantive" views. See, for example, Mackenzie and Stoljar, "Introduction: Autonomy Refigured," in their *Relational Autonomy*, pp. 20f.
27. For further discussion of this lower level of self-reflection, see Christman, *The Politics of Persons*, pp. 127–32.

28. A fuller defense of a version of this model of autonomy can be found in Christman, *The Politics of Persons*.

29. This point effectively echoes Rawls's distinction between psychological and institutional identity. See Rawls, *Political Liberalism*, pp. 30–31. Of course the use of representative models in normative principles in this way is not without controversy and complications.

30. Material in this section is adapted from Christman, *The Politics of Persons*, ch. 9. The literature on the issue of liberalism and culture has proliferated of late by both defenders of identity politics in various forms and by liberal voices raised in response. See, for example, Kymlycka, *Multicultural Citizenship*; Young, "Structural Injustice and the Politics of Difference"; Margalit and Raz, "National Self-Determination"; and Taylor, *Multiculturalism*. Liberal philosophers have also addressed this issue, but they do so in order to dilute or diminish the threat that group-based concerns pose for traditional theories of justice (Appiah, *The Ethics of Identity*; Sen, *Identity and Violence*; and Barry, *Culture and Equality*).

31. See, for example, Margalit and Halbertal, "Liberalism and the Right to Culture."

32. See Parekh, *Rethinking Multiculturalism*.

33. For discussion see Barry, *Culture and Equality*.

34. Interestingly, Rawls's slight shift in language from his earlier to his later work in defining a key aspect of freedom illustrates the path followed in the paper. For at one point he wrote that in being recognized as free, citizens of a well-ordered society must be seen as "self-originating sources of valid claims" ("Justice as Fairness"). But in *Political Liberalism* this was changed to "self-authenticating sources of valid claims" (p. 32). This marks the acknowledgment emphasized here that commitments that define one's identity but which one did not choose or create oneself are consistent with being autonomous. As he says in *Political Liberalism*, such "commitments and attachments" are such that "[i]f we suddenly lost them, we would be disoriented and unable to carry on. In fact there would be, we might think, no point in carrying on" (p. 31).

35. For arguments parallel to this, see Colburn, "Forbidden Ways of Life" and Crowder, "Two Concepts of Liberal Pluralism."

36. Gray, quoting Santayana, in "Reply to Critics,"p. 327.

37. See Young, *Justice and the Politics of Difference*.

38. *Ibid.*, p. 38.

39. Also, while I can't defend the claim here, there is also much overlap between autonomy in my sense and non-domination in the sense Philip Pettit uses to define republican freedom (see *Republicanism*). For some differences, however, see Christman "Freedom, Autonomy, and Social Selves."

40. Raz, *The Morality of Freedom*, ch. 15.
41. *Ibid.*, p. 407.
42. Wall, *Liberalism, Perfectionism and Restraint*, p. 8.
43. This sketch is meant to include any number of views, but for an approach from which it draws the most direct inspiration, see Cohen, "Deliberation and Democratic Legitimacy."
44. The reference to only autonomous persons here does not rule out plausible extensions to others (including non-humans).
45. I intend this list to refer to the work of Dworkin, Larmore, Gaus, and Habermas, respectively. See Dworkin, *Sovereign Virtue*; Larmore, *The Autonomy of Morality*; Gaus, *The Order of Public Reason*; and Habermas, *Between Facts and Norms*.
46. The first strategy refers to writers such as Dworkin (and perhaps Habermas) and the second to those espousing *political* justifications of state power such as Rawls.
47. As Habermas describes it, private and public autonomy are "co-original": see *Between Facts and Norms*. For discussion of this view, see Cohen, "Reflections on Habermas on Democracy."
48. This implies, by the way, that autonomy-based defenses of democracy must be committed to some form of *deliberative* democracy, as opposed to, for example, purely aggregative models. Procedures for the generation of social policy must involve the giving and receiving of reasons by way of cooperative interaction and communication for the people affected by the policies so generated to remain autonomous in abiding by them. Only if citizens have access to the reasons for the policies and can consider them in deciding whether or not to reflectively accept them can their autonomy remain protected. For discussion of a similar view, see Gaus, *The Order of Public Reason*.

7   Liberalism, neutrality, and democracy

The principle of state neutrality has figured prominently in recent philosophical debate over the character of liberalism as a political theory.[1] The principle holds that the state should be neutral among different conceptions of the good life and/or comprehensive doctrines that are held by members in the society to which it applies. Two questions about state neutrality are related, but can be distinguished. The first question concerns its interpretation. In what way, or in what respect, should the state be neutral? The second question concerns the grounding or support for the principle. What considerations, if any, speak in its favor? In this chapter I will be concerned mainly with the second of these questions. I will assume that an adequate interpretation of the principle of state neutrality is available, one that holds that the political institutions and the political decisions of a society should be justified in a way that does not presuppose the truth or correctness of any conception of the good or comprehensive doctrine that is controversial among its members. I want to discuss the prospects for grounding the principle of state neutrality, so understood, on the distinctively democratic value of political autonomy.

This will require me to characterize this value, to explain its democratic credentials, to show how it can support state neutrality, and to discuss its normative status and force.

The chapter aims to elucidate some of the interconnections between state neutrality and democratic values. It introduces a number of distinctions and contains several subarguments. The

An earlier version of this chapter was presented at the 2012 meeting of the American Section of the International Association for Philosophy of Law and Social Philosophy in Baltimore, Maryland. Thanks to Steven Scalet, David Lefkowitz and Sameer Bajaj for helpful comments.

argumentative strategy of the chapter overall is both constructive and critical. It is constructive insofar as it seeks to show that political autonomy is an attractive ideal and one that, while very demanding, is at least potentially realizable in the modern world. It is critical insofar as it seeks to show that this ideal cannot provide support for state neutrality without introducing independent considerations that, if sound, would do the main work in justifying the principle.

POLITICAL AUTONOMY

Political autonomy is a democratic ideal, but it is also a liberal ideal.[2] Properly understood, it can explain both why the so called liberty of the moderns and why that of the ancients are noninstrumentally valuable. Still, while it is a liberal ideal, political autonomy must not be confused with the ideal of personal autonomy. A person can be autonomous whether or not he lives in a political society that realizes political autonomy. To be sure, there are different conceptions of personal autonomy, and on some conceptions there are important connections between the two forms of autonomy. But I assume here that the realization of political autonomy in a political society is not a requirement for its members to be personally autonomous.

Unlike personal autonomy, political autonomy can be realized only in a democratic society. More precisely, it obtains only when those who are subject to political authority (i) participate, or have the option to participate, in its exercise (on roughly equal terms) and (ii) authorize it, or can authorize it, as reflecting their own will or reason. Political autonomy is thus a specifically democratic instantiation of political self-determination.

The roots of the value go back to Rousseau. He was its great champion and its most influential proponent. The solution to the fundamental problem of politics, Rousseau claimed, requires a people to fully achieve political autonomy. The fundamental problem, as he famously put it, is to "find a form of association that defends and protects the person and goods of each associate with all the common force" while at the same time ensuring that each associate "uniting with all, nevertheless obeys only himself and remains as free as before."[3] The solution to this problem is a political association with terms that it would be reasonable for each associate to endorse.

If each associate reasonably authorizes, or can reasonably authorize, the terms of the political association that protects and defends him, and if each associate participates in the rule of the association on roughly equal terms, then each will remain free. And when each associate remains free, political autonomy is achieved.

In describing political autonomy, and Rousseau's statement of it, I have left an important ambiguity in place. This concerns the nature of the required authorization. Must it actually take place among the associates, or is it sufficient if it could take place? And if the latter is the case, then what sense of possibility is expressed by the modal "could"? Depending on the answers given to these questions, the value of political autonomy will be more or less demanding, more or less difficult to achieve. Although the interpretive issue is not central to our discussion, a good case can be made that Rousseau believed that actual authorization was necessary. Call this the *actualist view*. By contrast, the *hypotheticalist view* requires only that it be possible for all associates to endorse the terms of the political association that defends and protects them.

The hypotheticalist view of authorization has become the favored view in recent discussions. Seeking to update Rousseau's social contract, Rawls claimed that in a democratic society – a society in which the people rule themselves and possess "an equal share" of its "coercive political power" – "political power should be exercised, at least when constitutional essentials and matters of basic justice are at stake, in ways that all citizens can publicly endorse in the light of their own reason."[4] The last clause in the preceding sentence expresses the hypotheticalist view. The fact that some citizens, who could reasonably endorse the basic terms of their political association, fail to do so would not, on this understanding, show that the society did not achieve political autonomy.

In this chapter I follow Rawls and other contemporary writers[5] in holding the hypotheticalist view to be the right view. There are several reasons for doing so. First, I want to consider the prospects for grounding state neutrality on political autonomy and the hypotheticalist view fits better with this ambition than the actualist view. Second, political autonomy on the hypotheticalist view is less utopian than it is on the actualist view. Finally, contemporary philosophers who have sought to defend state neutrality, such as Rawls and Cohen, have appealed directly to the value of political autonomy on the hypotheticalist view. To engage constructively with their arguments, we need to work with their understanding of the value.

The hypotheticalist view of authorization, as mentioned, must specify the sense of possibility implicit in the notion of possible endorsement. This is no easy task. The view also must specify whether the endorsement in question is permitted or required. This is a less difficult issue, for if the endorsement were merely permitted, then it would be too permissive. As Scanlon observed, many arrangements might be such that it would not be unreasonable for people to accept them, even if it also would not be unreasonable for them to reject them.[6] For this reason, on the hypotheticalist view, we should favor the stricter demand that the terms of the political association are ones that, reasonably, the associates are required to accept. This is equivalent to the claim that the terms must be such that no associate could reasonably reject them.[7]

This leaves the difficult issue of how to construe the "could" in the could not reasonably reject demand. The problem can be framed by distinguishing associates as they are from their idealized counterparts. If the terms of a political association are ones that the associates could not reasonably reject, then it is one that their idealized counterparts would accept. The problem then becomes how to fix the degree of idealization. Too much idealization will undermine the whole point of hypothetical endorsement. Too little will fail to capture the thought that the endorsement must be reasonable. Faced with this problem, many writers have sought to identify a set of background commitments that people in democratic societies could reasonably affirm. Idealization must not efface these commitments. Thus, on this common view, the requirements of what could not be reasonably rejected are indexed to the background reasonable commitments of democratic citizens.

What I am calling the common view can be developed in myriad ways. The details need not detain us. The key point for now is that the hypotheticalist view of authorization, at least as it has been defended by its recent proponents, presupposes reasonable pluralism with respect to background doctrines. Furthermore, any idealization that is imposed on reasonable endorsement must leave this reasonable pluralism in place. As these remarks suggest, the hypotheticalist view is closely aligned with contractualist principles of political legitimacy. Still, the democratic value of political autonomy should not be identified too tightly with contractualist political legitimacy for two reasons. First, it may be possible for a political association to satisfy the standard of contractualist political legitimacy while failing to realize political autonomy. Rawls hints at this possibility with the following suggestive example.

[S]uppose (we wildly imagine) that the Prussian chancellor of Kant's day, with the support of the King, acts to ensure that all laws enacted are in accord with Kant's principle of the social contract. If so, free and equal citizens would – let us say on due reflection – agree with them. Since citizens do not themselves freely discuss, vote on, and enact these laws, however, citizens are not politically autonomous and cannot thus regard themselves.[8]

Kant's principle of the social contract is a contractualist principle of political legitimacy, but, if Rawls is right, then it can be satisfied by citizens who are not politically autonomous. Political autonomy requires, in addition, that all citizens participate, or at least have the option to do so, in the process that generates the laws that apply to them. Second, it is possible to accept that political autonomy is a valid ideal and yet reject contractualist principles of political legitimacy. This claim may seem confused, since political autonomy presupposes that citizens can reasonably endorse the terms of their political association and the reasonable endorsement demand appears to express the requirements of contractualist political legitimacy. But, as I explain below, the appearance is illusory if political autonomy and contractualist legitimacy are values with a different normative status.

Political autonomy is a democratic value that is achieved when two conditions are jointly satisfied. There is no guarantee, however, that the two conditions – which I now christen the *participation condition* and the *collective authorization condition* – will not come into conflict. To illustrate, let us continue Rawls's example. Suppose that if the Prussian chancellor were to withdraw from his supervision of the laws and let the citizens themselves freely enact them, then the citizens would enact laws that violated Kant's principle of the social contract. In such unhappy circumstances, the value of political autonomy would not be attainable and a choice would need to be made as to which component of political autonomy – participation or collective authorization – should take precedence over the other.[9]

The possibility of this internal conflict shows that political autonomy can be realized only in societies in which the two components are jointly satisfiable. Yet even when political autonomy is attainable, pursuing it may conflict with the achievement of other goods and values. As will become clear in ensuing sections, this type of external conflict, as I shall call it, helps us to gauge the normative force of the value.

A final clarification should be mentioned up front. The two conditions I have distinguished can be satisfied in different ways. Consider the collective authorization condition. It can be held to apply only at the level of fundamental political institutions (namely, Rawls's constitutional essentials and basic justice), or it can be held to apply to all political institutions and decisions. Call the former view *modest* and the latter *robust*. Likewise, the participation condition can be held to apply only to fundamental constitutional decisions, such as the decision to establish a monarchy or a democracy; or it may be taken to apply to all laws.[10] Call the former view *constitutional* and the latter *comprehensive*. Combining these distinctions yields four interpretations of political autonomy.

| | | Participation condition | |
		Constitutional	Comprehensive
Collective authorization condition	Modest	(1)	(2)
	Robust	(3)	(4)

(1) and (3) require participation only at the fundamental constitutional level. In Rawls's example, let us imagine, contrary to historical fact, that the Prussian monarchy enjoyed the ongoing democratic endorsement of the Prussian people. Participatory assemblies of the sort Rousseau recommended periodically convened and endorsed it. If that had occurred, then perhaps it would have been sufficient for the participation condition to be satisfied, but if the Prussian citizens had established constitutional democracy and in addition freely discussed and voted on all the laws that bind them, then their realization of political autonomy would have been more substantial.

Presumably, that is why Rawls thought that the participation condition should apply to all laws.[11]

In what follows I will assume that the participation condition must be satisfied comprehensively.[12] That leaves (2) and (4). Why insist on modest rather than robust collective authorization? One reason for doing so is that modest authorization is more attainable than robust endorsement. Requiring citizens to all reasonably endorse every law may seem to set the bar too high. Against this concern, it can be said that if the fundamental political institutions meet the collective authorization condition, then all laws passed within these institutions do so as well. In effect, reasonable endorsement transmits down from the fundamental political institutions to ordinary law. Call this claim *transmission*. If we accept *transmission*, then robust authorization will look compelling. If we reject *transmission*, then we will need to confront more directly the concern that robust authorization is too demanding.

Presently, we do not need to decide this issue. Modest and robust political autonomy, we can allow, are both viable interpretations of the value. The choice between them, however, is not inconsequential for state neutrality. As we will see later, modest political autonomy may be easier to attain than its robust counterpart, but it will permit significant departures from state neutrality.

A PRELIMINARY OBJECTION

Many people will think that political autonomy is not achievable even on the modest interpretation. Unlike Rousseau's ideal republic, modern societies contain too much diversity to make the pursuit of the value a sensible goal. This is obviously an important concern, one I will address below. But a deeper objection to political autonomy should be addressed first.

Rousseau's vision of citizens giving the laws to themselves on equal terms may be inspiring, but inspiring visions can mislead. The objection holds that even if political autonomy were achievable for modern societies, it would not be desirable to pursue it in practice. Proponents of this objection – call it the *desirability objection* – can argue that the realization of political autonomy is not an appropriate goal for first-person political deliberation. Politics involves the exercise of power over others. As such, it is vital that the terms of political association be as just as they can be. For this reason, citizens should aim at justice in their political deliberations about whom or what to support. They should not favor participatory decision-making procedures if there is reason to believe that these procedures will be less good at yielding just outcomes over time than less participatory procedures. Similarly, they should not strive to meet the collective authorization condition, for doing so may lead them to compromise justice for consensus. In short, political autonomy, from the first-person deliberative perspective, is a distraction from the grave business of securing justice in politics.

The desirability objection raises a number of issues. Can political autonomy conflict with justice, or is it an essential component of justice? If the latter were true, then citizens would need to aim at political autonomy insofar as they aimed at justice. And, in fact, many contemporary writers contend that justice requires some form of democracy. They will insist that the satisfaction of the participation condition is a necessary element of justice. It might be claimed, in addition, that collective authorization is constitutive of just law. If a law is just, then it is reasonably endorsable by all and vice versa. But this latter claim, as we will see, is not one that proponents of political autonomy are in a good position to accept. We should allow that justice and reasonable endorsement, at least in principle, can come apart. A successful response to the desirability objection must not insist, then, that the pursuit of political autonomy can never conflict with what justice demands.

A successful response to the objection, however, is not hard to discern. Suppose, first, that citizens should not aim at political autonomy directly. They still could regard its realization as a valuable by-product of their politics. Comparing two political orders that are equally just, they could rank one over the other because it alone achieves political autonomy. But, second, if they can recognize the value of political autonomy in this indirect way, then they should be open to the possibility that it could supplant justice in some circumstances. A slightly less just political order that achieved political autonomy, for instance, might be preferable to the more just political order that did not. And if this were true, then good citizens would need, on occasion, to aim at political autonomy directly rather than at justice. Justice-loving citizens need not be fanatics about justice.

The basic lesson to draw is this. We can accept the desirability of political autonomy without determining its importance relative to other political values. If the pursuit of political autonomy and the pursuit of justice pull in opposing directions in a given set of circumstances, then we will need to decide how to balance them in these circumstances. That difficult issue will be taken up below. Yet even on the extreme assumption that political autonomy is always subordinate to all other political values, its achievement could still be regarded as desirable.

THE PRESSURE OF PLURALISM

Rousseau thought that political autonomy was achievable only in a small republic whose members adhere to a common civil religion and share a substantive conception of the good life. Such a political community is not a live option for us. Thus, the real concern behind the desirability objection may be not that political autonomy has no value, but rather that serious efforts to realize it in the modern world will be repressive and exclusionary.

A response to this concern must show that political autonomy is achievable in modern societies and that it can be achieved without enforced uniformity. Return now to the idea of reasonable pluralism discussed above. Building reasonable pluralism into the condition of reasonable endorsement was meant to show how political autonomy can be combined with the acceptance of pluralism. Rawls explained that in a well-ordered society "everyone has a similar sense of justice and in this respect a well-ordered society is homogeneous." But he emphasized that this does not mean that a well-ordered society must be homogeneous with respect to conceptions of the good or to other matters. The pressure of pluralism forces a retreat to justice, as it were. A politically autonomous society must be organized around a shared, or shareable, conception of justice and nothing more.

One might think that this retreat is a cause for disappointment. Rousseau had it right. A politically autonomous society must rest on both a shared conception of justice and a shared conception of the good. In such a society, all citizens would view their politics as an extension of their efforts to live well. Yet contemporary proponents of political autonomy do not view the retreat to justice as a lamentable retreat. Rawls explains:

Now this variety of conceptions of the good is itself a good thing, that is, it is rational for members of a well-ordered society to want their plans to be different ... Human beings have various talents and abilities the totality of which is unrealizable by any one person or group of persons.[13]

Matters are different with conceptions of justice. Here "we require not only common principles but sufficiently similar ways of applying them in particular cases so that a final ordering of conflicting claims can be defined."[14]

To defend this asymmetry (pluralism is good with respect to the good/bad with respect to the right), Rawls invokes Humboldt's ideal of a society that brings forth the full development of human talents. We should value other people's conceptions of the good since we cannot realize all that is valuable ourselves. "It is as if others were bringing forth a part of ourselves that we have not been able to cultivate."[15] Call this *Humboldt's claim*. Its truth would explain why political autonomy with pluralism (on the good)is not an ersatz version of Rousseau's ideal.

A problem now presents itself. Not every conception of the good is valuable in the way expressed by *Humboldt's claim*. Some conceptions of the good, including some which are consistent with justice, may be worthless. They may add nothing to the full development of human powers. Nonetheless, some of these conceptions could be reasonable in the sense implicated in the hypotheticalist view of the collective authorization condition.

The problem is not simply that *Humboldt's claim* does not line up neatly with this condition. It is rather that the appeal to this claim does not adequately express the accommodation to pluralism that is required. An adequate characterization of political autonomy for the modern political world, it is often said, must acknowledge the limited "scope of practical reason."[16] Reasonable people who live under free conditions can accept misguided conceptions of the good. That fact, if it is a fact, may be unfortunate, but it is a consequence of the limits of practical reason; and it must be acknowledged if the pursuit of political autonomy is not to become the dangerous business of enforced homogeneity that those who reject political autonomy suspect it will become.

It is proven hard to explain why practical reason is limited in this way, if indeed it is so limited. Rawls's well-known explanation invoked the "burdens of judgment." There are, he says, a number of factors that explain why good faith efforts by competent reasoners will lead them to disagree on questions of the good and on comprehensive doctrines more generally. (The burdens of judgment, at best, is a sketch of an explanation. More work would need to be done to fill in the sketch, but this chapter assumes that some such explanation could be given that would show that it is appropriate to index reasonable endorsement to certain background commitments to a conception of the good or wider comprehensive doctrine.) Yet if it is the limits of practical reason, and not the Humboldtian value of pluralism, that force the retreat to justice, then the retreat must proceed further. For the burdens of judgment, if accepted, also explain why good faith efforts by competent reasoners will lead them to disagree on questions of justice. This will be case, even if the reasoners in question are all committed to supporting a conception of justice that other citizens can reasonably endorse. A conception of political autonomy for the modern world, accordingly, must abandon the claim that every citizen should have a similar sense of justice. The homogeneity that Rawls claimed characterizes a well-ordered society could not come about under free conditions.

What is left after this further retreat? The popular answer among Rawlsians is that there exist a family of conceptions of justice, and that if any member of the family is selected by democratic means, then the institutions that this conception regulates will be such that they can be reasonably endorsed by all. Political autonomy is thus achievable, even in the face of disagreement over justice and the good. Call this *weak political autonomy* to contrast it with the strong political autonomy that is realized when citizens converge on a conception of justice.

Given the burdens of judgment explanation of reasonable pluralism, weak political autonomy will not be achieved unless citizens aim to achieve it. (It is extremely unlikely that it would result as a by-product of each citizen pursuing justice as he sees it.) Here, then, is the picture that we have arrived at. Imagine each reasonable citizen aiming at a conception of justice that, or so she believes in good faith, could be reasonably endorsed by all. Next, imagine them agreeing on a set of such conceptions, but disagreeing over which member of the set is the best. Still, since they agree on the set, they agree that any member of the set, if selected by the right kind of procedure and enforced, could serve as a legitimate conception of justice in the sense that it could be authorized by all. Under the pressure of pluralism, in the modern world this weak instantiation of political autonomy is likely as close as we can get to the Rousseauian ideal of citizens giving the law to themselves.[17]

GROUNDING NEUTRALITY

Thus far, I have been characterizing political autonomy, paying particular attention to how the value should be construed if its pursuit is to be even remotely feasible for modern societies. The aim has been to present political autonomy as an attractive and potentially realizable value for the modern world. The task now is to explain how it can ground the principle of state neutrality.

Some may think that the principle of state neutrality needs no grounding. However, unlike values such as equality or autonomy, state neutrality does not have direct and immediate appeal. That is why most proponents of the principle have felt the need to anchor it to deeper normative considerations, such as equal treatment or "respect for persons." Here I will assume that if the principle is sound, then there is an explanation for its value that appeals to deeper normative considerations. My concern is to investigate the extent to which the value of political autonomy contributes to the case for state neutrality. Many proponents of state neutrality foreground the coercive power of the state. They contend that it is disrespectful to coerce a person if one cannot justify the coercion to him in terms that he can accept. But the state's powers extend beyond its coercive powers and noncoercive state action, like coercive state action, can fail to be neutral. An attraction of grounding the principle of state neutrality on political autonomy – an ideal that demands that state authority, whether coercive or not, be exercised in the name of all citizens – is that it can ground state neutrality of broad scope. Yet, while attractive in this way, the appeal to political autonomy, as I have just noted, is not the only way to ground state neutrality. Given the limited focus of this chapter, no general conclusions about the soundness of the principle can be drawn.

The principle of state neutrality, as mentioned above, is subject to competing interpretations. The interpretation that has found favor with most proponents of the principle is *neutrality of justification* (NJ). Larmore provided an early statement of the view.

[P]olitical neutrality consists in a constraint on what factors can be invoked to justify a political decision. Such a decision can count as neutral only if it can be justified without appealing to the presumed intrinsic superiority of any particular [disputed] conception of the good life.[18]

Notice that NJ does not address the aims of those who make political decisions. This point will prove to be important.

There is a simple argument that ties NJ to the democratic value of political autonomy. It runs as follows: (i) For a political society to realize political autonomy, it must be regulated by a conception of justice that, while it may not be shared, can be reasonably endorsed by all its citizens. (ii) For a conception of justice to be reasonably endorsed by all citizens, it must be justified in a manner that does not presume the intrinsic superiority of any conception of the good or comprehensive doctrine. (iii) The principle of state neutrality imposes a constraint on political justification that is necessary for (ii) to be satisfied. Therefore (iv) state neutrality is necessary for the realization of political autonomy.

The simple argument, on inspection, is too simple. For one thing, it may not be true that every political decision implicates justice. If a conception of justice does not bear on some political decisions, then those decisions could be justified nonneutrally without compromising the reasonable endorsability of the conception of justice in question. For another thing, a conception of justice might be reasonably endorseable by all because there exists a range of complementary justifications for it. Each of the complementary justifications may appeal to controversial claims about the good, such that no justification could be endorseable by all, but the set of justifications would succeed in showing that all could reasonably endorse the conception of justice.

While interesting, these two problems should not distract us for long. The first one just requires us to be more precise about the scope of the principle of state neutrality. The principle may not apply literally to all political decisions. So long as there is symmetry between the domain of justice and the domain of state neutrality, then the simple argument can stand. The second problem commits us to the unattractive view that we can justify political decisions to one another by appealing to claims that are false and that we know to be false. This view is unattractive, since justification is not merely persuasive argument. It is argument that proceeds, or at least aspires to proceed, from true premises by valid derivations.[19] By prescinding from disputed and inconsistent conceptions of the good (as directed by premise (ii)), citizens can advance justifications for political decisions that avoid appeal to premises that they know to be false.[20]

There are two additional difficulties with the simple argument that are more serious. The first one is that even if it is true that competent reasoners can reasonably disagree over conceptions of the good and comprehensive doctrines, it does not follow that all such conceptions and doctrines can be reasonably accepted. There may be some conceptions of the good, for example, that (i) win support among a significant number of citizens, (ii) are consistent with the requirements of justice, and (iii) are not reasonable. The power of practical reason may be limited, but it is not radically limited. Conceptions of the good and comprehensive doctrines oriented around astrology or new age religions, for instance, may not be reasonably acceptable. If so, the state could treat these doctrines nonneutrally without jeopardizing its commitment to a conception of justice that could be reasonably accepted by all. This problem shows that political autonomy cannot ground the principle of state neutrality, as it is commonly understood. At most, it can ground a restricted version of that principle. The state must be neutral among all (reasonably acceptable) conceptions of the good and comprehensive doctrines, but it need not be neutral with respect to unreasonable ones.[21]

The second difficulty takes us back to the distinction between justification and aims broached above. Justificatory neutrality imposes "a constraint on what factors can be invoked to justify a political decision." But the collective authorization condition does not mention any such constraint. It holds instead that the institutions and decisions to which it applies must be such that they could be reasonably endorsed by all citizens who were subject to them. Yet an institution or decision presumably could be reasonably endorseable by all, even if it were actually justified in a way that could not be. For example, laws that recognize a right to religious freedom – laws that, let us assume here, could be reasonably endorsed by all – might be justified in practice by appeal to the truth of a particular religion. Now consider a more extreme case. The institutions and decisions of a democratic society are, in fact, reasonably endorseable by all citizens, but this fact is unknown in the society. In practice, the institutions and decisions of this society are justified by appeal to a particular conception of the good. This democratic society would violate state neutrality. Would it also fail to realize political autonomy?

We could respond to this difficulty by supplementing our characterization of political autonomy. Its realization requires not only that the collective authorization condition be satisfied, but also that it be publicly known that it is satisfied. Such a maneuver brings its own problems, however. In any actual political society, we should expect to encounter actual disagreement over whether the reasonable endorseability condition has been satisfied. The point of idealizing citizens was to show how reasonable endorsement is possible, even in the face of actual dissent.

Adding a public knowledge requirement pulls reasonable endorseability uncomfortably close to actual endorsement. The better response to the difficulty, I believe, is a more pragmatic one. Satisfying the collective authorization condition in a modern society is a demanding task, one that is very unlikely to be achieved unless citizens aim to achieve it. In aiming to achieve it, they should aim to present justifications for political institutions and decisions in terms that could be reasonably endorsed by other citizens. Aiming at the condition does not guarantee that it will be satisfied, but it makes it more likely that it will be satisfied.

This pragmatic response brings together the two distinct ideas expressed in Larmore's statement of NJ quoted above. A political decision that could not be justified without appealing to a controversial conception of the good would not be one that could be reasonably endorseable by all citizens. The best way in practice to ensure that political decisions meet this condition is for citizens to honor a constraint on the factors appealed to in justifying their political decisions. Thus supplemented, the simple argument grounds state neutrality, on the restricted construal of the principle,[22] on the democratic value of political autonomy.

NORMATIVE STATUS

Political autonomy can provide a measure of support for the principle of state neutrality. But there are different ways to understand the nature of its value. Most importantly, political autonomy can be understood to generate either requirements or, as I will put it, aspirations. This difference in the kinds of demands that a value generates, I will refer to as its normative status. Depending on its normative status, political autonomy provides a different kind of support for state neutrality.

Normative requirements are internally related to permissions. If some course of action is required for a particular agent on a particular occasion, then he is not permitted not to do it. Likewise, if a political society is required, in a given set of circumstances, to realize a certain value, then it is not permitted not to realize it. It is possible that political autonomy generates requirements for those societies capable of achieving it. For example, the value might explain why modern societies are morally required to satisfy the two conditions we have been discussing – the participation condition and the collective authorization condition. Failure to satisfy either condition would render illegitimate the exercise of political authority in these societies.

Many contemporary writers on politics claim that legitimate government must be democratic. Put more cautiously, they claim that, if democracy is possible for a society given its level of development, then it is required to be democratic. Similar strong claims are often made on behalf of the collective authorization condition. If political autonomy is the kind of value that generates requirements, then it could support these strong claims. By contrast, if political autonomy is an aspirational ideal, then it will not generate requirements to comply with its component conditions. The failure to realize political autonomy may be a shortcoming of the society, but it will not undercut the moral permissibility of the political authority exercised in the society. This point explains why, as I hinted at above, it is no contradiction to affirm the value of political autonomy while rejecting the contractualist principle of political legitimacy that requires political institutions to satisfy the collective authorization condition. The contractualist principle in question articulates a requirement for morally permissible institutions, but if political autonomy is an aspirational ideal, then it will not generate such a requirement.

Rousseau thought that political autonomy generates requirements. Any society that failed to realize political autonomy would be illegitimate. Rawls's view on the matter is harder to discern. The participation condition, he claimed, is a requirement of legitimate law.[23] But did he also believe that legitimate law must meet the collective authorization condition? Most commentators have thought the answer is "yes," since Rawls proposed a principle of legitimacy that includes the requirement that, at least with respect to basic justice and constitutional essentials, the exercise of political power must be reasonably endorseable by all citizens. But, intriguingly, Rawls articulated this principle of legitimacy in terms of the "fully proper" exercise of political power. And by using these words, it is possible that he meant to express a demand other than moral permissibility.[24] If so, then legitimate law (i.e., morally permissible law) would not need to satisfy the collective authorization condition. Full propriety would express an aspirational ideal rather than a moral requirement on the exercise of political power.

This interpretive question does not, of course, settle the substantive question of how best to understand the normative status of political autonomy. Putting aside Rawls's views, a strong case can be made that political autonomy should not be construed as generating moral requirements on the permissible exercise of political power. It is best viewed as an aspirational value. The case appeals to the very concern that guided the characterization of the value in response to what I termed the pressure of pluralism. That concern is that in characterizing the value of political autonomy we should be sensitive to its feasibility. The move from actualist to hypotheticalist collective authorization, the retreat to justice, and the retreat from strong to weak political autonomy were all spurred by the need to reconcile political autonomy with the pluralism of the modern world. For the pursuit of political autonomy to be a realistic and desirable political goal for modern societies, it must be characterized in terms that depart from the strong view articulated by Rousseau.

Aspirational values can be achieved to a greater or lesser extent. By contrast, values that generate requirements are best understood as ones that either are or are not realized. Thus, if political autonomy generates a requirement that all citizens must be able to reasonably endorse the terms of their political association, then if this requirement were not fully satisfied, the value would not be realized. But, if political autonomy instead generates aspirational demands, then as its two conditions are more fully satisfied, it will be realized to a greater extent. Plainly, if political autonomy is characterized as an aspirational value, then it will be more plausible to view it as a realistic political goal for modern societies. Its full realization may be very improbable, but a substantial realization of it may not be out of reach for those societies committed to it.[25]

I claimed above, however, that political autonomy is a democratic instantiation of political self-determination. Does this not imply that it must be fully realized to be realized at all? It does not, but it does imply that it must be realized to such an extent that it is plausible to speak of the citizens giving the laws to themselves. For the value to be achieved at all, then, each of its two conditions must be realized beyond some considerable, albeit difficult-to-state-with-precision, threshold. This ensures that political autonomy remains a demanding value for modern societies, even if it is granted that it is not so demanding as to be utopian.

Viewing political autonomy as an aspirational value reduces its power to support state neutrality. The realization of political autonomy becomes a desideratum, not a value that generates requirements, and this means that, at most, it can support state neutrality as a desideratum, one that (likely) can be defeated by other considerations of political morality.[26] This brings us finally to the issue of the normative force of political autonomy.

NORMATIVE FORCE

Requirements and desiderata are more or less stringent, more or less weighty. A maximally stringent requirement would be one that could never permissibly be infringed. A maximally weighty desideratum would be one that could never permissibly be outweighed by competing considerations. Dimensions of stringency and weight fix the normative force of a value. I have just claimed that political autonomy is best characterized as an aspirational value, one that generates desiderata rather than requirements. If it generates desiderata of maximal weight (assume here that there are no internal conflicts), then it will support a strong principle of state neutrality. However, few, if any, desiderata have this kind of force. Political autonomy is valuable, but it is not so valuable that it defeats all other normative considerations. To gauge its normative force, we need to consider possible conflicts between political autonomy and other values.

Return now to the desirability objection discussed above. This objection concerns the potential conflict between political autonomy and justice. It is possible that efforts to achieve political autonomy never obstruct efforts to achieve justice. This no-conflict view may be accepted by some proponents of political autonomy. However, as a general claim, it is not very plausible. Efforts to satisfy the participation condition, in some circumstances, will make it more likely that unjust decisions will be reached.[27] The same can be said of the collective authorization condition. That condition is satisfied, on the weak view of political autonomy, when one member from the set of reasonably endorseable conceptions of justice, after being selected by an appropriate process, regulates the fundamental political and legal institutions of a society. Now suppose that the selected conception, call it J_1, is one of several reasonably endorseable conceptions and that one of these alternatives, call it J_2, is a superior conception of justice. Next suppose that some of the most compelling arguments – compelling in terms of both their soundness and their motivational power – would be excluded by the principle of state neutrality that is grounded on the value of political autonomy. In this scenario, efforts to achieve political autonomy will impede efforts to achieve justice.

One response to these possibilities is to sidestep them. Perhaps political autonomy is a value that applies only under very favorable conditions. And perhaps part of what makes conditions very favorable is that political autonomy and justice do not conflict in the ways here envisioned. However, this response does not help us to think about the normative force of the value. A second response is to assign priority to one or the other value. Justice trumps political autonomy or political autonomy trumps justice. A third response is to deny any general priority to either value and to allow that sometimes one takes priority over the other and sometimes the other takes priority over it. On this third response, everything depends on the context and the issues in play.

The third response, in my judgment, is the best one; but it is also the response that provides the least guidance, for it is not clear how to determine the weights of conflicting values. Still, if either it or the view that justice trumps political autonomy is accepted, then political autonomy cannot support a general principle of state neutrality. At most, it can provide support for a modest idea: political institutions and decisions that satisfy the principle of state neutrality are desirable. Depending on the weight given to the realization of political autonomy and depending on how likely and how significant are the conflicts between justice and political autonomy, this support will be greater or lesser.

Over the course of this chapter, I have been drawing a number of distinctions to bring political autonomy into sharper focus. To review, these include:

Strong / Weak
Robust / Modest
Requirements / Desiderata
High Stringency or Weight / Low Stringency or Weight

I have argued that we should embrace weak over strong political autonomy. And I have claimed that political autonomy is best understood as an aspirational ideal that grounds desiderata, not requirements. I have remained neutral on whether political autonomy is best understood as robust or modest. (This issue, I have said, turns on the plausibility of *transmission*, which is a claim that cannot be addressed in this chapter. Many proponents of political autonomy, however, have accepted *transmission*. They have claimed that only the fundamental political institutions of a society must meet the collective authorization condition.) I have said almost nothing about how much weight the value of political autonomy has or about its capacity to override other values and ideals. I have claimed only that it is implausible to hold that it always overrides claims of justice.

Consider now a view that affirms the weaker fork in each of the above contrasts. Such a view would hold that political autonomy does not require its citizens to share either a conception of the good or a conception of justice, but only to view the conception of justice in force in their society as one that has been appropriately selected and one that is in a set of conceptions of justice that are all reasonably endorseable. Further, such a view would hold that the collective authorization condition need apply only at the fundamental political level. Finally, such a view would claim that political autonomy is an aspirational ideal that grounds desiderata, not requirements, and that its weight as an aspirational ideal is not high.

This view would not provide substantial support for the principle of state neutrality. It would permit the state to engage in nonneutral state action either (i) when such state action was consistent with the neutrally justified fundamental political institutions of the society or (ii) when such state action was justified by considerations or values that properly override the value of political autonomy. A proponent of this view would accept that political autonomy is a genuine value – and reject the desirability objection discussed above – but he would deny that anything as general as the principle of state neutrality could be derived from it. Contrast this view with a second one, which holds that political autonomy is weak and robust and that it is an aspirational ideal, but one with very significant weight. On this second view, political autonomy could provide substantial support for state neutrality.

Nothing I have said here tells us which of these two contrasting views have a stronger claim to acceptance. The more one thinks that efforts to realize political autonomy will obstruct the realization of other important political values, such as justice or the promotion of excellence, the more one will incline toward the first view. By contrast, those who accept the second view, in all likelihood, believe that the pursuit of political autonomy does not conflict significantly in practice with the pursuit of justice, and they likely believe, in addition, that there are independent reasons that establish that the state should not pursue other conflicting ideals, such as, for example, the promotion of ideals of the good. These prior beliefs and commitments, and not the value of political autonomy alone, will explain why they think that it can provide substantial support for the principle of state neutrality.

TAKING STOCK

This chapter has explored the relationship between state neutrality and political autonomy. I have argued that political autonomy is a genuine ideal, even for citizens living in modern societies. This ideal both reflects and brings together the democratic commitment that citizens should rule themselves and the liberal commitment that citizens should not be subjected to political institutions and decisions that they can with good reason oppose. I have also tried to show, however, that there is not a simple or direct argument from political autonomy to the principle of state neutrality. On some interpretations of the value, political autonomy permits nonneutral state action. And, as an aspirational ideal, political autonomy may be supplanted by the demands of justice or by other ideals.

No overall conclusion about the plausibility of state neutrality can be taken from my discussion. For some proponents of this principle, this chapter will merely confirm what they already knew. State neutrality rests not on the foundation of a distinctively democratic value like political autonomy, but rather on some other value or ideal, such as a principle of respect. Still, some progress has been made. A number of influential political philosophers recently have claimed that a properly liberal account of politics is both strongly democratic and committed to state neutrality. The appeal to political autonomy explains this connection. In a democratic society, all citizens have an equal share of political power – power that is both exercised in the name of all and aspires to be endorseable by all. Only by excluding nonneutral reasons from political justification can democratic citizens live up to this demanding aspiration. This is the view that this chapter has sought to clarify and to challenge.

NOTES

1. See the papers collected in Wall and Klosko, *Perfectionism and Neutrality*.
2. In saying this, I do not mean to imply that commitment to political autonomy is an essential element of liberalism. Many liberal political theories do not affirm it.
3. Rousseau, *On the Social Contract*, Book I, ch. vi.
4. Rawls, *Political Liberalism*, pp. 216–17.
5. See Cohen and Nagel for good discussions of political autonomy understood along these lines. Cohen's essays on Rawlsian liberalism and deliberative democracy are particularly valuable. See his *Philosophy, Politics, Democracy* and *The Arc of the Moral Universe*. See also Cohen's discussion of Rousseau in *Rousseau: A Free Community of Equals*. Nagel presents a perceptive account of the collective authorization condition in "The Problem of Global Justice."
6. For altruistic reasons it can be reasonable for people to accept an arrangement that imposes large and unfair costs on themselves relative to others, but plainly they are not reasonably required to bear these costs, for example. Scanlon is discussing moral contractualism, but the point he makes applies to our topic as well.

7. Henceforth, I will use the phrase "could reasonably accept" to mean "could not reasonably reject."
8. Rawls, "Reply to Habermas," p. 411.
9. One might conclude that neither component has value if both cannot be satisfied; but this would be an unusual view.
10. The former view was defended by Locke. The latter view is the common view among contemporary proponents of the value.
11. Rawls does not require ongoing democratic participation at the constitutional level. However, he does claim that while "those already living in a just constitutional structure cannot found a just constitution ... they can fully reflect on it, endorse it, and so freely exercise it in all ways necessary" ("Reply to Habermas," p. 403).
12. This assumption is harmless in the present context. Whether the participation condition should be satisfied constitutionally or comprehensively will not affect the argument for state neutrality that I shall be examining.
13. Rawls, *A Theory of Justice*, p. 448.
14. *Ibid.*
15. *Ibid.*
16. Cohen, *Philosophy, Politics, Democracy*, pp. 52–56.
17. The phrase is from *ibid.*, p. 336 (discussing a Rawlsian account of deliberative democracy).
18. Larmore, *Patterns of Moral Complexity*, p. 44.
19. The point about justification that I press here is controversial. Compare Raz, "Disagreement in Politics," pp. 41–43 with Gaus, *The Order of Public Reason*, pp. 287–92.
20. Assuming, of course, that the common ground shared by citizens consists of some true premises.
21. Nussbaum criticizes the standard Rawlsian view on precisely these grounds. See her "Perfectionist Liberalism and Political Liberalism." I reply to Nussbaum's critique in "Perfectionism, Reasonableness, and Respect."
22. I drop this important qualification in the remainder of this chapter, but it should be understood to apply.
23. At least for certain societies. As Rawls allowed in *The Law of Peoples*, legitimate law does not require democratic government.
24. See Copp, "Reasonable Acceptability and Democratic Legitimacy," pp. 258–59.
25. In suggesting that the full realization of political autonomy is utopian for modern societies, I am implicitly rejecting what might be termed the constitutive interpretation of reasonable endorsement. On this interpretation, one first identifies a conception (or set of conceptions) of justice

and then defines reasonable endorsement as endorsement of that conception (or to a member in the set of conceptions). This guarantees full realization of the reasonable endorsement condition, since anyone who does not endorse the relevant conception(s) counts as unreasonably withholding endorsement.

26. Thus, for example, if a policy can be adequately justified in two ways – one that complies with the principle of state neutrality and one that does not – citizens should favor the way that complies with the principle, since doing so allows them to better secure the desideratum of political autonomy.

27. This can be true even if the satisfaction of the participation condition is a requirement of justice.

III   Topics and concepts

8 Contemporary liberalism and toleration

Liberalism, historically, is closely associated with increased toleration, so it is unsurprising that a variety of contemporary authors
consider toleration to be "the substantive heart of liberalism."[1] The
precise role of toleration in liberalism, though, is unclear; different
liberals have different views. In this chapter, I will discuss three sorts
of liberal theories and indicate how they approach questions of toleration, arguing that one of them supports toleration of more sorts of
activities (including speech acts and lifestyles) than the others. While
I think this is reason to favor that sort of theory, I will not defend that
claim. Some reasonably think (and defend the view) that though
toleration is of value, its limits should be drawn more narrowly.

In the first section, I introduce the conceptual nature of toleration,
the nature of *state toleration*, and the two dominant ways philosophers might now be liberal theorists. With a nod to Rawls, I mark that
distinction by talking of comprehensive doctrine liberalism and political liberalism (hereafter, CDL and PL).[2] In the second section, I
consider the limits of toleration supported by the most prominent
CDL on offer – Rawls's early view. I turn to PL in the third section and
then consider another view – what I think of as a *thin* CDL – in the
fourth. In the final section, I conclude by briefly considering how the
three positions would respond to the paradox of liberalism. The
central claim defended throughout is that while PL might require
toleration of more sorts of activities than Rawls's earlier CDL, the
thin CDL discussed in the fourth section requires more than either
that CDL or PL.[3]

Thanks to Andy Altman, Cleo Grimaldi, Christie Hartley, Shanna Slank, Bus Van Der
Vossen, and Steve Wall, all of whom send previous versions of this chapter and provided
comments and criticisms that led to serious improvements.

CLEARING THE PATH: TOLERATION,
THE STATE, AND CDL VS. PL

An act of toleration, I claim, is an agent's intentional and principled refraining from interfering with an opposed other (or their behavior, etc.), where the agent believes she has the power to interfere.[4] If this definition is correct – and I think it is – it poses a problem for discussions of state toleration. Simply put, it is not clear that the state is the sort of entity that can act, let alone act in an intentional manner.[5] Non-intentional noninterference, though, is not toleration. So how can the state tolerate?

I suggest that when we talk about a state tolerating, we are speaking elliptically about a state wherein all agents of the state act on, or are legally required to act on, *a policy of toleration*. Of course, citizens may tolerate regardless of their state's policies, which apply only to agents of the state. When citizens tolerate, we can say there is *toleration within the state*. When there is a state policy of toleration, we can say there is *state toleration*. A policy of toleration would require noninterference by agents of the state in specific sorts of activities – whether those agents oppose the activities or not. If the agents oppose the activities, they must tolerate. If they do not oppose the activity, they simply must not interfere with it (conceptually, they cannot tolerate the activity). So, a state policy of toleration requires that certain sorts of activities be either tolerated or at least not interfered with by agents of the state.

A state policy of toleration requires clear rules indicating what sorts of activities are to be tolerated (or not interfered with) and what sorts of activities warrant interference. Such policies require noninterference with activities for which there is opposition, whether that opposition is from agents of the state or other citizens. For example, many in the United States oppose atheism and any statements of atheism. Whether or not current agents of the state oppose such statements, a state policy of toleration is possible. Similarly, there is likely opposition to the religious activities of any given religion practiced in the United States – and again, whether or not current agents of the state oppose such activity, a state policy of toleration is possible. Policies that require noninterference where there is no opposition, on the other hand, would not be considered policies of toleration.

One final – but large – piece of path clearing is needed: explaining comprehensive doctrine liberalism (CDL) and political liberalism (PL), with an eye toward exposing the different ways they endorse toleration. A comprehensive doctrine "includes conceptions of what is of value in human life, and ideals of personal character, as well as ideals of friendship and of familial and associational relationships, and much else that is to inform our conduct, and in the limit to our life as a whole."[6] These ideals "are to inform much of our nonpolitical conduct (in the limit our life as a whole)."[7] (The "in the limit" talk makes clear that doctrines can be more or less comprehensive.) A CDL is any liberalism that is essentially tied to (or is itself) a comprehensive doctrine; different CDLs are tied to different comprehensive doctrines. Some Kantians, with a rather robust view about moral autonomy, are CDLs. So too, though, are some utilitarians and natural law theorists, and so on. These CDLs could be in debate with one another to determine the best defense of liberalism (and perhaps the best form thereof). PL is meant to rise above such debate so long as the CDLs in question are reasonable.

Undeniably, there are plural comprehensive doctrines in contemporary liberal societies. The core political principles that all reasonable CDs accept are, collectively, the subject of an *overlapping consensus* and would be the *freestanding* principles of a PL society, not dependent on any particular CD or its metaphysical claims. "Person A may support political liberalism as the implication of her utilitarianism; person B may support it as the implication of his religious faith; person C may support it as the core of her less tightly organized hodgepodge of other moral commitments."[8]

Skeptical of getting agreement, PLs are unwilling to base principles of justice (or constitutional essentials) on metaphysical assumptions that reasonable others might reject. This constraint allows them to concentrate their concerns on the political arena. Refusal to rely upon controversial metaphysical claims is, thus, only one characteristic of political liberalism. A second is its limited domain. CDLs have commitments that affect aspects of their lives beyond the political and that they may believe should limit what others should be allowed to do. Millian utilitarians, for example, might advocate liberalism because it creates the most happiness. Such a CDL would also be committed to creating the most happiness possible, no matter where or when. An autonomist CDL (discussed in the next section), by contrast, insists individuals have moral autonomy throughout their lives. Political liberals, by contrast to both, make no such claims; in their view, "a political conception of justice should apply only to the basic structure of society."[9] Theoretically, individual PLs may endorse moral views and policies for all arenas of their own lives, simply insisting that this fact is irrelevant to the state. Though they thus might endorse a CD, they also insist that the only part of that CD that would matter for others (who do not endorse it) are the principles that are the subject of the overlapping consensus (which they also endorse). As one Rawlsian puts it, "[p]olitical liberalism distinguishes comprehensive doctrines, which include moral ideas that guide people in all aspects of their lives, from political conceptions, which comprise moral ideas and values expressed in political judgments."[10]

Once metaphysical commitments are rejected as grounding political principles, what is the political liberal left with? PLs insist that only "public reasons" can be used in political discourse.[11] Public reasons are those that *it would be reasonable for any citizen to assent to.*[12] They thus exclude all purely religious claims – since there will be citizens who would reasonably disagree with any such claim. They exclude, in fact, all metaphysical claims since these might be controversial – which here means "subject to rejection by those committed to some reasonable comprehensive doctrine." Different individuals may accept public reasons for different reasons, each finding grounding support for them in their own CD. The policies of toleration the PL will espouse are thus those that are justified by public reasons. CDLs, by contrast, willingly endorse some metaphysical claims (which claims depends on their CD) and these claims ground their political principles, including principles of toleration. Those endorsing such a view do not claim their metaphysical claims are uncontroversial. They simply insist on – and defend – their correctness. It may be an insistence on the value of autonomy, the value of happiness produced, or something else that grounds the relevant liberalism. (These do not exhaust the possibilities.[13])

On the face of it, advocates of PL seem likely to tolerate more sorts of activities than advocates of CDL. PLs, after all, will not try to defend the criminalization (or other legal interference) of any sort of activity without reasons acceptable to adherents of all existing reasonable comprehensive doctrines, including those they dislike or disapprove of.[14] By contrast, a CDL could argue for or against the criminalization of some activity based on reasons not acceptable to adherents of competing reasonable comprehensive doctrines. A utilitarian CDL, for example, might argue for the legal permissibility of abortion in cases of type X with empirical information that strongly supports the view that allowing abortion in such cases promotes overall utility.[15] It would not be reasonable, however, to expect a Roman Catholic (whether endorsing a CDL or not) to assent to reasons justifying a law permitting abortion.[16] A defender of either CD would thus support policies on the basis of reasons that are reasonably opposed by the other, seeming to demonstrate intolerance toward the other. PLs, by contrast, claim we should "accept or tolerate people's affirming and acting on the particular beliefs [e.g., those from their particular CDs] that provide them with reasons" and argue that "[p]ersons and principles of justice are unreasonable insofar as they do not tolerate or accept that false beliefs can provide others with good reasons for acting – good reasons insofar as these reasons fit with their rational plan of life and reasonable comprehensive views."[17] They would thus not support a policy justified by reasons specific to the Roman Catholic or utilitarian CDs.[18] It thus seems they would tolerate more sorts of activities than either CD.

With the CDL/PL distinction now clear, I turn to examining how each treats toleration.

ON COMPREHENSIVE LIBERALISM'S LIMITS OF TOLERATION (RAWLS'S EARLY VIEW)

Every political philosopher today recognizes the importance of John Rawls's *Theory of Justice*. With it, Rawls single-handedly reinvigorated political philosophy in the English-speaking world and introduced new terms and concepts into our discourse. Part of his brilliance was reinvigorating the idea of hypothetical consent. Classical contract theorists started with a state of nature, asking how people might exit it, consenting to civil society. Rawls considered the state of nature a mere example of an *original position* and offered, in its place, his *veil of ignorance* – a heuristic device wherein we seek to determine the principles of justice we would agree to if we did not know who we were.

The veil of ignorance is an impressive device for determining what we should each agree to (or *would* agree to if we donned the veil).

Critics argued, though, that the ability to think of oneself as the sort of being present behind the veil requires thinking of oneself as separate from all of one's ends, including commitments to others, desires, etc. That, it was (and often still is) thought, is impossible, requiring radical independence or *autonomy* of the self. It was also claimed that no agreement made behind the veil could have normative force for *us* since *we* are not the agents behind the veil. The important point here is that Rawls seems to have a contentious view of the individual grounding his liberalism, which, it is often thought, thereby promotes moral autonomy.

Behind the veil, Rawls argues, we would endorse two principles of justice. The first – the liberty principle – requires that each of us have the most extensive set of basic liberties compatible with everyone else having the same. The second requires that social or economic inequalities are just only if they are to the advantage of the least well off and all have fair equality of opportunity to attain the social (or political or economic) positions that correspond to the inequalities (the difference principle and equal opportunity principle).[19] Importantly, on Rawls's view, "by acting from these principles persons are acting autonomously; they are acting from principles that they would acknowledge under conditions that best express their nature as free and equal rational beings."[20] Hence, on this view moral autonomy is required – as it allows us to determine the principles of justice.

With some understanding of Rawls's 1971 view in place, we can ask the simple question: What does it require a just state to tolerate? Putting the point simply, X is to be tolerated if it is in accord with the two principles of justice that emerge from the original position. Some clarification. A state is just, on this view, if it is in accord with the two principles of justice and so long as the state is just, its laws determine what must be tolerated.[21] This means the state must not have a law requiring interference with X if that law would make the state fail to be in accord with the two principles.

Consider some examples. A society can be just in Rawls's scheme if its laws tolerate medical doctors earning substantially more than others, so long as this inequality makes it such that there will be more doctors than there would otherwise be so that even the least well off are more likely to receive medical attention when needed than they would otherwise be (and assuming the first principle is satisfied).

Similarly, a society can be just in Rawls's scheme if it tolerates homosexual marriage, marijuana use, and masturbation. A society *cannot* be just in Rawls's scheme if it tolerates a religious organization that forbids women from running for government office and requires they be subservient to men, allowing them fewer liberties. Similarly, a society cannot be just in Rawls's scheme if it tolerates a political order that grants economic rights to some and not others, nor if it tolerates an economic order that allows some to have political liberty but not others.

Imagine a religious organization develops, centered on the teachings of a previously unheard of wise woman. Her followers become faithful as adults – they were not raised in the religion, which did not exist before. Imagine, further, that her followers are (or were) all intelligent, freethinking, and autonomous and that they all intentionally and with full knowledge of the expected consequences give their informed consent to join the new organization. Imagine, finally, that these initiates agree to abide by the wise woman's teachings and to raise their children using techniques we might call "brain-washing" to guarantee *they* will be faithful to the wise woman's teachings when they become adults. The initiates would essentially be voluntarily and autonomously sacrificing their own autonomy and political liberties *and binding their children to the same*. Rawls's CDL would not tolerate such behavior as it treats autonomy as a value such that the promotion of non-autonomy cannot be tolerated.[22] Indeed, we might appropriately call Rawls's CDL *autonomist*.[23]

Now that we have some understanding of what Rawls's 1971 CDL would and would not tolerate, we move on to consider PL. Later, in the fourth section, I discuss a third position – what I think of as a *thin* CDL. First, though, take stock of a key factor: CDLs have independent commitments that dictate their approach to toleration and may have principles grounded in those commitments indicating when the limits of toleration have been broached. A PL is different.

POLITICAL LIBERALISM'S LIMITS OF TOLERATION

Despite offering (in his 1971 book, *A Theory of Justice*) what some think of as the best defense of liberalism in over a century, Rawls came to realize his view might face opposition as a CDL. What it needed, he thought, was to be supplemented with an account of what would make a state legitimate and stable. The result is his PL, a theory about how core political principles can be anchored in an overlapping consensus endorsed by all reasonable CDs. By virtue of that wide-ranging endorsement (read: consent), the PL society would be not only stable but also legitimate.[24]

Remarkably, Rawls believes PL results in an overlapping consensus on the principles of justice endorsed in his earlier view.[25] Given that the overlapping consensus is determined by the existing reasonable CDs and that these vary from society to society (and can change over time), this seems highly unlikely. If it were right, a PL society would presumably tolerate the same things as Rawls's CDL. Assuming this is not the case, the general question for PL is what sort of principles all who adhere to reasonable CDs would accept. For the PL, X should be tolerated if it is it in accord with public reason. Some clarification, once again. A state is legitimate, on this view, if justified by public reason.[26] So long as the state is legitimate, its laws determine what must be tolerated. This means the state must not have a law requiring interference with X if that law would make the state fail to be in accord with public reason. As standardly read, this requires that individuals have *political autonomy* but not moral (ethical) autonomy.[27]

The idea behind the political autonomy requirement is straightforward: Citizens must have the protected right to vote and perform other behaviors associated with living in a liberal democratic regime,[28] but in their private lives, they may, to put the point bluntly, be led by others. So, for example, those in the religious group discussed above (in the penultimate paragraph of the last section) would be free to act as indicated so long as the members retained their political rights. This presumably means they must be allowed to vote, to leave the religious group's compound, etc.[29] If they choose, though, to accept subservient roles on that compound, the PL state would tolerate it. This allows that both those whose reasonable CDs value (moral) autonomy and those whose reasonable CDs do not (or do not value it for some, usually women) can continue to live according to their CDs, with all being politically autonomous. PL "affirms political autonomy for all but leaves the weight of ethical autonomy to be decided by citizens severally in light of their comprehensive doctrines."[30] In PL, then, toleration's value seems weightier than that of moral autonomy. The laws of a PL state may tolerate groups that have members with less freedom within the group than other members – so long as they all have political autonomy (can participate as *autonomous citizens* with the state), they do not have to have full participation rights in the running of their own households, churches, or cultural groups. (PLs might oppose how such groups are organized even if they do not think the state should interfere.) Again, PL *seems* capable of tolerating more than CDL.[31]

Pluralism of CDs is an empirical fact of contemporary society – indeed, any society with freedom of conscience. This is due to what Rawls calls "the burdens of judgment."[32] Reasonable persons, on his view, recognize these burdens and how they make pluralism of CDs inevitable and thus support toleration and public reason.[33] All of this should be accepted. What must also be recognized, though, is that on this view, anyone insisting that their CD is the single true religious or philosophical CD and who cannot understand how others can reasonably disagree are, on this account, *unreasonable* and by virtue of that, excluded from the public reason bargaining table, as it were.[34] Of course, the PL state may include liberties that adherents of unreasonable CDs reject (and may reject some they want). This means that any promise of PL to accommodate *the real diversity* modern societies contain is doomed from the start. The real diversity of contemporary societies includes unreasonable CDs, and their views are not included in the crafting of public reasons. "We are not required ... to take seriously the political views of unreasonable persons."[35] For them, "the recommendation of political liberalism is to craft a limited exchange that avoids a confrontation of the beliefs that both illiberal and reasonable people tend to think are most important: the comprehensive beliefs."[36] In so doing, PL fails to show them respect as practical reasoners. To show them such respect requires believing it *worth helping them* to see the truth (or at least the good argument) behind the core liberal principles – and so believing they can come to see it. This requires willingly confronting their CDs in an open and honest attempt to convince them of liberal values[37] – and so openness to being convinced one is wrong oneself. Holders of unreasonable doctrines are instead "treated like the bearers of a pestilence ... excluded from the legitimation pool, that collection of citizens whose consent to the political system confirms its legitimacy."[38] PL thus "wins consent [and legitimacy] only by excluding from the outset those very persons whose illiberal convictions would lead them to reject the system."[39] Indeed, "the main aim of political liberalism is to address those who are committed to constructing terms of social coopera- tion that respect all persons as free and equal citizens."[40] Those not so committed need not be consulted.[41]

Two points should be clear here: (i) PL fails to respect adherents of CDs deemed unreasonable and (ii) given that lack of respect, PLs are quite happy to allow the existing diversity of CDs to evolve into a "reasonable pluralism" wherein all remaining CDs are reasonable. That is, PLs are comfortable with policies a consequence of which is the ending of unreasonable comprehensive doctrines. These policies may tolerate the unreasonable CDs insofar as they do not overtly call for their elimination, but such policies might have spillover effects destructive to those CDs.[42] This is not, on its own, a criticism of PL – certainly not a liberal criticism of PL. All liberals, after all, will have to limit the role of illiberal practices. Nonetheless, the second point is, on its own, worth attention as liberals – perhaps especially PLs – at least pay lip service to preferring to help diverse social (religious, moral, etc.) groups prosper.

A question should now loom for the PL: Might the spillover affects destructive to unreasonable CDs also be destructive of *reasonable* CDs, causing them a loss of adherents? Though a negative answer is surely implausible here, it may well be that reasonable CDs would also *gain* members in the process. After all, actual-world, well-educated people sometimes become *more* religious rather than less. It is an empirical question: Would reasonable CDs survive in a society com- mitted to basic political principles that are the subject of an overlap- ping consensus? More importantly, would adherents of reasonable CDs believe they would? If not, it would be surprising if they endorsed the principles about which there is hoped for consensus.[43] Two possi- bilities follow from this: either representatives of reasonable CDs will believe their CDs would survive in a PL state or a PL state would not obtain (since no one would endorse reasons supportive of principles that lead to their CD's failure). Put simply, either the subject of the overlapping consensus is consistent with a stable society of competing and diverse CDs or it is not; if not, a PL state cannot obtain. (There would be a diversity of CDs, but not in a PL state.)

Ignoring the possibility that a PL state might not be possible, it is important that the sort of toleration required by PL can leave CD groups eviscerated over the long term. This may not be an embarrassment to the PL. However, I would think our chief concern would be that people live well (what other legitimate concern can there be for the state?), and I think people can live well in groups committed to CDs that are not liberal. Indeed, I suspect some people *cannot live well* without such a group as I will discuss in the fourth section. I thus think it important that such groups be tolerated, where this means not merely that there is no intent to destroy such groups, but that there be no unnecessary intentional action *a known by-product of which* is their destruction. PL does not seem to offer this, despite claims of inclusiveness. Its commitment to political autonomy and rejection of the unreasonable as fit to participate in determining principles of justice prohibits toleration of more ways of life than PLs are apt to advertise. Whether it allows toleration of more ways of life than a CDL depends on the sort of CDL considered – likely more than autonomist CDL, but less than others.

Our conclusion about PL is unsurprising. Though it wishes to shed commitment to controversial claims, PL is, after all, a form of liberalism, and liberalism itself may be controversial. More to the point, it would seem that no matter what we do to make liberalism acceptable to groups not ordinarily part of its reach, liberalism must remain committed to the value of the individual. One PL recognizes this explicitly:

Liberalism, formulated as a strictly political doctrine ... forms a freestanding conception in regard to comprehensive moral visions of the good life, but it cannot coherently claim to be freestanding with respect to morality altogether. In particular, we would be wrong to suppose that the moral principle of *respect for persons* has the political significance it does because reasonable people share a commitment to it. On the contrary, the idea of respect is what directs us to seek the principles of our political life in the area of reasonable agreement. Respect for persons lies at the heart of political liberalism, not because looking for common ground we find it there, but because it is what impels us to look for common ground at all.[44]

For liberalism to be liberalism, it cannot be "political all the way down." It must accept that respect for persons matters morally.

Just what respect requires remains a question. I suggested above that it requires being willing to engage in honest dialogue seeking to persuade. Given concern to broaden the appeal of liberalism, the PL suggests we can make do with respect for persons as citizens (with political autonomy). As it turns out, this may not be the way of broadest appeal.

Let's take stock, briefly. CDL has independently defended policies of toleration. By contrast, the PL requires toleration of whatever the overlapping consensus demand be tolerated. A likely exception to this is a principle of respect for persons. We can now ask whether there might be a thinner moral principle – which would have broader appeal – to ground liberalism.

A *THIN* COMPREHENSIVE LIBERALISM'S LIMITS OF TOLERATION

According to Larmore, there must be a moral grounding to any defensible political theory. A moral grounding that is likely to receive universal assent, or as close to universal as possible, is desirable. Hence, the move many make to PL – the hope is that putting metaphysical claims (e.g., about personhood) to the side will result in a political view that all can accept. It would plausibly get more acceptance since more people believe reasonable persons must be respected than believe all individuals must be morally autonomous. PL is thus supposedly *thinner* than autonomist CDL, insisting only on political, rather than the more robust moral, autonomy.[45] PL is thereby meant to be more inclusive – the thinner the requirement, the more inclusive the view. But there are other forms of CDL – something oddly ignored in much of the literature about CDL and PL.

Autonomist liberals take autonomy (often Kantian) to be the core liberal value. Other CDLs are also *perfectionist* in the sense that they believe the right core values are those that lead individuals to the good. Autonomist liberals think autonomy is required for human perfection; other perfectionist CDLs flesh out perfection differently. A *non-perfectionist* CDL is also possible. This sort of CDL endorses a value, but not a value *meant* to lead individuals to the good even if it (intentionally or not) *enables* people to lead good lives. This is a liberalism that treats toleration as the single correct state policy,[46] not because of an overlapping consensus in favor of doing so, but because of a grounding value. In this section I discuss such a *thin* CDL that insists on neither moral nor political autonomy for all, showing how it may fare better than PL in terms of broadening the inclusiveness of liberalism.

Here is a moral principle: *suffering is bad*. This seems analytically true but also has normative bite since, prima facie, badness (again, analytically) should be avoided. It suggests states should be concerned to limit suffering. Ending suffering, of course, would be an overly burdensome requirement. There is suffering throughout the world, among humans and non-humans, and no state could hope to end it, even within its borders. Moreover, some sorts of suffering, while morally important, are obviously not political matters. The suffering of a broken heart, for example. The general concern is that people be able to live well – without suffering. The narrower, political, concern is that people not be prevented from living well – and made to suffer – by other agents. The state ought to work, then, to prevent the intentional infliction of suffering. This suggests a particular account of liberalism that takes *freedom from harm* to be the core political value, requiring that toleration's proper normative limit is the causing of harm (and so suffering).

According to this CDL, all behaviors are to be equally tolerated by the state so long as no harm is done to others. (The state thus ought to work to prevent harm – and perhaps punish harm-doers or otherwise work to bring about rectification of harms done.) John Stuart Mill wrote: "The sole end for which mankind are warranted, individually or collectively, in interfering with the liberty of action of any of their number is self-protection . . . the only purpose for which power can be rightfully exercised over any member of a civilized community, against his will, is to prevent harm to others."[47] This is the guiding idea of this CDL. A state committed to it does not seek to make people morally autonomous but leaves them to live as they wish.[48] Put differently, such a state leaves people to live according to their conscience,[49] whether their consciences are rationally and autonomously developed or the result of socialization and indoctrination. This CDL, in other words, requires respect for persons *as they are – which is to say it requires toleration of people acting on their own actual wishes*.[50] The limit, again, is behavior that is harmful – that is, we need not tolerate behavior that wrongfully sets back the interests of others.[51] Joey's stabbing innocent Rachel is a harm; a tree branch on my property falling on my head is not – though it is a hurt or setback of interests. In this CDL, conduct should be tolerated unless it causes or is likely to cause harm in this sense. On this view, laws are just if they are in accord with this requirement. This means the state must not have a law requiring interference except to prevent or rectify harm.

To be clear, this view does not deny autonomy is a value, but recognizes that it is not *valued by* or *important for* all. It is consistent with this to insist that autonomy has great intrinsic and instrumental value. However, that claim does not entail that all should be autonomous. Certainly, some who are not autonomous and do not value autonomy probably should – they may well live better lives if they were autonomous. But this is a contingent claim, and surely there are some for whom living autonomously means living less well than living non-autonomously – whether because they fare better in a group with others where no one is autonomous or because they themselves are not capable of meeting the challenges that autonomy raises. Kukathas gives us an example of the former – Australian Aborigines who "follow up The Dreaming" rather than determine for themselves what they should pursue.[52] Examples of the second sort, for better or worse, live all around us. These are individuals who despite extensive attempts to educate them, make life mistake after life mistake. They take out the wrong sort of mortgages, have children they cannot give appropriate attention to, spend money on frivolities when necessities are lacking, etc. Such individuals are striving (perhaps) to "make it on their own" but fail time and time again. Some will say that society failed to educate them well enough. It is unclear, though, why we should not instead think society failed them by trying to educate them so as to be autonomous.[53] Perhaps a different sort of education – one wherein they learned to abide by simple rules or mimic someone else – would have been better suited. Admittedly, this is conjecture, but conjecture is all we have here.[54]

The original Rawlsian CDL may seek to make people morally autonomous. PL explicitly seeks only to guarantee political autonomy, satisfied that people know they can vote and move (etc.) as they wish (this presumably provides respect for persons). Guaranteeing political autonomy, though, is likely to cause spillover effects wherein people become autonomous in more areas of their lives than PL ostensibly requires (it is also based on the idea that people are to be respected *as free and equal* as characterized in endnote 50). The thin CDL discussed here does not promote even the more minimal form of autonomy. Admittedly, there is a paradox in that if citizens are not autonomous, they can't (autonomously) decide if they want to be. This means that this form of liberalism cannot guarantee that individuals will pursue the lives they would pursue autonomously. This, in turn, means that their families or communities may retain a large degree of control over them. How can this be permissible? How can we sit back and allow families or religious or cultural groups to indoctrinate children such that said children would never choose to leave them or join some other group?[55] Simply put, we must allow that people are necessarily socialized by others and if an individual is socialized in such a way that she will not consider leaving her family or group, we must recognize that this is something important about *her* as the person she has become and we would fail to show her respect if we insisted that there is something wrong with her because *we think* she cannot possibly be consensually in her group.[56] We must accept that she does consent. We may, of course, condemn and seek to change the social-ization process,[57] but to insist that the individual would not consent *if she weren't who she is* is to engage in a *non sequitur*. More to the point here, forcing her to become autonomous would be harming her *as she is* by forcing her to live against her conscience; it would be to discount and set back the interests she currently has without concern for what she wants. This is not a way to show her respect; respecting persons *is* respecting them *as they are*.

The thin CDL discussed here tolerates more diversity than autono-mist CDL or PL because it accepts that if individuals are content with (acquiesce to) the lives they lead,[58] they should be tolerated as the people they are. They should be free to act *in accord with their conscience*. Both the individual who has her autonomy infringed against her will and the individual who has his autonomy *promoted* against his will have their interests set back. This thin CDL opposes both.[59] If, though, an individual opposes the way they are (presum-ably being forced to be) living their own life, they would be expressing autonomy and that should be protected – in such cases interference (by the state or otherwise) is permissible, in accord with the harm principle. There, toleration rightfully ends. Either way, people can live according to their conscience. This is interestingly in agreement with PL. "Respecting others as persons and as citizens involves allowing them to non-coercively decide their values and (within limits of justice) act on their chosen ways of life."[60] As already indicated, we might doubt that PL lives up to that promise.

Let's take stock one last time before concluding. CDL has independently defended principles indicating when limits of toleration have been transgressed. The thin CDL discussed in this section is no exception. Its principles, though, require much more toleration than the autonomist CDL discussed earlier. Indeed, it manages to require more toleration than PL as it does not insist on political autonomy or on treating people as free and equal (and has no bargaining table from which to exclude the unreasonable).

CONCLUSION

The view just discussed may not properly be a CDL since it doesn't tell people what to do in many areas of their lives (other than telling them that they ought not interfere with others). Indeed, some think it is the "distinctive and defining feature of political liberalism" that it not "invoke any particular conception of the good life,"[61] so this view may seem like a PL. Still, it is not a PL if PL only endorses values derived from an overlapping consensus – which, as we saw, Larmore denies. The core value of this CDL is the freedom from harm that is entailed by the respect given persons *as the persons they are* rather than the persons they could be if fully autonomous or otherwise perfected – and this is not a value derived from an overlapping consensus. It is a conception "of what is of value in human life"[62] taken broadly (though it offers no means of specifying how individual humans should live, leaving that to individuals, families, and communities, it provides a normative limit to what must be tolerated). Having such a value is, we are told, part of what it is to be a CDL. If, though, Larmore is right that even PL has a core value – respect for persons (presumably in an idealized form as being free and equal) – that is not derived from an overlapping consensus, then reliance on overlapping consensus to defend its core value is not a distinguishing feature of PL. If this is right, then the thin CDL discussed here may well be a form of PL. If that is the case, its insistence on respect for persons as they are rather than as they could be differentiates at least from Rawls's PL.

Whether the thin CDL discussed here is a form of PL or of CDL is not of much importance. We might call it *substantive* liberalism (SL), as it relies on a substantive defense of its core value – freedom from harm – and recognizes that value may be controversial. That value must be defended on objective grounds that all *should be able to accept*, but such acceptance is not essential to SL. SL does not insist that people are unreasonable (though they may be) if they reject it, but does not allow them to interfere with the state policy of toleration it requires (nor does SL justify any other state interference in their lives).

We conclude by briefly considering the paradox of liberalism. We can put the paradox simply: Persons living in a liberal state who are militantly anti-liberal should either be tolerated or not. If tolerated, nonliberalism – which limits toleration – is allowed. If not tolerated, the state is nonliberal. The paradox is supposedly embarrassing to liberalism since it is a commitment to toleration, which is curtailed either way.[63] The paradox supposedly shows that the range of toleration – and hence liberty – that liberalism allows is not so extensive. Can a liberal state outlaw those seeking to end its rule?

How would each of the three views discussed answer this question? Consider a fictitious aboriginal group in the United States whose members do not value autonomy but who act in accord with the dreams of their leader,[64] and who believe that doing so is necessary for salvation. To embellish the case further, imagine that the dreams require that all blue-eyed people must wait to eat until all of the brown-eyed people have eaten. This is the only way the blue-eyed are treated as second class, but it remains deeply ingrained in the group – accepted by brown-and blue-eyed people alike. The group members realize they can't enforce this rule on the rest of us, but they would if they could. They sometimes try political campaigns to pass a law making violation of the requirement a criminal offense (out of concern for the rest of us – they want us all to go to heaven and believe this requires abidance with this rule).

The three views – autonomist CDL, PL, and SL – are united in that they would not tolerate the passage of a law requiring abidance with the rule just discussed since it would impose a decidedly nonliberal requirement on unwilling agents. The autonomist CDL would not even tolerate an abidance requirement for those *within* the group since it would infringe their moral autonomy (autonomous choice to abide by the rule would be tolerated). The PL *might* tolerate the abidance requirement within the group if its members retained political autonomy and the democratic system was not otherwise hindered. The SL would tolerate the abidance requirement within the group so long as it involves no harm to others and all who are in the group are in it in accord with their own consciences so that they have no interests wrongly set back. The SL is not concerned to promote moral or political autonomy of any agent unless that agent has an actual interest in such autonomy – in which case, the interference permitted is the prevention of a harm that is the hindering of the relevant form of autonomy.

So, the blunt question: What should the liberal say to those seeking to end its rule? The CDL clearly has no qualms using state force to maintain the liberal regime. Unsurprisingly, though, the PL says the same thing. In that view,

> Democratic citizens and government officials ... can always argue about and contest the laws and the correct understanding of constitutional provisions, and even the alternative liberal conceptions of justice that are appealed to in public reason to justify laws. What they cannot do ... is contest liberalism itself, or provide reasons incompatible with a liberal constitution.[65]

The CDL will protect the liberal regime in the name of its underlying value – in the case of the autonomist CDL, that is autonomy and in the case of SL, it is freedom from harm. The former endorses a particular conception of the good life that some might reject, but the latter does not; it requires only that all non-harmful behaviors be tolerated. According to the SL, the state justifiably interferes to prevent harm – and this includes preventing an overthrow of the regime since such an overthrow would likely itself include harms and would leave a path for further harms (after all, the *raison d'etre* of the regime is harm prevention).

All three liberal theories we've discussed would respond to the paradox of liberalism by insisting on maintaining the liberal regime. The two CDLs (autonomism and SL) do this in the name of their underlying values; the PL does much the same – with its underlying value being political autonomy or respect for persons. This is no embarrassment for liberals; it is merely commitment to liberalism. Importantly, though, the theories we've discussed have different limits of toleration within that constraint. SL tolerates more than PL. PL likely tolerates more than the autonomist CDL. The question that cannot be answered here is simply "which view, with its limits on toleration, is the best view for a liberal to adopt?"

NOTES

1. Hampton, "Should Political Philosophy Be Done without Metaphysics?" p. 802. See also Kukathas, *The Liberal Archipelago*; Barry, *Culture and Equality*; and Tan, *Toleration, Diversity and Global Justice*.
2. This distinction is now common, though different names are used for each of the views. PL is often called *public reason* liberalism, for reasons that will become apparent. CDL is sometimes called *perfectionist* liberalism, as some believe that endorsement of any political principle that does not emerge from public reason is tantamount to an endorsement of a conception of the good. (As will be clear, I believe this is a mistake.) I should also note that I use the acronyms CDL and PL (and, later, SL) for both liberalisms and liberals (views and advocates). When I use "CD" it can be either a liberal or nonliberal comprehensive doctrine.
3. In a society with many people actively wanting to murder others, not tolerating that sort of activity would amount to not tolerating many acts. While I am inclined to think that a society with fewer reasons for non-toleration is a society with more toleration, this will depend on the nature of those reasons.
4. Cohen, "What Toleration Is." There I also argue that the act must take place in a "situation of diversity."
5. Margaret Gilbert, Michael Bratman, and others argue that groups can have collective intentions. Even if those views make sense of some groups having intentions, making the case that *states* can have intentions *of the same sort* you and I have is more difficult. I assume states do not have intentions in anything but an attenuated sense – agents of the state have intentions and they may want it to be *as if* the state has particular intentions – but my central claim does not depend on this.
6. Rawls, *Political Liberalism*, p. 13.
7. *Ibid.*, p. 175.
8. Mills, "'Not a Mere Modus Vivendi,'"p. 191.
9. Davis and Neufeld, "Political Liberalism, Civic Education, and Educational Choice," p. 50.
10. Cohen, "Truth and Public Reason," p. 12.
11. In 1999, Rawls backed away from this, allowing that such claims can be used in public discourse in nonideal circumstances if they are supplemented by public reasons "in due course." See "The Idea of Public Reason Revisited," pp. 584 and 591–94.

12. On a different sort of PL view, what matters is that all reasonable persons (and their CDs) accept the basic political principles of the society, though they accept those principles for their own (different) reasons. Rawls sometimes writes as if this is his view; talk of an "overlapping consensus" suggests it. See Wenar, "Political Liberalism," pp. 53–54. For clear statements differentiating the two sorts of views, see D'Agostino, *Free Public Reason*, p. 30 and Nagel, "Moral Conflict and Political Legitimacy," p. 218.

13. We cannot survey all CDLs here. Nor can we survey all PLs. It should be remembered, though, that the overlapping consensus that emerges in a society would depend on the extant CDs within it. At the theoretical level, though, how best to understand the process by which an overlapping consensus is derived is a matter for debate – William Galston, Jerry Gaus, Jurgen Habermas, and Charles Larmore offer important and interesting alternatives. (There is also disagreement about how best to interpret Rawls's PL.)

14. More precisely, they (or Rawlsian PLs, anyway) won't defend principles of justice and constitutional essentials that would support such criminalization (etc.) without reasons acceptable to all reasonable CDs.

15. I am not claiming there are cases of type X.

16. See Freeman, "Public Reason and Political Justification," p. 236.

17. *Ibid.*, p. 228.

18. It is not clear what this means for the abortion case specified. If there are no public reasons for laws against abortion, the PL would be unable to endorse such laws. But if there are no public reasons for laws *permitting* abortion, the PL would be unable to endorse *those* laws. This is an old problem in new guise: if law allows abortion, the Roman Catholic's view is rejected for purposes of law; if the law outlaws abortion, the utilitarian's view is.

19. See, for example, Rawls, *A Theory of Justice*, p. 302.

20. *Ibid.*, p. 515.

21. In addition to the choice of the two principles, Rawls discusses a "constitutional convention," a "legislative stage," and a stage wherein rules derived in the prior stages are applied and followed (*ibid.*, pp. 195–201). For simplicity's sake, I will assume the two principles and the constitutional essentials determine what is tolerated.

22. We can talk of a *contrast of autonomy and toleration*: if toleration is the preeminent value, autonomy and non-autonomy can both be tolerated; if autonomy is, non-autonomy cannot (cf. Tan, *Toleration, Diversity and Global Justice*, p. 51).

23. In his *Political Realism*, Rawls attributes this view to Kant and Mill: "the ethical values of autonomy and individuality, which may apply to the whole of life, both social and individual, as expressed by the

comprehensive liberalisms of Kant and Mill" (p. 78). The attribution to Mill is mistaken since "Mill was almost obsessively concerned ... with keeping the state out of any attempt to mould character" (Barry, *Culture and Equality*, p. 119).

24. See Rawls, *Political Liberalism*, pp. 29–35.

25. As an exception, he claims justice as fairness is but one of "a family" of PL views in "The Idea of Public Reason Revisited," p. 581.

26. More clearly, the core political principles must be justified by public reason, and the laws must be in accord with the core principles. For simplicity's sake, I will assume public reason determines what is to be tolerated.

27. Rawls, *Political Liberalism*, pp. 77ff.

28. See Rawls, "The Idea of Public Reason Revisited," p. 581.

29. *Ibid.*, p. 597.

30. *Ibid.*, p. 78.

31. This seems to me a *false promise of political liberalism* – one that cannot be fulfilled. See Wenar, "Political Liberalism" for further defense than I offer in what follows. See Gaus, *The Order of Public Reason* for perhaps the most impressive attempt to date to defend a version of PL (with many differences from Rawls's) that may avoid this problem. See especially pp. 359–68.

32. These include, but are not limited to, the facts that evidence is "conflicting and complex," that people disagree about the weight any given consideration should have, that concepts are vague, and that our upbringing affects how we assess evidence. (See Rawls, *Political Liberalism*, pp. 56–57.)

33. *Ibid.*, pp. 58–59.

34. Tan, *Toleration, Diversity and Global Justice*, p. 54.

35. Friedman, "John Rawls and the Political Coercion of Unreasonable People," p. 17.

36. Scalet, "Legitimacy, Confrontation Respect, and the Bind of Freestanding Liberalism," p. 96.

37. *Ibid.*, pp. 102–104.

38. Friedman, "John Rawls and the Political Coercion of Unreasonable People," p. 22.

39. *Ibid.*, p. 31.

40. Hartley and Watson, "Feminism, Religion, and Shared Reasons," p. 515.

41. PLs will say that holders of unreasonable doctrines are to be respected in a PL society – insisting, for example, that they have the rights and liberties accorded everyone else. The disrespect indicated above is, we can say, at a different level. CDs deemed unreasonable are given no truck in PL theorizing about what the state should be and those adhering to such CDs are thought to somehow be deficient in adhering to them.

42. Perhaps there will be policies requiring enough education so that all could be good citizens – for example, giving them the ability to critically reason (so as to vote well). This, combined with being taught they have state-protected civil rights (even against their own families and CD-groups), could lead them to exit their CD: upon critically analyzing their CD, they may find it lacking; given knowledge of their rights, they may exercise them. There is much written about this. See Gutmann, "Civic Education and Social Diversity" for an excellent defense of the claim here and Davis and Neufeld, "Political Liberalism, Civic Education, and Educational Choice" for some response (not meant as a full defense of PL).

43. Even parties behind a veil of ignorance would, I think, worry about the survivability of reasonable CDs, since they know the persons they represent might be committed to one (see Rawls, *Political Liberalism*, pp. 22–28 and 304–10).

44. Larmore, "The Moral Basis of Political Liberalism," p. 608, emphasis added. Ultimately, Larmore tells us, it is Rawls's liberal principle of legitimacy that does the moral work, "as it expresses in effect the idea of respect for persons" (*ibid.*, p. 610).

45. We can frame this differently, in terms more amenable to Larmore's argument. PL ultimately relies on respect for persons and this may well be a thinner requirement than moral autonomy. Whether it is as thin as political autonomy is meant to be, I leave to the side.

46. There are affinities between this approach and Dworkin's neutralist approach, which is another form of non-perfectionism.

47. Mill, *On Liberty*, p. 9.

48. It may be that this indirectly results in the development of autonomy in some, but only because they are left alone and people left alone often strive to improve themselves.

49. In this way, this thin CDL has antecedents in the writings of Baruch Spinoza, Pierre Bayle, and John Locke, as well as Mill. It also bears a resemblance to Kukathas's recent view in *The Liberal Archipelago*.

50. By contrast, an autonomist CDL – including that of early Rawls – requires respect for persons as autonomous agents, whether they are autonomous, want to be autonomous, or would be better off being autonomous. Even Rawls's PL seems to require respect for persons not as they are but as something more idealized – as free and equal, whether they are, whether they want to be, or whether they are better off that way. The CDL discussed in this section is, I think, "thinner" than both the autonomist CDL and PL precisely because its concern is with harm to persons *as they are* rather than persons in some idealized way. While it's true that what counts as harm – i.e., what counts as wrongful and a

setback to interests – is controversial, harm is the only element of this view that would be controversial, whereas the other views also require defense of their idealizations of persons. The idea for this endnote was prompted by discussion with Stephen Herman; I appreciate that discussion.

51. See Feinberg, *Harm to Others*, p. 36.
52. Kukathas, *The Liberal Archipelago*, p. 102, quoting Maddock; see also Lomasky, *Persons, Rights and the Moral Community*, pp. 42–47.
53. I here switch from autonomy as a capacity to autonomy as a goal (or success term). I do not think this is a problem as it is the fact that such people continually fail to succeed when acting on their capacity to act autonomously that suggests they do not sufficiently have that capacity.
54. I should add that what I say in this paragraph is not intended as a value judgment ranking those without autonomy lower than those with. The judgment is only that some can live *better* lives without living autonomously than they would live if required to be autonomous.
55. The remainder of the paragraph is adapted from Cohen, "What the Liberal State Should Tolerate Within Its Borders," pp. 503–504.
56. See Meyers, *Self, Society and Personal Choice*, p. xi.
57. I doubt we should seek to change the world such that are all are socialized to be autonomous – for the reasons just discussed.
58. While Rawls might oppose this in other arenas, he tells us that "traditional gendered division of labor within families ... adopted by people on the basis of their religion" could be "fully voluntary" ("The Idea of Public Reason Revisited," p. 599). Surely, this is nothing more than acquiescence.
59. The issue is somewhat more complicated because of the status of children. On this account, parents can raise their children as they wish *so long as they do not harm them*. Raising a child to be autonomous may have value, but absent an argument that it is necessarily wrongful and necessarily sets back the interests of every child to fail to do so, a policy of interference (educationally or otherwise) to make children autonomous will not be accepted. Of course, in particular cases, a parent will be wronging their child by not raising her to be autonomous. But, per the discussion above, it may also be that in particular cases, a parent wrongs a child by raising him to be autonomous.
60. Freeman, "Public Reason and Political Justification," p. 233.
61. Gutmann, "Civic Education and Social Diversity," p. 560.
62. Rawls, *Political Liberalism*, p. 13, quoted in the first section above.
63. This description is adapted from Cohen, "Toleration."
64. The group as specified is fictitious but modeled on Australian Aborigines mentioned above.
65. Freeman, "Public Reason and Political Justification," p. 241.

9 Liberalism and equality

"Liberalism is the conjunction of two ideals," Thomas Nagel once wrote.[1] The two he had in mind were roughly an ideal of free speech and individual liberty and an ideal of a democratic society controlled by its members, in which inequalities of wealth and privilege are not excessive. It is hard to know how to individuate and count ideals; perhaps Nagel's characterization already collects several. One might see liberalism as a jumble of disparate ideals, loosely held together, or alternatively as a bundle of ideals and values unified in one coherent doctrine. On either characterization, liberalism combines several distinct norms, and the perennial question is how to find a proper balance among them. Of course, nowadays and in the past, people use the term "liberal" with different meanings, sometimes with honorific connotation, sometimes pejorative. So focusing energy on the question "What's a liberal?" can seem a fool's errand.

In this chapter I simply stipulate that liberal political doctrines are those that affirm that people have moral rights to core individual freedoms, including freedom of thought, expression, and culture, freedom of organization and assembly and public protest, the rule of law including the right to a fair trial, wide individual liberty to live as one chooses provided one does not harm others, and rights of private ownership of resources, freedom of contract and market trading, and careers open to talents on a nondiscriminatory basis. These rights to freedom are assigned high priority and not easily overridden. All normally competent adult members of society equally possess these rights to basic freedoms. All of us have a duty to respect and, up to some point, to promote these individual rights, both when acting as individuals and when acting on others through the state.

An important division in liberalism centers on whether one regards these core rights and duties as matters of deontological rule that figure in the formulation of fundamental moral principles or whether, instead, they are seen as means to the further moral goals of promoting individual human flourishing, people leading good lives with goods fairly distributed. In the tradition of John Locke and Immanuel Kant, the liberal freedoms state basic moral requirements; in the tradition of John Stuart Mill, they are means, and the reasons for embracing them are a matter of empirical lore not basic moral principle. The position you take as to how the various components of the basic liberties should be weighed and balanced depends in part on whether you take them to be instrumentally or noninstrumentally morally valuable (or both).

Another important division in liberal thought is between those who affirm and those who deny that what we owe one another includes a strong, expansive, and stringent beneficence requirement. This division tends to coincide with splits between left-wing and right-wing liberals, and overlaps somewhat with the different distinction between egalitarian and nonegalitarian liberalisms that is the subject matter of this chapter.

Everyone equally possesses the core moral rights to individual liberties. On this point there is general agreement. Does the best, most compelling and appealing version of liberal doctrine encompass requirements of equality of other sorts? If so, which equalities matter? On these questions, opinions diverge widely. Below I list and characterize some types of equality that some versions of liberalism embrace. In the rest of the chapter, I look at what might be said for and against egalitarian liberalisms.

1. Some embrace democratic political equality: each person has a right to an equal vote in majority-rule elections that select (a) top political officials who administer the laws and public policies and (b) the legislators who will (perhaps in conjunction with some top elected administrators) determine the content of public policies and laws.

2. Some embrace (usually in addition to 1) the idea that to some degree there should be equality of rank, power, and status among members of society and that in these ways members of society should relate as equals.

3. Some embrace the idea that to render the core freedoms substantive and not merely formal, society should be arranged so that all have adequate material means and developed skills so as to be able to make effective use of these freedoms. All should have substantive or real freedom, where one has the real freedom to go to Paris just in case there is some course of action one can choose and execute such that if one chooses and executes this course of action one gets to Paris and if one does not choose and execute it, one does not get to Paris. Having "adequate" material means and skills might be interpreted as having them at a good enough threshold level or as having them at an overall equal or close to equal level.

4. Some embrace, beyond equality of opportunity as nondiscrimination and careers open to talents, a norm of substantive equality of opportunity. In a weak form this requires that all have some opportunity to become qualified in the ways that render one successful in competitions for positions of special advantage, such as student slots in colleges and universities, access to business loans for entrepreneurial purposes, and desirable posts in business firms and public agencies. In a strong form this requires that all individuals with the same native talent and the same ambition to succeed should have the same chances of competitive success (independently of their social class, sex and sexual orientation, ethnicity and supposed race, and so on).

5. Some embrace an egalitarian or prioritarian beneficence norm that requires that actions be taken and institutions and practices arranged to help those who would otherwise be worse off than others in well-being prospects. Such a norm might demand flat equality of condition (or priority-weighted maximization of condition) or instead equality of opportunity for well-being (or priority-weighted maximization of such opportunity). The measure of people's condition for an equality norm might be resource holdings or some other alternative, rather than well-being.

These various ways in which core liberalism might be enriched – or corrupted, depending on your point of view – by egalitarian infusions are overshadowed by two possible extensions of the scope of application of the doctrine. The two extensions are across space and across time. Liberalism in normative political theory is a doctrine developed in the context of reflection and deliberation about suitable political arrangements and basic institutions for a single sovereign nation. Questions about secession and immigration reveal that taking a unified nation-state as the unit of analysis takes a lot for granted. But anyway the ideas that people have basic rights to liberty that others should respect and needs that should prompt concern in others do not seem to encounter any natural barriers to their extended application. The rights do not stop at any borders.

This point is already explicit in John Locke's *Second Treatise of Government*, standardly regarded as a canonical text in the liberal tradition. The natural moral law that regulates our dealings with one another binds us regardless of positive law or convention.[2] But his emphasis is on limited government and on the conditions that must hold if consent to government is to make sense.

On the face of it, the rights and responsibilities and entitlements that liberalism posits hold without spatial limit, for practical purposes across the entire globe, and without temporal limit, giving us duties to future generations. However, once you actually try to extend the principles in these natural ways, their character is significantly altered, in ways that we are just beginning to acknowledge and understand. Although liberalism is transformed when it becomes a doctrine of global and intergenerational justice, and surely should be so transformed, this chapter remains focused on the case of a single nation-state in isolation.

The question arises, on what basis do we regard all persons as possessing a fundamental equal status and deserving some form of equal concern? If we say, we are all human, the claim looks narrowly chauvinistic. If we say, any being that possesses (enough) rational agency capacities is a person, and on this basis qualifies for a fundamental equal status, it is not clear why differences among persons along the various dimensions of rational agency capacity above whatever threshold is deemed to mark the personhood level do not render persons fundamentally *unequal* in status and deserving of *unequal* concern. This is an important and unsettled question, but not one this chapter considers.

AUTONOMY

To make effective use of the freedoms and opportunities a liberal society provides, individuals must be educated and socialized so that they have capacities to choose well and to be resolute in carrying out chosen plans and must also be disposed to exercise these capacities. To fulfill the responsibilities of democratic citizenship, individuals need civic virtues including abilities to understand public affairs and the disposition to pay attention to them. In a word, individuals need to become autonomous.[3] These are platitudes, but the policies they demand are controversial.

An aspect of egalitarianism appears on this scene if one affirms that society is obligated to bring it about, so far as is practically possible, that each individual becomes autonomous or self-governing at least at a threshold level. On that view, we owe everyone equally a good enough level of autonomy. That view is controversial. Liberals in the libertarian camp (both left libertarians and right libertarians) can accept that parents, who choose to act in ways that may foreseeably bring a child into existence, have duties to raise the child properly, but tend to deny that the rest of us have any back-up or complementary child-rearing duties. This is an important instance of the division in liberalism between those who accept and those who deny that beneficence duties are central parts of the enforceable core of morality, not merely supererogatory optional frills.

The moral requirement to protect and promote each individual's autonomy has implications for child rearing. The duty to raise children so that they become autonomous applies first to parents or recognized guardians of the child. For those who accept a general beneficence requirement to ensure that all children are properly raised, society at large has a duty to help with child rearing and, as part of that duty, to promote children's autonomy. A plausible empirical surmise is that the duty requires training children in critical reasoning skills and encouraging them to think for themselves and acquainting them with the wide variety of values and principles and doctrines that have been foundational for different people's choices and ways of life. Arguably training for autonomy also involves inculcating in children some particular plausible set of values as well as the disposition to scrutinize it and to revise it as seems fit. Some see here a potential conflict between the duty to train for autonomy and the claimed right of any competent parents to raise their children as they choose within broad limits, this right being understood to encompass a right to do whatever they deem necessary to ensure that children internalize and follow the parents' ethical outlook. This conflict pretty much disappears if the right to indoctrinate one's children in one's own cherished values is strictly subordinate to the prior right of the child to become an autonomous individual. The parents and society (all of us regarded collectively) both have the duty to foster autonomy in the child, and the duty of society becomes stringent if the parent lacks the will, the competence, or the resources to do this effectively.

The duty to promote autonomy is a close companion of the duty to secure the child's right to an open future.[4] I could be disposed and able to choose well, but lack the skills to prosper in any but a very narrow range of life choices. The right to an open future is the right to be trained in general-purpose skills so that a fair share of the options that are open for choice in the society one inhabits are within one's reach and grasp. Here the right to an open future in its egalitarian guise – everyone equally has a right to a good enough set of opportunities, or to a set of opportunities equally as good as anyone else's – blends into substantive equality of opportunity norms.

EQUALITY AS NO-MASTERY

John Locke vigorously affirms a conception of equality in chapter 2 of his *Second Treatise of Government*:

To understand political power right, and derive it from its original, we must consider, what state all men are naturally in, and that is, a *state of perfect freedom* to order their actions, and dispose of their possessions and persons, as they think fit, within the bounds of the law of nature, without asking leave, or depending on the will of any other man.

He immediately adds that this is

A *state* also *of equality*, wherein all the power and jurisdiction is reciprocal; there being nothing more evident, than that creatures of the same species and rank, promiscuously born to all the same advantages of nature, and the use of the same faculties, should also be equal one amongst another without subordination or subjection.[5]

Call this conception *equality as equal no-mastery*. No person is initially subject to the authority of any other person, and none is required to obey the commands of any other person. Each is perfectly free to live as she chooses and act as she chooses within the limits of the moral law.

Locke's ideas stated here cast a long shadow on subsequent liberal thought. Switching the metaphor, I note also that the tensions between the different thoughts banded together in this short passage reverberate throughout the rest of Locke's own *Second Treatise* and beyond.

One thought is the rejection of natural aristocracy and natural privilege. The justification of political authority, whatever it might turn out to be, cannot amount to telling the peasants, the order of society works out well for the nobles and the high-born, and it is morally appropriate that you low-born types labor for their benefit. The justification of imposing a social order and a set of social duties on people has to appeal to principles that give equal consideration to the interests of all affected people, regardless of their rank, social position, class status, or initial place in any social hierarchy. Social arrangements must be justifiable to all in terms of fair and impartial moral principles. A different thought is that so long as you act in ways that do not violate the natural moral rights of others, no others have the right to coerce you to induce you to behave as they wish, unless you agree by your free voluntary choice to be subject to the will of specific others.[6]

The two thoughts are potentially in tension. If all persons were fully rational and moral, then they would only voluntarily agree to social arrangements that include a government that promotes the common good and that respects and protects everyone's fundamental moral rights, if these are the arrangements that would be singled out by moral principles that are justifiable to all in terms of fair and impartial moral principles. But suppose, as is surely the case, that we are not all fully rational and moral and that individuals differ widely in the degree to which they are fully rational and moral. Then some of us by free and voluntary choice may subject ourselves to a government that does not promote the common good and respect and protect human rights. It might well be that under a wide range of circumstances some of us would not freely and voluntarily agree to the authority of a government that would be well functioning in moral terms.

Locke himself fails to acknowledge the tension and clearly give priority to one or another element in equal no-mastery. He emphatically asserts that no one is bound to obey government decrees except by his free and voluntary consent.[7] But he develops a notion of tacit consent according to which it seems that simply being the recipient of benefits that a tolerably just government supplies can generate obligations to conform to the laws the government enacts independently of any action or choice that amounts to voluntary acceptance of benefits. This formulation read literally seems to withdraw the free and voluntary consent requirement for political obligation and to anticipate principles of fair play and effective rights protection as possible grounding for political obligation.

EQUALITY AND "POLITICAL LIBERALISM"

The Lockean norm of equal no-mastery can be interpreted in still another way that yields a distinct and different liberal ideal of equality. The idea here is that we are all free and equal in the sense that no one has the right to impose her own interpretation of moral requirements on others who disagree.[8] When people disagree, insisting that "this is what morality demands" and forcing compliance with that is simply self-aggrandizement or rule by the stronger.

Pushed too far, this idea is ludicrous. It is surely not wrong to force me to desist from killing innocent people even though my conscience tells me that God demands human sacrifice. The ideal then is transmuted into the claim that people should not be forced to conform to moral rules that can only be justified by appeal to principles that some people can reasonably reject. Applied to the state, this ideal becomes a norm of liberal legitimacy: it is morally illegitimate to wield state power in ways that can only be justified, if at all, by appeal to principles that some people subject to this coercion can reasonably reject.[9]

There is an ambiguity in the liberal legitimacy norm as just stated. On one interpretation, it states that some moral disagreement is not rationally resolvable, and that at the end of the day, after the most ideal and protracted scrutiny and deliberation, fully reasonable people will disagree about the correctness of some candidate moral principles, and no principle that cannot attract unanimous acceptance among fully reasonable people is a proper basis of state policy.

To this, one might wonder how fully reasonable people could disagree in perpetuity, rather than recognize that none of the views under dispute can be known to be uniquely correct. Further, if this is so, why not say that organizing society on the basis of any set of principles that does no worse than any other candidate set at attracting the assent of the fully reasonable is morally permissible?

On a second interpretation, the liberal legitimacy norm says that if people's ethical views are reasonable enough, even if not fully reasonable (that is, would not survive full rational scrutiny), it would be illegitimate, hence wrong, to use state power to force them to conform to rules against their conscientious beliefs. Again, an ambiguity surfaces. "Reasonable enough" can mean "close in content to what is really reasonable." But if my incorrect views are close in substance to what is being enforced, why think there is anything seriously problematic about forcing me to conform? "Reasonable enough" can mean "reasonable enough in the process of one's practical reasoning." However, if my reasoning is moderately good (though imperfect) but leads me to embrace (say) racist views that are egregiously wrong, again, it is not clear at all that there is anything even slightly morally wrong with coercing me to conform to the nonracist better views.

A third interpretation of reasonable rejectability avoids this last implication.[10] On this interpretation, reasonable rejectability is a mixed idea that combines insistence on a moral minimum and an epistemic norm: Views that are egregiously, flagrantly wrong, or morally beyond the pale, cannot be the basis for a reasonable rejectability claim, and in addition views that are reached by evidence-gathering and argument-assessing practices that do not meet a threshold standard of epistemic acceptability cannot be the basis of a reasonable rejectability claim. So perhaps racist views no matter how reasonable the epistemic process of their formation cannot be the basis of a reasonable rejectability claim. This third interpretation invites the objection that views that are morally wrong, but just short of qualifying as egregiously wrong, and epistemic processes that are inadequate, but not so bad as to fail to meet the good enough standard, can form the basis of a proper reasonable rejectability claim. However, using state power to enforce correct moral norms that are reasonably rejectable in this sense can still be morally acceptable.

EQUAL DEMOCRATIC RIGHTS

Liberals, by and large, are democrats. They favor a democratic state, in which top public officials and the legislators who (by majority vote) enact laws are selected by majority rule, with each adult citizen having an equal vote, and in elections conducted against a background of secure freedom of speech and assembly and freedom of political organization. There are many varieties of democratic political constitution. A political society can be more or less democratic, depending on the degree to which the features mentioned in this characterization are present. A society might be regarded as more or less democratic, depending on the degree to which one or more further conditions are satisfied: (i) Equal influence: All citizens with the same political talent and skill and the same ambition to influence political outcome have the same chances of influencing political outcomes. (ii) Wide scope: No issues are kept separate from control by elected legislators and top elected public officials and decided by some nondemocratic process. (iii) Deliberative politics: Political arrangements and public culture render it the case that significant political decisions are made only after extensive and wide-ranging political discussion in which all citizens are participants. (iv) No time gap: When majority rule in the relevant jurisdiction shifts concerning some substantive issue or on the question of whether an elected official or legislator should remain in office, public policies and laws immediately shift and unwanted officials and legislators are immediately replaced. Bringing about greater fulfillment of one of these democratic desiderata can require lesser fulfillment of others.

What justifies democracy? One view is that when conscientious citizens who are morally decent disagree about what public policies should be enacted and what candidate individual right should be politically enforced, the only fair way to proceed is to have a discussion and then take a vote, with all having an equal vote and majority rule settling the issues under review.[11] On this view, democracy gives each person living in a political community an equal say in political power, and giving some an unequal say would be intrinsically unfair.

This defense of the right to an equal say invites two criticisms. One is that if democracy is justified for an ideal community of conscientious voters, the justification does not smoothly carry over to actual circumstances in which members of society are not ideally conscientious, and majority rule can enact violations of people's moral rights. A second criticism is that even if voters are conscientious and try to vote for the common good, they may well fail to discern it, due to failure of moral insight, ignorance of relevant empirical facts, or inability sensibly to incorporate their factual knowledge into the determination of appropriate public policies and laws. So perhaps political power rightly belongs to conscientious moral and political experts, those who are most knowledgeable about the matters that bear on correct policy choice and disposed to use their knowledge to advance the common good.

An instrumentalist justification of democracy holds (1) that political arrangements should be set so that over time the consequences of their operation are morally better than the consequences that would be brought about by installing and maintaining any alternative political arrangements and (2) the consequences of installing and maintaining political democracy would be morally better than those that would result from the operation of any alternative regime. Claim 2 can be supported by showing that democracy tends to select better policies than alternative regimes, that installing democracy has other morally desirable effects such as improving the democratic citizens or by fostering wide social solidarity and diminishing people's sense of alienation from government authority, or by noting the difficulties of constructing elite rule mechanisms that do not in practice draw incompetent or immoral agents into elite rule roles.[12] An instrumentalist justification of democracy offers a method for deciding to what degree a political society in given circumstances ought to be democratic along various dimensions: put in place and sustain the version of democracy whose consequences will be best.

Hybrid views are possible. David Estlund argues that of the political systems that would not be morally illegitimate in virtue of being reasonably rejectable, democracy has epistemic virtues, and is likely to lead to the selection of better laws and public policies, and is justifiable on that basis.[13] He argues against rule by moral experts on the ground that any specification of a procedure to implement this idea would be reasonably rejectable in that it might conceivably operate in a way that was biased against the interest of some citizens. This defense of political democracy by appeal to the political liberalism legitimacy norm may be vulnerable to the criticisms of political liberalism already mentioned in this chapter under that heading.

A commitment to democracy can form the basis of a wider egalitarian ideal. The idea here is roughly that people ought to be treated as equals by giving each a democratic say in political decision making and by establishing and sustaining social and political arrangements that enable all members of society to relate as equals, on the footing of equal social status. In recent political thought this democratic equality ideal can be traced back to writing by Michael Walzer and more recently has been developed and defended by Elizabeth Anderson and by Samuel Scheffler.[14] Advocacy of equality of democratic status is, like any advocacy of equality for its own sake, subject to the leveling down objection, to be described below.[15]

EQUALITY OF CONDITION

Throughout its history, for better or worse, liberalism in its many ramifications and variations lacks a firm commitment to equality of condition. This is the idea that all persons deserve equal well-being or equal material resources (or equality according to some other measure of one's condition) and that social arrangements should promote and sustain this equality across persons. Put another way, the egalitarian ideal is that inequalities in people's condition should not be excessive, and that beyond the acceptable range, the greater the gap between the haves and the have-nots, the morally worse the situation is. A comment by George Orwell expresses the egalitarian conviction: "A fat man eating quails while children are begging for bread is a disgusting sight."[16]

The affirmation of the moral imperative of equality of condition is historically associated with left-wing criticisms of liberalism and capitalism. In the nineteenth century, the radical Karl Marx is an egalitarian and the liberal John Stuart Mill is not.[17] The same dialectic resounds in recent political philosophy. Thus G. A. Cohen faults the liberal political theorists John Rawls and Ronald Dworkin for embracing doctrines according to which a just society is fully compatible with the institutions of capitalism.[18] If the economic domain is organized around private ownership of resources and the free market, differences in people's initial wealth endowments, abilities, and luck in their circumstances and in the outcomes of their choices are bound to militate against equality of condition. Cohen upholds the intrinsic moral desirability of equality of condition and denies that a society that tolerates significant equality of condition can be fully just. It should be noted that although Cohen denies capitalism can be fully just, he does not rule out the possibility that in the actual circumstances we face, some form of capitalist institutions might deliver more justice than any feasible alternatives.

The picture just sketched is somewhat cartoonish and over-simplified but roughly correct. Qualifications need to be made and important details added. For starters, inequality of condition might arise from an initially equal (or fair) distribution followed by people choosing to use their resources in ways that would not seem to trigger any social justice demand for redistribution to restore equality or condition. Perhaps some are prudent ants who labor and save and some are imprudent grasshoppers who frolic and spend, as in Aesop's fable. Perhaps all engage reasonably in high-stakes gambling activity in which some win, some lose. Perhaps some reasonably pursue lucrative activities such as banking and lawyering and others reasonably pursue nonlucrative activities such as poetry and teaching. Suppose the result of these diverse choices is that both groups end up with lives they want, but with unequal bank account balances. In none of these examples, including others that might be adduced, does the demand for equality of condition that would undo the predictable results of these different choices as they play out in a fair framework for interaction much resemble a plausible demand for justice.

In response, the left-wing criticism of liberalism can be reformulated or perhaps just rephrased. The revised critics of liberalism hold that it is morally bad – unjust and unfair – if some are worse off than others through no choice or fault of their own. Justice requires equality of condition except insofar as inequality of condition obtains and those who are worse off than others are reasonably held responsible for their choices and for their overlooking of available choices that led to their being worse off. Here one is responsible for one's choice just in case any shortfall in one's condition that results from the choice does not trigger any obligation on the part of others to undo the shortfall. This position, known as luck egalitarianism, can be fitted out with various bells and whistles that introduce modulations in the ideal of personal responsibility that is attached to equality of condition.

The revised egalitarian – now luck egalitarian – critique of liberalism may have become more plausible in the character of the ideal that it upholds, but it now becomes an open question whether liberalism can accommodate the left-wing critique simply by accepting the revised ideal.[19] Maybe some version of luck egalitarianism should be added to the set of ideals and norms, the proper balancing among which determines the ideal shape of liberal principles.

Take the vexed and still poorly understood relationship between liberalism and the endorsement of capitalist institutions including robust private ownership of resources and the organization of economic life by voluntary, mutually beneficial agreements among private owners. Maybe some version of liberalism that takes luck egalitarianism on board will endorse a social democratic organization of society, in which a market economy based on private ownership delivers outcomes that are continually adjusted by tax and transfer policies that take resources from the more fortunate members of society for the benefit of the less fortunate. Maybe the residual inequalities of condition in such a system are ones that should elicit our acceptance not our resentment or indignation.

REAL FREEDOM

Another wrinkle in the picture comes into view when we ask what sort of freedom the liberal should anyway be upholding. Recall the Anatole France quip to the effect that the law in its majesty equally forbids rich people and tramps to sleep under bridges. A law that is formally impartial may bear down with cruel force on some people and not others depending on their circumstances. In other words, the equal freedoms and civil liberties that are at the core of the liberal ideal might turn out to be merely formal and not substantive. So let us distinguish formal and real (or effective) freedom. One is formally free to perform a given act just in case no applicable law forbids doing it and no one would interfere (in certain ways that count as wrongful) if one were to try to perform the act in question. One is really free to perform a given act just in case, if one chooses to do it, there is some available course of action one can choose and execute that will result in one's successful performance of the act.[20]

Simply marking this distinction is not to dismiss formal freedom as unimportant. It would be oppressive for state officials to forbid us from going on a pilgrimage to Lourdes from misplaced concern for our souls or from climbing Mount McKinley from hatred of outdoor activities even if we lack the money for passage to Lourdes or the ability to attain the McKinley summit. But real freedom also matters.

Among recent political theorists, John Rawls and Amartya Sen have perhaps done the most to show how a concern for real freedom might help us improve our understanding of social justice as interpreted within a framework of liberal ideas.[21] Rawls has a broader and a narrower proposal. The broader proposal appears in the course of his elaboration of the idea of a political conception of justice that can gain the acceptance of all reasonable people even though they disagree with each other in their ultimate moral values and their ideals of human good. His surmise is that justice demands that citizens regard one another as free and equal, that civil liberties and democratic rights be affirmed, and that institutions and practices are arranged so that all are enabled to gain access to sufficient material resources so that they can effectively make use of their liberties and freedoms. This formulation points toward the idea that justice demands that all have access to resources that enable them to have "enough" real freedom. This raises the question, how much is enough? Rawls's narrower and more specific proposal is known as the *difference* principle. This holds that provided basic freedoms are protected and provided that substantive equality of opportunity obtains (on which, see below), institutions should be set to make the worst-off social group as well off as possible, in terms of primary social goods. These are multipurpose resources, which any rational person will want. They include wealth and income, freedoms and opportunities. Rawls also affirms an alternate formulation of his principle of justice in distribution. This says that inequalities in primary social goods are unacceptable unless they are to the maximal advantage of the worst-off social group.

Sen criticizes the primary goods idea on the grounds that people differ in native abilities, and more broadly, in capacities that enable them to transform resources, in given circumstances, into achievements and enjoyments that they have reason to value.[22] For a simple example, suppose that two persons are similar in aims and traits except that one lacks functioning legs and the other has normal legs. With the same allotment of primary social goods, one must spend her resources on wheelchairs or other mobility devices, the other will get this for free and be able to attain greater fulfillment of her aims. The example generalizes, because people's traits vary along many dimensions in ways that matter. Justice requires taking account not only of the piles of resources people get but also of what each will be enabled to do with the resources she gets. In other words, primary goods are not the right measure of someone's condition for distributive justice purposes. Sen urges that we should measure people's condition in terms of their capacities to achieve functionings (ways of being and doing) they have reason to value.

The capability approach to social justice that Sen presents is further developed in writings by Martha Nussbaum.[23]

EQUALITY: DESIRABLE FOR ITS OWN SAKE OR INTRINSICALLY? REPLACEABLE BY PRIORITY?

The debate between the primary goods advocate and his critics is about how to assess people's condition for purposes of determining what we owe to them by way of egalitarian justice requirements. Any answer to this question of measurement can be paired with various answers to the question of what principle specifies just treatment of people according to this measure. A straightforwardly egalitarian principle holds that everyone should have the same, or equal opportunity for the same. Another candidate answer within the broadly egalitarian family is sufficiency: everyone should have enough, or have access to enough.

The proposal that equality is per se morally desirable, even as one value among others, is subject to the leveling down objection.[24] If equality is valuable, then achieving equality by making better-off people worse off without making worse-off people in any way better off would be in one way morally valuable, even if not acceptable all things considered. The objection is that leveling down is in no respect desirable, so equality cannot be per se valuable.

A perhaps apocryphal story is told of an egalitarian activist, call him Fred, in an Israeli kibbutz during the early days of the Israeli state in Palestine. The kibbutz members live communally and are committed to equality of condition. Late one night a chink-chink-chink sound is heard in the communal kitchen. Upon investigation it turns out that what people are hearing is Fred systematically knocking the handles off the unchipped cups in the communal kitchen. He had noticed some cups had lost their handles, inducing an inequality, and he was acting to restore equality of condition. This is the leveling down spirit.

If equality of condition is not per se morally valuable, then neither is luck egalitarianism – equality of condition modified by some doctrine of personal responsibility – per se morally valuable. The leveling down objection at this point appears to leave the left-wing critique of liberalism in a shambles.

These appearances may be deceiving. Left-wing criticisms of liberal institutions and the behaviors of individuals in liberal societies do not tend unequivocally to insist on equality of condition as noninstrumentally morally valuable. When Orwell finds it repulsive that people are sitting in restaurants eating fancy food while people elsewhere are living in horribly grim conditions, he is surely envisaging that there are alternative social arrangements in which the well-off people share resources with the badly off and the condition of the badly off dramatically improves. Also, a slightly subtler point, surely Orwell is also supposing that there is some rearrangement that would improve the condition of the worse off that would be stable through time. He is not recommending redistribution with the expectation that the worse off will enjoy a temporary rise in well-being at the expense of the rich at the cost of permanently lowering everyone's standard of living in the long run. In the simplest case, Orwell is surely not saying that if the quails you are eating right now would rot if it were attempted to transfer them to the starving children, you should still cease eating them right now and throw them in the garbage.

It is possible to hold onto an ideal of equality of condition while insisting that equality should not be pursued when doing so conflicts with the Pareto norm, such conflict being the objectionable feature of leveling down. But if one countenances interpersonal comparisons of advantage, equality still shares an objectionable feature of sufficiency. Neither gives moral weight to advantages gained for better-off persons, or for those who are already assured of remaining above the threshold of sufficiency. Achieving a tiny amount of gain for one worse-off or below threshold person does not plausibly have strict lexical priority over achieving any amount of gain, however large, for any number of persons however large who are already better off or above the sufficiency threshold. Accepting this point naturally suggests accepting a prioritarian morality, which holds that it is morally more valuable to achieve a small same-sized benefit for a person, the worse off the person would otherwise be over the course of her life.

At this point the left-wing critique of liberalism is reconfigured. There are two left-wing versus right-wing continua. On one scale we register the degree to which beneficence, the norm that urges us to help people lead better lives even though we have neither harmed them nor stand in social relations with them, is morally required, with right-wingers denying that any degree of impartial beneficence is ever morally required. On another scale we register the degree to which attaining a benefit for someone is more valuable, the worse off the person would otherwise be. Right-wingers give little or no priority to aiding the worse off.

These considerations cross-cut the personal responsibility component of luck egalitarianism. To see the point, consider how a moral case for aiding someone based on beneficence and priority considerations might be amplified or dampened by the individual's moral responsibility for her present plight. To illustrate, suppose one is morally responsible for actions that result in one's present condition, the more one is morally blameworthy or praiseworthy for those actions, depending on their quality. An unforgiving stance on moral responsibility holds that being morally responsible for one's present bad plight renders one ineligible for aid come what may. A stern stance on moral responsibility holds that if one's behavior is faulty, and one could have behaved well, one's moral responsibility is not diminished by the degree to which it would have been difficult or painful to do the right thing. A stance on moral responsibility for purposes of deciding what we owe to one another can be variously unforgiving and stern.

I have suggested that equality is valuable neither intrinsically nor for its own sake. At most it is valuable as a means. The dispute between egalitarians and nonegalitarians does not disappear, but is better construed as differential embrace of (1) beneficence obligations, (2) a prioritarian understanding of beneficence,[25] and (3) a soft conception of personal responsibility. In this way the egalitarian critique of liberalism becomes assimilated to liberalism as one of its branches.

In passing, notice that intramural disputes among liberals regarding the strength and character of sensible egalitarian commitment are likely overshadowed by disputes concerning the morally mandatory scope of social justice principles. Do liberal principles of justice apply globally across national borders and across time to encompass the interests of distant future generations? Many liberal philosophical arguments work to confine the writ of social justice to each separate political society considered in isolation. Cosmopolitans oppose this truncation of liberal morality.

EQUALITY OF OPPORTUNITY, FORMAL AND SUBSTANTIVE

Liberals standardly are portrayed as rejecting equality of condition. This chapter supports that portrayal. They are also standardly portrayed as embracing equality of opportunity. This bears examination.

Liberalism tends to hold that one should be free to do whatever one likes with whatever one legitimately owns so long as one does not thereby wrongfully harm others. But in entering into interactions with others in the economic marketplace, duties of nondiscrimination apply. If I am selling skis, it is wrong for me to sell to men but refuse to sell to would-be women customers, and wrong to insist on hiring white heterosexual males regardless of the qualifications of others who would apply for the job in my firm I am trying to fill if I would let them do that. The equal opportunity norm of *careers open to talents* requires that in seeking applicants for desirable job openings in public and private firms, bank loans to be used for business or investment purposes, and student slots in higher education institutions, applications should be open to all and judged on their merits, and selection made on the basis of merit (roughly, the question to be asked is, selecting which candidate would do most toward advancing the morally innocent aims of the enterprise?). This nondiscrimination norm is an element of a fair framework for cooperative interaction among individuals.

Careers open to talents could be fully fulfilled in a society in which none but children of the wealthy or of an hereditary aristocratic class ever become qualified, because only their parents can afford the costs of education to gain qualifications. If lower-class parents lack the competences needed to pass along technical qualifications to their children, again, careers open to talents could be fulfilled even though members of large social groups have no chance to succeed in social competitions and never do succeed.

A large issue is raised here. Consider the issue as it arises within a single society. When parents bring it about that a child is born, clearly parents (or substitute guardians appointed by mutual agreement with parents) have special duties to nurture the child and help it gain good life prospects. What do the rest of us owe the child, or those playing the parent role, in this process? Public education financed by general tax revenues represents a moral judgment that all of us together have duties to see to it that each and every child has some substantial opportunity to develop her native talents and become qualified for success in later social competition. Head Start programs and child care programs for poor working parents reflect the same concern. There is little consensus in modern societies as to what the exact shape and strength of the duty to help parents and children is.

Rawls, innovative on this issue as on many social justice issues, proposes a strongly egalitarian principle of substantive equality of opportunity, called *Fair Equality of Opportunity* (FEO). This principle requires that provided basic civil liberties are respected, as a first priority, justice requires that institutions and practices be set so that all persons with the same native talent potential (genetic endowment) and the same ambition (aspiration to succeed in competition and willingness to work to succeed) should have identical chances of competitive success (in contests and other interactions regulated by careers open to talents). This principle in a sense legislates a classless society – at least, one in which social privilege and advantage are not passed along from parents to children. One might suppose the implementation of this principle is limited by a morally required respect for the freedom of parents to give their own children a leg up in social competition by lavishing special nurturance and training on them, but in principle, whatever well-resourced parents do to help their children could be entirely offset by philanthropic and public policy programs that provide exactly offsetting advantages to children of parents who are not well resourced. So in theory, fulfillment of FEO could coexist with wide and deep parental partiality expressed in acts of favoring their own children (all such acts being counterbalanced by acts of others).

FEO is clearly controversial. But there are objections to it that do not consist merely of footdragging recalcitrance to help our neighbors and our neighbors' kids. First, FEO is a principle that mandates a type of equality, so it is vulnerable to the generic criticism of equality already canvassed. Why insist on equality of opportunity if the alternative is inequality favoring better-off children but in ways that also promote the real freedom advantages of the worse-off children who are getting the short end of the stick? Suppose we amend FEO so that it does not require movement to suboptimal outcomes and violation of Pareto. But FEO constrained by Pareto is also suspect.

Second, consider FEO from the standpoint of people who have low abilities and are not going to benefit from extra social resources expended to help their abilities to blossom. Suppose that instead of expending social resources to fulfill FEO, ensuring that talented persons of lower-class, middle-class, upper-class, and upper-upper class backgrounds end up with identical competitive prospects, we could instead expend extra social resources to help low-ability people become more qualified for decent jobs, and to structure the work environment so that more decent jobs are available to them. Such expenditures would be in violation of FEO, but would help the worse off, and perhaps the worse off among the worse-off members of society, to thrive. I'm all for such expenditures.

Third, notice that the broad issue with which we began discussion in this section was what do the rest of us owe to parents and their children by way of helping with child rearing. Even if FEO were adequate as a principle to guide just preparation of individuals for success in social competition (I have claimed it is not), it would not be a complete guide to just public policy regarding education and socialization.

This issue has to be central for any normative political theory, liberal or not. The liberal endorses strong protection of wide freedom of persuasive speech on any topic relevant to how we should live, in part because a social environment of robust free speech will help the individual see flaws in her current aims and desires and life plans and improve them. To benefit from free speech, individuals need an array of critical thinking skills and complementary virtues so they can benefit from the hubbub of expression to which they will be exposed. These considerations have a bearing on what individuals in childhood are owed by way of education and socialization.

In much the same way, a just education prepares people not just for the labor market and the economic sphere, and not just in skills needed to function as good citizens, but in skills and virtues needed for a happy and rewarding life. Even if I have less native talent than anyone else in society and will never win in any social competitions no matter how much education is lavished on me, so FEO is irrelevant to the issue, what am I entitled to by way of educational provision? Surely society owes me a good education? What is that? One answer (canvassed earlier in this chapter under the "Autonomy" heading) is that the child has a right to an open future and many accessible options. Here is an alternative answer: Each person is owed an education that will facilitate her leading a life filled with genuine goods in the actual circumstances she will face. Each of us needs to be able to identify not only what is abstractly worthwhile, but also what suits us, given the strengths and limits of our particular nature, and to form a character that leads us to successful pursuit of what suits us, within the constraints of what we owe to others.

Which answer is better? Settling this issue would require adjudicating the degree to which a sensible liberalism should impose on us a duty to promote not merely freedom and opportunities but the actual achievement of genuinely good lives for people. On this issue, as on others, liberalism is still contested terrain.

NOTES

1. Nagel, "Libertarianism Without Foundations," p. 137.
2. Locke, *Second Treatise of Government*, ed. Macpherson, p. 8.
3. There are many conceptions of autonomy. In the text the autonomous person is identified as one who chooses well and controls her own will so that she acts effectively as circumstances permit to fulfill her values and implement her choices. In this sense a person could be autonomous, and self-governing, even if she lacks any opportunity to act on her choices and values. For a broader conception of autonomy, see Raz, *The Morality of Freedom*, ch. 18.
4. See Feinberg, "The Child's Right to an Open Future," pp. 76–97.
5. Locke, *Second Treatise of Government*, ch. 1.
6. This reading of Locke yields Lockean libertarianism. See Nozick, *Anarchy, State, and Utopia*. Strictly speaking, Nozick's brand of libertarianism does not qualify as liberal according to my initial characterization, because the Nozickian libertarian denies there is any duty to

promote, as opposed to respect and honor, individual moral rights. We can regard the Nozickian as a limit case, situated at the far edge of the range of liberal doctrines. Nozick's libertarianism also does not encompass a duty to establish a just state, so does not clearly embrace the elements of liberalism in my characterization that presuppose the existence of a state that enforces certain rights. Of course nothing substantive hangs on what is or is not included in my stipulative characterization of core liberal rights.

7. For vigorous defense of the idea that actual individual consent is required to render it the case that the state wields power legitimately over the individual, see Simmons, *Moral Principles and Political Obligations; On the Edge of Anarchy;* and *Justification and Legitimacy.* See also Simmons and Wellman, *Is There a Duty to Obey the Law? (For and Against).*

8. A thorough exploration of this idea is in Gaus, *The Order of Public Reason.*

9. On political liberalism and the associated idea of public reason, see Rawls, *Political Liberalism;* also Larmore, *Patterns of Moral Complexity.*

10. I thank Steven Wall for advancing the ideas discussed in this paragraph.

11. Waldron defends this position in his *Law and Disagreement.*

12. A locus classicus of instrumentalist argument for democracy is Mill, *Considerations on Representative Government.*

13. Estlund, *Democratic Authority.*

14. See Walzer, *Spheres of Justice;* Anderson, "What Is the Point of Equality?"; and Scheffler, "What Is Egalitarianism?". See also Pettit, *Republicanism.*

15. The leveling down objection asserts that if one holds that equality is valuable for its own sake one must hold that achieving equality by making better-off people worse off without improving the condition of worse-off people is at least in one respect good (it achieves equality, after all) even if achieving equality in this way is undesirable all things considered. If status among a group of people is purely comparative, so that if one person gains status, another must lose, then the leveling down objection does not apply. But if status has a dimension that is noncomparative, then the leveling down objection applies. Suppose that everyone in society can be assigned high status (all equally have dignity and worth) or low status (none have dignity and worth). Suppose the present situation is that some are assigned high status and some low status. There is no way to raise the status of the low-ranked; they will inevitably lack dignity and worth. But without improving the absolute status of those who now have low status, we can bring about a lowering of the

status of some who have high status, so that they come to lack dignity
and worth. With this framework in place, we can render some worse off
in status without anyone else better off in status, so the leveling down
objection applies to the idea that achieving equality of status by degrading some and giving dignity to none is in one respect improving the
situation.

16. Orwell, *Homage to Catalonia*.
17. Marx, "Critique of the Gotha Program"; Mill, *Utilitarianism*.
18. Cohen, *Rescuing Justice and Equality*; also Cohen, "Expensive Taste
    Rides Again." The liberal views that Cohen is criticizing are articulated
    in Rawls, *A Theory of Justice* and in Dworkin, *Sovereign Virtue*, esp. chs.
    1 and 2.
19. On luck egalitarianism, see Temkin, *Inequality*; Nagel, *Equality and
    Partiality*; Dworkin, *Sovereign Virtue*; Cohen, "On the Currency of
    Egalitarian Justice"; and Arneson, "Equality and Equal Opportunity for
    Welfare."
20. The conception of real freedom as stated in the text may not be fully
    adequate, as is revealed when one notices that according to it one could
    qualify as really free to do X (if one were to choose to do X, there is a
    course of action that one could follow that would result in one's success-
    fully doing X) even if one is unable to choose to do X – and indeed, even if
    one's inability to choose to do X is brought about by some other agent's
    deliberate action intended to degrade one's ability to choose to do
    X. Different examples of this phenomenon might elicit different judg-
    ments. We might balk at describing Sally as really free to become a
    lawyer if antifemale socialization impedes her ability to choose to
    become a lawyer. On the other hand, we might allow that I am really
    free to jump on a table and dance the polka while naked in front of my
    students, even though I could not choose to do that, given the strength of
    my reasonable conviction that this would be a stupid and offensive
    action. (I owe my awareness of this possible flaw in the stated idea of
    real freedom to Steven Wall.)
21. Ronald Dworkin's ideal of equality of resources also contributes to our
    understanding of the distributive element in egalitarian social justice.
    Two seminal essays that he published in 1981 are included as the first
    two chapters of his *Sovereign Virtue*.
22. Sen, *Inequality Reexamined* and Sen, *The Idea of Justice*. Sen also argues
    that welfare is an inadequate conception of people's condition for pur-
    poses of deciding what we owe to one another according to distributive
    justice. But by "welfare" he has in mind either "preference satisfaction"
    or "pleasurable experience." Even if his argument on this point is correct,
    this still leaves open the possibility that welfare or well-being objectively

construed is the appropriate measure for purposes of the theory of justice. See Sen, "Equality of What?".

23. Nussbaum, *Sex and Social Justice* and Nussbaum, *Frontiers of Justice*.
24. See Parfit, "Equality or Priority?". A thorough recent discussion is in Holtug, *Persons, Interests, and Justice*.
25. The formulation in the text assumes that a prioritarian norm is not vulnerable to the leveling down objection. I would uphold that assumption. But for a contrary view, see Temkin, "Equality, Priority and the Leveling Down Objection." On equality, priority, and the leveling down objection, see Holtug, *Persons, Interests, and Justice*, ch. 8.

10 Disagreement and the justification of democracy

The justification of democracy in political society is often thought to rest in significant part on the fact of disagreement in that society concerning the common good and justice. Democracy is thought of as a way of treating persons as equals in the context of that disagreement. Indeed, democracy is purported to be an intrinsically justified way of dealing with disagreement on matters of public concern in the context of collective decision making. In fact I think this is a widely held intuition in modern democratic societies. At the same time, many think that in order for this justification to work, it must be the case that the views of persons have "equal claims to rational acceptance" and that persons are equally willing and able at the job of coming up with good ideas about the common good and justice.

But the idea that the intrinsic justification of democracy rests on such equal claims to rational acceptance and equal abilities seems manifestly to undermine the idea that there is an intrinsic justification. It seems plainly true that citizens' views have no such equal claim to acceptance and that citizens' abilities and willingness to discern the common good and justice vary a great deal. And to complete the puzzle, it is clear that citizens disagree about the claims to rational acceptance of the different views advanced in society and about the abilities of their fellow citizens. The normal position of any particular citizen is that some persons' views are clearly better supported than others and that some citizens are more able than others.

I thank the participants in the conference on Disagreement at the University of Alberta May 2013 and in particular Howard Nye for stimulating discussion on the arguments of this chapter. And I thank Andrew Williams and Steven Wall for comments on an earlier draft of this chapter.

In this chapter, I want to vindicate the intuition that democracy has intrinsic value. I will revisit the structure of the argument that democracy has intrinsic justification with the above puzzles in mind. I will attempt to articulate the intrinsic justification of democracy with the help of the idea that the justification must proceed from the public standpoint. I will discuss some of the difficulties people have seen in this latter idea as well.

I will proceed by discussing the ideas of democracy and its intrinsic value first. I will lay out the difficulties some contemporary authors have seen with this idea. Then I will discuss the idea of a public standpoint and why it ought to be adopted by citizens in considering the question of how to establish justice among themselves by means of law and policy. And I will articulate the justification of democracy from this public standpoint and assess whether the assertions that citizens have equal claims to rational acceptance or that citizens have equal abilities in discerning the common good and justice are required for that justification. Finally, I will discuss the worries some have had concerning the public standpoint and I will close with a discussion about whether my approach actually does vindicate the idea that democracy has intrinsic value.

THE INTRINSIC VALUE OF DEMOCRACY

By "democracy" I mean a process of collective decision making for a political community in which the principal stakeholders participate as equals in an essential stage of the decision making and in which that participation plays a central role in the creation of law and policy for that community. Democracy requires equality among stakeholders considered distributively and the sovereignty of stakeholders considered collectively. This is meant to be an open definition and not to settle any normative questions.

Along with other theorists, I have attempted to define an ideal of equality in collective decision making for a political community in which the stakeholders have an equal say in the process.[1] In this ideal, individuals have equal political power to participate in political decision making when there is continued disagreement and a collective decision is desirable. Individuals also have equal opportunities to influence the processes of negotiation and deliberation that precede decision making and equal opportunities to hear arguments and proposals in the process. Further details of this account needn't detain us here. Suffice it to say here that this ideal is one that can be approximated to a greater or lesser extent. And there may be a minimum threshold as well. I have described a conception of minimally egalitarian democracy elsewhere in which people have equal voting power, equal opportunities to run for office and form political associations, and where the voting of citizens determines who is in power and how they rule. Such an association must adhere to the rule of law as well.[2] The idea is that a society that possesses this minimally egalitarian character has some intrinsic value and the more egalitarian the society becomes along the spectrum from the threshold to the ideal, the more intrinsic value it has.

The thought behind the intrinsic value of democracy is that there is value in making decisions in this egalitarian way that is not entirely accounted for by appeal to the outcomes of the decision-making process and that this value is one that can be weighed against the values or disvalues of the outcomes. By "outcomes of the decision-making process," I mean the legislation and the effects of that legislation as well as the effects on the characters and lives of the participants. The intrinsic value of democracy is grounded in the intrinsic justice or fairness of making decisions in this particular egalitarian way in the circumstances of disagreement and in light of the interests in shaping the social world we live in.

In this respect, to assert that democracy has intrinsic value is not to subscribe to fair proceduralism, as David Estlund has defined it. With respect to democracy and majority rule in particular, Estlund says "fair proceduralism mainly claims – that the justification of majority rule rests on its procedural fairness and not on *any* procedure-independent standards for outcomes"[3] (italics mine). In my conception of the intrinsic value of democracy, there are a number of outcome standards that play a role in justifying democracy. First, we have a collective procedure in order to decide a question. Second, the function of political decision making is to advance the common good and justice among persons, and the thought is that we do better on this score when we make collectively binding decisions. Third, persons have interests in being able to shape the social world in which they live (even if they are not always trying to advance their interests), and these interests are advanced in a democratic decision-making process. The idea behind the intrinsic value of democracy is that a certain way of pursuing these aims is intrinsically valuable in light of the importance of the aims and in the light of the facts of disagreement and the interests of these equal participants. Democracy's intrinsic value consists in its affording equality in the means by which people pursue their aims.[4]

Steven Wall argues that only if the views of citizens have equal claims to rational acceptance can the argument for giving each citizen an equal say be correct. Only under these circumstances could it make sense to accord equal respect to each of the said views. And so only under these circumstances can it make sense to take seriously the interests each has in advancing her or his own views and accord each an equal say. As he puts it: "only ... those who have views that have an equal claim to rational acceptance have an equal claim to have their views treated with equal respect."[5] But Wall rejects the argument for equality seemingly on the grounds that, for the most part, citizens' views do not have equal claims to rational acceptance. He says that "it ... does not show that all citizens have an equal claim to have their political views treated with equal respect."[6] I want to contest the asserted necessary condition on the justification of political equality and replace it with a different though not entirely dissimilar condition, which I think does hold.

I think there is something right in the assertion of the necessary condition, but it is importantly vague or ambiguous. The first key ambiguity that is relevant to the issue here is the question of what a claim to rational acceptance is and what an equal claim is. Call this the question of the nature of the claim to rational acceptance (or the *claim issue*). The second ambiguity is the question: Whose rational acceptance is being claimed? Whose rational acceptance is the citizen making a claim to when she asserts her view? Call this the question of the appropriate subject of rational acceptance (or the *subject issue*).

I will discuss the subject issue first by assuming a conception of the claim to rational acceptance. I will assume that to say that a view makes a claim to our rational acceptance is to say that there is genuine epistemic reason or justification for accepting the view. And to say that two distinct views make equal claims to rational acceptance is to say that they are equally justified or supported by reasons. Let us call this idea the *equal justification condition.* Once we have discussed the issue of the subject with this limited conception of the claim, I will then articulate the claim issue more clearly.

I want to discuss a related asserted necessary condition on the justification of political equality, and that is the *equal cognitive ability condition.* This condition asserts that the intrinsic justification of political equality for a group of persons presupposes that those persons have equal cognitive abilities with regard to the main topics of democratic discussion. And it is asserted by some that the justification of political equality is defeated by the fact that this condition does not hold.[7]

Wall's negative judgment on the idea that views make equal claims to rational acceptance rings true for two different kinds of perspectives. The first perspective is that of each individual citizen. Since citizens disagree with each other on matters of the common good and justice and have reasons for their disagreement, it is certainly the case that they will not have reason to think that other citizens' views have equal claims to rational acceptance by them. Each citizen has reason, from within her own standpoint, for thinking that some viewpoints are superior to others. They may think that other citizens' views are not as well supported as their own. And many citizens also think that the views of some citizens are better supported by reasons than others' views are. Indeed, some citizens may reasonably take their cues primarily from opinion leaders they think highly of and not others. So from the particular standpoint of each citizen, the idea that the views of citizens have equal claims to rational acceptance will usually be thought to be preposterous.

Citizens also think that people have different abilities and dispositions with regard to being able to justify and articulate reasonable political visions. They believe that their fellow citizens' abilities and dispositions are unevenly distributed. Some are better at articulating and justifying compelling political visions. They may be better because of differences in native talent, or they may be better because they have spent more time and resources in the efforts to articulate and defend their views. Some occupy roles in the division of labor in society that give them the time and resources to articulate and justify their views. And of course some citizens are suspected of not being motivated by a concern for the common good. They are thought to be disposed to make arguments for the wrong kinds of reasons. These are perfectly natural and reasonable thoughts for citizens to have, and they are encouraged by the intense spirit of contestation that animates democratic politics.

So from each citizen's particular point of view, the viewpoints of other citizens do not have equal claims to rational acceptance and some citizens are regarded as being more able and/or more willing to articulate and defend reasonable political views. This is the reality of disagreement in a democratic political society. To ignore this phenomenon or to deny it would be untrue to the nature of democratic politics and would undermine the credibility of a normative democratic theory. Such a theory is clearly not worthy of our allegiance.

We can also think of a kind of absolute perspective or standpoint that in some sense determines the absolute worth of the justification of some view. This might be the standpoint of the perfectly rational being, that knows all and that understands all and that makes no mistakes in reasoning.[8] It is traditionally the divine standpoint. And in this case also, there is likely to be a significant amount of difference in the claims of the different views that citizens hold to the rational acceptance of this kind of being. Ordinary citizens are all likely to fall very far short of the standard that this kind of being imposes on its own beliefs. But some may be a little closer than others. Furthermore, ordinary citizens do aspire to come as close as possible to this divine standpoint at least other things being equal. And when an ordinary citizen asserts that her view is more justified than some other, she is asserting that her justification is closer to the absolute standard than the others are. In that sense, some citizens' views may have superior claims to rational acceptance than others.

Notice also that from this absolute standpoint, it should be clear who has the greatest ability to come to the views that have the strongest claim to rational acceptance. No doubt different people will have greater abilities on some issues and in some contexts than others, so there will likely not be anyone who dominates in all areas. But there will be some absolute truth about these matters. It might even be true from this absolute standpoint that there is good reason for some persons, who have significantly greater ability, to be given greater power than others at least in the contexts in which they have greater ability and motivation.[9]

Here too, I think, Wall's negative judgment about the equal claims to rational acceptance from this standpoint would seem to be quite reasonable. And so if political equality rests on citizens' views having equal claims to rational acceptance or on the idea that citizens have equal abilities, then we should reject political equality.

THE PUBLIC STANDPOINT

But I think that the ideal of political equality rests on different, though not entirely unrelated, grounds. To explain these grounds I will introduce a standpoint I have discussed in my work, which is distinct from that of both the absolute standpoint and the standpoint of each citizen. I call this the public standpoint or the egalitarian standpoint. I will lay out my conception of this public standpoint, including its function and its internal features. Then I will say why it is important that people adopt this standpoint under certain circumstances. I will then say how adoption of this standpoint bears on the justification of democracy and the equal justification condition and the equal abilities condition.

First, let me say why I think talk of standpoints is important. When a group of persons attempts to establish justice among themselves, they must do so on the basis of their own judgments. This is the case even if there is, as I believe there is, an absolute conception of justice, the truth or objective validity of which is independent of people's judgments.

We establish justice among ourselves by means of law, policy, and social norms. Law, policy, and norms impose a distribution of benefits and burdens (though not necessarily coercively) on persons for the sake of establishing a unified framework of social and legal norms among persons. Because people disagree about justice and because of the need to clarify and precisify norms in order to coordinate with each other, a unified scheme of rules is necessary for the achievement of any of the serious concerns of justice and the common good. These rules are not constitutive of justice; they are merely the instruments by which persons attempt to establish justice as best they can among themselves.

Law, policy, and norms are justified in part by appeal to principles of social justice. These principles are capable of guiding persons in the construction of a political system and guiding the criticism of the structure of a political system. They assert rights and duties that are reasonably action-guiding for persons. And they can serve as the bases of criticisms that people make of the political system they live in. What I want to say is that the public standpoint is the position from which the basic principles of social justice are justified, and these principles establish the framework in which more particular conceptions of justice may be advanced among citizens.

The problem we face as human beings is how to establish justice among ourselves. And the way we must do this is by using our judgment to establish it. Hence, we must justify the norms we establish on the basis of our own views of the matter. The question, "who's to judge?" becomes relevant at this stage. So the question is: whose judgment is to determine how we are to establish justice among ourselves?

Now the absolute standpoint is unavailable to us as cognitively limited human beings. We must engage in the activity of judging the justice of our community from the limited standpoints we occupy. Even if it were true that a god could see that our community is just if it were set up in a particular way, this would be of very little help to us. This perception would be beyond our ability to appreciate as a whole. Each of us would pick out parts of it and ignore the rest.[10]

The public standpoint is the standpoint of the group of persons who are involved in the effort to establish justice and pursue the common good among themselves. It is not the standpoint of any particular citizen or that of a perfectly rational being. We have a choice then between the particular standpoints of individuals and the public standpoint.

As I am understanding it, persons are concerned with the public standpoint when they are concerned that everyone can see that they are being treated as equals in light of the facts of cognitive limitations such as cognitive bias, fallibility, disagreement and diversity of interests, and the fundamental interests persons have. The standpoint is shared. I have said that it is the standpoint of the group and not merely of any particular citizen member of the group. It is a standpoint one occupies when one tries to take everyone's views into account and discern a principle that everyone can agree treats them as equals given the facts and interests described above. The public standpoint, I contend, does not side with any particular citizen on the issues that it deals with. Hence, one does not characterize the public standpoint in terms of any one of the views of the citizens. So the public standpoint embodies a certain impartiality with regard to the citizens of the society. In a sense, this impartiality is toward the views of different citizens. So, in characterizing the public standpoint we must filter out all the controversial views of citizens except a certain group of beliefs that ought not to be controversial: these latter views will be the ones that are justified from the public standpoint.

The public standpoint is a standpoint that is limited by imperfect rationality in the creation of beliefs. Human beings, in their individual and their collective efforts, always fail to achieve perfect rationality. Individuals are deeply fallible and biased and have very limited resources for figuring out the truth, particularly when it comes to matters of justice and the common good. The content of the public standpoint can be understood as what we as a group can see to be the case, and what we as a group can see to be the case will inevitably be limited by the cognitive limitations of human beings generally.

There is a sense in which the public standpoint embodies a version of the idea that persons' judgments have equal claims to rational acceptance. Each person's claim to see that they are treated as an equal is as important as anyone else's claim. I will argue below that this will not require that each person's beliefs are equally justified but only that each person's judgment concerning how they are treated is necessary to establishing the appropriate justification. Each person has a kind of veto. If they don't see themselves as being treated as an equal, they can deny that the relevant principle is public principle. The idea here is that each person's view has a sufficient claim to rational acceptance in order to derive the veto for that person.

The public standpoint is the standpoint from which we evaluate whether persons are being treated as equals, in the sense that they are being treated in a way that equally advances their interests. So the principle of equality of advancement of interests itself is not at issue here. The question the public standpoint helps to answer is when is it that people can see that they are being treated as equals?

Now I want to say that each person can occupy both the particular standpoint that they have and the public standpoint. They can see the world both from their own point of view and from the more impartial point of view of the public standpoint. Citizens have reasons to occupy both standpoints simultaneously. Usually the public standpoint takes a certain precedence over the particular standpoints in the sense that the citizen is not willing to advance the particular views she has unless it is done within the framework established by the public stance.

I think we do this all the time. We look at our views as correct and try to advance them in political life, but we also take a stance on ourselves as one among many equals and thus advance our views in a way that is compatible with others doing the same. But it is important to note that we do not sacrifice our particular standpoint to that of the public in the sense that we deny for political purposes any aspect of our views that is not shared. We legitimately attempt to advance our particular views within the framework established by the public stance.[11] The public standpoint endorses this constrained pursuit of our aims.

There are a number of questions that need to be answered about this public standpoint. First, why occupy the public standpoint? Second, what is the content of the views that are accepted from within this standpoint and how are they derived? Third, when and why does it have precedence over my particular standpoint? The answers to the first and second questions can help us see how democracy has intrinsic importance as political equality. The answer to the third question helps us see why democracy has authority in controversial matters. I will not pursue that question here.

THE REASON FOR ADOPTING THE PUBLIC STANDPOINT

The public standpoint embodies a kind of impartiality that we can have when we step outside of ourselves and see ourselves as one among many within the community. I can believe that the view of justice and the common good that I want to advance is the best view while also seeing that others have their conflicting views and that the structure of the collective deliberations and decision making must treat all of us equally.

Why should we accept that we should treat different citizens with impartiality and treat their views with a certain kind of impartiality? The idea is that this limited impartiality is justified for the purpose of designing the basic institutions that frame our decision making. The most basic consideration behind this argument is that persons have equally important fundamental interests in being able to shape the social world that they live in by their own lights. To the extent that they shape the social world in which they live in accordance with their judgments about how best to do so, treating their judgments with sufficient respect is necessary to treating them as equals regarding the fundamental interests they have in shaping that world.

What are these interests? Given a level of disagreement and given the facts of plurality of interests, fallibility, and cognitive bias, each person has fundamental interests in correcting for the cognitive biases of others. Each person will have good reason to think that in a world shaped by others, their interests will be given short shrift. They must be able to see that they are treated as equals. In addition each person has fundamental interests in being at home in the world they live in. They have interests in being able to make sense of the social world they live in and orient themselves in it. A world that only others are able to grasp is not a home and will be alienating to the person who cannot see how it is treating her. By virtue of this alienation her interests are set back.

This does not require that we think of conflicting judgments as equally justified. It does not even require that we think that every person is as able and willing as every other person to devise good conceptions of social justice and the common good. What it does require is that we think that appeal to every person's judgment is necessary if we are to treat them as equals.

But why aren't my fundamental interests in being treated as an equal better advanced in some cases by a system that gives those who are more enlightened than I am the power to determine how I am to live? The enlightened ones have a better appreciation of the requirements of equality than I do, so presumably I am treated more as an equal when their judgments are implemented even if I disagree. Who cares if I don't see that I am treated as an equal if in fact I am being treated as an equal? To be sure, there is no guarantee that the enlightened person is going to be successful at treating me as an equal because even they are fallible and biased. Indeed, it may even be true that the unenlightened person may arrive at a better conception of equality than the enlightened by some kind of accident. But it still seems appropriate to put one's bets on the enlightened person over the others if one is genuinely concerned with equality.

The trouble here is that the difference between the enlightened and the unenlightened is not that great, and so there is little plausibility to the idea that the enlightened will have such a greater appreciation of equality than the unenlightened. This is especially so because of the peculiar features of each person's interests. Since each person's interests are quite distinct in a number of ways from those of others and equality requires equal advancement of those interests, the likelihood of an enlightened person, with the degree of difference we expect among persons, being able to grasp some person's interests better than the person in question is pretty small. And so even if there is a sense in which a person can appreciate the genuine requirements of equality better than another, the interests of that other are going to be left out of the picture when we simply allow a particular group to determine what equality is for the purpose of establishing justice in the group. Hence, the likelihood is that the person's interests in question will be given short shrift in some important way.

The epistemic access that each person has to her own interests and the cognitive biases that interfere with their understanding of others' interests (along with the idea that equality involves advancing those interests) suggest that the epistemic differences between persons on these matters is not likely to be very great and that a person's interests will be neglected if they do not participate. This would not be compatible with equality in the sense I have advanced here. And, of course, there is always a lot of disagreement among even the enlightened about what equality and interests require.

I want to argue that given the setback of these fundamental interests, each person whose interests are set back in this way will have reason to think that she is not being treated as an equal. Now I want to assert here that each person has a fundamental interest in being recognized and affirmed as an equal among his fellows. This interest cannot be met if this person lives in a world that can be seen by others to be treating them as equals but which she cannot see to be treating her as an equal.

To establish justice merely on the basis of one's own point of view, therefore, is to treat one's fellows as inferiors in the sense that one treats one's fellows as if their interests do not count for as much as one's own. The reason this happens is that the establishment of justice brings about a certain distribution of interests. And given the idiosyncratic nature of interests, establishing justice without reference to the public standpoint will leave out the interests of those who are not included. Their interests will not be advanced. To the extent that this is an expected feature of acting merely from the particular standpoint of a particular person, the other is being treated as an inferior. Again a god or a perfectly rational being does not face this dilemma and can see everything clearly from a perfectly rational standpoint, but that is not our situation.

These observations provide a rationale for adopting the public standpoint for each person. Given the centrality of judgment to the establishment of justice among persons and given the distinctive interests each person has in seeing that she is being treated as an equal, we have a reason for each person, insofar as she is concerned with treating others as equals in the establishment of justice, to adopt the public standpoint as a way of treating others as equals in the establishment of justice.

Here I want to reiterate the idea that the reason to adopt the public standpoint is not grounded in the idea that each person's view of equality has an equal claim to rational acceptance. Each person's view of equality has a sufficient connection with her interests, which cannot be adequately grasped by others, to imply that the imposition of a conception of equality that does not take that person's view of the matter into account cannot be said to be treating that person as an equal. As long as a person holds a conception of equality that meets some minimum standards, that person has a claim to a veto of a principle of social justice. Hence, basic principles of social justice must be justified from the public standpoint.

I want to make two observations about this argument for the public standpoint. One, the need for adopting the public standpoint is grounded in the fundamental principle of equality and the interests of persons in addition to the basic factual situation people find themselves in when they attempt to establish justice among themselves. But despite this relation of grounding, the idea is that it introduces a distinctive level of practical reasoning about how people ought to treat each other. One way to characterize this is that reasoning from the public standpoint gives us a morality of imperfect information while reasoning from the absolute standpoint is the morality of perfect information. We cannot do without both of these levels of reasoning. Two, my argument here is not meant to imply skepticism about particular conceptions of the good or about particular conceptions of justice. To the extent that there is a skeptical element in my argument, it is skepticism regarding our ability to understand each other's distinctive interests that animates the need for the public standpoint.

JUSTIFICATION FROM THE PUBLIC STANDPOINT

I have argued that from the public standpoint, the basic principles of social justice are the principles of democracy and basic liberal rights as well as an economic minimum. But I will focus on the argument for democracy here. And I will focus on this argument with particular attention to whether the argument requires the ideas that each citizen's views have equal claims to rational acceptance and each person is equally able and willing to think about justice.

When thinking about the principles that guide the design of social and political institutions, persons will have two distinct kinds of considerations in mind. First, they will want a system that is effective in advancing the interests of all the members in the society and advancing them in reasonably equal ways. But second they want to have a scheme that treats them as equals in a way that they can see to be treating them as equals. They must think about this in the light of extensive disagreement, cognitive bias, diversity of interests, and fallibility on everyone's part. Furthermore they will take account of basic interests in shaping the social world that each person has.

What basic principle of social justice has the property of treating persons as equals in ways that they can see treats them as equals despite the disagreements that people have regarding how equality is to be implemented? I want to argue that at least one necessary condition that can be established in this context is that persons are to have an equal say in the collective decision making by which law and policy are devised. This is the appropriate egalitarian way of dealing with disagreement given the facts and interests noted above. Any way of making collective decisions that left some group out or that gave substantially and clearly less power over the method of collective decision making could not but be seen by that group as anything but treating that group as second-class citizens, unless it was clearly justified by appeal to the principles of democracy, liberal rights, and an economic minimum outlined above. It has to suggest this to them, I think, because they are taking into account the fallibility and cognitive biases of persons, their basic interests in correcting for cognitive bias and being at home in the world, and the basic plurality of interests among persons.

Here we need to proceed slowly. One might think that all this argument requires is that people be included in decision-making processes in some way, such as playing a part in something like a plural voting scheme. My argument for adopting the public standpoint was merely an argument for inclusion, so why can't that work in this context? The basic reason is that a collective decision-making system cannot work effectively as a system of unanimity. It must work as some sort of majoritarian system for making decisions. Inclusion is a sufficient protection for the distinctive interests of persons in a scheme of unanimity, which scheme characterizes the public standpoint. But it does not protect the equal interests of individuals in the context of majoritarian decision making. And I want to say that some kind of scheme of majoritarian decision making is necessary in light of the extent and degree of disagreement a normal political system will have. A demand for unanimity will simply choke the system and paralyze it.

What I want to say here is that only equality of say can be seen by all to protect persons' interests as equals in a system of majoritarian decision making. This will demand that the system be genuinely majoritarian and that persons have equal votes in this system. It will also demand that persons have equal opportunities for influence in the processes of negotiation and deliberation that characterize democratic societies.

It will be noted that the argument I have offered has some empirical components. One of them is that the possession of political power advances the interests of the person holding it. And this was the basis of the thesis that someone who is excluded from power or who has significantly less power will not be able to see that they are treated as equals. This is clearly an instrumental claim. But the fact that assertions about the instrumental importance of the possession of political power play a role in the justification of political equality does not show that the justification is instrumental. It only shows that political equality is equality of things that have instrumental value to the possessors. The justification of democracy is that the equal distribution of these instrumentally valuable things is intrinsically justified.

Let us see how this gives us an intrinsic value for democracy. The intrinsic value is internal to the public standpoint and not to other standpoints. The nature of the intrinsic value is that democratic decision making is not justified in the public standpoint by reference to any particular end state. The reason for this is that the particular views that could serve as possible end state justifications of collective decision making are not accepted from the public standpoint. Only the sense that persons are not treated as equals in the contexts of the facts and interests of disagreement when they are not given an equal say is justified publicly.

To be sure, some outcome standards are generated from within the public standpoint. The easiest way to see this is that the public standpoint justifies democracy, and so it will provide grounds for rejecting actions that have the effect of undermining democracy. And just as it does not permit democracies to undermine democracy, so it does not permit democracy to undermine certain basic liberal rights and an economic minimum, because these too are justified from the public standpoint. I also think that a limit on the possibility of persistent minorities can be established by this argument. These limits, I contend, are grounded in the same basic principle of public equality as democracy is, which is why they can provide such firm limits to democratic authority.[12]

However, these outcome conditions only specify the boundaries within which democratic decision making has intrinsic value. They do not provide a full account of the outcomes democracy is meant to achieve. They show that the intrinsic value of democracy is conditional, not that it is nonexistent.

Within the limits established by the public standpoint, the idea is that there are no justified outcomes established within the public standpoint that can serve to justify democracy. All judgments about end states, apart from those specifying democracy, liberal rights, and an economic minimum, are controversial and thus cannot serve as grounds for democracy or liberal rights. This is so even though instrumental considerations are playing a role in justifying democracy, namely that political power is instrumentally valuable. The equal distribution of this political power is justified because political power has instrumental value, but the equality is justified because, in the light of the instrumental value of political power, persons cannot see that they are treated as equals if they are not given equal power.

But why can't someone say in response to these arguments that there is an outcome standard in play here? The critic can say that the basis of the argument above is that since political power has instrumental value, individuals cannot see that they are treated as equals when they do not have political equality, because they have good reason to think that inequality of political power will set their interests back relative to those of others. The particular way in which their interests will be set back may be unknown or obscure and the assertion may be merely probabilistic, but it is nevertheless by reference to a probable and problematic outcome that the person objects to political inequality in the public standpoint.

I am not convinced that this criticism can work. From the public standpoint, my sense is that there will be some disagreement on whether the political inequality actually does produce inequality in the outcome. Some may think that it is to the advantage of the person with less political power that others have more power. Others may think that the person will get better than equal outcomes if he has equal political power. It is likely that a conscientious egalitarian will think in his own case that inequality of political power will end up treating him worse than others, but this needn't be the case with others. So from the public standpoint, there will not be a clear outcome-based verdict in favor of political equality.

Of course, we have a situation in which many are likely to be dissatisfied with the outcome standpoint if political equality is chosen. But this is going to be true of any collective decision rule. The point is that given this disagreement and given the facts of disagreement (diversity of interests, fallibility, and cognitive bias) and the interests in shaping the social world one lives in, the natural point for persons to settle on as a way of equally advancing the interests of all is a principle of political equality.

I think this is in part an empirical judgment, or at least it can receive some confirmation from empirical data. And one basis of confidence that one might have that collective decision making must be made democratically if it is to treat people as equals in a way that they can see that they are being treated as equals is as follows. The vast majority of people who live under democracies greatly prefer it to other forms of government, and the great majority of people who do not live under democratic government also prefer democracy, though not by as great a margin. This does not show what reasons they have for preferring democracy, so the evidence is relatively weak with regard to a specifically egalitarian conception of democracy.[13]

EQUAL JUSTIFICATION OR ABILITIES

I argued above that the adoption of the public standpoint need not imply a judgment that people have equal abilities or that their views have equal justification. Here I want to ask whether the argument for democracy from the public standpoint requires that persons' views have equal claims to rational acceptance or that people have equal abilities? I don't think so.

Let us start with the abilities claim. Why wouldn't the public standpoint choose a system of plural voting in which the most talented would be given more power than the less talented? I think the basic reason for this is that from that public standpoint, we will not be able to determine who are the most talented since talent is judged by the worth of the judgments people have and people disagree about the worth of these judgments. It is not that no one thinks that some are more talented than others. Each has her own view of who is more talented. It is not even that from the public standpoint there isn't some idea that some are more talented than others. The problem is to figure out who are more talented. And this cannot be done from the public standpoint. But the idea is not that everyone has equal abilities, but rather that the public standpoint does not take a stand on who has the most abilities. And in the absence of a defensible stand on this question, any giving of more power to some rather than others would seem to violate the equal importance of each person's interests. There is no other possible basis for giving more power to some if there is no defensible way to establish in the public standpoint that some are better than others.

But someone might object: Why not have a plural voting scheme that gives more votes to the more educated against a background of robust equal opportunity to become educated? This gets fairly close to the egalitarian standard I have suggested. And there is a sense in which the kind of egalitarian democracy I am recommending does have something like this since people can exercise their equal rights by giving more credence to some rather than others and of course by voting for some persons rather than others. The account of democracy does permit the existence of elites as long as those elites are in their positions because of popular backing by equal citizens.

The answer to this objection is that in order to develop such a system we will need two theses that are the legitimate objects of controversy. First, the idea that those with more formal education are more competent than those with less is problematic, at least when we focus on the role of citizens as choosing the basic aims of the society.[14] Second, the particular requirements needed to establish the qualifications will inevitably be controversial. This particular way of choosing elites is not compatible with people seeing that they are treated as equals. It seems to me that the more egalitarian way is to allow elites to arise from the democratic process itself.

So the intrinsic value of democracy does not rest on a judgment that people are equally talented. It merely requires that from the public standpoint we take no stand on this and that in the absence of a stand, equality of say is the appropriate way publicly to realize equality among persons.

I think something like this can be said concerning the issue of whether citizens' views have equal claims to rational acceptance from the public standpoint. The idea that people's views have equal claims to acceptance cannot be made out in the public standpoint. This isn't because people's views have unequal claims to rational acceptance. It is because there are no appropriate grounds from the public standpoint to determine who has superior claims to rational acceptance, at least once we have established the basic requirements of public equality. Any proposed grounds are going to be controversial and thus can be vetoed in the public standpoint. What this means is that, from the public standpoint, there is no stand on most of the claims to rational acceptance that people take.

That there is no such stand can be seen from the following fact. People can think, without inconsistency, that some people's views are better than others and that some people are better able to understand justice and the common good while also according the equal right to each to have their own opinions on these matters.

INSTRUMENTALISM IN A DIFFERENT GUISE?

The argument I gave that each ought to adopt the public standpoint has an instrumental ring to it. The interests of some will be neglected if their points of view are neglected. Some have suggested that this implies that my argument for democracy is a kind of indirect instrumentalist argument. The idea is that instrumentalism is the underlying moral idea and the justified rules are merely means for achieving non-democratic aims such as the protection of other rights or the interests of persons. The suspicion is that we are saying that we should be thinking or acting as if democracy were intrinsically valuable because such thinking or acting is instrumentally valuable. This does not seem compatible with the claim that democracy is intrinsically valuable.[15]

I think there is something right about this way of looking at the argument. But it is not clear to me that the argument I have given above doesn't vindicate the intuition that there is something intrinsically valuable about democracy. First, the adoption of the standpoint and the propositions apprehended within the standpoint need not share the same features in this respect. Just because the standpoint is defended in an instrumental way, it does not follow that the values defended in it are instrumental. Much depends on the way in which the public stance is instrumentally valuable. If the public stance is instrumentally valuable because it gives us an improved view of the subject matter, then it is quite possible that the truths concerning the subject matter apprehended in the public stance are not merely instrumentally valuable. If I use binoculars to see a particularly beautiful object that I cannot see otherwise, my use of the binoculars is instrumental but the beauty of the objects need not be merely instrumental. In this case, the instrumental value of the perceptual aid is that it gives me improved epistemic access to the features of the relevant object. The features are there in the object independent of the aid. And normally, without the aid, I would be able to get a view of these same features, for example by getting closer to the object.

Contrast this kind of reason for adopting a standpoint with another entirely instrumental reason. Suppose that I adopt a standpoint such as the use of binoculars because I want to show off my ownership, and skill in the use of, the binoculars to someone else. I am not interested particularly in what I see through them. But what I see through them is also of instrumental value in that it displays the power of the binoculars and my abilities and thus advances my aim of impressing the other person. In this sense the value of what I see is instrumentally valuable because it furthers the instrumental value of showing off my binoculars. The value of using the binoculars is entirely incidental to their normal function, which consists in improving the view. This is a purely instrumental use of the visual aid, and it suggests that the values of the things perceived are instrumental as well, at least in this context.

The value of adopting the public standpoint is not incidental to the point of adopting a standpoint as it is in the show-off case. The public standpoint gives us a better view of equality at least in one important respect. So the adoption does not have the kind of incidental instrumental value as in the show-off case.

Still, the perception of the intrinsic values of democracy and liberal rights from the public standpoint has one of the features of the perception-of-beauty case but not the other. I have argued that the standpoint gives us an improved view of our relations with others. It is able to incorporate their views of what is just, which (I have argued) enables us to include a more adequate grasp of their interests in our conception of equality. The greater adequacy of our grasp of the interests is something that can be assessed independent of the stance, otherwise we wouldn't have an argument for it. However, the perception of the intrinsic value of democracy is not entirely stance independent. It is possible to think that democracy has intrinsic value from the particular viewpoints of persons, but the argument above suggests that one can derive the intrinsic value of democracy from the public standpoint even if one did not already have it in the particular standpoints.

We might compare the public standpoint on equality to viewing certain movies with 3D glasses. The 3D glasses help us see the aesthetic value of the movie (let us suppose) and hence have a kind of instrumental value in giving us access to the aesthetic value, but the value thus perceived in the movie is not something that can be perceived without the 3D glasses. Here, too, the glasses give us an improved view, but the view is not stance independent. The aesthetic merit of the movie does not thereby become instrumental even though it is dependent on the adoption of an instrumentally valuable visual aid.

I don't think that this gives us a demonstration that the intrinsic value of democracy is perceived from the instrumentally valuable public standpoint, but it does show us that the instrumental value of adoption of the public standpoint does not defeat the intrinsic value of democracy, and it suggests how the intrinsic value claim is supported. The instrumental value of the public standpoint derives from its ability to give an improved view of equality (improved because it enables us better to accommodate the interests of each) even though that improved view of the intrinsic value of equality is not stance independent.

However, I am not convinced the discussion ends there. Adopting and arguing from within the public standpoint has a powerful expressive value as well. Indeed that expressive value is internal to the adoption of the public standpoint. Each person can see that he is being treated in accordance with a principle that each accepts as a realization of equality. We affirm our egalitarian attitudes toward each other by adopting this stance and reasoning from it. The public standpoint is uniquely suited to achieving this expressive value because it is the standpoint from which everyone can see that they are being treated as equals by others and where each knows this. It is also exceedingly hard to have this affirmation and expression without it. What this implies is that when we take the public standpoint, the adoption of the public standpoint itself acquires intrinsic value because of its inherently expressive value. It may be that we can argue our way into the public standpoint only by showing how it gives us an improved view of equality but once we are in the public standpoint we can see that the adoption of the public standpoint is itself intrinsically valuable because it gives us a mutually recognizable way of expressing our equal status.

Second, with these points in mind, once we adopt the public standpoint, we have arguments for democracy, basic liberal rights, and an economic minimum. We also have possible instrumental arguments for institutions that can protect these public values such as constitutions with constitutional courts. So we can distinguish between intrinsic and instrumental arguments within the public standpoint. Furthermore, the public standpoint creates the basic framework of institutions for a society, within which individuals can contest each other's conceptions of justice and the good openly. So even if there is an instrumentalist background, the pervasiveness of the public standpoint in justification, and the fact that it can distinguish intrinsic and instrumental values within it, suggests that what we have here is a distinctive layer of moral reasoning from which the sense that democracy has intrinsic value may be sufficiently well vindicated.

CONCLUSION

In this chapter I have tried to defend the idea that democracy has intrinsic value by appeal to the idea that it has intrinsic value from the public standpoint. Once we conceive of the nature and basis of the intrinsic value of democracy in this way, objections that the value of democracy depends on spurious assertions of the equal claims to rational acceptance of people's views or on the equally problematic idea that people are equally able and willing to understand what justice requires in political society are shown to be groundless. I have also attempted to show how the argument for the intrinsic value of democracy works despite the fact that there are premises appealing to the instrumental value of democratically available resources. And I have tried to show how the intrinsic values of democracy and liberal rights are compatible with the fact that the initial adoption of the public standpoint may be for instrumental reasons.

NOTES

1. See my *The Constitution of Equality*. See also Cohen, "Procedure and Substance in Deliberative Democracy"; Brighouse, "Egalitarianism and Equal Availability of Political Influence," and Dahl, *Democracy and Its Critics* for some representative egalitarian accounts of democracy.
2. See my "An Instrumental Argument for a Human Right to Democracy" for this conception of minimally egalitarian democracy.
3. Estlund, *Democratic Authority*, p. 82. Estlund says that only procedures that satisfy full anonymity (i.e., that are blind to all the personal features of the participants) can satisfy fair proceduralism because any standard that does not satisfy this condition would have to be partly justified by reference to procedure-independent outcomes. I am not convinced that this conception of fair proceduralism is coherent, since even a fully anonymous procedure is used for the purpose of producing an outcome and hence the procedure rests to that extent on a procedure-independent standard.
4. I think Estlund can agree with this, since he says that "We should not say that procedures, including majority rule, are not fair simply because they are not fully anonymous. Rather, procedures can mix fairness and other principles, remaining fair, among other things" (*ibid.*, p. 81.) I discuss Estlund's views on this in more detail in "Estlund on Democratic Authority."

5. Wall, "Democracy and Equality," p. 435.

6. *Ibid.*

7. This is one of the main themes running through Richard Arneson's work in criticism of the intrinsic worth of democracy. See his "Democracy at National and Workplace Levels" and "Democracy Is Not Intrinsically Just," pp. 40–58, as well as his "The Supposed Right to an Equal Say." Wall also suggests this in "Democracy and Equality," p. 426.

8. This seems to be the perspective that Arneson appeals to in his "Democracy Is Not Intrinsically Just," p. 51. There he writes of the reasonable person who "makes no cognitive errors and deliberates with perfect rationality."

9. A thesis Arneson asserts in "Democracy at National and Workplace Levels."

10. If the arguments in the rest of the chapter are sound, then the god will have reason to think that the scheme cannot be just unless it can be seen to be so by the citizens.

11. In this sense, the public standpoint is less restrictive than Rawls's and others' conception of public justification, which tends to exclude viewpoints that are not shared or permits them only when they are used in the service of advancing a shared position. See Rawls, *Political Liberalism* for the classic formulation of this. See my "Must Democracy Be Reasonable?" for a critique of the restrictive view.

12. I argue extensively for these limits in chapters 4 and 7 of my book *The Constitution of Equality.*

13. See Gallup International: The Voice of the People 2005 for polling data on this.

14. I defend this account of the role of citizens in modern democracies as a way of reconciling the requirement of political equality with the need for a division of labor in collective decision making in *The Rule of the Many* and more recently in my paper "Rational Deliberation among Citizens and Experts."

15. I thank Amanda Greene and Howard Nye for pressing this objection.

11 Liberalism and economic liberty

INTRODUCTION

Can the state decide how much people must be paid for their work, say, by setting a minimum wage? Can it limit how many hours people may work in a day or week? Can the state require that people must be licensed to sell medical services, alcohol, or groceries? Can the state require that people save for their own retirement, or that they contribute some determined amount to medical insurance? Can the state levy taxes to provide putative public goods such as roads or national defense, or to fund medical care or housing for the needy? These are questions about economic liberty. They require us to consider what authority the state has to regulate economic activity.

We can consider these questions in a slightly different way. If we approach the authority of the state in terms of the authority of citizens to regulate themselves as a collective, then it is natural to view questions about what the state can do in terms of what free and equal citizens can justify to each other. Can citizens justify to each other imposing requirements about the wages they must be paid or the hours they can work? Can citizens justify to each other the requirement that various professionals must be licensed? Can citizens justify to each other mandatory saving for retirement or mandatory participation in an insurance scheme?

These two ways of asking questions about economic liberty invite two different approaches to answering them. Asking the questions in the first way invites reasoning that foregrounds the social results of free economic agency. On this line of reasoning, economic liberties are seen as means to the achievement of social goals such as peace and prosperity. Asking the questions in the second way, by contrast, foregrounds the possibility that economic agency may be a morally charged forum of self-expression. On this line of reasoning, economic liberties are expressions of the respect that is due every member of society as a free and equal citizen. By a liberty, we understand a sphere of human agency that ought to be legally respected and protected. Liberties obligate citizens to respect and protect the activities of their fellow citizens in some sphere of agency.

What aspects of economic activity ought to be protected as liberties in this sense? The main schools of liberalism divide over this question. In this chapter, we provide a map of the various divisions of liberalism, showing in every case how the problem of economic liberty functions as an exacting conceptual tool that separates rival schools of liberalism from each other. To begin, we need a better understanding of the source of disagreement: what, precisely, is this divisive problem of economic liberty?

THE SIGNIFICANCE OF A LIBERTY

The problem of economic liberty can be understood along two dimensions: the first concerns *what* significance economic liberties should have; the second concerns *why* they should have this significance. The significance of a liberty is a function of two variables: weight and scope. The *weight of a liberty* is the importance it should be accorded in political deliberation vis-à-vis other societal considerations that might inform the exercise of political authority. The weightier the liberty, the more significant it is, meaning that fewer or stronger societal considerations can justify regulating the sphere of agency protected by this liberty.

For liberals, all spheres of human agency carry a presumption of liberty: No sphere of human agency can be politically regulated without sufficient and impartial justification. How to cash out the presumption of liberty more precisely is a hard question. Let us simply stipulate that the presumption of liberty is carried by any legislation that is democratically enacted in accordance with a constitution the principles of which are acceptable to all citizens.

The presumption of liberty is the lowest weight a liberty can have. Indeed, a sphere of agency protected merely by the presumption of liberty is a liberty only in a minimal sense of the word, since it can be regulated as needed to pursue other social values. The weightiest a liberty can be, by contrast, is absolute. An absolute liberty is a sphere of agency that cannot be regulated for any reason except to secure that same liberty for all. There is a continuum of weights between the presumption of liberty and absolute liberty. The most important of the categories on this continuum is the category of basic liberties.

A basic liberty can be regulated only to secure that an adequate scheme of basic liberties is equally secured for all citizens. A basic liberty is weightier than the presumption of liberty, since the sphere of agency it protects cannot be regulated to maximize productive output or for whatever other interest carries the majority of citizens of the day. A basic liberty is less weighty than an absolute liberty, since it can be regulated to ensure that an adequate scheme of basic liberties is provided for all (and not only to ensure that the particular type of liberty in question is provided for all, as with absolute liberties).

The *scope of a liberty* is the set of activities falling within the protected sphere. The scope of a liberty must, accordingly, be defined relative to its weight. If a liberty is absolute, the scope of that liberty is the set of activities that cannot be regulated for any other reason than to provide the liberty in question. Likewise, the scope of a basic liberty is the set of activities that may be regulated only to secure an adequate scheme of basic liberties for all. Since the presumption of liberty covers all activities not already within the scope of absolute or basic liberties (assuming for simplicity that these exhaust the options), it makes little sense to talk about the scope of a liberty protected merely by the presumption of liberty. This is part of the reason why spheres of agency protected merely by the presumption of liberty are liberties only in a minimal sense.

The *significance of a liberty* is a function of its weight and scope. The significance of a liberty falls a on a scale between minimally significant at one end (mere presumption of liberty) and supremely significant at the other end (absolute weight and of wide scope). Freedom of speech, for example, is currently given high significance in most liberal democracies: it is constitutionally entrenched and it protects a wide range of speech-acts from government regulation. Whether freedom of speech should be given this significance is, of course, a normative question that must be decided by reference to principles of justice.

ECONOMIC LIBERTIES

Economic liberties are liberties of the person as an economic agent. We can identify four categories of economic liberties corresponding to the main spheres of economic agency:[1]

1. Liberties of working (of the person as laborer): liberties to employ one's body, time, and mind in productive activities of one's choice and according to the terms one has freely consented to (such as to donate, sell, trade, and buy labor).

2. Liberties of transacting (of the person as entrepreneur): liberties to manage one's own affairs, to buy and sell goods, to save and invest, to start, run, and close a commercial enterprise such as a business or farm, and to engage in the activities of running such an enterprise: to hire workers, buy and use land, display, advertise, and sell one's products or services.

3. Liberties of owning property (of the person as owner): liberties of acquisition, holding, and transfer of property (whether personal or productive), of using and developing one's property for commercial and productive purposes, to sell, trade, invest and bequest one's property.

4. Liberties of using property (of the person as consumer): liberties to use, consume, destroy, or otherwise do as one pleases with one's goods, resources, and services.

But how significant are these economic liberties? Some liberals maintain that liberty of contract as a liberty of working is both wide and absolute. Thus, contractual relationships can be regulated only to secure freedom of contract for all (if so, even contracts of workers in the sex trade cannot be regulated, except to secure liberty of contract for all). Conversely, other liberals maintain that freedom of contract is of limited weight and so can be regulated in pursuit of a fair and efficient distribution of opportunities and resources, or for reasons of public safety (in which case, contracts in the sex trade could be regulated for a wider range of reasons).

Let's say that a conception of economic liberty is an account of what economic liberties should have what significance. A theory of economic liberty is a conception of economic liberty together with its justification. We use a notion of thickness to help us compare different conceptions of economic liberty. The thickness of a conception of economic liberty depends on the three identified variables: range, weight, and scope. The wider the range of economic liberties that are given higher weights and wider scope, the thicker is that conception of economic liberty.

In light of the preceding, we can map different conceptions of economic liberty on a continuum of thickness. At one extreme we find the maximally "thick" position that the full range of economic liberties are extremely significant. Call this economic rights absolutism. At the other extreme, we find the "thinnest" liberal position that the full range of economic liberties are protected merely by the presumption of liberty. Call this economic rights minimalism. Between these two extremes lie a number of possible conceptions. For example, one might argue that all or some of the economic liberties are basic, but no economic liberties are absolute.

This map is, of course, incomplete in several ways. Cardinal ranking seems out of the question, and even an ordinal ranking must be incomplete. For example, there is no way to say whether the just mentioned conception is thinner or thicker than a conception that holds some economic liberties absolute and the rest are protected merely by the presumption of liberty. These problems aside, we now have a rough measure for sorting different liberal theories of economic liberty: namely, according to the thickness of their conception of economic liberty. This approach allows us to distinguish the three main divisions of liberalism: libertarianism, classical liberalism, and high liberalism.[2] (Later in the chapter we consider two nonliberal approaches to economic liberty: socialism and market-anarchism.)

LIBERTARIANISM, CLASSICAL LIBERALISM, AND HIGH LIBERALISM

Libertarians affirm a thicker conception of economic liberties than do classical liberals, who, in turn, affirm a thicker conception than do high liberals. Speaking generally, libertarians maintain that most of the economic liberties are absolute;[3] classical liberals maintain that more or less the full range of economic liberties are basic liberties;[4] and high liberals maintain that almost the full range of economic liberties are protected merely by the presumption of liberty.[5]

These different conceptions of economic liberty generate different accounts of distributive justice. Libertarians tend to think that distributive justice is fully realized by the protection of economic liberties and that any state redistribution of resources impermissibly violates economic liberties. Thus, Nozick's famous opening to *Anarchy, State, and Utopia*: "Individuals have rights ... So strong and far-reaching are these rights that they raise the question of what, if anything, the state and its officials may do."[6] On Nozick's interpretation, these rights include the full range of economic liberties and are given more or less absolute weight.[7] So economic rights severely limit what the state and its officials may do – primarily, the state should secure that (natural and acquired) rights are respected for all.

Classical liberals also tend to think that distributive justice is realized by protecting the economic liberties: Distributions that emerge as the unplanned consequence of voluntary interactions are, by that very fact, distributively just. Nevertheless, classical liberals are more open to state regulation of economic liberties. Regulation of one economic liberty can enable the exercise of another. For example, classical liberals have no problem with regulation that prevents monopolies or other market failures (more on this topic below). Similarly, economic liberties may be regulated in order to maintain other basic liberties.

High liberals, finally, tend to think that distributive justice is a concern of justice that is distinct from and has priority over the protection of the economic liberties. High liberals affirm a thin conception of economic liberty, where most economic liberties are protected merely by the presumption of liberty. Economic liberties ordinarily can and should be regulated in pursuit of distributive justice and other social goals.

PHILOSOPHICAL FRAMEWORKS

Why do these different schools of liberalism affirm these different conceptions of economic liberty? To find out, let us examine the philosophical framework characteristic of each school.

There are three main liberal philosophical frameworks: natural rights theory, consequentialism, and contractualism. A natural rights liberal maintains that some rights and liberties are innate and inviolable, though they may be alienable by crime or free consent. A consequentialist liberal treats rights and liberties as means to some independently defined end (such as happiness or human perfection).

A contractualist liberal approaches rights and liberties as parts of the terms of social cooperation that must be reasonably acceptable to all citizens conceived of as free and equal members of society. In this manner, different philosophical liberalisms view economic liberties through different lenses, each with a distinctive conceptual tint.

Conceptually speaking, the two levels – framework and school – are only loosely connected. A consequentialist liberal, for example, might defend a classical liberal or a high-liberal conception of economic liberty. Yet, there are philosophical strains. Thus, a consequentialist liberal would find it hard to support economic rights absolutism, since the indirect nature of a consequentialist approach to liberties looks fit to establish only a conditional absoluteness.

The preceding explains why we find no less than three distinct sorts of disagreement about economic liberty among liberals. There is the first-order disagreement about what is the right conception of economic liberty. But this dispute is rooted in two second-order disagreements. First, a disagreement about what framework – natural rights, consequentialist, or contractualist – provides the appropriate lens through which to consider the significance of economic liberties (call this inter-framework second-order disagreement). And second, a disagreement about what the right conception of economic liberty is, given an agreed-upon framework (intra-framework second-order disagreement).

For many decades, the main pattern of linkages between frameworks and schools was stable. Libertarians typically defended their conception from a natural rights framework. Classical liberals tended to support their conception on broadly consequentialist (utilitarian) grounds. And high liberals typically supported their conception from a contractualist framework. Yet, increasingly, this pattern is being disrupted. In the following we first look at the traditional tendencies and then tour one main site of disruption.

NATURAL RIGHTS LIBERTARIANISM

Libertarianism is the position that most or even all of the economic liberties are supremely significant and as such cannot be restricted or regulated, except to ensure that they are protected for all.[8] Normally, this position is defended from within a natural rights framework based on a claim of original self-ownership, or on a principle of natural liberty.[9]

There is a wrinkle here. On some libertarian theories, economic rights absolutism is compatible with just about any sort of state. A natural extension of the self-ownership idea implicit in the libertarian position is that persons may and can alienate their rights by free consent. In the extreme a person may contract to become slave to another – in that case, the other has authority to decide on her behalf. The free alienation of rights can create interpersonal authority that allows persons to use force against each other in ways that were otherwise impermissible. Likewise, a group of persons may well decide to create political authority that is authorized to collect taxes, regulate labor, and so on. So, on this picture, though the economic rights are *originally absolute* (prior to legal deeds by which interpersonal authority is created), their alienability means that they must be respected and protected only insofar as there are no past contracts to the contrary. So, on such a natural rights framework, whether and how a state ought to respect and protect economic liberties depends on the past contracts of the members of society.

Libertarianism has had a hard time asserting itself as an equal member of the liberal family. (Some have even questioned whether libertarianism is a liberal philosophy at all.)[10] One difficulty for libertarians has been the challenge of articulating an attractive natural rights framework. Some libertarians look to Locke for their arguments, but Locke relied on questionable assumptions about the status of humans as parts of God's creation and plan.[11] And even if Locke had not relied on controversial metaphysical premises, he explicitly rejects the sort of economic rights absolutism that libertarians defend.[12] Others have looked to Kant's theory of autonomy and the idea that all persons are ends in themselves and have sought to show that Kant's theory implies a very thick conception of economic liberty. Yet, Kant rejected this implication,[13] and it is, in any case, doubtful that respect for autonomy implies anything close to economic rights absolutism. Contractualists have argued that Kant's theory of autonomy requires that economic liberties be regulated and restricted insofar as this is necessary to secure a fair distribution of opportunities and goods.[14]

Another set of problems concerns what many people have seen as unattractive commitments of libertarianism. If economic rights are absolute, there is very little the state is morally permitted to attempt to do to protect the weak from exploitation or to provide for those who through no fault of their own are unable to provide for themselves. Some libertarians bite this bullet. Others advert to the space thus reserved for charitable activity. But the lack of *moral permission* for the state to address such issues is a feature of libertarianism that gives many people pause.

Moreover, if freedom of contract is both absolute and of wide scope, as some libertarians argue, then it allows contracts of prostitution, slavery, and perhaps even the sale of vital bodily organs (say, one's heart). These permissions raise deep concerns, especially when combined with the absence of state support even for those who through no fault of their own find themselves in extreme need. The misfortunate might face a choice between starvation and a contract of slavery. The libertarian position appears to sanction such a choice and even to require that the state use its power to enforce such contracts.[15]

UTILITARIAN CLASSICAL LIBERALISM

One of the oldest and most successful defenses of economic liberties has been that the free exercise of economic agency tends to minimize waste, maximize the productive output of society, secure an optimal distribution of goods and resources, and avoid the dangers of concentrated governmental power. Despite the allure of planning, the spontaneous order that emerges from the free interactions of self-interested agents is, perhaps paradoxically, a more reliable route to peace and economic prosperity.[16] Classical liberals have thus defended economic liberties on utilitarian grounds as indispensable or efficient tools for promoting general well-being.

Given certain empirical assumptions, this line of reasoning offers an indirect utilitarian defense of a moderately thick conception of economic liberty. The indirect utilitarian argument does not support treating economic liberties as special or giving them absolute weight. Rather, the economic liberties are treated as members of the set of liberties that must be given special weight in order to secure a good society. Such liberties can be regulated for the sake of designing the scheme of basic liberties that best serves the purpose. Indirect utilitarian liberalism in this manner tends to support the classical liberal conception of economic liberties – typically, that the full range of economic liberties should be treated as basic rights, but not as absolute.

The indirect utilitarian justification invites a certain laxness even when it comes to the basicness of economic liberties. After all, utilitarian justification is highly fact sensitive. Classical liberals have not been hostile to regulating economic agency, if it turns out to better serve the good of society, as we have already noted regarding the threat of monopoly.[17] Nor have classical liberals been averse to the state being involved in the provision of public goods (Smith himself saw the provision of public goods as one of the central functions of government).[18] Classical liberals such as F. A. Hayek and Milton Friedman have supported tax-based support for education and welfare programs insofar as these are reliable means to secure an educated workforce, peace, and stability, and perhaps for other moral reasons as well.[19]

Thus, in classical liberalism, the economic liberties are not quite basic, since they can be regulated by reference to the underlying values – but in this the economic liberties are once again on a par with the other (more or less basic) liberties. So another way to distinguish classical liberalism from libertarianism and high liberalism is to say that classical liberals tend to view economic liberties as of equal significance with other traditional liberal liberties such as freedom of thought, speech, and the rights of bodily integrity. By contrast, libertarians and high liberals both single out the economic liberties: libertarians by treating the economic liberties as *more* significant than other traditional liberties; high liberals by treating them as *less* significant.

The instrumentalist defense of rights and liberties has been something of an Achilles heel for classical liberals. Applied to political questions, this framework inherits all the ills of indirect utilitarianism in general. Classical liberals working in this framework are vulnerable to challenges from less liberally inclined utilitarians: if what we really care about is promoting happiness, then we (or the state) should violate rights if doing so promotes happiness – say, if we can violate rights secretly, or if it appears that the benefit of rare violations outweighs the slight instability they cost.

Conversely, less utilitarianly inclined liberals have argued that the utilitarian argument fails to capture the true importance of liberties, especially given the conditional nature of utilitarian justification. The importance accorded to rights is typically signaled precisely by their ability to trump utilitarian, or social averaging, considerations.[20]

Moreover, the indirect utilitarian argument seems unable to establish that the basic liberties should be equally provided for all members of society. At least, it makes the commitment to equal liberty dependent on empirical facts. If unequal liberty maximizes utility, the indirect utilitarian argument seems to require a principle of unequal liberty, an outcome that seems wholly incompatible with the ideals of the liberal tradition.[21]

The underlying concern of these criticisms is, of course, that the utilitarian framework mistakes why we should care about liberty in the first place. From a Lockeian or Kantian perspective, the liberties (or at least the more significant liberties) are not instruments to other social ends. They are norms grounded in the status and value of individual agency.[22]

Of course, not all utilitarians are classical liberals (or liberals, for that matter), and not all classical liberals are utilitarians. Below we shall see how classical liberalism can be restated on grounds closer to the Kantian view of why liberties matter. First, however, let's consider the more traditional Kantian interpretation of the significance of economic liberties, namely, the contractualist high liberalism offered by John Rawls.

CONTRACTUALIST HIGH LIBERALISM

According to contractualism, the principles of justice are the principles that free and equal rational persons would agree to as the fundamental terms of social cooperation.[23] Rawls designs the original position to identify these principles.

Rawls invites us to imagine parties selecting principles of justice while operating under a set of information constraints.[24] These constraints famously include a "veil of ignorance" that makes the parties unaware of particular facts about those they represent and the society they inhabit. Along with some general facts, the parties know that they have a conception of the good and an interest in securing the means for pursuing it. Significantly, the parties also have a higher-order interest in securing for those they represent the preconditions for the development and exercise of the two powers of moral personality – the capacity to form, revise, and pursue a conception of the good and the capacity to develop and exercise an effective sense of justice.[25] The original position ranks candidate principles of justice according to how well the parties can expect their interests to be satisfied in a society well ordered by these principles. The highest-ranking principles are the principles of justice.

Rawls argues that the original position will issue as first principle of justice that "Each person is to have an equal right to a fully adequate scheme of equal basic liberties which is compatible with a similar scheme of liberties for all."[26] He also argues that the basic liberties have priority over any other social concerns – including the requirements of distributive justice set out in the second principle.[27]

The exact scheme of basic liberties protected by the first principle can be defined by reference to the higher-order interests of the parties. For Rawls, the basic liberties are all and only those liberties necessary for the adequate development and full exercise of the two moral powers.[28] If a liberty is not necessary for the development and exercise of one of the moral powers, then that liberty is protected merely by the presumption of liberty. Thus, as we have seen, it can be regulated as required by the second principle or in light of other social concerns.

Rawls argues that only two categories of economic liberties are basic:[29] first, the right to hold and have exclusive use of personal (nonproductive) property. Rawls suggests that this liberty is necessary for the adequate development and exercise of both moral powers. Second, liberty of occupation is required by freedom of association and in general for the adequate exercise of the second moral power.[30] Apart from these two, Rawls thinks that the activities of economic agency can and should be regulated as needed to realize the fair value of political liberties, equality of opportunity, and a fair and efficient distribution of income and wealth.

Unfortunately, Rawls does not say much about why he concludes that most economic liberties are not basic. In general, his argument must be that such liberties are *not* necessary for the adequate development and exercise of the two moral powers.[31] But the details of this argument are unclear. This lack of clarity in Rawls's argument invites doubt that he has really established what he claims. In the following we shall see how neoclassical liberals exploit the gap between Rawls's basic ideas and conclusions to argue that the contractualist framework leads to a classical conception of economic liberties, one which recognizes a wider range of economic liberties as basic rights.

NEOCLASSICAL LIBERALISM

Like classical liberalism, neoclassical liberalism defends the position that more or less the full range of economic liberties are basic and thus should be regulated only as needed to secure an adequate scheme of basic liberties for all.[32] Neoclassical liberals differ from classical liberals in three ways.

First, and most important, they work from a contractualist framework. Instead of working within the consequentialist (or econometric) framework of traditional classical liberals, neoclassical liberals argue that the principles of justice are those that could meet with the consent of all citizens conceived as free and equal.

Second, because they work within the contractualist framework, neoclassical liberals offer an alternative definition of what makes a scheme of basic liberties "adequate." For traditional classical liberals, recall, adequacy is defined relative to the end of maximizing happiness or prosperity. The adequate scheme of basic liberties is that which best serves this end. By contrast, neoclassical liberals define adequacy in terms of the proper development and exercise of the powers of moral personality. The adequate scheme of basic liberties is the set of liberties necessary for the exercise of these moral powers.

Third, while classical liberals such as Hayek support a variety of social programs, they reject the idea of social justice. Officially at least, traditional classical liberals support a tax-funded safety net and system of educational supports only insofar as such policies support utilitarian aims (such as social stability).[33] Neoclassical liberals, by contrast, follow high liberals in affirming an ideal of distributive (or "social") justice and in maintaining that liberal justice requires a direct concern for the least well off members of society.

Neoclassical liberals, in short, are like classical liberals in that they maintain that the full range of economic liberties are basic. But they are like high liberals in that they defend their conception of economic liberty from a contractualist framework that also issues distinct requirements of distributive justice. Whether the political implications of neoclassical liberalism are closer to those of classical liberalism or high liberalism is a matter of dispute. On one hand, neoclassical liberals such as John Tomasi affirm a thick conception of economic liberty: There is an important domain of economic agency that cannot be restricted even to secure equality of opportunity or to improve the lot of the least well off. On the other hand, equality of opportunity and improving the lot of the least well off are recognized as distinct requirements of justice that outweigh other social considerations (such as efficiency).[34]

How do neoclassical liberals get to the classical liberal conception of economic liberty from the contractualist framework that is usually thought to support high liberalism? Recall the incompleteness of Rawls's argument that most economic liberties are protected merely by the presumption of liberty. This lack of argument invites the charge that Rawls's exception of the economic liberties from the scheme of basic liberties is unjustified.

Tomasi offers a three-pronged version of the charge of unjustified exceptionalism.[35] First, given that liberal thinkers traditionally include the economic liberties among the basic liberties, the burden of proof is on those who claim that they are not on the list. But high liberals offer little argument to lift this burden. Second, to show that the economic liberties are not basic, high liberals would have to show that the economic liberties are not necessary for the adequate development and exercise of the two moral powers. However, if we look at the arguments that high liberals give for why other basic liberties are necessary for the moral powers, these arguments seem to apply equally to the economic liberties. The economic liberties protect essential interests in security and independence, and the various spheres of economic agency – the activities of the human being as a worker, as entrepreneur, owner, and consumer – can be as central to personal identity as the religious and political aspects of our existence. Finally, the argument that Rawls offers in defense of including the eonomic liberties of personal property and freedom of occupation on the list of basic liberties seems to apply equally to other economic liberties. The freedom to sell, trade, and donate one's labor seems no less essential to the moral powers than freedom to choose one's occupation. People define themselves, and express their values, not only by *what* work they choose to do, but also by the *way* they choose to work.

If the economic liberties are as necessary for the adequate development and exercise of the moral powers as the liberties that high liberals claim are basic, then high liberals ought to embrace the conclusion that a fuller range of economic liberties are basic – to not do so is unjustified exceptionalism.

High liberals would reject this charge of unjustified exceptionalism.[36] First, Rawls does not defend freedom of occupation because people define themselves by their choice of occupation, but because it is needed to exercise the other basic liberties, such as freedom of association. More generally, the neoclassical argument interprets the criterion of basic liberty to mean that any sphere of agency that might be central to some reasonable conception of the good should be protected as a basic liberty. Yet, even if Rawls's criterion of basic liberty needs clarification, it is clear enough that he does not share this interpretation of the criterion. Rawls's criterion is not primarily about protecting whatever conceptions of the good citizens may have, but about securing the conditions necessary for the adequate development and exercise of the moral powers, including the capacity to devise and pursue a conception of the good. Thus, it might be argued that Tomasi's claim that the economic liberties are as important for some conceptions of the good as the liberties Rawls affirms as basic is beside the point, and the charge of unjustified exceptionalism misses the target.

However that debate shakes out, both camps have work to do. High liberals need to clarify the criterion of basic liberties and explain why most economic liberties are omitted by this criterion. Neoclassical liberals must either show why the economic liberties are basic by the high-liberal criterion, or offer an argument for why we should abandon the high-liberal criterion in favor of a criterion by which the economic liberties are basic.

TWO CHALLENGES TO LIBERAL THEORIES OF ECONOMIC LIBERTY: SOCIALISM AND ANARCHISM

All liberal views rely on a distinction between liberty and what we might call "freedom." Liberty is the set of liberties that the state ought to respect and protect. Freedom is the set of options available to a person. For liberals, the abilities and means needed to exercise one's liberties and thus to be more fully "free" are conceptually external to those liberties. One can have a liberty even if one lacks the abilities or means needed to fully exercise it.[37] On this approach, a person too sick to go to church has no less religious liberty than a healthy person. Her inability means that her possibilities for exercising that liberty are limited, so that she, in that sense, is less free to practice her religion than the healthy person. Similarly, a poor person has the same economic liberties as a rich person, even though she has fewer economic options.

On the liberal approach, the state should protect liberty, not promote freedom. At most, the state secures the background conditions of freedom by protecting and respecting liberties and securing conditions of distributive justice – however conceived.

Socialists reject the liberal distinction between liberty and freedom and they object to what they see as a liberal conflation of "inability" and "lack of means." Lack of means, especially pecuniary means, presents *legal* restrictions on the exercise of a liberty.[38] These objections support two criticisms of liberal theories of economic liberty.

The first criticism is aimed at classical and neoclassical liberal conceptions of economic liberty (libertarians are immune and high liberals tend to agree): If a basic liberty is enjoyed only when the necessary means for its enjoyment are available, then the economic liberties can and should be regulated with the aim of ensuring that all citizens have the means for enjoying the full scheme of basic liberties, whether or not the economic liberties themselves are basic. For socialists, a thorough regulation of the activities of economic agency is consistent with taking the full range of economic liberties as basic.

The second criticism targets all liberal conceptions of economic liberty: If having a liberty means having access to the means necessary to exercise it, then having an economic liberty means having access to the means necessary to engage in that sphere of economic agency. The right to property is not, as liberal thinkers tend to define it, primarily a negative right that protects holders of property against certain types of interference from others.[39] The right to hold property is, rather, just that: an equal right to actually hold property. But if the liberties of ownership require that all members of society have more or less equal access to ownership of property, then the economic liberties can be protected and respected only in a system of public ownership and production.

Socialists, accordingly, agree with liberals that the state has an important role in protecting economic liberty (at least until the last stage of history, where the state can wither away).[40] However, socialists maintain that liberals mistake this role. When the liberal state

"respects" economic liberty, people are barred from taking democratic measures to secure true economic liberty for all. When the
liberal state "protects" economic liberties, it enforces an oppressive
system of entitlements that keeps the majority of society from access
to economic liberty. Socialists thus argue that liberal theories of
economic liberty serve as part of the ideology that justifies using
the state as a means of oppression, rather than liberation.

Interestingly, market anarchists agree with the socialist claim that
the liberal state is a means of oppression. But they reject the socialist
idea that the state could serve a role in securing economic liberty.
Indeed, market anarchists argue that it is *impossible* for a state to
protect and respect economic liberties.

Market anarchists affirm a principle of non-aggression: It is impermissible to use violence, or to threaten violence, against other people
or their property.[41] The non-aggression principle requires that people's control of their own lives and property be respected, so long as
their actions do not themselves violate that principle. According to
market anarchists, the non-aggression principle leaves no room for
the state, which inevitably uses threats of violence to subject individuals to laws with which they do not agree and is funded through
the seizure of property ("taxation").[42] Just as it would be wrong for
one person to force rules upon or steal from his neighbor, so it is
wrong for the state to do so. Market anarchists see the state not as a
solution to the problem of aggression, but rather as a major contrib-
utor to it.

Market anarchists believe that economic liberties of working and
ownership ought to be protected. But they say that protection must be
left to individuals or, more precisely, to groups of individuals working
together voluntarily. Collective entities resembling a state, entities
that provide constituents with goods ranging from defense to health
insurance, and even courts and property law itself, may emerge and
persist – so long as all involved consent to its rules. Market anarchists
argue that, more successfully than the state, the free market can
provide competitively priced and effective property rights protection.

CONCLUSION

The central problem of economic liberty concerns which economic
liberties should be given what significance and why. Whole schools of

liberalism divide over this problem: The defining differences between libertarians, classical liberals, and high liberals are differences in their conceptions of economic liberty. Traditionally, the different conceptions of economic liberty were supported by different philosophical frameworks – libertarians defending a thick conception of economic liberty from a natural rights framework; classical liberals, a moderate conception of economic liberty from a utilitarian framework; high liberals, a thin conception of economic liberty from a contractualist framework. So long as disagreements about economic liberty were primarily inter-framework disagreements, liberal debates about economic liberty proceeded mostly in terms of the opposing sides identifying faults and weaknesses in the philosophical frameworks of their opponents. While this has led to more refined philosophical frameworks, it has had less of a refining effect on the arguments that lead from philosophical frameworks to conceptions of economic liberty.

But the landscape is changing. Increasingly, we see intra-framework disagreements. We focused on a prominent example, namely, the neoclassical challenge to high liberalism: that the contractualist framework supports a classical liberal conception of economic liberty. We expect and hope that intra-framework disagreements such as this will lead to refinement of the arguments offered in defense of the different conceptions of economic liberty. Such refinements are needed, not only to clarify the relation between philosophical frameworks and liberal conceptions of economic liberty, but also to allow liberals to respond to the challenges mounted by socialists and market anarchists.

The problem of economic liberty does more than separate scholars into rival intellectual schools. As much or more than any other issue, the problem of economic liberty also divides liberal citizens into rival and contending groups. This is yet another reason for liberals, and their critics, to attend more closely to the problem of economic liberty.

NOTES

1. Here we follow Nickel, "Economic Liberties," pp. 156–57.
2. The distinction between these three schools has been drawn in a number of different ways: see Freeman "Illiberal Libertarians"; Freeman,"Capitalism

in the Classical and High Liberal Traditions"; Tomasi, *Free Market Fairness*; Tomasi and Brennan, "Classical Liberalism"; Mack and Gauss "Classical Liberalism and Libertarianism."

3. For paradigmatic statements of libertarianism, see Nozick, *Anarchy, State, and Utopia* and Narveson, *The Libertarian Idea*.

4. Early versions of the classical liberal conception of economic liberty were offered by David Hume and Adam Smith. More recent varieties are offered by Hayek, Friedman, and Epstein.

5. The use of the term "high liberalism" to designate this subset of the liberal family was introduced by Freeman in "Illiberal Libertarians". Among its members Freeman counts John Stuart Mill, T. H. Green, John Dewey, and John Rawls. The family also includes many contemporary liberals, including Ronald Dworkin, Joshua Cohen, Bruce Ackerman, Thomas Nagel, Charles Larmore, Corey Brettschneider, and Samuel Scheffler.

6. Nozick, *Anarchy, State, and Utopia*, p. ix.

7. It might be said that Nozick backs away from natural rights absolutism in his discussion of risk and compensation in chapter 4 of *Anarchy, State and Utopia* (see Sobel, "Backing Away from Libertarian Self-Ownership"), but for the purposes of illustration we ignore this complication.

8. Different libertarianisms work with different theories of property and original acquisition and their conceptions of economic liberty vary with these theoretical underpinnings. Thus, right- and left-libertarians might disagree about which economic rights are natural rights, about what sorts of unilateral, bilateral, and omnilateral moves are necessary and/or sufficient for just changes to the distribution of rights, and thus also about the legitimate roles and extent of the state. For a brief overview of some of the moving parts in these debates, see Vallentyne, "Libertarianism."

9. For backing and qualification of this generalization, see Zwolinski, "Libertarianism." Nozick is commonly cited as a self-ownership theorist. A prominent liberty-based argument for libertarianism is Narveson, *The Libertarian Idea*.

10. Rawls, *Political Liberalism*, p. lviii; Freeman, "Illiberal Libertarians."

11. Locke, *Second Treatise of Government*, esp. chs. 4–5. See also Waldron, *God, Locke, and Equality*.

12. See Locke, *Second Treatise of Government*, §§73 (on inheritance), 120 and 138–39 (on regulation of property), 142 (taxation).

13. See section 1 of the division "Public Right," in Kant, "Metaphysical First Principles of the Doctrine of Right." See also Ripstein, *Force and Freedom*, chs. 8–9.

14. For an interpretation of Kant that supports this claim, see Guyer, *Kant on Freedom, Law, and Happiness*, chs. 7–8.

15. von Platz, "Absolute Freedom of Contract," pp. 107–10.

16. Smith, *An Inquiry into the Nature and Causes of the Wealth of Nations*; Hayek, *The Constitution of Liberty*; Friedman, *Capitalism and Freedom*; Epstein, *Principles for a Free Society*.

17. For example, Hayek, *The Constitution of Liberty*, pp. 264–66; Friedman, *Capitalism and Freedom*, pp. 27–30, 132–33.

18. Smith, *An Inquiry into the Nature and Causes of the Wealth of Nations*, IV, p. ix.

19. Hayek, *The Constitution of Liberty*, chs. 19, 24; Friedman, *Capitalism and Freedom*, chs. 6, 11, 12.

20. Cf. Dworkin, "Rights as Trumps," pp. 153–67; Nozick, *Anarchy, State, and Utopia*, pp. 28–33.

21. Rawls, *A Theory of Justice*, rev. edn., p. 185; Rawls, *Justice as Fairness*, p. 96.

22. One might dispute that Locke agrees with this characterization of rights, since in his natural law framework the right promotes peaceful and good society. Yet, though the right is conducive to the good, that is not, for Locke, what makes it the right: "the rightness of an action does not depend on its utility; on the contrary, its utility is a result of its rightness" (Locke, *Essays on the Law of Nature*, p. 215).

23. Rawls, *A Theory of Justice*, rev. edn., p. 10; see also Freeman, "Social Contract Approaches."

24. Rawls, *A Theory of Justice*, rev. edn., §24 and pp. 110, 137–38; Rawls, *Political Liberalism*, pp. 22–28, 70; and Rawls, *Justice as Fairness*, §§6, 11, 25–26, 35.

25. Rawls, *Political Liberalism*, pp. 73–75; Rawls, "Kantian Constructivism in Moral Theory," pp. 312–13.

26. Rawls, *Political Liberalism*, pp. 5, 291. This version of the first principle contains several changes to the principle that Rawls made in light of criticism of the principle as it was stated in the first edition of *A Theory of Justice*; see Hart, "Rawls on Liberty and Its Priority" and Rawls's reply to Hart in *Political Liberalism*, Lecture VIII.

27. Rawls, *A Theory of Justice*, rev. edn., §39.

28. Rawls, *Justice as Fairness*, pp. 45, 112–13, 169; Rawls, *Political Liberalism*, pp. 24, 74, 187, 293, 308–25; Rawls, *A Theory of Justice*, rev. edn., p. xii; Rawls, "Reply to Habermas," esp. pp. 409–19.

29. See Rawls, *A Theory of Justice*, rev. edn., §§42, 43, 82; Rawls, *Justice as Fairness*, p. 114; Rawls, *Political Liberalism*, pp. 228, 232, 298, 335, 338, 363.

30. Notably, most often free choice of occupation is not included among the basic liberties in the list of primary goods; cf. Rawls, "Social Unity and Primary Goods," p. 362; likewise *Political Liberalism*, pp. 181, 308.

31. Rawls says this about some economic rights in *Political Liberalism*, p. 298; *Justice as Fairness*, p. 114.
32. The term "neoclassical liberal" was coined by Brennan and Tomasi in "Classical Liberalism." Nickel was one of the first to defend economic liberties along neoclassical lines; see "Economic Liberties." More systematic defenses of neoclassical liberalism are offered by Gaus in *The Order of Public Reason*; "On Justifying the Rights of the Moderns"; and "Coercion, Ownership, and the Redistributive State"; and Tomasi in *Free Market Fairness* and "Democratic Legitimacy and Economic Liberty."
33. Hayek, *Law, Legislation, and Liberty*, vol. II.
34. Freeman has criticized Tomasi on this point. See "Can Economic Liberties be Basic Liberties?" See also Tomasi, "Reply to Freeman."
35. Tomasi, *Free Market Fairness*, ch. 4.
36. The discussion in this paragraph draws on von Platz, "Are Economic Liberties Basic Rights?"
37. Hayek, *The Constitution of Liberty*, pp. 16–19; Narveson, *The Libertarian Idea*, pp. 20–21; Rawls, *Political Liberalism*, pp. 325–26. Rawls's distinction between liberty and the worth of liberty is supposed to answer the socialist critique (*Political Liberalism*, pp. 324–31; *Justice as Fairness*, pp. 148–50).
38. This challenge has historical credentials almost as impressive as those of liberalism itself. For a recent and very clear presentation of it, see Cohen "Freedom and Money." Alex Gourevitch uses a similar argument to contend that liberal theories of economic liberty are both confused and inconsistent ("What is Economic Freedom?" working manuscript presented at the Brown Political Theory Workshop, April 2012).
39. The classical statement of the incidents of the right to property is Honoré's "Ownership"; see also Gaus, "Property and Ownership."
40. Cf. Engels, "Anti-Dühring," p. 713.
41. Rothbard, *For a New Liberty*, p. 27.
42. *Ibid.*, pp. 47–48.

12 Liberalism and religion

FROM THE TWO-RULES DOCTRINE TO FREE EXERCISE AND NO ESTABLISHMENT

In a letter of 494 to the emperor Anastasius, Pope Gelasius I declared that "two there are, august Emperor, by which this world is ruled: the consecrated authority of priests and the royal power." The idea that Gelasius here expresses is that pope and emperor, church and state, are distinct authority structures whose essential difference is that they have jurisdiction over two distinct domains of human activity. This represents a sharp break with the classical view of society as having a single unified governance structure with authority over the lives of the subjects as a whole, including their religion.

In his tract of two years later, *On the Bond of Anathema*, Gelasius elaborated his idea. Church and empire each have a distinct "sphere of competence," a distinct "jurisdiction." Christ himself, says Gelasius, "made a distinction between the two rules, assigning each its sphere of operation and its due respect." The emperor has governance over "human" or "secular" affairs. The pope, along with his bishops and priests, has governance over "divine affairs," over "spiritual activity."[1]

The doctrine that Gelasius articulated in these passages came to be known as the "two-rules" doctrine. From the time he wrote his letter until a century or so after the Protestant Reformation, the framework employed in the West for discussing the relation of the state to religion and the church was almost always this doctrine. The fact that there was near-consensus on the doctrine among theorists by no means eliminated conflict, however. The vagueness of the secular/spiritual contrast resulted in endless controversies over

I thank Steven Wall for very helpful comments on an earlier draft of this chapter.

applications of the doctrine; and, as one would expect, the doctrine was almost always being violated somewhere or other either by the state intruding into what the doctrine clearly declared to be church affairs, or by the church intruding into what the doctrine clearly declared to be state affairs.[2]

The doctrine assumed that the church in a given area is unified and that its membership, for all practical purposes, was identical with the body of those who were subjects of whatever was the government in that area. What differentiated church and state was not a difference in those they govern but a difference in the activities that fall under their governance. Jews were an exception; they were subjects of the government but not members of the church. Their anomolous position put them at risk.

The two-rules doctrine assumed a perfectionist view of the state as it did of the church: State and church together aim at perfecting the people in virtue and piety. This assumption remains implicit in Gelasius' letter and tract; in numberless later writings it is stated explicitly. From the many passages that could be quoted on the matter, let me select one from John Calvin. Calvin is emphatic in his insistence on the importance of distinguishing the two rules. "These two, as we have divided them, must always be examined separately; and while one is being considered, we must call away and turn aside the mind from thinking about the other. There are in man, so to speak, two worlds, over which different kings and different laws have authority."[3] As to the task of government, this is what Calvin says:

[Government] does not merely see to it ... that men breathe, eat, drink, and are kept warm, even though it surely embraces all these activities when it provides for their living together. It does not, I repeat, look to this only, but also prevents idolatry, sacrilege against God's name, blasphemies against his truth, and other public offenses against religion from arising and spreading among the people; it prevents the public peace from being disturbed, it provides that each man may keep his property safe and sound, that men may carry on blameless intercourse among themselves, that honesty and modesty may be preserved among men. In short, it provides that a public manifestation of religion may exist among Christians, and that humanity be maintained among men.[4]

Let us now jump from 496, the year of Gelasius' tract, to 1579, twenty years after the fourth and final edition of Calvin's *Institutes*, when there appeared a tract with the title, in English translation, *A Discourse upon the Permission of Freedom of Religion, called Religions-Vrede in the Netherlands*. Though the author presents himself as Catholic, the predominance of scholarly opinion nowadays is that he was the prominent Huguenot, Philip du Plessis Mornay. Here is what the author says in one place:

> I ask those who do not want to admit the two religions in this country how they now intend to abolish one of them ... It goes without saying that you cannot abolish any religious practice without using force and taking up arms, and going to war against each other instead of taking up arms in unison against Don John and his adherents and delivering us from the insupportable tyranny of the foreigners. If we intend to ruin the Protestants we will ruin ourselves, as the French did. The conclusion to be drawn from this is that it would be better to live in peace with them, rather than ruin ourselves by internal discord and carry on a hazardous, disastrous, long and difficult war or rather a perpetual and impossible one. Taking everything into consideration, we can choose between two things: we can either allow them to live in peace with us or we can all die together; we can either let them be or, desiring to destroy them, be ourselves destroyed by their ruin ... As we cannot forbid these people to practice their religion without starting a war and cannot destroy them by that war without being destroyed ourselves let us conclude that we must let them live in peace and grant them liberty.[5]

The argument is eloquent and poignant. The situation in The Lowlands is that the religious unity that once prevailed is gone. Many have left the Catholic Church and become Protestant. Any attempt to recover the hegemony of the Catholic Church by force of arms would require appalling bloodshed, devastating the Catholic population as well as the Protestant and leaving both at the mercy of the Spaniards. The only option is to tolerate the Protestants, live at peace with them, and together fight Don John.

It was the impossibility of undoing the religious fission caused by the emergence of Protestantism that forced Europeans to consider some form of political community alternative to Christendom and its two-rules structure. Initially they played with the idea of mini-Christendoms, each political unit enforcing its own preferred religion. But within a relatively short period even that project proved impossible. An entirely new way of dealing with religion was imperative.

The new way that gradually and haltingly emerged is now one of the bedrock principles of all liberal democracies. It received its first clear political expression in the First Amendment to the US Constitution: "Congress shall make no law respecting an establishment of religion, or prohibiting the free exercise thereof."[6]

This represents a stunning rejection of the two-rules structure. Instead of the state being enjoined, in conjunction with the church, to seek the perfection of the citizens with respect to religion, the First Amendment *protects* the people *against* the state with respect to the practice of their religion. The First Amendment goes on to say that Congress shall not abridge the right of the people to assemble peaceably. No doubt the authors of the amendment were thinking along the same lines about religion as they were about peaceable assembly. Citizens have a *right* to exercise their religion in accord with their own conscience; they have a *right* to be free from governmental establishment of religion. What is coming to expression here is the new idea of a rights-limited state as opposed to the old idea of a perfectionist state. The two-rules doctrine had also limited the state with respect to religion; however, it was the jurisdiction of the church that limited the state, not the rights of citizens.

CONTROVERSIES CONTINUE

In modern liberal democracies Protestants and Catholics are not killing each other as they were when the author of *A Discourse upon the Permission of Freedom of Religion* wrote his tract. The relation of the state to the religion of its citizens, however, remains the site of controversy. Our controversies take different forms from the form they took in former days, and they are conducted in different terms. In former days the controversies were almost always jurisdictional controversies between church and state; nobody asked whether some governmental policy amounted to impermissible establishment of religion. But controversy continues. Religion remains a problem for the state.

What is it about religion, and what is it about the liberal democratic state, that results in religion continuing to pose quandaries to the state, and those quandaries, and the state's handling of them, in turn causing controversies in the public? That is the question whose answer I wish to pursue for a time.

All liberal democracies forbid, or place substantial restrictions on, the state's infringing on the free exercise of religion. And they all forbid, or place substantial restrictions on, the establishment of religion by the state. They do not all use these terms, but they all do what can be described in these terms. The particular character of the restrictions differs considerably from one liberal democracy to another, with the result that the quandaries posed to the government by religion differ somewhat, as do the controversies generated by those quandaries and by the government's handling of them. In recent years the French have had an intense debate over where to permit and where not to permit Muslim women to wear veils in public; the United States has not had such a controversy. But I suggest that it is essentially the same features of religion and of the liberal democratic state that generate the quandaries and the resultant controversies. To get at the issues, let me use my own country, the United States, as my example.

Some of the quandaries presented by religion to the liberal democratic state are basically definitional controversies. Does this policy on the part of the government count as an establishment of religion or does it not? Does this act on the part of certain citizens count as an exercise of their religion or does it not? If it does, does this law or policy on the part of government count as an infringement on their free exercise or does it not? (The term the First Amendment actually uses is not "infringing on" but "prohibiting.")

In the United States, these definitional quandaries have tended to be framed in terms of how the two religion clauses of the First Amendment are to be interpreted. The term "establishment of religion" has especially raised issues of interpretation. The term was derived, of course, from the term "established church." It turns out that what constitutes establishment of religion is far less clear than what constitutes establishment of a church.

By no means are all the quandaries and controversies definitional, however. There may be little doubt that some law or policy on the part of the government is an example of establishment of religion; nonetheless, it may be a point of controversy as to whether or not it is permissible. So too, there may be little doubt that some law or policy on the part of government is an example of infringing on someone's exercise of his or her religion; nonetheless, it may be a point of controversy as to whether or not it is permissible. Let us see why this is.

CONTROVERSIES GENERATED BY THE FACT
THAT THE RIGHTS ARE PRIMA FACIE

Most if not all of the religions present in Western liberal democracies are exercised by members of the religion participating in communal rituals and engaging in acts of private devotion. One would think that such forms of exercise would pose few quandaries to the liberal democratic state. It's easy to see that these activities count as exercise of the religion in question; and usually it will be easy to tell whether or not some law or policy infringes on their free exercise. But things prove not to be as simple as one might have expected.

Here's why. The two religion clauses of the First Amendment have the rhetorical flavor of being the articulation of absolutes: Congress shall make *no* law respecting an establishment of religion and *no* law prohibiting the free exercise thereof. That is not, however, how the courts have interpreted these clauses. They have interpreted them as articulating *prima facie* rather than absolute *ultima facie* prohibitions on governmental action – or to view it from the other end, as articulating *prima facie* rights of citizens vis-à-vis the government rather than absolute *ultima facie* rights. One's *prima facie* right to the free exercise of one's religion can be outweighed by some other, more weighty, right. The currently operative formula, as I understand it, is that the government may substantially burden a person's exercise of his or her religion if it demonstrates a compelling need to do so and if it uses the least restrictive means available.

Whether or not a person's right to free exercise of his or her religion is, in fact, outweighed in a given case is very much a judgment call on the part of the courts. These judgment calls are invariably controversial, and liberal democracies differ considerably in how they make the calls. To know what the American government is actually prohibited from doing by the two religion clauses, one cannot just exegete the language of the clauses; one has to look at the long and complex series of often-convoluted court decisions as to which infringements on free exercise and which violations of no-establishment are permissible and which are not.

Suppose that the members of some religion have come to the conviction that they are called by God to offer the occasional child sacrifice in their communal rituals; should they be allowed to do so? No liberal democracy would permit them to do so. But suppose that it is the long-established practice of some group to use certain mind-altering drugs when performing their rituals. Should this be permitted? The answer in this case is less obvious. When a case of this sort was presented to the US Supreme Court in the form of the use of peyote in the rituals of a certain Native American tribe, the Court ruled that the government, in the interest of public health, could forbid the use by the public of peyote and other drugs even though this clearly resulted in infringement of the religious practices of the tribe in question.

The quandaries posed to the government by the communal rituals and private devotions of the religions present in society pale before the quandaries posed by the fact that seldom is the exercise of a religion limited to such activities. Almost always the exercise of a religion spreads out into everyday life, sometimes in surprising ways. In order to exercise their religion as they believe it should be exercised, groups establish faith-based hospitals, adoption agencies, educational institutions, relief agencies, development agencies, housing agencies, and social justice organizations. To exercise their religion as they believe it should be exercised, they do such things as pray and wear religious garb in public and post the Ten Commandments in public places. To exercise their religion as they believe it should be exercised, they resist doing such things as serving in the military, getting vaccinated, educating their children beyond elementary school, working on Saturdays or Sundays, or employing members of other religions or of same-sex couples in their businesses and organizations.

It's easy to see that such forms of religious exercise will regularly pose quandaries to the government. Suppose the government decides that recitation by schoolchildren of the Pledge of Allegiance enhances national unity; is it permitted to require recitation of the Pledge by all schoolchildren even though reciting the Pledge would violate the religious convictions of Jehovah's Witnesses? When the US Supreme Court was faced with this question, it determined that this was not permissible.

We do not have to dredge the past for cases of this sort. Suppose the government, in the interest of public health, decides that insurance plans should offer contraceptive medicines and devices. It turns out, however, that some institutions and organizations are opposed on religious grounds to including contraceptive medicines and devices in the insurance plans they offer their employees. So suppose that the government, after exempting churches, synagogues, and other organizations that offer distinctly religious services, decides to require institutions and organizations to offer their employees such plans even though offering such plans would violate the religious convictions of certain faith-based hospitals, colleges, universities, and so forth? Is this permissible? If not, would it be permissible if the government allowed such institutions to offer plans that make contraceptive medicines and devices available but do not require the institution itself to pay for those?

The courts have required that, when possible, the government offer reasonable accommodations and exemptions when passing general laws aimed at securing public health, safety, and order whose effect is to infringe on the free exercise by some group of its religion. The question in the case of Obamacare has been whether the exemptions and accommodations proposed are sufficient. Of course, the state can no more pass laws whose *intent* it is to infringe on the exercise of someone's religion in daily life than it can pass laws whose *intent* it is to infringe on the performance of communal rituals and private devotional practices. But over and over the courts have found in favor of some law aimed at public health, safety, or order that has the effect of prohibiting or infringing on the free exercise of religion. The right to free exercise and the right to no-establishment are no more than prima facie rights.

CONTROVERSIES GENERATED BY WHAT NON-ESTABLISHMENT IS TAKEN TO REQUIRE

Another source of quandaries for the government and of controversies in the public is the fact that certain ways of securing non-establishment arguably treat some religious people unfairly and infringe without good cause on the free exercise of their religion. To develop this point, let me select for discussion some of the issues that have faced the courts when applying the religion clauses to elementary and secondary schools.

In the interest of having an educated citizenry, all of the American states in the nineteenth century established elementary and secondary schools that are governed by school boards elected by the public and supported by public tax funds. Eventually the courts interpreted the non-establishment clause as requiring that the instruction offered by these schools be neutral with respect to all the religions present in American society; more generally, it required that the schools refrain from any activity that would indicate approval or support for some particular religion, for religion in general, for some particular form of secularism, or for secularism in general. They must, for example, refrain from engaging in prayer or the devotional reading of some group's sacred scripture, and they must refrain from in any way sponsoring such activities.

Now add the presence in society of one or more groups of religious people who are opposed on religious grounds to having their children educated in such schools. Some of these citizens insist that the idea of an education that is neutral with respect to all the religions present in American society is pure fantasy. There can be no such education, they insist; education is inevitably shaped by some worldview. And they have come to believe that the worldview shaping the education in their local public school is one to which they are opposed and to which they do not want their children exposed.

These are joined by other citizens whose position is that even if the educational program of the local public elementary and secondary schools is religiously neutral, they are nonetheless opposed on religious grounds to having their children educated in such schools. They believe that it is their religious duty to have the education of their children shaped at relevant points by their own religious worldview and set within a devotional context.

A number of groups of these like-minded people get together to establish their own schools. They hire teachers who share their religious convictions and institute a program of education that expresses those convictions. The courts permit them to do this, but insist that public funds continue to go exclusively to the public schools, which are mandated to offer a religiously neutral education. One might call this the *no-support* policy: no financial support for religiously committed schools.

Throughout most of the second half of the twentieth century, the no-support policy guided the decisions of the US Supreme Court. The court was repeatedly confronted with quandaries concerning the application of the policy; for example, if the public school system provides busing for the students of non-public religiously oriented schools, does that count as lending support to those schools, and hence as governmental establishment of religion? And if it does, is it nonetheless permissible because the prima facie right of the citizens to non-establishment is outweighed by some other right? The fact that the court was repeatedly confronted with such quandaries did not deter it from using the no-support policy to guide its decisions.

The no-support policy raises a substantial question of fairness. On the face of things, it seems unfair that those who find the education offered by the local public school satisfactory – whether because it offers a neutral education and that's what they want for their children, or because it offers an education shaped by some worldview and they share that worldview – should get free education for their children, while those who are religiously opposed to their children receiving that sort of education must themselves pay for alternative schooling.

The standard response to this charge of unfairness is first to describe religious people as asking for their own preferred supplement to public school education, and then to go on to say that there is no more reason why I should pay for the religion-supplement that you want for your child than that you should pay for the ballet-supplement that I want for my child.

The reply to this response by those who desire a religiously oriented education for their children should be obvious: what they desire for their children is not a religion-supplement to the education offered by the public school; what they desire is a devotionally framed and religiously oriented education.

The no-support policy also raises a serious question as to whether it has the effect of impermissibly violating the free exercise clause. The courts recognize that the imposition of a financial burden on someone's exercise of his or her religion may constitute an illegitimate infringement on its free exercise; whether it does or not depends on the particular form that the imposition takes. Obviously, those who find the education offered by the local public school religiously unsatisfactory and opt for an alternative pay a heavy financial price for this particular exercise of their religion; pretty clearly that is an infringement on the free exercise of their religion. But is it an impermissible infringement? That would seem to depend on whether there is an alternative way in which the state can achieve its goal of an educated citizenry, a way that does not constitute an establishment of religion and also does not infringe on the free exercise by some citizens of their religion.

There is such an alternative, namely, what one might call the *equal-support* policy. On the equal-support policy, the state distributes funds to all schools equally regardless of their religious or non-religious orientation. The state establishes educational criteria that all schools must meet if they are to receive funding; no doubt these will sometimes prove controversial. And all schools must obey the laws of the land with respect to child abuse and the like. But in its distribution of funds, the state is religion-blind.

The equal-support policy would seem to satisfy the requirement of no-establishment at least as well as the no-support policy, while at the same time being arguably more fair and clearly infringing less on free exercise. It's relevant to note that some European countries – The Netherlands, for example – do in fact follow the equal-support policy in their funding of schools.

The arguable unfairness of the no-support policy, and its infringement on the free exercise by some citizens of their religion, has led municipalities and states in recent years to chip away at the policy with such strategies as vouchers, charter schools, and the like. Over the past decade or so, the courts have tended to look more kindly on these strategies than they did previously. As I read our present situation, the American people, along with its legislatures and judiciary, are moving, in halting and confused ways, away from the pure no-support policy in the direction of the equal-support policy.

This change is discernible not only in the relation of the government to elementary and secondary schools but also in its relation to a number of other types of faith-based institutions. As noted earlier, we in the United States have faith-based adoption agencies, faith-based relief organizations, faith-based hospitals, and so forth, on and on. Traditionally the government followed a no-support policy toward all of these. In recent years there has been a halting and cautious move toward including faith-based organizations and agencies in the government's distribution of funds for the support of adoption, relief, development, and the like.

The equal-support policy poses its own quandaries, however. The main problem is that the religious convictions of faith-based agencies rather often lead them to run afoul of one or another anti-discrimination law. Almost all faith-based organizations employ some form of religious discrimination in their hiring policies; they view that as essential to their being the sort of faith-based organization they are. That sort of discrimination has not in general been prohibited. But what if some faith-based adoption agency refuses to arrange for the adoption of children to same-sex couples on the ground that to do so would violate its religious principles? Or if some faith-based hospital refuses to perform sterilization procedures on the ground that doing so would violate its religious principles? Or if some faith-based educational institution refuses to allow onto its faculty those living in homosexual relationships because doing so would violate its religious principles? It is such forms of discrimination by faith-based institutions that pose deep problems for implementing the equal-support policy.

In short, though the emergence of the liberal democratic state put to rest the religious wars that wracked Europe after the breakup of Christendom, it has by no means ended quandaries confronting the state over how it should treat its citizens with respect to their religions, and it has by no means ended controversies in the public over those quandaries and how the government handles them. It is my view that we must expect that this is how it will always be. Religion will always pose problems for the liberal democratic state.

RELIGIONS MUST SHAPE UP IF THEY ARE TO LIVE WITHIN THE LIBERAL DEMOCRATIC STATE

I do not claim to have highlighted the sources of all the quandaries that religion poses to the liberal democratic state, but I want now to turn our attention in the opposite direction. The religious fracturing of Europe and the subsequent wars of religion forced the gradual emergence in Europe, over the course of the seventeenth and eighteenth centuries, of a new form of state. This change could not have happened without Europeans also changing their religious convictions in certain ways. There had to be a mutual accommodation: the state to the religions of its citizens and the religions of the citizens to the new form of state.

The point, of course, is that some religions are not compatible with the liberal democratic state. Richard Rorty remarks in one place that the "happy, Jeffersonian compromise that the Enlightenment reached with the religious ... consists in privatizing religion – keeping it out of" the public square.[7] That seems to me not correct; religion in liberal democracies has not, in general, been privatized. But that some sort of accommodation had to take place on the part of religion to the state, as well as on the part of the state to religion, is indubitable. I am speaking of a different and deeper form of accommodation than that which consists of accepting certain qualifications on free exercise. Let me develop this point by presenting a form of religion that is through and through incompatible with the liberal democratic state.

In the *New York Times Magazine* of March 23, 2003, there was a rather lengthy analysis by the journalist Paul Berman of the thought of the Islamic scholar, Sayyid Qutb.[8] Qutb was an Egyptian intellectual who spent some time as a student in the United States (Colorado) and then returned to Egypt. He was imprisoned for more than ten years by the Egyptian government and executed in 1966. While in prison he wrote a commentary on the Koran called *In the Shade of the Qur'an*. Let me summarize a bit of his thought, basing my summary on Berman's article. Whether or not Berman's interpretation is correct on all points is irrelevant to my purposes here.

A central component of Qutb's writing was socio-political analysis of a type familiar to us in the West for almost two centuries now. The analysis begins with a recitation of the sorrows of life in modernized societies. I quote Berman:

Qutb wrote that, all over the world, humans had reached a moment of unbearable crisis. The human race had lost touch with human nature. Man's inspiration, intelligence and morality were degenerating. Sexual relations were deteriorating "to a level lower than the beasts." Man was miserable, anxious, and skeptical, sinking into idiocy, insanity, and crime. People were turning, in their unhappiness, to drugs, alcohol, and existentialism.

Qutb admired economic productivity and scientific knowledge. But he did not think that wealth and science were rescuing the human race. He figured that, on the contrary, the richest countries were the unhappiest of all.

Those are the symptoms. Qutb's diagnosis is the same, in its general structure, as that of all our great Romantic social theorists: the once-upon-a-time unity of human life has been fractured by modernization. Qutb perceives what he calls a "hideous schizophrenia" in modern life. The root cause of our unhappiness is the fragmentation resulting from that schizophrenia. Qutb's originality lies in his particular way of filling in the details of this now-familiar sort of structural analysis. Christianity is the principal cause of fragmentation, with Judaism now playing a supporting role. Intrinsic to Christianity is a split between the spiritual world, on the one hand, and the physical, biological, and social world, on the other. The sorrows of modern life are the result of that split. Qutb's narrative goes as follows. The teachings of Judaism were "divinely revealed by God to Moses and the other prophets. Judaism instructed man on how to behave in every sphere of life – how to live a worldly existence that was also a life at one with God. This could be done by obeying a system of divinely mandated laws, the code of Moses" (p. 28). Eventually Judaism withered into what Qutb called "a system of rigid and lifeless ritual." God then sent a new prophet, Jesus, who penetrated to the essence of the Mosaic code and proposed some reforms. Rather than the Jews in general acknowledging Jesus as a prophet and accepting the reforms he proposed, intense controversies erupted between old-line Jews and the followers of Jesus, resulting in what Qutb called "this unpleasant separation of the two parties" (ibid.).

As a consequence of this antagonism, the early Christians distorted the true teachings of Jesus by emphasizing his divine message of spirituality and love while rejecting its context, namely, "Judaism's legal system, the code of Moses, which regulated every jot and tittle of daily life" (ibid.). They "imported into Christianity the philosophy of the Greeks – the belief in a spiritual existence completely separate from physical life, a zone of pure spirit" (ibid.). The subsequent history of Christianity and of its influence has been the playing out, in ever new ways, of that original split between the spiritual on the one hand, and our daily life on the other.

Christianity lost touch with the physical [and social] world. The old code of Moses, with its laws for diet, dress, marriage, sex and everything else, had enfolded the divine and the worldly into a single concept, which was the worship of God. But Christianity divided these things into two, the sacred and the secular. Christianity said, "Render unto Caesar what is Caesar's and unto God what is God's." Christianity puts the physical world in one corner and the spiritual world in another corner. Constantine's debauches over here, monastic renunciation over there. (ibid.)

Europe's scientific and technological achievements have enabled it to impose its "hideous schizophrenia" "on peoples and cultures in every corner of the globe." That is the root of our present-day worldwide misery – the root of "the anxiety in contemporary society, the sense of drift, the purposelessness, the craving for false pleasures" (*ibid.*).

One can anticipate the cure that Qutb proposes. In true Islam there is a vision of the wholeness of life; in true Islam there is no schizophrenia between the sacred and the secular, church and state, the spiritual and the physical; in true Islam there is no split between God's laws and our daily lives. It's all one. True Islam must be recovered. Christians and Jews have mounted a gigantic campaign against true Islam, attempting to annihilate it. With their liberal democratic ideas in hand they have attempted "to confine Islam to the emotional and ritual circles, to bar it from participating in the activity of life, and to check its complete predominance over every human secular activity, a pre-eminence it earns by virtue of its nature and function" (*ibid.*). That campaign must be resisted by Islam with all the resources at its disposal. Sharia must be reinstated as the legal code for society as a whole so that God's law can once again hold sway for all of everybody's life. Only then will divinity and humanity be once again united. Only then will there be justice, peace, true freedom, and happiness.

It's obvious that Islam, as Qutb understands it, is incompatible with liberal democracy. But what exactly are the fundamental points of conflict? What are the fundamental structural principles of social organization that Qutb rejects but that he would have to accept if he were to regard liberal democracy as a legitimate political structure?

The first and most fundamental structural principle is that religious institutions in all their forms – church, mosque, synagogue, whatever – are distinct from political institutions in all their forms. Liberal democracy requires that fundamental sort of duality, that fundamental sort of institutional separation.

An important part of what made it possible for liberal democracy to emerge in the West was that for more than a millennium the West had accepted this principle of institutional separation; the two-rules principle presupposed the separation. So there is something right in Qutb's analysis of Christianity. For fifteen hundred years Christians in the West have lived with the institutional duality of church and state. And even in the East, where church and state were traditionally far more intertwined than they were in the West, neither the primate nor the emperor was under the authority of the other; they were frequently at loggerheads with each other.

I judge Qutb to be mistaken, however, in his assumption that this institutional duality has been a matter of intrinsic conviction on the part of Christians in general. I do not doubt that sometimes it was; but often it was more a matter of expediency than of conviction. I see nothing in Augustine's thought, for example, that commits him in principle to the duality.

Likewise Qutb is mistaken in his claim that Christians have regarded God's law as holding only for that area of life governed by the church and not for that governed by the state. Those who said that the state was to be concerned with secular matters did not mean that God's law had no application to government; Calvin was not eccentric in remarking that God's rule takes two forms, one for the church and one for the state. Nonetheless, Qutb is correct in his claim that there has long been an institutional separation of church and state in societies shaped by Christianity. And that separation is indispensable to the existence of a liberal democratic polity.

What does the institutional separation of religious institutions and the state actually come to? What are the tell-tale signs of this duality? Three, I would say. First, religious institutions do not have their powers delegated to them by the state, the state does not have its powers delegated to it by religious institutions, and neither of these has its powers delegated to it by some higher institution. Second, nobody has political authority by virtue of holding an office in some religious institution, and nobody has an office in some religious institution by virtue of having political authority. And third, religious institutions and the government each have their own distinct "powers," their own distinct jurisdiction.

A second fundamental structural principle of a liberal democratic society is, to put it rather vaguely at first, that the state is the polity of all its citizens equally no matter what their religion. This fundamental principle of equality of membership has two aspects. First, in its distribution of benefits and burdens, liberties and restrictions, the state is not to favor one religion or brand of secularism over another. (This is part, at least, of what non-establishment comes to.) And second, everyone is to have equal voice in determining the personnel and conduct of the state. One's religion or lack thereof is to make no difference to one's political voice.

It is these two aspects of equality of membership, even more than the institutional separation of church and state, that give to life in a liberal democracy the peculiar "schizophrenic" character that Qutb finds so offensive. The state is not to favor believers over infidels; it must refrain from cultivating true piety. And the voice of the infidel carries the same weight in the affairs of state as the voice of the believer.

Before the breakup of the religious unity of Europe in the sixteenth century, Christians for the most part did not accept these two aspects of equal membership. It was their slow, halting, and often reluctant acceptance of them that made possible the emergence of liberal democracies in the West. European Christianity accommodated itself to the new political structure. And Christians came to accept the ongoing piecemeal accommodations required by the infringements on religious freedom judged permissible by the courts.

FURTHER ACCOMMODATION?

In this final section of my chapter, I want to call attention to the presence in liberal democracies of voices that find the accommodations of religion to liberal democracy that I have thus far noted inadequate. These voices hold that religion endangers peace, justice, and the stability of liberal democracy even if it has accommodated itself to the structural principles of liberal democracy and even if religious people do accept those infringements on the free exercise of religion that the courts judge permissible. These voices call for a further shaping up on the part of religion. For the most part they do not propose that laws be enacted to bring about this further shaping up; they hope that moral suasion will do the work.[9] Let me order these voices, starting with those that call for a more limited form of shaping up and concluding with those that call for a more radical form.

John Rawls and his followers hold that it is acceptable for citizens to employ reasons drawn from their own particular religion when debating significant political issues in public and when making decisions on those issues; but if they do, they must "stand ready" to employ reasons for the positions they favor that are drawn from what

Rawls calls "public reason." What exactly Rawls means by "public reason" is the subject of a literature that is by now massive; for our purposes here it will be sufficient to say that public reason, as Rawls understands it, consists of principles, drawn from the governing idea of liberal democracy, for the just distribution of benefits and burdens, civil rights and duties, by the state. Those who affirm liberal democracy, rather than merely putting up with it, implicitly embrace such principles, whatever be their religious disagreements. Accordingly, appealing to such principles when debating and deciding significant political issues enhances the stability of a liberal democratic society; resting content with employing our diverse religious reasons endangers that stability.

In all liberal democratic societies there are religious people who are not in the habit of debating and deciding political issues on the basis of reasons drawn from public reason. It is their habit to debate and decide political issues on the basis of reasons drawn from their own particular religion. For some, this is more than a mere habit; they believe that this is what they *ought* to do.

Many of those who are in the habit of debating and deciding political issues on the basis of reasons drawn from their own particular religion know no other way of debating and deciding such issues; this is the way they learned in their families and in their religious institutions. They don't know how to appeal to public reason. Satisfying the Rawlsian injunction requires of them that they shape up by acquiring the ability and the willingness to debate and decide significant political issues on the basis of reasons drawn from public reason.

Richard Rorty urges a more stringent form of shaping up. In an unpublished essay consisting of remarks he made upon receiving the Eckhart Prize and titled "Religion after Onto-Theology: Reflections on Vattimo's *Belief*," he asserts that ecclesiastical institutions, "despite all the good they do – despite all the comfort they provide to those in need or in despair – are dangerous to the health of democratic societies, so that it would be best for them eventually to wither away." The dangers posed to democracy by institutionalized religion are "particularly evident," he says, in present-day United States, where "Christian fundamentalists whose support has become indispensable to right-wing American politicians are undermining the secularist, Jeffersonian, tradition in American culture." The danger to our liberal democracy is not that fundamentalists are threatening to overthrow the US government; the danger is that they support legislation restricting behavior that other groups in society regard as completely acceptable – abortion and homosexual activity, for example.

The danger can only be averted by religion shaping up so that it becomes entirely personal and private. The religion of one's inner life can be of whatever form and intensity one wishes; no harm there. It is when religion leaves the sanctuary of the inner life and tries to shape the state and other social institutions in accord with its convictions that it endangers the liberal democratic society. To repeat a passage that I quoted earlier: the happy "Jeffersonian compromise that the Enlightenment reached with the religious ... consists in privatizing religion – keeping it out of" the public square.

In John Hick and his allies in the discussions on religious pluralism, one finds a yet more radical proposal for shaping up. Both Rawls and Rorty propose setting bounds to religion as we find it. Religion must shape up so that it no longer appeals exclusively to its own resources when debating and deciding significant political issues, or it must shape up so that it no longer speaks on institutional matters in general. Within those bounds, religion is free to take whatever form it wishes. In his well-known book, *Interpretation of Religion*,[10] Hick urges that particularist religions, rather than learning to live within bounds, should reinterpret their particularisms so that they are no longer exclusivist.

Hick holds that any "axial" or "post-axial" religion that does not accord equal religious significance to all other such religions perforce harbors within itself the threat of coercion and violence, thereby being a menace to peace.[11] To cite just one example: As long as Christianity harbors a supersessionist attitude toward Judaism, there can be no enduring peace between the two religions. The solution is for each axial and post-axial religion to regard all such religions as alternative ways of engaging The Real, with none of them giving us the literal truth of the matter, and for each to concede that all are equally successful in achieving salvation for their adherents.

A fourth, and yet more radical, version of the line of thought that I am delineating says that a particularist religion, whatever its form, content, or self-understanding, poses a danger to the liberal democratic society. It must wither away. Rather than shaping up by living within the bounds of public reason, by living within the bounds of the inner life, or by reinterpreting its particularism in non-exclusivist fashion, religion, on this fourth view, must shape up by transmuting itself into non-particularist religion.

This is what Jacques Derrida proposed in some of his late writings. In his reflections on "the return of religion" that seemed to be occurring at the time, Derrida proposed to undertake "a program of analysis for the forms of evil perpetrated in the four corners of the world 'in the name of religion.'"[12] His analysis led him to the conclusion that violence is the inevitable political consequence of what he calls "determinate" religion. The violence may not be what those of us less given to hyperbole than Derrida would call "violence"; it may simply be what we would call "coercion" – though let it be added that often it does take the form of violence.

The solution is for determinate religion to be transmuted into "religion without religion." Take an example. A structural feature typical of the religions that interested Derrida is the messianic structure; adherents of the religion look forward to a day when justice and peace shall reign. "Religion without religion" would be religion in which all determinate content had been abstracted from such messianic anticipation, leaving only the pure structure. Such religion would be "structural messianism," "messianism without content," or simply, "the messianic." A condition of the elimination of political "violence" is the transmutation of present-day religions into a religion in which messianism is purely structural; determinate messianisms necessarily harbor the threat of "war."

The great grey eminence behind this way of thinking is Immanuel Kant, though it must at once be added that the religion Kant proposed was by no means a religion of pure structure and no content; it was a *determinate* religion without being a *particular* religion. Kant explicitly shared with the other thinkers we have canvassed here the conviction that particular religion is a danger to peace, justice, and the stability of liberal democracy. If "eternal peace" is to arrive, particularist religion must wither away. Kant did not consider whether reining it in would be sufficient, nor did he consider the possibility of religions reinterpreting their particularisms so that they were no longer exclusivist. Since what Kant says about the menace of particularist religion is as vivid as Kant's writing ever gets, let me quote him at some length:

The so-called religious wars which have so often shaken the world and bespattered it with blood, have never been anything but wrangles over ecclesiastical faith; and the oppressed have complained not that they were hindered from adhering to their religion (for no external power can do this) but that they were not permitted publicly to observe their ecclesiastical faith.

Now when, as usually happens, a church proclaims itself to be the one church universal (even though it is based upon faith in a special revelation, which, being historical, can never be required of everyone), he who refuses to acknowledge its (peculiar) ecclesiastical faith is called by it an *unbeliever* and is hated wholeheartedly; he who diverges therefrom only in part (in non-essentials) is called *heterodox* and is at least shunned as a source of infection. But he who avows [allegiance to] this church and yet diverges from it on essentials of its faith (namely, regarding the practices connected with it), is called, especially if he spreads abroad his false belief, a *heretic*, and, as a rebel, such a man is held more culpable than a foreign foe, is expelled from the church with an anathema ... and is given over to all the gods of hell. The exclusive correctness of belief in matters of ecclesiastical faith claimed by the church's teachers or heads is called *orthodoxy*.[13]

The solution to these evils of religion is the withering away of "positive" religions and their replacement with a purely rational religion, that is, a religion whose content is grounded in reason alone and not in the particularities of revelation, mania, or tradition. As humankind progresses toward full rationality, this is the religion that it will increasingly embrace. Such religion, though determinate in content, will nonetheless not be a *particular* religion since it will enjoy universal acceptance; it will therefore not be a danger to peace and justice. The coming of such religion, shared by all on account of their common rationality, will finally bring about "the world of an eternal peace."[14]

The line of thought that I have been highlighting runs deep in the mentality of modernity. Religion remains a danger to peace, justice, and the stability of the liberal democratic society. It must, accordingly, shape up in ways that go beyond what is required for living within the structural principles of liberal democratic society and beyond accepting those infringements on its free exercise that the courts judge permissible.

My response is twofold. First, I see no prospect whatsoever of religion in general disappearing, or of all particular religions disappearing, or of all determinate religions disappearing, or of all particular and determinate religions reinterpreting themselves so that they are no longer exclusivist, or of all particular and determinate religions becoming privatized, or of all adherents of particular and determinate religions refraining from appealing exclusively to the resources of their own religion in debating political issues and making political decisions. That religion is often a danger to peace, justice, and the stability of our liberal democratic societies is beyond doubt. I think we have no choice but to deal with those dangers in ad hoc fashion when and where they arise. There is no prospect of averting them all in advance.

Second, I judge that these views, should they become widespread, would themselves be a danger to liberal democracy; they are, in that way, themselves illiberal. If a sizable number of citizens come to believe that particularist religion that interprets itself in exclusivist fashion is a menace to peace, justice, and the stability of liberal democracy if it goes beyond the interior life and seeks public expression, then they will be strongly tempted to go beyond moral suasion and press for laws aimed at curtailing what they see as the threat.

NOTES

1. My quotations from Gelasius are all from the translations to be found in O'Donovan and Lockwood, *From Irenaeus to Grotius*, pp. 178–79.
2. The standard documentary history of the conflict between church and state is Ehler and Morrall, *Church and State Through the Centuries*. Ehler's *Twenty Centuries of Church and State* is a less detailed telling of the story. Tierney's *The Crisis of Church and State* fills in the details for the medieval period. There is as yet no comparable detailed and comprehensive history for the Reformation period. (I owe these references to John Witte.)
3. Calvin, *Institutes* III. xix.15; trans. Ford Lewis Battles.
4. *Ibid.*, IV. xx.3.
5. *Discours sur la Permission de Libertē de Religion, Dicte Religions-Vrede au Pais-Bais* (1559), p. 163.
6. That the free exercise of religion is one of the bedrock principles of liberal democracy is incontrovertible; whether the non-establishment of religion is also one of its bedrock principles is subject to doubt. The fact that establishment tends to become more and more innocuous in those polities that honor free exercise but not non-establishment seems to me to

argue in favor of also regarding non-establishment as a bedrock principle, though indeed less fundamental than free exercise. What this claim implies is that some European states, such as England, are not yet full-fledged liberal democracies, and that others, such as the Netherlands, became full-fledged liberal democracies only gradually. (Steven Wall pointed out to me the need for this explanation.)

7. Rorty, *Philosophy and Social Hope*, p. 169.
8. Berman, "The Philosopher of Islamic Terror." Subsequent page numbers are given in the text.
9. An exceptionally vigorous and aggressive development of the thesis that religions in liberal democracries must shape up in ways that go beyond their acceptance of the structural principles of liberal democracy and of court decisions declaring the permissibility of certain infringements on the free exercise of religion is Macedo, *Diversity and Distrust.* "Diversity must be kept in its place," says Macedo (p. 3).
10. Hick, *Interpretation of Religion.*
11. The period extending from 800 to 200 BCE has come to be called "the axial age" in world religious history. Axial religions are those that emerged during that period, for example, Judaism, Buddhism, and Confucianism. Christianity and Islam are post-axial religions. Hick regards pre-axial religions as inferior to axial and post-axial religions.
12. Smith, "Determined Violence," p. 197. The quoted phrases that follow are all taken from Smith's article.
13. Kant, *Religion Within the Bounds of Reason Alone*, pp. 99–100.
14. *Ibid.;* the last words of Division One of Book Three.

13　Liberalism and multiculturalism

How do liberalism and multiculturalism relate to one another? As stated, the question seems impossible to answer in a univocal manner. Both "liberalism" and "multiculturalism" denote theoretical constellations more than they do well-delineated concepts. My intention in this chapter is therefore not to attempt to provide an answer any clearer than is allowed by the terms in which the question is formulated. Instead, I will provide the reader with a thumbnail sketch of the contours of the debate as to the proper way in which to construe the nature of the relationship between the two, as that debate has developed in recent decades in the philosophical literature. Rather than providing stipulative definitions of the correct ways in which to understand the concepts involved, I will, as it were, allow the protagonists to the debate to speak for themselves. This will allow us to appreciate how the ongoing debate has affected the manner in which theorists have modified their understandings both of liberalism and of multiculturalism in order to arrive at a plausible conceptualization of what an appropriately liberal multiculturalism would look like. Having gone through the main stages in the debate, I will examine one of the theoretical roads not taken by contributors to the theoretical literature on liberal multiculturalism that may give rise to a more satisfactory position than the ones thus far assayed.

I

There are just about as many liberalisms as there are liberal theorists. But if one thing unites liberals, it is a commitment to what may be termed political individualism. Political individualism is the view that the justification of states, and of state policies, must ultimately be grounded in some aspect of the good of individuals. Whether that

305

good is cashed out in terms of individual interest, individual consent, or in terms of some more morally ambitious notion such as individual flourishing, is one of the questions that liberals argue about. However, this core commitment is sufficient to generate the view, common to all liberals, that groups cannot be viewed by liberalism as possessed of any kind of irreducible value. Groups matter only to the extent that they matter to individuals. They cannot therefore be independent sources of moral claims. The commitment to this form of individualism is a constraint on all recognizably *liberal* forms of multiculturalism.

The individualism inherent in liberalism's core commitments has given rise in some theorists to the idea that liberal justice should have to do exclusively with the protection of individual rights, and with the setting up of rules that justly adjudicate between individual claims to opportunities and resources. When members of groups make claims to distributions of rights, resources, and opportunities *qua* group members that differ from those that would result from taking individuals alone into account, or when they make claims on behalf of groups to *soi-disant* group rights, those claims are to be rejected by liberals, or so it would seem. What liberal regimes have to offer to groups on this view is the full complement of individual rights, including civil rights to freedom of association, of conscience, of religion, and the like, which are essential building blocks in the associational lives of individuals. On this view of the relationship between liberalism and groups, liberal states should go no further than ensuring that all individuals are protected in their decisions to associate, or not to associate, with others. The "free market" that would ensue from these protections being rigorously enforced may lead to some groups thriving, and to others withering away. But the result of the exercise by individuals of their liberal civil rights should be of no particular concern to the liberal state. John Rawls's invocation of Isaiah Berlin's idea that there can be no social world without loss is emblematic in this connection:

No society can include within itself all forms of life. We may indeed lament the limited space, as it were, of social worlds, and of ours in particular, and we may regret some of the inevitable effects of our culture and social structure. As Sir Isaiah Berlin has long maintained ... there is no social world without loss – that is, no social world that does not exclude some ways of life that realize in special ways certain fundamental values. By virtue of its culture and institutions, any society will prove uncongenial to some ways of life. But these social necessities are not to be mistaken for arbitrary bias or for injustice.[1]

As we shall see, the emergence of a more robust liberal multiculturalism can be traced to the critique of what some have seen as the mistaken inference according to which what I have here termed political individualism necessarily excludes any modification to the exclusively individualistic schedule of rights that theories like Rawls's put forward. Indeed, the development of a liberal multiculturalist position can be seen as emerging from the overcoming of a purported liberal "blind spot" with respect to groups. But given the degree to which this reading of Rawls has become orthodox,[2] it is worth pausing for a moment to ascertain the resources that the kinds of liberal regimes that would emerge from the application of Rawlsian principles would give rise to for multiculturalists. Is the liberalism of individual rights really as antithetical to multiculturalism as some have supposed? To begin to do this, we must provide a bare bones conception of multiculturalism to match the rather stripped down vision of liberalism that has been put forward thus far. Any multicultural theory is in my view committed to the idea that, at a minimum, states should interpret the requirements of social integration in as parsimonious a manner as possible. Liberal regimes appropriately worry about the social conditions that must be satisfied in order for the core institutions of the state to function as they should.

According to a view that has gained some prominence in recent decades, for example through the work of Robert Putnam, democratic institutions can function only if they are underpinned by a fund of "social capital."[3] Some theorists have in recent years worried about the degree of compatibility between a socially diverse society and a society whose members are willing to sacrifice some of their material well-being for the sake of others. They have claimed that distributive justice and multiculturalism may well stand in some degree of tension with one another.[4]

Now, it seems clear that a society cannot tolerate a complete absence of fellow feeling and solidarity among its members. Let us accept that there are sociological conditions for the realization of just principles through political institutions. A society cannot achieve the requisite degree of cohesion simply because its members are all Rawlsians.

A multiculturalist, according to the minimalist conception I propose, is someone who believes that the state should enact policies designed to achieve the requisite degree of social cohesion in as parsimonious a manner as possible. Specifically, it should draw as clear a line as possible between social integration on the one hand, and cultural integration, on the other. Social integration has to do with the possession by citizens of cultural traits that allow them to function as full members of public institutions, and that contribute to those institutions functioning justly. For example, it seems unexceptionable that the state should ensure that all citizens possess the linguistic wherewithal with which to understand the communications that the state directs toward them. Linguistic integration of the requisite kind will unavoidably have an impact on the degree and intensity of linguistic diversity that obtains in a society. But such integration seems justified by considerations of social cohesion.

Cultural integration refers to any policy designed to reduce the degree of cultural variety in a society in ways that are not justified by the requirements that justify social integration. That is, policies which aim to shape the linguistic, cultural, religious, or ethnic identities of citizens in ways that are not required in order to achieve the threshold of social cohesion required for the smooth functioning of institutions fall into the category of what I have here referred to as cultural integration.

Multiculturalism in the minimalist form I am referring to here involves the denial of cultural integration, but the acceptance of measures of social integration. With this definition in hand, we are in a better position to appreciate the contribution that even a Rawlsian liberal regime can make to multiculturalism. As is accepted by all, an orthodox liberalism provides citizens with invaluable tools with which to pursue their lives as cultural beings, inasmuch as it affords them liberal civil rights that provide bulwarks against the use to which the state might be put by intolerant majorities. But inasmuch as it is committed to the view that no group should be provided with the institutional means with which to tilt the balance toward itself in terms of its possession of inducements and policies designed to attract and to preserve membership, that commitment extends to the state even in its pursuit of apparently less nefarious objectives.

Indeed, states have historically used the policy levers at their disposal in order to erode minority cultures, and in order to construct a shared identity among the diverse members of their populations. This process, which has come to be known as "nation-building," can in certain circumstances be quite in keeping with the liberal ethics that has been described here. "Nation-building," that is, may simply refer to the policies through which states attempt to achieve social integration. But that has not been the most typical kind of case in the history of Western nation-building. European and North American states (to name but these) have throughout the nineteenth and twentieth centuries employed the levers that have been at their disposal to construct thick national identities. This has involved among other things the prohibition on teaching minority languages, the erosion of the pre-existing institutional bases upon which the viability of minority groups rested, and so on. Clearly, such policy measures are just as difficult to reconcile with the liberal commitment to individualism as are the methods that groups that do not possess a monopoly on the use of legitimate coercion would employ in order to "police" the identities of their members.

If this is the case, then it follows that *liberalism is by its very nature minimally multicultural*. It is so, first, because it provides citizens with the individual civil rights that they require in order to conduct their associational lives as they see fit, and second, because it is by its very nature opposed to cultural, as opposed to more modestly social, integration.

A final note before considering those liberal theorists who purport to move beyond the rather timid multiculturalism that the orthodox liberalism of someone like Rawls allows. In *A Theory of Justice*, Rawls argues that "self-respect" is the most important of the primary goods. Rawls seems to ground this claim in the plausible idea that in order for citizens to be able to carry out their plans of life, it is as important that they think well enough of themselves to consider their plans worth carrying out as it is that they possess more recognizably tangible primary goods such as money and opportunities. Now, Rawls does not believe that individual agents can acquire a sufficient fund of self-respect endogenously. Individuals must also possess social bases of self-respect. It is important that "for each person there is some association (one or more) to which he belongs and within which the activities that are rational for him are publicly affirmed by others."⁵ Now, Rawls assumes that "in a well-ordered society ... there are a variety of communities and associations, and [that] the members of each have their own ideals appropriately matched to their aspirations and talents."⁶

This assumption seems baseless, however. There is nothing about "well-orderedness" as Rawls defines it that guarantees or even renders it more likely that this fortuitous match will eventuate. A society is well ordered, on Rawls's view, just in case "everyone accepts and knows that the others accept the same principles of justice, and their basic social institutions satisfy and are known to satisfy these principles."⁷ As we have seen, Rawls's principles of justice purport to set up fair background conditions against the backdrop of which citizens are to lead their associational lives. The fair "cultural marketplace" that is given rise to when these conditions obtain may, as Rawls acknowledges in invoking Berlin, lead to some ways of life being more difficult to pursue than others.

Rawls's views, on the one hand, about the need for social bases of self-respect, and on the other, about the need for the liberal state to prescind from doing anything more to ensure that groups will continue to possess sufficient numbers of members to make them viable, stand in some tension to each other. The claim that a well-ordered state will in virtue of its well-orderedness give rise to a perfect match between aspiration and association in this context appears like little more than philosophical wishful thinking. The view according to which each person requires the social bases of self-respect should move Rawls's theory toward the view that certain reasonable plans of life, which would fare badly in a pure cultural marketplace, may require being propped up by the state in some way. I clearly do not have the space to delineate exactly how Rawls's theory would have to be modified in order to accommodate this adjustment. Suffice it to say, in the present context, that even a theory as supposedly closed off to anything but a minimal multiculturalism as Rawls's is meant to be possesses some interesting, unexploited resources for a more robust multiculturalism.

II

The inference that seems to be present among orthodox liberals, according to which from the fact that liberalism should affirm political individualism it follows that liberal states' policies should only affirm a minimal, as opposed to a more robust multiculturalism, was put into question by post-Rawlsian philosophers who recognized that individuals can flourish in the manner privileged by liberals only if they are placed in the appropriate social conditions. In particular, these theorists noted that liberalism, at least in one of its most important variants, tends to place the autonomous individual chooser at its core. Autonomous choosing cannot be exercised in a vacuum, however. Individuals choose from within a socially constituted repertoire, rather than making up options for themselves, or drawing them from social settings with which they have no contact. Support for autonomy would thus seem to entail support for those social forms that make autonomous choosing possible.

In an essay entitled "Multiculturalism," Joseph Raz argued that the connection between autonomy and social forms supports an argument for multiculturalism. Now, multiculturalism is in Raz's view also the logical implication of moral universalism in a context of social diversity. It requires that we "learn to think of our societies as consisting not of a majority and minorities, but as constituted by a plurality of cultural groups."[8] But multiculturalism is also in Raz's view an implication of the moderately perfectionist position according to which the capacity of individuals to choose worthwhile options depends upon their being members of a thriving, viable cultural group. "People's well-being consists in their success in valuable relationships and activities. Their social and other skills to engage in activities and pursue relationships derive from their own cultures, and their sense of their own dignity is bound up with their senses of themselves as members of certain cultures."[9]

Now, the connection between autonomous choosing and group membership is affirmed in Raz's work, but its exact political implications are there left undefined. Raz writes in a rather undifferentiated manner about "groups" and about the indebtedness of individuals to the groups to which they belong for the capacity they possess to realize important aspects of human flourishing. But he says nothing of the kinds of groups that are capable of realizing these functions in people's lives. Is the political implication of Raz's view that the state should somehow promote all groups as central to the development and exercise of individuals' capacity for autonomous choosing? This would lead to a Pandora's box, since societies are made up of all kinds of "groups" of all shapes and sizes. Even were we to restrict our purview to ethno-cultural and religious groups (the groups that are most commonly at issue in discussions of multiculturalism), it is unclear whether all of these types of groups function in the lives of their members in exactly the same way. If the justification of multicultural support for groups is that they underpin the ability that individuals have to lead lives of (worthwhile) autonomous decision making, does this justification apply equally to large national minorities, such as the Québécois, the Catalan, and the Scots, and to small ethnic minorities born of immigration? Does it apply to the "lifestyle" groups with which many individuals increasingly identify?

It would seem when this set of questions is raised that the two theoretical supports for multiculturalism assayed by Raz come apart. While moral universalism on the face of it provides us with no reason to discriminate among groups for state support, since what matters is that no particular group within society be given asymmetrical recognition or support by the state, the concern with the promotion of autonomy does seem to warrant some degree of differentiation among groups.

Raz's insight concerning the connection between autonomous choosing and group membership was systematized in the work of Will Kymlicka to answer precisely this concern. Kymlicka reiterates the move made by Raz, which consists in showing that individual choosers can exercise their capacity for choice only in a social context that provides them with a range of meaningful options upon which to exercise their choosing capacity. But Kymlicka argues that the promotion of autonomy can be achieved only by certain kinds of social forms, which he terms "societal cultures." A societal culture is, in Kymlicka's view, "a culture which provides its members with meaningful ways of life across the full range of human activities, including social, educational, religious, recreational, and economic life, encompassing both public and private spheres." Moreover, Kymlicka stresses that such a culture must be "institutionally embodied – in schools, media, economy, government, etc."[10] For Kymlicka, the paradigm case of a societal culture is therefore an involuntarily incorporated minority nation, one that has managed despite its incorporation in a larger political entity to maintain important aspects of its culture, its language, and its institutional infrastructure. Prime examples, as seen above, include such societies as Quebec, Catalonia, and Scotland.

Such groups are, in Kymlicka's view, prime candidates for group-differentiated rights. Kymlicka recognizes that large societal cultures in which such minority nations find themselves enmeshed exercise a centripetal pull upon members of smaller cultures simply in virtue of their larger numbers. All things equal, it is more attractive to be a member of a larger rather than a smaller culture, because of the greater opportunities for business, culture, and romance that membership in such larger cultures affords. Members of large cultures need not put any particular measures in place in order to ensure that their cultures will remain viable. Smaller cultures, especially ones that have been politically incorporated, face an uneven playing field because of their numerical disadvantage. The kinds of group-differentiated rights that are in Kymlicka's view justified by this asymmetry are the kinds of measures that might protect minority nations against the corrosive power of the larger cultures that surround them. Quebec's enactment of a policy requiring immigrants to educate their children in French schools would be an example of the sort of multicultural measure that Kymlicka has in mind. In general, Kymlicka believes that the connection between autonomy and group membership in the case of national groups warrants the granting of powers of self-government that such groups can use in order to protect their culture against the threat of assimilation.

The kinds of multicultural groups that typically form as a result of immigration cannot perform the same autonomy-enhancing functions in the lives of their members, in Kymlicka's view. First of all, Kymlicka observes that immigrant groups typically do not possess the territorial concentration or the institutional infrastructure needed to qualify for the kinds of group-differentiated rights that appropriately attach to societal cultures.[11] Moreover, as Kymlicka notes repeatedly, immigrants typically move not with the intention to recreate their cultures of origin in new surroundings. "They typically wish to integrate into the larger society, and to be accepted as full members of it."[12] Moreover, in Kymlicka's view, majorities have a legitimate expectation that immigrants will integrate, since in most cases the decision to immigrate is one that is taken voluntarily.[13] To the extent that immigrant groups have a legitimate claim to some form of accommodation on the part of the state,[14] this will take the form of "polyethnic rights" – which can take the form of active measures on the part of the state to enforce anti-discrimination norms, of funding for ethnic associations, and of exemptions from laws and practices that place a significant burden on their ability to express aspects of their cultures of origin (especially religious practices and rituals) – the principal function of which is not to allow immigrant groups to self-govern in the way that minority nations appropriately do, but rather to facilitate the process of integration.[15]

I introduced Kymlicka's important work by showing how it allowed us to solve one of the problems that Raz's view gives rise to. That problem had been that though Raz makes plain that one of the reasons why liberals should affirm multiculturalism has to do with the connection between the autonomy that liberals have traditionally wanted to promote and group membership, he is somewhat vague as to the kinds of groups that can plausibly be seen as effectively promoting autonomy. Kymlicka's work provides us with a way of distinguishing between groups along this dimension, and it establishes a fairly clear line between societal cultures on the one hand, and other ethno-cultural groups, such as immigrant groups, on the other. (In later work, Kymlicka also argues along similar lines that groups formed on the basis of lifestyle or of physical particularities do not qualify as autonomy-supporting in the requisite manner.)[16]

Now putting aside the question of whether Kymlicka is correct in his claim that societal cultures are uniquely situated with respect to their capacity to promote autonomy effectively among their members, we can see that the Kymlickean framework poses a problem from the point of view of the other normative bases that in Raz's view underpin the liberal commitment to multiculturalism. In Raz's view, as we have seen, moral universalism applied to the modern state requires that we view political society not as made up of a national majority – which would be possessed of various prerogatives simply in virtue of its majority status – and of minority groups whom the majority can place under obligations of integration or of assimilation, but rather as made up of different groups that are all symmetrically situated from a moral point of view, and whose members can all legitimately form the expectation of being self-governing to a significant degree. For example, Raz believes that a multicultural society should provide all groups with the right to educate their children according to their own norms and in their own languages.[17]

From this point of view, the multiculturalism defended by Kymlicka seems somewhat timid. It is so for at least two reasons. First, Kymlicka decidedly does want to privilege the prerogatives of national groups to control the process of immigration selection and integration. As we have seen, the voluntariness of the decision to immigrate in Kymlicka's view establishes a normative asymmetry between immigrant groups and the members of the "receiving" nation. Second, and relatedly, the decision to ground group-differentiated rights in the capacity of certain groups to promote and sustain the autonomy of their members means that the framework developed by Kymlicka will at best have nothing to say about the diversity that actually characterizes modern societies (aside from affirming the minimal multiculturalism that flows from the application of core liberal rights), and at worst, it will be corrosive of that diversity. As William Galston has put it in an influential article, "if choice and critical reflection are the dominant public values, then society will be drawn down the path of interfering with groups that do not accept these values."[18] This fear is at least in some significant measure confirmed by Kymlicka's own treatment of the problem of illiberal minorities in *Multicultural Citizenship*. There, he writes that immigrant groups can legitimately be compelled to respect liberal norms, and that liberal states should abstain from engaging in such compulsion in the case of historically established illiberal immigrant groups to which more expansive accommodations have been granted solely in virtue of the legitimate expectations that these accommodations have generated over time, rather than in virtue of the legitimacy of the claim to accommodation itself.[19]

Theorists like Galston and others[20] who are dissatisfied with the implications of an autonomy-based liberalism like Kymlicka's, but who have nonetheless wanted to ground their espousal of multiculturalism in recognizably liberal norms have appealed to other liberal values in order to ground a more capacious multiculturalism. They have, in particular, argued for a multiculturalism grounded in the values of toleration and conscience. It is to these variants of liberal multiculturalism that I now turn.

III

Mildly perfectionist autonomy liberals like Will Kymlicka and toleration liberals such as Chandran Kukathas, William Galston, and Jeff

Spinner-Halev can be seen as differing in two principal respects. First, toleration liberals are typically pluralists about the values realized through associational life that warrant the liberal state granting groups some degree of autonomy over certain aspects of the lives of their members, whereas autonomy liberals, while they may recognize that individuals may join groups and take part in their practices for all sorts of reasons, hold that the degree to which group life both is the object of autonomous choice and helps to sustain the capacity for such choice is crucial to its claim to respect. William Galston puts the matter tersely: "properly understood, liberalism is about the protection of diversity, not the valorization of choice."[21] Second, and relatedly, these two species of liberal differ as to what they see as the principal threat to the liberty of individuals. Autonomy liberals, focused as they are on the importance of promoting the capacity for autonomous decision making, are suspicious of groups, most notably (but not exclusively) religious groups that attempt to realize values in group life that may actually be antithetical to autonomy as it is construed by liberals. They also tend to view the state as best situated to ensure (for example through its control of public school curricula) that the individual interest in developing a capacity for autonomous decision making will be realized. Conversely, toleration liberals are suspicious of liberal states.

Galston again expresses this position most succinctly: "liberal societies not infrequently act in ways that reduce diversity ... and ... they can refrain from so acting without ceasing to be liberal."[22] In their view, either liberal states are overtly perfectionist and seek to promote values that might corrode the viability of groups focused around values other than autonomy, or they claim to be neutral as between rival conceptions of the good but actually insidiously promote certain ways of life by default. They are skeptical of the modern state as an effective vehicle for moral socialization and tend to idealize intermediate groups such as Churches and other civil society associations as "havens in a heartless world."

To the extent that they are toleration *liberals*, however, theorists such as Galston, Kukathas, and others, have had to find a way of integrating some account of individual consent into their picture of group life. Toleration liberals claim that a plurality of values can be realized in different kinds of groups present in civil society, and that autonomy liberals provide an unattractively narrowed view of group life by restricting their account of the kinds of groups worth defending within the theory and the practice of liberal multiculturalism to groups that promote autonomy among their members. Some groups may very well defend traditions and customs that are hostile to the acquisition by their members of too much autonomy, and the toleration liberal is of the view that some of these customs and traditions realize values that are worthwhile, even though they are in tension with the value of individual autonomy. But to go from that claim to the much stronger claim according to which the state need not in any way ensure that membership in these groups is voluntary would risk placing defenders of this kind of view well beyond the bounds of a recognizably liberal theory.

Clearly, the kinds of groups that toleration liberals have in mind in distancing themselves from autonomy liberals like Kymlicka are not ones that members join willingly. Religious groups, ethno-cultural groups typically possess an historical rootedness that makes it the case that members are born into them rather than joining them as one would join, say, a numismatic association. Voluntariness of membership will therefore for toleration liberals have to be vouchsafed not by conditions being placed upon entry into a group, but by assurances that continued membership is not coerced. Liberal states will therefore on this account have to make sure that members of groups that do not promote autonomy are nonetheless possessed of robust *exit rights*. Given the presence of the right, guaranteed by the state, to leave a group without undue duress, the decision to remain within the group should be seen by the state as just that, a *decision*. Where exit rights are present but remain unexercised, the liberal state as imagined by the toleration liberal has done as much as it can or ought in order to ensure that membership is voluntary.

Here, the toleration liberal confronts a dilemma.[23] For there are exit rights, and then there are exit rights. A minimalist conception of such rights, such as that defended most notably by Chandran Kukathas, requires simply that individuals not be blocked in their attempts to leave the confines of the group.[24] However, as has been noted by other toleration liberals, most notably William Galston, an exit right construed in as minimal a manner risks remaining purely formal, a right that exists in theory, but not in practice. One can imagine three sorts of further guarantees that a state might want to impose in order to give an exit right substance. First, a person might be said to possess an exit right in the full sense only if she satisfies a certain number of cognitive conditions, concerning most importantly the existence of options – the option to exit, to be sure, but also the option to pursue different ways of life as well. Second, the existence of exit rights might be taken to depend upon groups not being able to impose significant exit costs upon individuals. For example, groups that purport to own all property collectively, or who insist upon an individual's private belongings reverting to group authorities upon departure, arguably make option all but impossible for members, and so there is an argument, grounded in a concern for exit rights being more than purely formal, for the liberal state to impose limits on the material costs that groups can impose upon exiting members.

Third, and perhaps most significantly, groups can impose psychic and emotional costs upon members who may form a desire to leave. Even where the first two conditions have been dealt with, for example through imposed curricula in schools and through a prohibition on groups imposing their own property regimes, socialization may occur inside groups in ways that make members feel as if the options that are objectively at their disposal are not really options *for them*. It is hard to see what measures the state might put into place to counteract psychic obstacles of this sort.

One can imagine toleration liberals being placed on a continuum. At one extreme lie theorists like Kukathas who would impose very minimal conditions upon exit rights. The mere fact that an individual is not being physically coerced into remaining within the group would, according to this minimal condition, suffice to claim that he has a full right to exit. The state's responsibility on this view would not go any further than ensuring that the individual is not forcibly constrained to stay. At another extreme lie theorists who claim that the state should do all that it can to counteract the three categories of obstacles that I have just briefly described, and thus to ensure that members of groups are possessed of substantive, rather than merely formal, exit rights. Thus, Galston recognizes that substantive exit rights would include conditions to do with knowledge of alternatives and the capacity to assess them, with the psychological conditions required in order for individuals to be able to conceive of living a different life, and with the ability to exercise at least some of the options that are theoretically available.[25]

Theorists who lie close to the former end of the spectrum I am imagining would be hard pressed to characterize the multicultura-lism to which they arrive as liberal. The society they envisage would in effect be denying members of particularly illiberal communities the kinds of liberal protections that are due to all other members of society. Such views are morally unattractive inasmuch as they fail to recognize that in so doing they are failing to address the concerns and needs of the most vulnerable members of these groups, their "internal minorities" – women and children in particular.[26]

But the theorists who, like Galston, lie closer to the latter end of the spectrum face a different problem, that of distinguishing their position from that of autonomy liberals. The latter group of theorists after all does not typically put forward a substantive conception of autonomy. That is, they do not believe that the only conception of the good worth promoting is that of the maverick or of the non-conformist. Though some autonomy liberals like Joseph Raz are also moderate perfectionists, in that they believe that some concep-tions of the good lack worth and ought in virtue of this fact be discouraged by the state, their perfectionism is pluralist. They do not believe that only groups that promote a substantive conception of the good deserve promotion. Rather, autonomy liberals tend to believe that the liberal state should institute measures designed to ensure that citizens are possessed of sufficient *procedural* autonomy. Procedural autonomy has to do with the *manner* in which choices are made, rather than with the substance of those choices. They believe that conceptions of the good, and of corresponding groups, come to acquire value for individuals in virtue of having been chosen in the right way. Conditions on (procedurally) autonomous choice tend to include absence of coercion, sufficient information about options, and perhaps also the ability concretely to act on some of those options.[27]

When autonomy liberalism is understood procedurally, it seems clear that it differs from toleration liberalism at most in emphasis rather than in substance. Both sets of theorists believe that the state ought to use the policy levers at its disposal – in the area of education for example – in order to provide citizens with the capacity for procedurally autonomous choice. The justifications for this impera-tive are somewhat different. Autonomy liberals emphasize self-authorship, and the ability of individuals freely to choose conceptions of the good and their corresponding group memberships, whereas toleration liberals focus on conditions for meaningful exit rights. (In practice, these justifications may ultimately come to the same thing. Indeed, it seems plausible to claim that in real-world conditions, the capacity of agents for self-authorship will manifest itself through the ability that people have to question the memberships they are born into, and to act on the basis of these questionings.)

Let us take stock of the point we have reached: We have seen that liberal theorists have in recent years adopted a variety of theoretical postures with respect to multiculturalism. Some liberals have noted that liberalism is naturally sympathetic to a minimal multiculturalism. To the extent that liberalism implies the denial of cultural integration, and to the extent that liberal regimes strive to provide their citizens with the full range of liberal civil rights, which citizens make use of in their associational lives, liberalism according to some does not require any amendments in order to give rise to a plausible multiculturalism.

This position has been criticized because it is excessively sanguine as to the capacity of an unfettered cultural marketplace to sustain worthwhile groups and associated conceptions of the good. Some liberals have therefore sought to provide liberal multiculturalism with additional theoretical supports. The most widely discussed of these attempts, those of Joseph Raz and of Will Kymlicka, stress that some groups that might not survive should be supported by the state because they are the condition for agents being able to exercise their capacity for autonomous choosing.

This position in turn ran up against the objection that some groups may be less able and/or less willing to promote the capacity for autonomous choice than others, but that this should not necessarily disqualify them from state support. On a pluralist view of what conduces to individual well-being, groups can embody worthwhile values without necessarily promoting autonomy. We turned to toleration liberalism as a version of liberalism compatible with a more capacious multiculturalism. We concluded that toleration liberalism retains its connection to liberalism through the notion of exit rights, and that they are caught on the horns of a dilemma with respect to these rights. A purely formal construal risks making the theory difficult to reconcile with liberalism, inasmuch as it fails to provide minority group members with standard liberal protections, while a more substantive conception of exit rights, which includes not just the formal right but also the satisfaction of conditions lending substance to the right, risks being indistinguishable from autonomy liberalism, at least inasmuch as that version of liberalism construes autonomy procedurally rather than substantively. Indeed, the educational requirements that would need to be satisfied in order for the exit rights of a toleration liberal like Galston to be guaranteed risk being just as corrosive to groups and communities that do not cleave to an autonomist ethic as the "education for autonomy" that autonomy liberals recommend. Indeed, they might end up being indistinguishable in practice, though their rationales might differ somewhat.

Does this mean that liberal multiculturalism of necessity will tend not to be able to make room for groups that, though they realize values in the lives of their members, are difficult to reconcile with autonomy, even procedurally construed? Are we stuck with the dilemma of, on the one hand, affirming a more robust multiculturalism but sundering the connection with liberalism, or, on the other hand, putting forward a more recognizably liberal, but much more moderate multiculturalism, one that would fall afoul of the concern voiced by the likes of Galston, to the effect that liberal society tends to erode diversity?

IV

I believe that there is a significant "road not taken" among liberal multiculturalists, one which further research in the field would do well to explore. To show what direction it might take us in, I want at this point to bring out a shared assumption which seems to be made both by autonomy and by toleration liberals, and indeed by opponents of any form of liberal multiculturalism, be it autonomy or toleration-based. That assumption is that groups are static entities to which people can choose to belong or not to belong, and that individuals therefore exercise their agency with respect to groups by choosing to join or to exit. What is not considered by this way of construing the relationship between individual agency and cultural groups is the possibility that part of what exercising autonomous agency requires is that one be able to do so *within* the groups to which one belongs. That agency can take the form of adopting roles and functions that have been defined within the group, but inflecting them on the basis of one's individual understanding of the norms that govern them. Or it can take the more radical form of challenging roles and authority structures, remaining "internal" to the culture of the group by appealing to values or narratives that are criterial for membership, but which one feels are badly reflected by present arrangements. Liberal multiculturalists have by and large opted for a multiculturalism of "exit" – one in which one acts through deciding on whether or not to join, or whether or not to continue one's membership. They have – with exceptions that will be mentioned below – by and large chosen not to develop a multiculturalism of "voice," one in which state policies are geared not only toward the protection of the capacity that people have to join or leave, but also toward supporting individuals in their ability to be agents within the groups to which they belong, rather than adopting a univocally submissive posture toward group norms defined by others.[28]

The cost of insisting upon the "exit" option within theories of liberal multiculturalism can be seen in considering the debate that was touched off by the publication of Susan Okin's *Is Multiculturalism Bad for Women?* Okin famously argued that the kinds of measures for which multiculturalists have tended to militate have sought to exempt group practices from the liberal protection of individual rights.[29] As many of these exemptions have to do with the way in which gender roles are policed, these exemptions bear particularly hard on women. Multiculturalism is thus in Okin's view (a view that she tempered somewhat in later papers[30]) bad for women, for the reason that it would hand them over to the patriarchal authority structure that tends to dominate minority cultural groups. Far from being candidates for protection or support from the liberal state, such groups should be allowed to wither away.

What was missing from Okin's argument was any appreciation of the fact that what many women who belong to cultural minorities might actually want is not the stark alternative of either accepting group norms and authority structures in their most conservative form, or abandoning them altogether, but rather to be able to exercise some say over the way in which these norms and structures develop. Many women, after all, identify with the ethno-cultural or religious group into which they are born, or to which they have chosen to belong, even as they experience some aspects of the life of the group in question as oppressive. A liberal-feminist multiculturalism, it might be argued, should attempt to sustain these women in acquiring voice, and thus in becoming able to exercise agency, *within* groups rather than assuming that the exercise of agency will consist in deciding to belong or not to belong to groups whose nature and functioning lie beyond the reach of agency.[31]

One response to this argument might be to claim that though a "multiculturalism of voice," as we might call it, is preferable to a "multiculturalism of exit," the former lies beyond the reach of policy. Even autonomy liberals are loath to intervene in the internal lives of groups and associations in the manner that Okin's arguments suggest they should. They tend to pin their hopes on the gradual liberalizing effects that living in close proximity with others will have, or on the impact that the state's control over certain aspects of the educational curriculum might produce. Looking at the issue of potentially oppressed "internal minorities" from the point of view of the state, it might seem that providing individuals with the wherewithal to be able to exercise their option to exit is preferable, all things considered, to intervention into the internal functioning of groups

To this the following responses seem apposite. First, it bears repeating that what the "exit rights" strategy does is not provide many people with alternative tools with which to obtain what they want, which is to be able to exercise their cultural agency *within* groups with which they identify, but rather an outcome that many of them may well view as suboptimal.

Second, there may very well be areas of overlap between the exit rights strategy and policies that seek to alter the internal functioning of groups, and thus, between a multiculturalism of exit and a multiculturalism of voice. This is because the border separating what lies within a group's purview and what lies outside of it is itself a matter of policy. Consider the vexed question of education. To what degree should groups, say religious communities, be allowed to organize the education of their children on the basis of their values and beliefs? For many groups, one of the central purposes of associational life is to induct children into the community and thereby to ensure intergenerational continuity. Though the home and places of worship are central to this purpose, and are rightly considered to lie beyond the reach of state intervention (except in extreme cases in which harm to children is uncontroversially involved), education has always been a contested site. Even non-perfectionist liberal states have tended to believe that the interests of children dictate that cultural groups not have complete dominion over the way in which schooling is organized. Many cultural groups have, however, felt that the work of intergenerational cultural transmission could be complete only on condition that they have at least some substantial say on crucial aspects of curriculum. Thus, when the state arrogates the right to educate children to itself partly on the grounds that in so doing it is making it easier for them to exercise their exit rights, it is affecting the "internal lives" of groups in a fairly profound way, by defining what counts as lying within the purview of group authority in ways that many groups see as deeply problematic.

Third, a multiculturalism of voice need not result solely from interventions. The intervention/permission dichotomy is too simplistic a construal of the full range of liberal policies available to the state. The state has a number of policy levers at its disposal through which it can incentivize a greater degree of openness to the voice of internal minorities on the part of ethno-cultural groups. Let me in closing mention three possibilities in this connection.

First, and perhaps most modestly and feasibly, the state can be more attentive than it sometimes is to the manner in which its policies tend unwittingly to reinforce unaccountable hierarchies and static conceptions of cultural groups. For example, one of the ways in which the state can support cultural groups, rather than consigning them to the vagaries of the cultural marketplace, is to fund its ethno-cultural organizations, to grant tax-exempt status to its religious organizations, etc. One of the effects of these otherwise (arguably) justifiable policies is, first, to identify as interlocutors those persons who already occupy positions of authority within the organized community. Members of internal minorities, or people who are on the fringes of organized community life (and whose marginal status may very well be the result of their having been unable to acquire any measure of "voice" on the inside) will simply not be on the radar for governmental agencies eager to cut down on administrative complexity. It is far simpler to seek out individuals who are already in positions of authority than to connect with those who may be less institutionally visible in virtue of their marginal or oppressed status.

Another effect of otherwise defensible policies of financial support might be to reinforce fairly static and highly differentiated community groups. By this I mean that in seeking to support community X from the potentially corrosive force of the cultural marketplace, the state may be inclined to seek out, among all community groups that it might transact with, groups that are "most distinctively" X. Support for multiculturalism might come to be seen by state bureaucrats as sitting ill with support for groups that, for example, celebrate *métissage* and complex identities, and that therefore may come to blur the boundaries separating them from other groups.

These two tendencies in interaction may lead to the state's policies of financial support having the unintended effect of supporting conservative forces within cultural communities, and compounding rather than counteracting forces already present within community groups that oppose the taking up of voice by traditionally oppressed or marginal members. A first way in which states can affect the incentive structure within which members of groups structure their internal lives is simply to avoid the default administrative impulse which is to identify persons who already possess authority within well-delineated groups.

At the extreme, and this is a second policy lever that states might employ to incentivize some degree of openness of groups to a plurality of internal voices, states might make financial support conditional upon the relaxing of orthodox authority structures. Or in a more nuanced manner, it may peg funding levels to a group's willingness to open its decision-making structures to those individuals who fit the description that has led us to question the adequacy of the "multiculturalism of exit" that has become something of an orthodoxy among liberal multiculturalists. That is, states could tie funding to how well a group treated its members who wished to exercise cultural agency by remaining within the group rather than choosing to remain within a group over whose internal functioning it has no say, or leaving it altogether.

A third policy lever, one that has been explored in the pathbreaking work of Ayelet Schachar, would leverage the fact that many groups that make up the multicultural landscape of modern societies seek a limited degree of self-determination. That is, they seek to be able to exempt themselves from laws and policies that obtain in society at large, and to govern themselves at least with respect to policy domains that are felt to be of particular importance to the life of the community. Rather than meeting these requests for exemption and self-determination with either blanket acceptance or refusal, states can incentivize changes within groups that might accommodate the needs for voice of internal minorities and dissidents by making the granting of exemptions conditional upon some degree of openness of internal deliberative and decision-making processes. Institutional design might also allow individuals to benefit from partially over-lapping jurisdictions by "forum-shopping."[32]

V

Liberal multiculturalism has been at something of an impasse in recent years. This has led some theorists to eschew the liberal framework altogether, in favor of either a radically democratic, "agonistic" political philosophy through which to account for the diverging claims of groups, or a framework grounded in the claim to "recognition."[33]

While these frameworks clearly have something important to contribute to the elaboration of a plausible multicultural theory, my claim in this paper is that, because of the way in which the debate about multiculturalism has been joined by liberal theorists, the resources of liberalism to illuminate the manner in which the state should regulate the coexistence of diverse groups within society have not been fully exploited. In particular, I have emphasized the impor-tance of making central to the liberal exploration of these matters the notion of "cultural agency," and the political conditions that are required in order to sustain it. The hope is that this notion can form the basis of a new liberal multiculturalist research agenda.[34]

NOTES

1. Rawls, "The Priority of Right and Ideas of the Good," p. 462. Cf. *Political Liberalism*, p. 198.
2. It is present, for example, in Will Kymlicka's seminal *Multicultural Citizenship*.
3. Putnam, *Bowling Alone*.
4. This concern has been explored in the essays collected in Banting and Kymlicka (eds.), *Multiculturalism and the Welfare State*.

5. Rawls, *A Theory of Justice*, rev. edn., p. 387.

6. *Ibid.*

7. *Ibid.*, p. 397.

8. Raz, "Multiculturalism," p. 197.

9. *Ibid.*, p. 200.

10. Kymlicka, *Multicultural Citizenship*, p. 76.

11. *Ibid.*, p. 96.

12. *Ibid.*, pp. 11–12.

13. *Ibid.*, p. 96. I have criticized this aspect of Kymlicka's argument in "Immigration and Reciprocity."

14. Joseph Carens has argued that Kymlicka's framework actually does not provide adequate grounding for the polyethnic rights that Kymlicka describes. See his "Liberalism and Culture," pp. 35–47.

15. Kymlicka, *Multicultural Citizenship*, pp. 30–31.

16. Kymlicka, *Finding our Way*.

17. Raz, "Multiculturalism."

18. Galston, "Two Concepts of Liberalism."

19. Kymlicka, *Multicultural Citizenship*, p. 170.

20. See, *inter alia*, Kukathas, *The Liberal Archipelago*; Spinner-Halev, *Surviving Diversity*.

21. Galston, "Two Concepts of Liberalism," p. 523.

22. *Ibid.*, p. 522.

23. I have developed this point at greater length in my "Value Pluralism, Toleration, and Autonomy."

24. Kukathas, *The Liberal Archipelago*.

25. Galston, "Two Concepts of Liberalism," pp. 122–23.

26. For the problems associated with internal minorities in liberal multiculturalist theories, see the papers collected in Eisenberg and Spinner-Halev (eds.), *Minorities within Minorities*.

27. The *locus classicus* of the distinction between substantive and procedural conceptions of autonomy is Dworkin, *The Theory and Practice of Autonomy*.

28. The voice/exit distinction obviously refers to the seminal work of Hirschman, *Exit, Voice and Loyalty*.

29. Okin, *Is Multiculturalism Bad for Women?*

30. See, for example, Okin, "Multiculturalism and Feminism."

31. For an example of the form that this kind of internal critical cultural agency might take within the context of Islam, see, for example, Ahmadi, "Islamic Feminism in Iran."

32. Schachar, *Multicultural Jurisdictions*.

33. Examples of the former approach might include Laden, "Negotiation, Deliberation, and the Claims of Politics"; examples of the latter are

grounded in the work of Taylor and his seminal essay *Multiculturalism and the Politics of Recognition;* and Honneth, *The Struggle for Recognition.*

34. I have begun to explore this agenda in my "Le paradoxe du multiculturalisme libéral."

14 Liberalism and nationalism

Liberalism and nationalism are two distinct ideologies that emerged in Europe following the French Revolution, although both have deeper roots in European intellectual history. These ideologies continue to characterize and shape political developments into the twenty-first century and remain a concern of contemporary liberal political theorists such as Hayek, Berlin, Rawls, Taylor, Miller, and Tamir who wrestle with the extent to which they are complementary or antithetical. There have certainly been liberal philosophers in the twentieth century who have seen nationalism as one of the most potent threats to liberalism. Yet there have been self-proclaimed liberal nationalists, and some of the most important figures of nineteenth- and twentieth-century European liberalism such as Mill, Weber, and Berlin have been sympathetic to the importance of national identity. There have also been national-liberal political parties in Western democracies. This chapter will explore the diverse responses to national claims within the liberal tradition and the extent to which these two perspectives can be reconciled.

The history of liberalism and liberal ideas and the history of nationalism provide ample opportunities to confuse and conflate any exclusive definition of each complex tradition or theory. Nevertheless, one can profit by using John Breuilly's characterization of nationalism as involving three distinct positions: that nations as groups exist; that they have value to their members and in themselves; and that because of this value they have a claim to some form of political autonomy.[1] A definition of liberalism is equally controversial but using the structure of Breuilly's analysis whilst replacing nation with individual to characterize liberalism is instructive. Although liberal theorists differ over how far liberalism is fundamentally a social theory or a substantive ethical and political philosophy, both positions acknowledge that it is individualist; that it regards individuals as real, as having fundamental value, and in consequence as having a claim to moral and political self-determination, usually characterized in terms of rights to freedom and equality.

The debate about the compatibility of liberalism and nationality has been at the heart of the philosophical disputes between individualists and communitarians and between cosmopolitanism and particularism as approaches to political rights and values. This chapter will also address the extent to which these distinctions show that liberalism and nationalism are antinomies or merely dichotomies of a larger whole.

To make sense of the recent debates between liberalism and nationality, it is necessary to explore the philosophical sources of liberalism before its emergence as an ideology in the nineteenth century and then examine the way in which national identity is incorporated into the liberal political thought through the particular examples of John Stuart Mill[2] and Lord Acton. This history sets the context for Isaiah Berlin's[3] rehabilitation of nationality within liberal theory and its use by contemporary liberal philosophers such as David Miller, Charles Taylor, Will Kymlicka, and Yael Tamir who have sought to emphasize national identity against the perceived individualistic cosmopolitanism of John Rawls's *A Theory of Justice*.

The chapter will conclude by arguing that the Berlin-inspired reconciliation of liberalism and nationality is unsustainable and that Rawls's notion of a *Law of Peoples*[4] provides a better account of the claims of political community within liberalism than that of liberal nationalists, without at the same time collapsing into an unrealistic form of cosmopolitanism.

PRE-NATIONAL LIBERALISM

As an ideology, liberalism emerged in Europe in the wake of the French Revolution but as a philosophical approach to politics it originated in the eighteenth century. Although it would be naïve and anachronistic to claim that Locke, Kant, Hume, and Smith were liberals in any straightforward sense, it is nevertheless possible to identify sources of liberalism in the complex philosophies of each thinker.[5] These four thinkers help to identify two distinct strands in the development of liberal thought that have a bearing on the way in

which groups are accommodated within a liberal theory and importantly how the idea of nationality features within liberalism. It is
worth bearing in mind that the modern concept of a nation was
unavailable to all four thinkers.

John Locke and Immanuel Kant are two familiar sources of liberalism as an ethical or moralistic approach to politics and are used as
ideal types by contemporary libertarian and egalitarian philosophers
to explain and defend their respective theories of justice or individual
rights. Both Locke and Kant distil and transform an earlier tradition of
natural jurisprudence that sought to explain political authority and
the claims of individuals in respect of it. Although Locke's contract
theory appears to provide a textbook account of the construction of
political institutions by pre-political individuals agreeing to transfer
their natural and moral powers, his theory is actually much more
complex. Contract theory is methodologically and ethically individualist, and it is this feature that is at the heart of liberalism. Individuals
are the basis of social institutions and practices and are therefore
ontologically prior to social institutions and associations. This is
often considered a hopelessly naïve sociology: a fact appreciated by
Locke who tries to draw the sting from just such a critique offered by
Sir Robert Filmer's *Patriarcha* in the first of his *Two Treatises of Civil
Government*. Yet although Locke is an individualist, his main concern is not explaining the origin of political institutions but instead
justifying and legitimizing political authority in the face of pre-social
individual rights and liberties. These rights and liberties are real, but
they are indeterminate in the absence of authority and institutions
that can adjudicate and enforce rights claims. Kant, although not
strictly a contract theorist, also extends aspects of this individualistic
account of the state even further in using the idea of public right as
the basis for the juridical state that confers determinacy on individuals' private right claims. The modern state is required by the existence of individuals who share a common space (in Kant's sense a
finite globe) and who make claims of right as part of exercising
agency. Kant and Locke are therefore concerned with the idea of a
juridical entity and its normative authority and legitimacy and not
with the origins of actual political institutions. Indeed Locke's
account of the contractual emergence of political authority and the
state is accompanied by a separate historical sociology of the emergence of political societies.[6] Kant's position is also neutral on the

historical emergence of actual political communities. Although Locke and Kant do not deny the existence of intermediate institutions between the individual and the state, they account for these in individual terms and most importantly they do not regard such intermediate institutions or associations as having a normative status that is irreducible to the rights and ethical status of the individuals who compose them. Two things follow from this. First, there is no normative role for a nation in Locke's and Kant's political theory. Both acknowledge the idea of a people and attach significance to it in their international political theory,[7] but in each case it is clear that this is a juridical entity that is coextensive with the state or political community. To suggest, as does Meisels, that a territorially bounded juridical community is a root of the nation[8] is misleading and potentially leaves the concept of nation to be so broad as to be meaningless. Second, the idea of a state derived from individual rights and liberties as either a philosophical presupposition or as a practical implication exhausts the idea of political community. The ethically individualist liberalism that can be derived from natural jurisprudence and which is exemplified in the political thought of Locke and Kant is primarily a "state-focused" political theory where the state is the implication of a philosophy of rights, obligations, and their sanctioning powers. Any accommodation between this variant of liberalism and national identity must therefore subordinate the claims of nation to the prior ethical and political claims of individuals as rights bearers. Yet the juridical individualism of Locke and Kant also challenges any simplistic identification of liberalism with a universalist-cosmopolitanism that claims that the primary obligations of individuals are to all other individuals irrespective of geographical and cultural distance. Both Locke and Kant acknowledge that there are ethically significant political communities that are not straightforwardly captured by the idea of a voluntary association, but they regard these as features of a complex moral economy of individual rights and liberties and not as implications of fundamental ethical communities as moral particularists claim.

As we have seen, this juridical source of liberal individualism in natural jurisprudence can accommodate an historical and sociological account of political communities, but it subordinates this to the prior logic of moral norms. However, the liberal tradition also involves a different account of liberalism as a social theory as opposed to an ethical philosophy. This social theory tradition is closely associated with the ideas of David Hume and Adam Smith, although as with Locke and Kant one must again caution against a simplistic claim that Hume and Smith are liberals.

Hume and Smith have accounts of liberty, rights, and legitimate institutions, but unlike the tradition of natural jurisprudence they do not assert the priority of these normative claims. Instead, they provide accounts of the emergence of moral and political practices and norms as consequences of uncoerced social interaction. Hume challenges the tradition of natural jurisprudence with his naturalistic philosophy and conventionalist account of the emergence of private property, promise keeping, and the associated artificial virtue of justice.[9] Government, in turn, also evolves to support and enforce the sanctions of justice when society becomes more complex and the opportunity to avoid the consequences of non-compliance with societal norms arises. Hume argues that the simple idea of the evolution of conventions provides the basis for the norms that characterize moral and political life. Hume turns from philosophy to history in his later works[10] and develops an historical account of freedom in the context of the particular institutions of the English Constitution. Hume's idea that a system of liberty emerges as a complex social practice and not as a serious of rational deductions from normative premises gave rise to a conception of conjectural history that is developed and expanded in the work of other Scottish Enlightenment thinkers such as his friend Adam Smith.

Smith's *Lectures on Jurisprudence*[11] provides an anthropological account of law and government emerging through four stages of development from a primitive hunter-gatherer lifestyle through pastoral and agricultural forms of society and into the fourth and final stage of commercial or civil society. Each stage involves a greater degree of social complexity through a process of historical and cultural evolution. Smith's social anthropology and conjectural history provides a developmental account of liberty as a social practice exemplified in a society of private property, security of contract, and commercial exchange. Smith's account of liberty is essentially negative as it emphasizes a neutral role of government as a guarantor of the system of natural liberty through its provision of defense against external enemies and its protection of property and the rule of law. As with the tradition of natural jurisprudence and contract theory, the role of the government is to enforce the law and punish infractions of the rights and liberties of its subjects, but the crucial difference is that these liberties are the result of an evolving social system. The key to maintaining that social system of natural liberty involved maintaining the balance between institutions within society. For Smith the emphasis is on civil society, commerce, and trade as the ultimate guarantors of natural liberty and not the primacy of a sovereign state. Society is not equivalent to the state, and Smith is more concerned with the role and scope of government than with theorizing the state as a juridical implication of natural and fundamental rights or ethical claims.

Hume and Smith provide a model of a liberal order as a commercial society where the boundaries between polities are porous and open to trade and commerce rather than a closed juridical system of rights. This model does not deny that individuals have particular attachments or that they find significance in the fellowship of other individuals in groups and associations, but it does deny a place for intermediate natural communities of significance such as nations that have a natural claim of authority over individuals. Indeed, it was argued, the idea of commerce as the spread of material culture and civilization had a tendency to break down barriers between people and establish relationships of interdependence and mutual regard which undermined classical ideas of republican liberty and solidarity. And it was precisely for this reason that Rousseau, a contemporary and correspondent of Smith, considered the ideas of commerce and trade as incompatible with the maintenance of a general will.[12] The theorists of civil society, such as Smith, who shaped the ideas of classical liberalism emphasized liberty in opposition to government and saw the state as a necessary instrument for enforcing contract and property rights but not as the expression of a popular will or as constituting a people: The state as the institutions of government and the law fits within the idea of society and is not coextensive with it. Similarly the boundaries of society are merely accidental and contingent having a particular history, and at least according to these thinkers they were likely to become less important as trade and commerce established social connections among those previously isolated.

Although neither Locke, Kant nor Smith deny the possibility of individuals associating into groups that are distinguished by language and tradition, they do not provide any ethical or sociological support for the view that nations are real entities of any kind in the same way that they insist that individuals are real entities both methodologically and ethically. Concepts such as territoriality, sovereignty, self-determination, and "people" may appear to serve as building blocks for nationalism or the vehicle through which national identity is exercised, but they need not be seen as place-holders for a nationalist completion of an abstract and incomplete liberal theory, as we can see when these ideas return to the center of liberal political philosophy in the twentieth century. Yet for much of the intervening period, nationalist critics of liberalism, starting with Herder in the 1790s and some liberal nationalists, made precisely the claim that liberalism was abstract and incomplete without the addition of the reality of national identity and national groups.

MILL AND THE RISE OF LIBERAL NATIONALISM

Herder developed a Counter-Enlightenment critique of universal rationalism and an ideal of cultural history that was to profoundly affect many early nineteenth-century Romantic thinkers because of his theories about the expressive role of language and the concept of culture as the expression of the natural unit of a nation.[13] The idea that language is a vehicle that expresses the collective life of mankind has influenced contemporary thinkers such as Isaiah Berlin and Charles Taylor and has played a role in the development of contemporary communitarian critiques of individualistic liberalism.

Much of Herder's cultural nationalism was aesthetic as opposed to political, but it influenced subsequent philosophers such as J. G. Fichte (1762–1814) in the wake of the French Revolution and it captured the spirit of national liberation that was unleashed in the wake of Napoleon's assault on the *ancien régime* powers and in the anti-French reaction to Napoleonic imperialism. With the defeat of Napoleon and the attempt to reestablish an imperial order in Europe, the struggles of peoples for national liberation and self-determination grew. Rising political leaders such as the Hungarian Lajos Kossuth (1802–94) in central Europe, Giuseppe Mazzini (1805–72) in Italy, and Daniel O'Connell "the Liberator" (1775–1847) in Britain appealed to the concept of a nation as the basis for their struggle for independence from the pre-revolutionary imperial order. National struggles such as that of Greece against the Ottoman Empire inspired Romantic poets such as Lord Byron and political radicals such as Jeremy Bentham to campaign for rights to political self-determination, and in Byron's case also inspired him to join the national struggle, fighting against the Ottoman Turks. Mazzini founded a group named Young Italy in 1834, which argued for a second revolution to extend national liberty and self-determination as the earlier French Revolution had extended individual liberty. Many of these new nationalist leaders drew on liberal ideas of political self-determination and individual liberty in their struggles against the old order. The early nineteenth-century rise in nationalist sentiment combined Romantic ideas of national identity and solidarity with liberal ideas of political liberty, individual freedom, and constitutional government. Although the concept of the nation and national identity originated as an aesthetic critique of Enlightenment rationalism and individualism, in the writings of Herder it took the events following the collapse of the French Revolution in Europe and South America to bring liberalism and nationalism together as a political movement. Mazzini, Kossuth, O'Connell, and Simon Bolivar in South America were all influenced by liberal political ideas and espoused ambitions for liberal constitutional orders in place of political absolutism. Indeed, for much of the early nineteenth century liberalism and nationalism were interconnected. This had an important impact on the subsequent development of liberal political theory and gave rise to the idea of liberal nationalism, an idea that is given its most forceful anglophone statement in the nineteenth century in the political theory of John Stuart Mill (1806–73).

Mill's position in the liberal canon is unchallengeable yet deeply controversial. Mill's *On Liberty* (1859) remains one of the iconic texts of the liberal canon, yet his defense of liberty on utilitarian premises is potentially self-undermining. His *Principles of Political Economy* (1848) is a classic statement of liberal political economy and remained a standard work in the field until the late nineteenth century, yet the chapters on socialism are also seen as marking a rupture in the classical liberal tradition that paved the way for the state interventionism of new liberalism.[14] His utilitarianism, libertarianism, and political economy all build upon the ideas of his liberal predecessors, but Mill also famously drew on the thought of

Romantic thinkers and developments in nineteenth-century French and German philosophy. His 1861 *Considerations on Representative Government* is an important contribution to liberal engagement with the rise of democracy and develops the idea of representative democracy originated by Jeremy Bentham. Chapter xvi of Mill's work marks an important milestone in liberal thinking about government and the state, as it involves an explicit statement about the place of nationality. Mill writes:

A portion of mankind may be said to constitute a Nationality if they are united among themselves by common sympathies which do not exist between them and any others – which make them co-operate with each other more willingly than with other people, desire to be under the same government, and desire it should be government by themselves or a portion of themselves exclusively.[15]

He goes on to explain the origin of a spirit of nationality in terms of language, race, or descent and possibly even geography, but most importantly he departs from purely essentialist accounts of national origins of the sort found in Herder and Fichte by focusing on the history of "political antecedents," what one might re-describe as a political tradition. In the short opening section of chapter xvi, Mill intimates many of the ideas that were to characterize accounts of liberal nationalism and theories of the place of nationality in twentieth-century liberal and democratic politics.

For Mill nations are real in the sense of being groups and entities that act in the world and make political claims, but he also retains his methodological individualism by seeing nations as groups of individuals who share common ends, desires, or preferences. Nationality works through the aspirations and beliefs of the individual members of groups, and as such he rejects any methodological or ontological claim about the priority of national groups over individuals. In this respect he intimates the idea of "imagined communities" developed by Benedict Anderson.[16] Imagined communities (Mill uses the phrase "communities of recollection") are real, but they are real because they are thought into existence in the acts and discourse of those who use the idea of nationality as a ground of identification. There is no attempt to modify the ontological individualism that underpinned Locke's and Kant's conception of a people or Smith's moral and political economy: individualism remains central to Mill's philosophy and to liberalism. Nor, however, is there any need to modify or reject individualism as Mill simply combines the liberal idea of a people with the sociological or historical category of the nation: "Where the sentiment of nationality exists in any force, there is a *prima facie* case for uniting all the members of the nationality under the same government."[17] Mill's argument also prefigures the later functionalist account of nationalism developed by the twentieth-century liberal sociologist Ernest Gellner.[18] Gellner argued that nations are primarily a feature of modernity and are associated with the practice of state-building. Nationality is a mechanism through which states consolidate their power, secure their legitimacy, and seek to reproduce themselves. Mill explicitly links the idea of nationality to self-government, but more importantly he uses the idea of the nation as a way of securing political stability and effective and efficient government. The wider point of chapter xvi was not simply to acknowledge the fact of nationality but to recognize how it could support a liberal representative government in the face of the rise of democracy. Mill saw nationality as a way of taming the more dangerous and destabilizing tendencies of a democratic order by tying together disparate individuals into a single political entity focused around a common set of self-legitimizing institutions and practices. The liberal benefit of a national state is that it made possible the minimization of coercive legitimation as well as the liberal ideal of "soft" or non-invasive government.[19]

Where a nation existed and where it could sustain a minimally invasive and coercive political order, Mill acknowledged that there should be a right of national self-determination as an extension of the general right of self-government. Nevertheless, he remains a liberal first and a nationalist second. Although nations have a prima facie claim to self-determination and self-government, they do not have a conclusive claim. Indeed, Mill is often criticized by defenders of nationalism for an arbitrary distinction between the nations that he approves of and which should have rights to self-determination and those nations he is critical of which should subordinate themselves to dominant nations. Minority nations that have been absorbed into larger nation-states, such as the Bretons in France, Basques in Spain, or the Welsh and highland Scots in Britain, are described as "inferior and backward," and Mill suggests that such nations should be assimilated into the privileges of a "civilised and highly cultured people." All nations are not equal, and he makes no claim that they should all enjoy the same rights and privileges. Mill's support for a hierarchy among nations is consistent with his views about the differential development of peoples and his controversial views about the educative and progressive role of British imperial rule in India.[20]

ACTON AND THE LIBERAL REACTION TO LIBERAL NATIONALISM

Mill's liberal accommodation of nationality established a paradigm of liberal nationalism that has been developed and defended by some contemporary liberals, but it would be incorrect to see his position as the sole dominant strand of liberal discourse on the nation in nineteenth-century anglophone thought and the later liberal tradition. Mill's utilitarian liberal nationalism was one of the subjects of Lord Acton's essay on nationality[21] in which Acton mounts a liberal critique of liberalism and the idea that states and nations should be combined in single entities.

Coming from an old recusant Catholic family, Acton (1834–1902) is a curious figure in English liberalism: being educated into a European Catholic culture and civilization does not look a promising context for a defender of free institutions. Yet despite Acton's Catholicism, he was a close correspondent of the great liberal W. E. Gladstone and was thoroughly integrated into English liberal culture, which he celebrated in his historical writings, contrasting English liberalism with rationalist anti-clerical liberalism inspired by the French Enlightenment. Acton acknowledged the importance of national identity as an historical artefact, but he criticized the way in which elites used an abstract and artificial conception of the nation to construct an ideology of nationalism and to assert that it alone should be the principle of unity within a state. It was precisely this point that brought Acton to criticize Mill's argument that all members of a nation have a prima facie claim to be brought under one government. Acton saw Mill's argument as a threat to freedom and a liberal order by its strengthening of the power of government and the state and by its single criterion of political inclusion. Against this partisan idea of state nationalism, Acton asserted the importance of political pluralism and suggested that multi-nation states such as Great Britain and Austria-Hungary were more likely to ensure political and individual liberty than states with an homogenous national culture which in most cases will be a dominant culture imposed upon minorities. It was for this reason that he supported the Confederacy against the Union in the United States' Civil War.

Acton's liberalism reflects the conception of civil and commercial society as an evolving order of natural liberty familiar from Smith and the Scottish theorists of commercial society rather than the political monism of the social contract tradition in Locke or Kant. Although Acton's Catholicism ensured that he remained committed to a universal natural law, he rejected the modernist tendency of post-Hobbesian contract theorists to connect the law of nature with the modern sovereign state. A liberal order was not achieved by the rise of a system of sovereign states and the consolidation of state power but by a plural order of powers within and between states that balanced and dispersed political power. Where Mill feared the rise of the democratic masses and their capture of the state, Acton saw the rising power of the state as the primary problem.

Freedom was essentially a social order of dispersed power and not ultimately a condition of individuals under a sovereign state. The latter was a confidence trick performed by absolutists such as Hobbes and Bodin and which had deceived the likes of Locke, Kant and their successors such as Bentham and Mill. As a Catholic Acton's political sensibility was partly shaped by his membership of a recently oppressed minority in Britain and a culture that challenged the idea of the primacy of state sovereignty as a recent modernist invention that threatened a culture of freedom rather than guaranteeing it: He was the author of two provocatively titled essays on the idea of freedom in antiquity and freedom in the Christian world which show that freedom has evolved and developed and is not the gift of the modern sovereign state.[22] The state remained the greatest threat to freedom and the biggest danger from the state was its capture and domination by a partial faction or elite. For Acton the post-revolutionary rise of nationalism represented precisely this threat against the traditional orders and institutions that balanced and limited state power.

By the end of the nineteenth century, the Millian paradigm of liberal nationalism had apparently won against the liberal pluralism of Acton, becoming the dominant liberal discourse, especially following the policy of the US President Woodrow Wilson to advance liberal nationalism in the face of the breakup of the continental European empires in the Versailles Treaty after World War I. The redrawing of the European map, and that of the Middle East following the collapse of the Ottoman Empire, applied the Millian and Wilsonian idea that states and nations should converge (except in the case of the Kurds which became a source of instability and remains such to the present day). But the consequences of the Wilsonian settlement also precipitated a liberal challenge to liberal nationalism that reflected Acton's liberal pluralism. Perhaps unsurprisingly, some of the most forceful twentieth-century liberal critics of nationalism were Austrians such as F. A. Hayek and Karl Popper.

Hayek and Popper developed their political philosophies in the context of the collapse of the Austro-Hungarian Empire and the rise of state nationalism in central Europe. Following World War II, they both became prominent liberal critics of totalitarianism, but whilst this was primarily directed against the threat of Soviet Communism, Hayek in particular also challenged the idea of nationalism as a threat to a liberal international order. In *The Road to Serfdom* (1944), Hayek directs his attention at Nazism arguing that it combined socialism with nationalism. Where many critics of Nazism have tended to downplay the role of nationalism in the face of the peculiar version of genocidal racism that led to the Jewish Holocaust, Hayek was quite clear that nationalism was a central and dangerous element of totalitarianism which challenged the idea of an open international order by its principle of national uniformity as a criterion of collective organization and inclusion. Hayek's critique of nationalism is similar to that of Acton, indeed Hayek was quite explicit about his intellectual debt to Acton in the development of his mature liberal theory in *The Constitution of Liberty* (1960).[23] As a theorist of liberalism as a spontaneous order that is undermined by the imposition of an arbitrary and partial political conception of a collective good, Hayek's social theory could regard national identity only as an artificial construction imposed on a people. That said, like Acton he did not deny the existence of national fellow feeling: the problem was not the matter of fact, which Hayek could hardly deny although he was skeptical of claims about its significance, but the way in which it was used to justify a partial collective ideology.

Where the Millian paradigm had elided the social fact of national identity and fellow feeling with the normative claims of the sovereign state, Acton and Hayek rejected this strategy as a false ideological form of politics. The struggle within liberalism over the place of national identity remains a special case of the struggle over the place of the state in a liberal order. Mill and Acton, just as Locke and Smith, hold opposite positions in that debate. Hayek's position alongside Acton and Smith has placed him outside the main debates within academic liberalism, which has followed Isaiah Berlin and John Rawls in returning the discussion of liberalism to the context of a juridical state.

LIBERAL COSMOPOLITANISM AND THE CRITIQUE OF LIBERAL NATIONALISM

The experience of mid-twentieth-century European history, as mediated through the writings of classical liberals such as Hayek, has been unpromising for liberal nationalism. The debate about the compatibility between nationality and liberal values has returned to the heart of liberal political theory since the 1990s and has been spearheaded by David Miller, Will Kymlicka, Yael Tamir, Charles Taylor, and Margaret Moore, all of whom can be situated in debates that are inspired by two dominant late twentieth-century political philosophers, Isaiah Berlin and John Rawls.

Berlin is one of the most elusive of contemporary liberal political philosophers; a passionate defender of negative liberty and value pluralism through works that purport to be the history of ideas; he is a critic of nationalism as a manifestation of the politics of resentment, but he is at the same time a defender of national identity and national belonging.[24] Some scholars have explained Berlin's sympathy for liberalism and the value of national identity in his own conflicted attempts to reconcile his adopted Englishness with his Latvian Jewish background and later Zionism.[25] Although there is a danger in biographical reductionism, Berlin's own philosophical position is not incompatible with such interpretations. Berlin was an antisystematic political thinker as befits his philosophical training in Oxford realism and ordinary language philosophy.

Political philosophy is necessarily a second-order reflection on a first-order moral and political language that is given by experience, tradition, and practice and not derived from pure reason. It is not a science and does not have its own peculiar body of knowledge.

The political theorist's task is to analyze and explain the origins of that political language, and this involves the deployment of philosophical (or logico-linguistic) analysis and historical reflection and criticism. This requires the political theorist to sift through our moral and political experience to make the best possible sense of it. This focus on the grammar of a political or moral language can nevertheless draw our attention to features of moral and political experience that do not fit with systematization or logical coherence. For Berlin, one of the facts of moral experience is the ubiquity of conflict at the level of values and commitments, thus it is by no means incoherent both to value liberal principles and to recognize the claims of national belonging. Indeed, one of Berlin's criticisms of nationalism is that it reduces national sentiment to a single exclusive or monistic ideology.

Berlin's value pluralism is also manifest in his preoccupation with the ideas of anti-liberal and anti-enlightenment thinkers;[26] many of whom shape the development of Romanticism and nationalist politics in the nineteenth century and who influence the communitarian philosophy of some of Berlin's more famous students such as Charles Taylor.[27] Although he remains a liberal in politics and personal life, Berlin's recognition of the significance of national identity inspired other Jewish liberal political philosophers, such as Avishai Margalit, Joseph Raz, and most importantly Yael Tamir, to develop complex perfectionist versions of liberalism. Berlin's impact on Tamir's book *Liberal Nationalism*[28] is openly acknowledged and profound, yet Tamir pursues the relationship between liberal values and national (particularly in her case Zionist national) identity in much greater depth including the vexed political claims to recognition and self-determination.

Tamir addresses the issue of national self-determination by distinguishing between a cultural and a political claim and suggests that many nationalists conflate the two. The former acknowledges the importance of culture as a source of identity, values, and language, whereas the latter connects these with exclusive control of territory and collective political agency. Furthermore, she acknowledges the ubiquity of cultural pluralism within modern states. From these two premises she concludes that the recognition of national identity does not entail a claim or a right to political self-determination. As such she acknowledges the force of the liberal criticism of the nationalist's claim to reconcile national culture with political and territorial claims of the sort that underpinned Wilsonian nationalism, whilst at the same time not denying the importance of national belonging within individual and social identity. Mill's liberal nationalism had only ever asserted a contingent connection between the existence of national identity and political autonomy: Tamir's argument is not just a more forceful assertion of that contingency; instead, she refocuses attention on nationalism as a form of culturalism, thus linking her argument with liberal multiculturalists such as Will Kymlicka. Similarly, she does not deny the third element of Breuilly's typology of nationalism but just redirects attention from a narrow identification of nation and state to address other ways of accommodating national cultural claims, such as providing internal protections and through the distribution of resources within a state. Tamir's argument is thus consistent with the fundamental perspective of post-Berlinian liberal theory, which takes the statist character of the domain of politics for granted and sees the task of the political theorist in moralistic terms as the justification of norms of distribution within pre-existing states. This Berlinian-inspired liberal nationalism challenges the individualistic cosmopolitanism of Hayek and classical liberals that attaches no great significance to culture and identity. This is also the background presupposition of another great contemporary liberal philosopher, John Rawls, although Rawls is often considered a target of contemporary liberal nationalism as he inspires a more radical liberal cosmopolitanism that undermines the significance of states, nations, and cultures in its Kantian focus on free and equal individuals and their rights.

Rawls's three great works of political philosophy make virtually no reference to the idea of nationality,[29] and his theory of justice returns to the social contract tradition of Locke and Kant. Like Berlin, from whom he drew some inspiration, Rawls does not offer a theory of the state or an account of the political processes through which real politics manifests itself. Instead, the task of the political philosopher is reduced to an ethical one of regulating the distribution of the benefits and burdens of social cooperation. To this end, Rawls argues that social or distributive justice is the first virtue of political institutions and the primary concern of political philosophers. Consequently, Rawls cannot have anything to say about the justness of a state system or how territory should be divided between states and national groups: All of these issues are either presupposed as settled or are outside the scope of philosophical resolution. It is precisely this denial of the place of national identity that has encouraged political philosophers who are sympathetic to the issue of social justice to reintroduce the claims of nation and nationality into liberal arguments. Foremost among these is David Miller, who argues that Rawls either presupposes an established national community or requires the cultivation of national identity to motivate the form of redistribution that social justice requires.[30] Miller's argument ranges beyond commentary on Rawls and advances an account of national identity as both a political fact and a basis for social and political cohesion within a modern state, but he differs importantly from Tamir in acknowledging that national identity can form the basis of political rights and that these curtail the individualist cosmopolitanism that some commentators have argued follows from Rawls's theory of justice as fairness.[31]

Rawls's apparent failure to acknowledge that he presupposes a territorially defined national political community at the heart of his theory of social justice is not the only reason why his theory has attracted criticism from liberal nationalism; a further reason is provided by the original choice situation in which his two principles of justice are identified. A Theory of Justice employs the idea of a social contract in two important senses. First, the social contract is a metaphor for a political society as a scheme of social cooperation agreed between individuals who differ about fundamental ends and goals. In other words, it assumes that the common good is the problem and therefore that it cannot be presupposed as a way of solving problems of social cooperation. To this extent, Rawls repeats Berlin's claim about the ubiquity of pluralism. The social contract also functions as a device for choosing or legitimating the two principles that he claims constitute justice as fairness. To this end he imagines an original choice situation in which representative individuals choose the principles that govern the distribution of the benefits and burdens of social cooperation. To ensure that they do not merely choose what is in their narrow self-interest, they are required to choose behind a hypothetical veil of ignorance that denies them knowledge about their specific conception of the good, but also crucially about features of their particular identity. Thus, individuals would know nothing about their gender, culture, religion (if they have one), or nationality.

This model of individual choice behind a veil of ignorance has inspired a rival tradition of communitarian criticism often associated with thinkers such as Charles Taylor. The communitarian critics claim that choosers or selves who are unencumbered by the elements of their identity denied to them behind the veil of ignorance would either not be able to choose at all, or more importantly they would cease to be selves or individuals in any recognizable sense. For communitarians we are constituted as selves through identity-conferring practices such as culture, morality, nation, and religion, and without these there would be no individuals. This argument, often called the "social thesis," claims that our identities are socially constituted and that the isolated individual of classical liberal theory, especially that of Locke and Kant, is a mere philosopher's fiction or an abstraction taken too far. Although some communitarians have taken this argument to undermine liberalism, many liberals have sought to accommodate the social thesis within liberal discourse. It can be found at the heart of Tamir's defense of the importance of national identity and in Will Kymlicka's arguments for cultural recognition and protection in his liberal multiculturalism. As we have seen, this argument also reflects Berlin's rejection of an "inner citadel" view of the liberal self and his commitment to cultural and value pluralism. If the cultural sources of self-identity are preconditions of autonomous choice, then liberals need to cultivate and protect those valuable contexts of choice as a condition of a liberal and autonomous life. Rawls is therefore criticized for being too Kantian and anti-perfectionist in his conception of liberalism. Liberal nationalism positions itself as a modest liberal communitarian position that avoids the dessicated individualism of Rawls's Kantian liberal cosmopolitanism.

The argument thus far has been to show how the liberal nationalist argument has become interwoven with the discussion of two of the most important recent liberal political philosophers. What has not been done is assess whether this engagement has enhanced liberal theory or weakened the claims of nation within liberalism. In the closing part of this section, I will argue that the concessions contemporary liberal nationalists have won in these arguments are either weak or nonexistent.

Kymlicka and Tamir both deploy the culturalist or "social thesis" argument to support the claims of national identity, and whilst this makes a good point about the social context of choice and identity formation, it can at best make nationalism a contingent element in that process. When confronted by the claims of rival nations in the context of multi-nation states, or when having to adjudicate between the claims of national recognition and of social justice, egalitarian liberals such as Kymlicka and Tamir side with universalist-liberal values over the claims of nation or of culture. Tamir's cultural theory offers a weak defense of the nation as her liberalism requires the priority of just treatment, and where liberalism has to choose between culture and freedom or equality, it will always chose the latter values. If all that is being claimed is that liberalism can accommodate liberal versions of nationalism, then the point is true but trivial. If something stronger is being claimed on behalf of national identity, then the culturalist argument for national recognition becomes more problematic. Miller and Moore[32] do indeed make stronger claims for national recognition, although Miller's recognition of claims to rights to national self-determination or secession is heavily qualified, but they face the problematic challenge of why national cultural claims should automatically trump the claims of other cultural groups. The argument that national identity is special and prior to other group identities because it creates the bases of solidarity that sustain functioning states and democracies is open to the challenge that it is either circular or false as it defines as a nation whatever holds a state together, including in multi-nation states such as the UK or states like the USA where the idea of the nation is largely meaningless unless it refers to constitutional patriotism. If we interpret the nation in liberal nationalism to be so broad as to accommodate the ideal of constitutional patriotism or the bases of political obligation in a stable multi-nation state such as the UK, then we exhaust it of any explanatory content and contradict precisely the claims of the culturalist argument deployed by Tamir, Kymlicka, and ultimately Berlin, which sees a richer tradition of language and culture at the heart of national identity.

Yet in rejecting the claims of nationality within liberalism, we should not assume that this consigns liberalism to a dessicated cosmopolitan individualism or a universalist utopia. In weaving between individualist cosmopolitanism and national particularism in his last work, John Rawls recovers the idea of a law of peoples to regulate a global order. *The Law of Peoples* is a short, pregnant, and complex work which recovers ideas that are at the origins of liberalism in the ideas of Locke and Kant. Rawls's primary task is to extend the contractarian perspective of his political liberalism to the international and global realm and show why he posits a two-level contract theory – between individuals within political communities and between peoples at the global and international level – rather than through the global extension of his idea of a closed domestic society, as some of his cosmopolitan followers had argued. At the heart of the second level of contract is the notion of a people that is distinct from the idea of an existing state or a nation. The crucial point is that existing states and nations may both count as peoples, but such an overlap is wholly contingent as the idea of a people is a normative and juridical category. In choosing to conceptualize political communities and their interrelationships in terms of a law of peoples, Rawls recovers the tradition of Locke and Kant that distinguishes between the moral and juridical conceptualization of political relationships and the historical or anthropological facts of political experience. It is precisely this distinction that is overlooked by contemporary liberal nationalism. Furthermore, by acknowledging the idea of a political community between the individual and the global realm, the juridical idea of a people undercuts the nationalist claim that liberalism is too preoccupied with individuals and their rights to make sense of political experience.

CONCLUSION

Liberalism and nationalism are at best uneasy companions. Liberalism's social ontology denies the primacy of nationality as an account of political community, and its ethical theory denies the moral primacy of nation or any other kind of community or association above the claims of individuals to equal concern and respect. Consequently, liberalism can accommodate the claims for national recognition only on liberal terms. As we have seen, that does not deny that the national fellow-feeling of a liberal people sustains the free institutions and personal rights and liberties of a liberal order. All that said, the positive relationship between liberal and national ideals and values is politically contingent and in the long run unstable, although how unstable is an historical and empirical as opposed to a philosophical question. Some liberal theorists assumed that the logic of liberalism is that of a cosmopolitan order where the personal liberty and free movement of individuals dilute the ties of identity groups and national identity. It is precisely for this reason that nationalist politics often involves language protection policies, special social provision, and other restrictions on individual behavior to sustain the bases of national identity from the challenge of cosmopolitan culture and economic globalization. These provisions can be benign, although they clash with some core tenets of liberalism; however, where they are benign they also have unfortunate consequences for national identity as the more a nation becomes a liberal civic nation the less significance the idea of national identity has as a source of solidarity. This does not mean that solidarity becomes less important for liberals, but it does suggest that accounts of liberal solidarity can dispense with appeals to the social fact of national belonging and identity as their justification.

Although liberalism can accommodate a place for national identity, where stronger claims are made for national identity, as in most traditional political nationalisms, the uneasy relationship completely breaks down. Liberalism cannot and need not support nationalist claims for the national communities to be states and for significant national groups to secede from existing states to achieve national self-determination. In the last analysis liberalism is a person-regarding political philosophy, and insofar as it needs to accommodate rights to group self-determination this must be for person-regarding reasons alone. Such arguments are not well served by being confused with ideas of nationalism or nationality. The challenge for liberalism remains the same as it was for the early precursors of liberalism, such as Locke or Kant; to distinguish the legitimate claims of groups of individuals to organize their affairs collectively, from the idea that there are national communities which have a claim to recognition and self-determination that are not reducible to the rights and interests of their members.

NOTES

1. Breuilly, "On the Principle of Nationality," p. 77.
2. Mill and Acton are discussed as exemplars because of the clarity of their engagement with national identity and its political salience. It is not claimed that Mill or Acton exhaust the discussion of liberalism and nationality within discourse of nineteenth-century liberalism.

3. Berlin, "Nationalism."

4. Rawls, *The Law of Peoples*.

5. Until recently histories of political thought made precisely this claim, whereas almost all recent scholarship has attempted to extricate these thinkers from behind the shadow of liberalism. See Sabine, *A History of Political Theory;* Laski, *Political Thought in England from Locke to Bentham;* and compare with Dunn, *The Political Thought of John Locke* and Winch, *Adam Smith's Politics*.

6. See Waldron, "John Locke."

7. Locke, *Second Treatise of Government*, §§145–46. Kant, "Metaphysical First Principles of the Doctrine of Right," §§53–55.

8. Meisels, *Territorial Rights*, p. 159.

9. Hume, *A Treatise of Human Nature*.

10. Hume, *A History of England*.

11. Smith, *Lectures on Jurisprudence*. Smith's lectures were delivered between 1750 and 1764 at Glasgow University but were not published during his lifetime.

12. Rousseau, *On the Social Contract*.

13. Johann Gottfried Herder (1744–1803) was a student of Kant but was also influenced by J. G. Hamman (described by Isaiah Berlin as the "magus of the north").

14. Gray, *Liberalism*.

15. Mill, *Considerations on Representative Government*, chapter xvi.

16. Anderson, *Imagined Communities*.

17. Mill, *Considerations on Representative Government*, pp. 546–53.

18. Gellner, *Nations and Nationalism*.

19. This is a perspective held by contemporary defenders of nationalism; see Calhoun, *Nations Matter*.

20. See Varouxakis, *Mill on Nationality*, pp. 19–20 and Parekh, "Decolonising Liberalism," p. 91.

21. Acton, "Nationality," pp. 270–300.

22. Acton, "The History of Freedom in Antiquity" and "The History of Freedom in Christianity."

23. In establishing the Mont Pelerin Society in 1947, Hayek had originally suggested that it be called the Acton-Tocqueville society to indicate its commitment to a non-statist classical liberalism.

24. Much of Berlin's work comprises essay-length studies of philosophers and political thinkers that differ significantly from the methodologically self-conscious writings of many professional historians of ideas. Nevertheless, Berlin's provocative, reflective, and critical readings are often genuinely insightful contributions to political thought irrespective of whether historians of ideas would regard them as genuine history. Berlin is more

properly considered a practitioner of a form of political thinking that proceeds through reflection on the ideas of past thinkers as opposed to a practitioner of historical synthesis. See Crowder, *Isaiah Berlin*.

25. See Dubnov, *Isaiah Berlin* and for a critical response, Cherniss, *A Mind* in *its Time*.

26. Berlin, *The Crooked Timber of Humanity* and *The Magus of the North*.

27. Taylor, *Sources of the Self*.

28. Tamir, *Liberal Nationalism*.

29. Rawls's *A Theory of Justice* makes only one reference to nation in 538 pages and this is in the context of just war; his *Political Liberalism* makes no reference to nation or nationality, while his final book, *The Law of Peoples*, does refer to nationality but in purely cultural terms following Tamir.

30. Miller, *On Nationality* and Miller, *National Responsibility and Global Justice*.

31. See Caney, *Justice Beyond Borders*. Caney along with Thomas Pogge regard Rawls's later *A Law of Peoples* as a betrayal of the individualist cosmopolitanism of his early work on justice as fairness, whereas nationality theorists such as Miller think that Rawls is insufficiently attentive to the place of a nationality within liberal theory.

32. See Moore, *The Ethics of Nationalism* for a more forceful defense of the culturalist argument for national recognition that is prepared to challenge liberalism.

IV Challenges

15 Feminist critiques of liberalism

Feminism and liberalism have a complex and fraught history. On the one hand, first- and second-wave feminists rooted their basic rights claims in the venerable tradition of arguments for political liberty and equal citizenship. Although the principle of liberty has been given various interpretations (e.g., positive or negative), the idea that freedom is a fundamental individual right and that any limitation on it must be justified (e.g., the social contract) is core to liberalism as a prominent strand of historical political thought. In this way, liberalism has been an invaluable resource for feminists in the long struggle for political freedom and against the arbitrary power of men over women.

On the other hand, even a cursory look at the history of liberalism shows that it has often enough been an obstacle to the very thing that its fundamental commitment to equal liberty would seem to promote. Many early modern and modern liberal thinkers have either excluded women from the social contract on the basis of some putative deficit (e.g., in reasoning), or grudgingly included them while holding fast to traditional gender roles and, in some cases, to male (husbands' and fathers') power over women (wives and daughters) in the family. Indeed, so captivated have classical liberal thinkers been by the "natural" social and cultural logic of binary gender differences that even John Stuart Mill – whose fierce contestation of male power led him to advocate state intervention into "the domestic life of domestic tyrants" – did not begin to question domestic life organized around the gendered division of labor.[1]

In our own time, when traditional gender roles have been challenged by feminists and forms of arbitrary rule can no longer publicly be defended, liberals have been divided on how to address forms of social inequality that make a mockery of equal liberty but are not directly caused by the formal legal and political barriers that have been the historical focus of liberal critique. Although so-called social justice liberals (e.g., John Rawls and Ronald Dworkin) are far more willing than their classical predecessors to balance the core demand for liberty with concerns about tenacious forms of inequality, they remain curiously blind, if not indifferent, to the gendered structure of family life and the crushing costs for women's liberty. Contemporary liberal thinkers do not argue for this division in the way that classical theorists openly did, but they nevertheless take for granted "the mature, independent human beings as the subjects of their theories without any mention of how they got to be that way," as Susan Okin wryly observes.[2] The vastly disproportionate share of women's work in producing those subjects remains mostly ignored by contemporary liberal theorists of whatever stripe, though it drastically influences women's own chances of becoming the very independent human beings capable of exercising liberalism's *raison d'être*, namely, liberty.

In light of the tenacity of de facto gender inequality in the face of the de jure gender equality that characterizes contemporary liberal democratic societies, liberal theory's blind spot on that which disproportionately prevents women from realizing liberty is troubling. It presents a genuine problem for feminists as they consider the limits and possibilities of the liberal tradition. As we shall see, for some feminists liberalism is a theoretical and political dead end, for it cannot call into question the private/public distinction in which the hidden gendered division of labor has its life.[3] To do so, say these critics, liberals would have to abandon the terrain of the very distinction that underwrites fundamental liberal principles regarding the liberty of the individual in relation to the power of the state. For other critics, liberalism requires a feminist critique, only this critique would not declare liberalism dead for feminism but would instead expose the implicit feminist commitments in any liberalism worthy of the name.[4] "Liberalism properly understood, with its radical refusal to accept hierarchy and its focus on the equality and freedom of individuals, is crucial to feminism," declares Okin.[5] Liberalism still offers great resources to feminism, but it also needs feminism to live up to its best ideals.

FEMINIST CRITIQUES OF EARLY MODERN AND MODERN LIBERAL THOUGHT

Some of the most trenchant feminist critiques of liberalism begin with early modern arguments for natural rights based in the capacity for reason, for it is here that the whole question of arbitrary rule was first critically raised. In *A Vindication of the Rights of Woman* (1792), Mary Wollstonecraft, writing against the world-historical background of the French Revolution, famously took up the idea of natural, God-given rights to mock those thinkers (e.g., Rousseau) who would restrict their exercise to men alone. At the center of Wollstonecraft's argument is a sustained interrogation of the claim that women are more emotional than rational. If women are indeed guilty of excessive sentiment, she concedes, this is reflective not of their feminine nature but of gender convention and cultural constraint. Though the raw material of reason is present in both sexes at birth, the vast differences in their education lead each human being's natural rational powers to develop in men and atrophy in women. "My own sex, I hope, will excuse me, if I treat them like rational creatures, instead of flattering their *fascinating* graces, and viewing them as if they were in a state of perpetual childhood, unable to stand alone," she writes.[6]

Wollstonecraft's apparent defense of a gender-neutral capacity for reason, which transcends all historical contingencies, has been crucial to the reception of her as a liberal feminist.[7] Like liberal thinkers, she is often read as primarily concerned with individuals and rights. Although it is true that Wollstonecraft was focused on both, the distinctive character of her political voice is lost when she is assimilated to liberal feminism. For one thing, Wollstonecraft wrote in the context of the Pamphlet Wars of the 1790s, an important historical fact that leads some readers to interpret her thought as universalist in scope and more properly radical egalitarian and utopian than liberal.[8] For others, Wollstonecraft's political views would be more aptly called radical republican and their vehicle was a brilliant use of revolutionary and feminist rhetoric.[9] She was a defender of the rights of women, but she did not understand rights solely as legal artifacts that are mostly focused on securing the (negative) liberty of the individual vis-à-vis society and the state. For Wollstonecraft, rights were more closely aligned with a form of participatory democracy in which having rights does not exist apart from the practice of claiming rights. "Viewed as a rhetorical and political artifact, Wollstonecraft's appeal to rights is figured as a claim for revolutionary and feminist transformation where rights themselves are understood as part of a broader democratic project that is seldom explored," as Angela Maoine writes.[10]

Many of the themes regarding women's subjection to men and the artificial character of proper femininity were addressed over a half a century later by another key figure in the liberal tradition: John Stuart Mill. Together with his wife Harriet Taylor, Mill challenged the Victorian figure of the "Angel in the House," which denied women any public voice and made of them the domestic keepers of morality. Extending many of the principles of *On Liberty* (1859), which examines the question of when and under what conditions the state or society has the right to interfere with the liberty of an individual, Mill exposed the fallacious logic at work in the nineteenth century's vast social, economic, political, and legal apparatus of male power.

Like Wollstonecraft's 1792 *Vindication*, Mill's *The Subjection of Women* (1869) is a tour de force of feminist argumentation and rhetoric. Inspired by his companion and deceased wife Taylor, Mill powerfully challenged the idea that women were by nature deficient in reasoning or in any other way incapable of the kind of self-development that he took to be crucial to the defense of individual liberty. He blamed custom, especially sex-specific education, and explained the tenacity of the status quo in terms not only of formal legal constraints on women's liberty but also of the psychology of male power:

All causes, social and natural, combine to make it unlikely that women should be collectively rebellious to the power of men. They are so far in a position different from all other subject classes, that their masters require something more from them than actual service. Men do not want solely the obedience of women, they want their sentiments. All men ... desire to have, in the woman most nearly connected with them, not a forced slave, but a willing one ... They [men] have therefore put everything in place to enslave their [women's] minds.[11]

Notwithstanding his staunch support of women's rights, including suffrage, Mill's feminist thought is compromised by his deep and at times obsessive concern with the procreative habits of the unemployed poor. Like most of his European contemporaries, Mill subscribed to temporally progressive yet always endangered narratives of civilization. He worried that British society would be driven back into barbarism by what he called the "animal power of multiplication."[12] Thus, his support of the 1834 Poor Law Amendment Act was at once a rebuke to conservatives, who held that charity destroys the incentive to work, and an acceptance of the idea of self-willed pauperism, which underwrote new restrictions on relief. To those reformers who would raise wages in order to reduce working hours, the otherwise socialist sympathizer Mill countered that work is the only antidote to excessive sensuality and lust. Left to itself, an unregulated working-class sexuality would "call into existence swarms of creatures who are sure to be miserable, and most likely to be depraved ... [Furthermore, such] conduct ... is a degrading slavery to a brute instinct in one of the persons concerned, and most commonly, in the other, helpless submission to a revolting abuse of power."[13]

The consequence of Mill's concern about the disruptive effects of sexuality was an attenuated feminism that could not shake off the idea of female sexual modesty as a kind of safeguard against those who "follow their brute instincts without due consideration."[14] This positioning of women as the guardians of the well-ordered society deeply limited Mill's ability to question the gendered division of labor, even as he clearly saw the pernicious effects of a wholly domestic existence on women's self-development and thus on their exercise of liberty.[15] As time went on, he became more and more invested in the idea of a select class of individuals, "the higher natures," who came to symbolize what liberal theory needed to defend. He could not shake, finally, the belief in an asexual domesticated femininity as the anchor of a civilized liberal culture that could allow individuals who had the capacity for self-restraint to develop freely.

Concerns over the disruptive effects of sexuality have been central to early modern and modern liberal political thought. As Carole Pateman argues, though liberalism centers on the idea of humans as rational beings who are naturally free and equal and whose consent is therefore necessary to any form of rule, it has always posited exceptions. Historically, women have been seen as an exception, women who "by virtue of their very [sexual] natures, are a source of disorder in the state."[16]

In her now classic feminist work, *The Sexual Contract*, Pateman shows how women get excluded from the category of fully rational beings and thus from free and equal political status. The other face of the social contract, which tells the story of men's equal natural freedom vis-à-vis the patriarchal Father, is the justification of men's power over women. Contrary to the assumption that the social contract challenges the very idea of arbitrary rule, it actually re-encodes patriarchal right (the power of fathers) as conjugal male sex-right (the power of husbands over wives), argues Pateman. This is true even in the case of Hobbes, who was alone both in granting mother-right (the power of the mother over the child in the state of nature) and in holding that there is no natural dominion of men over women. Notwithstanding this radical stance, Hobbes went on to justify conjugal right, the right of men to power over and property in their wives. "Hobbes's patriarchalism is a new, specifically modern form, that is conventional, contractual, and originates in conjugal right, or, more accurately, sex-right; that is, in men's right of sexual access to women, which, in its major institutional form in modern society, is exercised as conjugal right," writes Pateman.[17] Likewise, even an outspoken critic of patriarchalism such as John Locke, who explicitly rejected paternal right as the basis for political right, had no problem holding to husbands' conjugal right over wives. Conjugal right is redefined as nonpolitical and in this sense is taken off the table, so to speak, for rethinking the basis of political power.

Pateman's account of the gender subtext of social contract theory raises significant questions for feminists who are either friendly toward or critical of liberal political thought. She reveals as illusory the contract's status as a gender-neutral concept for understanding modern forms of political power. In Pateman's view, the contract is relevant not only in its classic historical form as a way of justifying political rule, but also in contemporary contractual arrangements such as wage-labor, surrogate motherhood, prostitution, and marriage. All of these contracts have in common the idea of property in one's person and all of them are defended as valid (if at times problematic) human arrangements based on liberal principles. What Pateman suggests, however, is that being in a contractual relationship by no means guarantees one's free status, either in the act of "contracting-in" or in the exercise of the terms of the contract itself. On the contrary, the social contract's modern form is one that reasserts the male/female relation as one of domination and subordination. Thus, even in cases where women appear to have property in their own bodies and to be freely contracting out a service of some kind (e.g., prostitution), they are in reality subject to forms of power that sustain the fundamental male/female relation as master/subject. Contract, then, is a ruse for concealing an original form of subordination.

FEMINIST CRITIQUES OF CONTEMPORARY LIBERALISM

One of the problems raised by Pateman's critique of classical social contract theory is whether the dyadic "master/subject model is adequate for analyzing gender inequality in late capitalist societies," as Nancy Fraser puts it.[18] Likewise Wendy Brown holds that in our own time "both liberalism and women's subordination may well be sustained without contract."[19] In Fraser's and Brown's respective accounts, there are larger structural forces that do not appear in the form of one individual (a man) exerting an authoritative will over another (a woman), but that strongly support men's power as a sex-class. The assimilation of contract to command can blind us to forms of power that disadvantage women but do not follow the master/subject model. Modern marriage, for example, may well fit certain aspects of Pateman's critique: for example, some jurisdictions do not recognize marital rape. Yet to focus on such legal disabilities can distort our understanding of how gender power works. To return to a point made earlier, we might well miss "the structural and processual constraints" on women that Susan Okin has characterized as "a cycle of socially caused and distinctly asymmetric vulnerability by marriage."[20] These constraints, we recall, include a gendered division of labor that is not part of any actual marriage contract but that significantly limits women's educational and work opportunities.[21]

The invisibility of this work and the actual dependence on it of the supposedly unencumbered (masculine) liberal subject is occluded by liberalism's separation of public and private spheres. Liberalism is neither the first nor the only political philosophy to separate private from public realms.[22] "Distinctions between public and private have been and remain fundamental, not incidental or tangential, ordering principles in all known societies save, perhaps, the most simple."[23] Although liberals do not agree on where the boundary between public and private should be drawn, all nevertheless accept the necessity of the distinction itself to any theory that can properly be called liberal.[24]

The consequences of this distinction from a feminist point of view cannot be underestimated. For one thing, it tends to conceal forms of power that greatly limit women's liberty and equality. These include not only the gendered division of labor described above but also forms of violence (e.g., domestic violence, marital/partner rape and date rape, stalking, etc.) that significantly limit women's freedom of movement and ability to claim the political rights that are formally theirs. The public/private dichotomy can also blind us to the non-consensual work of care, making such work appear voluntary.[25] "[T]he autonomous subject of liberalism requires a large population of nonautonomous subjects, a population that generates, tends, and avows the bonds, relations, dependencies, and connections that sustain and nourish human life," comments Brown.[26] The problem, however, is that the actual non-autonomy that characterizes the lives of these (mostly female) subjects is barely visible within the liberal framework of public and private that is understood in terms of consent and choice. Taking for granted that individuals are free to move from one realm to the other as they choose, liberalism's private/public distinction blinds us to constraints that appear to be extra-political, and this would include the family. As we saw with John Locke, the argument for distinguishing paternal power from political power sought to free sons from the rule of the Father (kings), but it treated conjugal right (the rule of husbands over their wives) as fully nonpolitical.[27]

To properly grasp the nature and extent of the constraints under which women as private caretakers labor, feminists have argued that we need to interrogate the understanding and deployment of consent as a key term in liberal theory. In her work on political obligation, Nancy Hirschmann has argued that the very idea of consent as the basis of legitimate political obligation is based on liberal ideas of the abstract – read male – individual. "In asserting that the individual can and does create all of her relationships and all of her obligations, consent theory abstracts people from their social circumstances and ignores the reality that social relationships do in fact influence, shape, and make possible the human capacity for autonomy."[28] Hirschmann not only implicitly agrees with Okin about the blind spot in liberalism when it comes to the invisible labor of women that is involved in producing an autonomous being; she also sees this blind spot as symptomatic of liberalism's flawed understanding of what binds people together in a political community. The obligations they incur by virtue of being born cannot be properly described as a matter of choice without significantly distorting the character of human relations. It is not a matter, then, of extending contractual relations into the private sphere, but of rethinking what it means to have obligations to others in the first place.

FEMINIST CRITIQUES OF LIBERALISM'S "ATOMISTIC MAN"

Hirschmann's book exists in a long line of feminist critiques of the figure of "atomistic man," that is, liberalism's masculinist ideal of unconnected and unencumbered individuals.[29] Within feminist jurisprudence in particular, as Linda McClain has written, liberalism is typically viewed by its critics as having "exalted rights over responsibilities, separateness over connection, and the individual over community."[30] Insofar as these critics put forward an alternative vision to what they see as liberalism's masculinist conception of "separate, atomistic, competing individuals," this tends to be articulated in terms of "interdependency, connection, responsibility, and caring," writes McClain.[31] Notwithstanding the harm done to women, the domestic labor performed by them becomes, in the view of these critics, the basis for rethinking the nature of human relationships in ways that start with the individual as always already embedded in community. Liberal social contract theory is rejected in favor of models emphasizing care and mothering. Indeed, comments McClain, "the goal is often expressed as supplementing or replacing an 'ethic of justice,' based on conceptions of rights and rules, with an 'ethic of care,' based on notions of responsibility and relationships."[32]

What Martha Minow has called "the relational turn" in feminist work was rooted in a range of books, published mostly in the 1980s, which endeavored to articulate an alternative account of women's ways of knowing and being in the world that did not see these as somehow deficient or flawed in comparison with men's. Carole Gilligan's *In A Different Voice* (1982), Robin West's *Love, Rage and Legal Theory* (1989), and Sara Ruddick's *Maternal Thinking* (1989) all found in women's experience a deep sense of connectedness to others and a moral sensibility that reflected not "detachment, objectivity, universality, and abstraction but instead empathy, engagement, subjectivity (or intersubjectivity), and contextuality."[33] Although universal claims about women's experience have fallen out of favor in recent years, the view of liberalism as a male-centered discourse premised on a highly abstract conception of individuals taken out of any social context still resonates with many feminists.

Consider John Rawls's description of the "original position" in his magnum opus, *A Theory of Justice* (1971). The "veil of ignorance" that conceals from individuals their particular place in society, including attributes such as one's sex, has been described by feminists as embodying "an atomistic view of the person that is contrary to the reality of human connection."[34] Indeed, in the view of Iris Marion Young, one of the most vocal feminist critics of Rawls's veil of ignorance and its "ideal of impartiality," the impartial thinker "aims to adopt a point of view outside concrete situations of action, a transcendental 'view from nowhere' that carries the perspective, attributes, character, and interests of no particular subject or set of subjects. This ideal of the impartial transcendental subject denies or represses difference in three ways": (1) "it denies the particularity of situations," (2) it "seeks to master or eliminate heterogeneity in the form of feeling," and (3) it reduces "the plurality of moral subjects to one subjectivity."[35] Thus, although Rawls's critique of utilitarianism for not taking into account the plurality of moral subjects leads him to insist on the plurality of selves in the original position, argues Young, the reasoning in which they engage "is nevertheless monological."[36] In other words, "each subject reasons in terms of its own interests alone with full knowledge that there is a plurality of others doing the same with whom it must come to agreement." There is no "discussion among them."[37]

In McClain's view, feminist critiques such as Young's, which characterize the ideal of impartiality as the hallmark of liberalism's "atomistic man," are based on a "caricature" of liberal thought. Though this caricature may well have a basis in fact, especially when it comes to early modern and modern liberalism, she writes, it is not an accurate portrait of "contemporary versions of liberalism, most prominently the work of both John Rawls and Ronald Dworkin."[38] For example, far from being the device of abstract individualism that feminist critics of Rawls claim it to be, Susan Okin holds that the veil of ignorance "forces each person in the original position to take the good of others into account," as Rawls himself puts it.[39] Rather than "think from the position of *nobody,*" one must try to "think from the position of *everybody,* in the sense of *each in turn,*" Okin writes.[40] What is more, comments McClain, Okin "contends that persons could not go through the exercise of the original position unless they were motivated by care, empathy, and concern for others ... Thus Okin challenges the distinction between an ethic of justice and an ethic of care and suggests that the latter is necessarily present in the persons Rawls imagines as engaging in the exercise of the original position."[41]

Okin and McClain are critical of liberalism, but also highly sympathetic to its "key concepts of rights, autonomy, equality, fairness, and justice."[42] In their view, these concepts are not necessarily tethered to a view of individuals as atomistic, unencumbered by obligations to others, and unaccountable to public scrutiny – and they are concepts that are absolutely crucial for feminism. Okin and McClain's defense of Rawls against his feminist critics, then, by no means amounts to an unqualified endorsement of his work in particular or liberal theory in general. There are genuine problems in liberal conceptions of the family and gender relations, which need to be exposed and addressed, but so too are there resources for doing so in their view.

In Rawls's later work we find formulated an explicit commitment to equality as the fundamental relation in which men stand to women. "The adult members of families and other associations are equal citizens first: That is their basic position. No institution or association in which they are involved can violate their rights as citizens," writes Rawls.[43] In the case of families, he adds, that "[s]ince wives are equally citizens with their husbands, they have all the basic rights, liberties, and opportunities as their husbands; and this, together with the correct application of the other principles of justice, suffices to secure their equality and independence."[44] He also acknowledges that insofar as the family "inculcate[s] habits of thought and ways of feeling and conduct incompatible with democracy ... the principles of justice ... can plainly be invoked to reform the family."[45] And he recognizes that women's vastly disproportionate contribution to child-rearing represents a "long and historic injustice" that needs to be politically addressed.[46] Notwithstanding these claims, Rawls seems bound to his earlier claim, in *A Theory of Justice*, that the principles of justice "are not to apply to the internal life of the many associations within [the basic structure of society], the family amongst them."[47] Consequently, the division of labor within the family must be tolerated so long as it is "fully voluntary and does not result from or lead to injustice."[48] As Okin remarks, "this is more than a little puzzling."[49]

Rawls is aware of and sympathetic to feminist critiques, but the criterion of voluntariness that he, like most, liberals holds out as the test according to which to decide whether injustice is at play is woefully inadequate for understanding the maintenance of men's power over women. For one thing, he assimilates families to other private voluntary associations, as if exercising the right of exit were the same for a family as it is for a university or a church.[50] He imagines a scenario in which we would be able to say, with more or less perfect certainty, that any existing gendered division of labor in the family is indeed voluntary and thus that the family is just. "That even the voluntary gendered division of labor in families might compromise the equality of girls and women through the inculcation of gender stereotypes seems not to have occurred to him," comments Tracy Higgins.[51]

To Rawls's claim that "[w]e wouldn't want" families to be regulated by principles of distributive justice, Okin replys, "why not?"[52] If we take seriously a critique made long ago by John Stuart Mill, namely, that families are "schools of despotism," we can see why thinkers concerned with the survival of liberal democracy do well to attend to what happens behind the veil of privacy. As Okin reformulates Mill's concern: "How could the social institution in which, as Rawls acknowledges, small children's first inklings of justice emerge in the context of their love and trust for those who care for them, forming the basis for moral development, not itself be based on internal justice?"[53] Whether this can be done through extending liberal principles is, of course, at the heart of the debate between liberal feminists and their critics. The problem concerns not only liberalism's unyielding adherence to the distinction between public and private spheres but also its application of a gender-neutral principle of equality that may not be neutral at all.

EQUAL TO WHOM?

The principle of equality that liberals articulate and defend has been at once appealing and troubling for feminists. On the one hand, equality has served as a banner for many important feminist struggles of the eighteenth, nineteenth, and twentieth centuries, including suffrage, property law, and wages. The increasing acceptance of liberal democratic principles in advanced industrial societies provided a common idiom in which women's political voices could be heard. Rather than being labeled "merely subjective" ("the female complaint"), women's claims to an equal share in governing resonated with a broader vocabulary of equality as part of liberal democratic common sense.

Although it is tempting to see this expansion of the equality principle to women as just that – an expansion – there are good reasons to pause and consider what such a view entails. Some feminists have been critical of the idea of equality as an expanding principle, for this view tends to go hand in hand with the idea that equal rights expand by themselves, thanks to a certain logic that is implicit in rights. Occluded in this view is the hard, fragile, and highly contingent work of feminist politics. There is no guarantee that the principle of equality will be extended to groups not already included in its purview, any more than there is a guarantee that whoever currently is not included never can be. Thus, feminists insist on attending to the actual practices of feminist politics, rather than assuming that liberal principles have a logic and temporality of its own.[54]

Another worry raised by feminists regarding equality is that the gender neutrality that is supposedly equality's aim and basis is merely a ruse for sustaining androcentric ideals. As we saw earlier, many feminists are highly critical of the atomistic individual at the heart of liberalism, an "individual" who is gender neutral in name only. To strive for equality is to strive for equality with men, which is to say, to strive to be more like men. For men have more or less defined what it means to be a citizen, a worker, a property owner, a juror, and so forth. In a world in which one's sex/gender is indeed a crucial basis of social differentiation, can we really consider legal and political subjects as gender neutral without blinding ourselves to crucial facts?

In *The Female Body and the Law* (1988), Zillah Eisenstein asks feminists to consider what drives the debate over whether to stress equality or, instead, difference. This is an impossible choice, which has more or less defined the history of all three waves of feminism. Any answer is already overdetermined by a legal system in which the male body and the masculine subject are the norm. In practice this means that any attempt to take account of sexual difference will be interpreted as a reinscription of masculinist ideals of proper femininity; and any attempt to claim equality will result in women being treated as if they were men. Equal-protection law is in fact gendered masculine but it conceals its gendered nature under the guise of neutrality.[55] This keeps feminism in a perpetual state of the impossible choice: equal *or* different. The only way out of this dilemma, argues Eisenstein, is to "pluralize the meaning of difference and reinvent the category of equality."[56] Rather than take male/female as the marker of difference, we need to acknowledge differences among women themselves and men themselves. "[In] the engendered view of difference, differences among women are silenced and difference between men and women privileged; the sameness among women is presumed and the similarity between men and women denied."[57] The pregnant body becomes for Eisenstein a way to decenter the male body that is at the heart of but also concealed by equality doctrine: "it reminds us of at least the potential difference between females and males that makes sameness, as the standard for equality, inadequate. In a more general sense it reminds us of diversity."[58] Men do not become pregnant but neither will all women.

If "sex equality is not enough for feminism," to borrow Merle Thornton's phrase, that is because feminism knows that equality is a principle that treats likes alike and unlikes differently. "Equality is a concept that can only be applied to two (or more) things in some specified respect. There has to be a characteristic which both have in respect of which they are said to be equal ... Equality implies commensurability," observes Thornton.[59] That is another way of saying, with Eisenstein, that equality leads to the assimilation of women under an androcentric norm.

Writing in a similar vein, feminist legal scholar Catharine MacKinnon explains that law presents the situation of women and men as if from a place of neutrality, what she calls "the point-of-viewlessness" of law.[60] The principle of legal equality is not only insufficient for feminism but occludes the reality of gender power with the idea of gender neutrality, which is really just a disguise for androcentric law, law that takes the masculine subject as the norm. "Objectivist epistemology is the law of law. It ensures that the law will most reinforce existing distributions of power when it most closely adheres to its own highest ideal of fairness."[61] For women to be recognized under equal protection doctrine, they have first to be seen as like men. "Socially, one tells a woman from a man by their differences, but a woman is recognized to be discriminated against on the basis of sex only when she can first be said to be the same as a man ... Sex equality becomes a contradiction in terms, something of an oxymoron," MacKinnon declares.[62]

Furthermore, argues MacKinnon, gender difference is really gender dominance, men's power over women. This power is hidden when the equality principle is applied, for it appears that men and women are equally positioned. Apart from real biological differences (e.g., only women get pregnant), women are situated differently in relation to the social effects of bodily differences, which include access to wealth, power, and influence due to centuries of discrimination. Turning a blind eye to gender, which is what contemporary no-fault divorce and child custody laws do, is often to the detriment of women. If gender, which is to say past discrimination's effect on women, is ignored, men will simply look like the better parent: they make more money and have more of the sorts of things that courts consider when deciding custody.

Consequentially, if the law treats men and women as equal, that is, as the same, the reality of women's unequal status is invisible. "But if they ask to be treated like women, they provide justification for unequal treatment by admitting that they are different than men. MacKinnon thus explains why contemporary feminism appears to be divided against itself, why it is said that feminism cannot decide whether women want equality or special treatment," writes Denise Schaeffer.[63] The problem with liberal neutrality is that it cannot treat women as women without violating its own principle, and yet to treat women as the same leaves invisible the very real differences in power and situation that make a mockery of equal status under law.

From the perspective of feminist legal historian Ute Gerhard, however, "equality remains indispensable as a standard of justice" and "enjoying equal rights does not presuppose assimilation into

men's status and lifestyle."[64] The assumption that the equality principle is androcentric and that it can take account of women only to
the extent that it occludes their specific situation is premised on a
misunderstanding of the meaning of equal rights.

Equality is neither an absolute principle nor a firm standard, but a "relational
concept." It expresses a relationship between two objects, people, or conditions and determines the respect in which they are to be viewed as equal.
That is, equality must first be sought, demanded, and established, and it
presupposes that the objects being compared are different from each other.
Otherwise, the principle of equality would be unnecessary and absurd.
Logically, this can only involve partial equality, that is equality in specific
respects. Absolute equality would mean identity. If one were to demonstrate
this mathematically, the formula for identity would be a = a, while equality
would be expressed as a = b.[65]

Gerhard sees that Aristotle's concept of equality – treating likes alike
and things that are unalike unalike in proportion to their unalike-
ness – has caused conceptual confusion and led many feminists to
assume that women must first be seen like men in order to be treated
as equal to men. But even Aristotle's formulation, she argues, leaves
open the question as to "who or what decides which characteristics or
particularities suggest comparison or equal treatment and in respect
of which traits difference is determined."[66] There is no logical rule
according to which the principle of equality can be applied. Instead,
comparison is "the result of an assessment, a value judgment, whose
criteria may very well be controversial."[67]

To appreciate the complexity of every claim to equality, Gerhard
suggests, we need to focus not on the social objects being compared
(e.g., a and b, men and women), as if they alone determined the
standard of comparison, but on the social subjects making the comparison and the historical context in which they judge. By shifting our
attention to context and the specific situation of those making the
comparison, Gerhard reminds feminists that the standard for adjudicating equality claims does not inhere in the object itself; it cannot be
found by way of a logical operation. Rather, each claim to equality
requires subjects to make political judgments that may be based on
precedent but are nonetheless not knowable in advance of any claim.
Such a judgment does not appeal to a standard that is inherent in the
comparison of two objects. "It is dependent on the context and the

perspective of those making the comparison should by no means be oriented towards only one of the objects to be compared. It requires a third party."[68] What lawyers call a "*tertium comparationis*," writes Gerhard, "tells us that the standard of comparison cannot be found in either one of the two sides but requires a third, impartial point of view. This means that equal rights for women cannot take men as the guideline; it cannot mean 'attaining the status of men.'"[69]

GENDER AND THE PROBLEM OF EQUAL POLITICAL REPRESENTATION

The problem of legal equality and gender neutrality described above can be approached from a related angle, namely that of political representation and participation. On the whole, liberal political thought has emphasized the importance of diversity and difference, even as it has championed the principle of equality under law. For the most part, diversity has been understood in terms of value pluralism, that is, as the diversity of ideas. As Anne Phillips observes, "[t]he diversity most liberals have in mind is a diversity of beliefs, opinions, preferences, and goals, all of which may stem from the variety of experience, but are considered as in principle detachable from this."[70] This understanding of diversity has important consequences for how liberalism understands political representation, argues Phillips, "for when difference is considered in terms of intellectual diversity, it does not much matter who represents the range of ideas."[71] Consequently, "men may conceivably stand in for women when what is at issue is the representation of agreed policies or programs or ideals. But how can men stand in for women when what is at issue is the representation of women *per se?*" she asks.[72]

To the extent that liberals consider the issue raised by what Phillips calls "the politics of presence," they tend to subordinate it to a "politics of ideas" and to think of these ideas as connected to different social groups. For the most part, the question of fair and equal group representation is considered within the larger framework of liberal neutrality, that is, how to balance what John Rawls, in *Political Liberalism* (1993), argues to be the incommensurable but equally rational claims of competing "comprehensive doctrines" or worldviews.[73] For Rawls, such incommensurability need not lead defenders of liberalism to despair. A political arrangement can be

worked out which creates an "overlapping consensus" around fundamental principles of fairness and justice. Conceptualizing the problem of diversity in terms of beliefs or doctrines, Rawls understands
the issue of the "proper representation" of the point of view of free
and equal citizens in terms of a politics of ideas, not a politics of
presence: "he does not at all mean that there should be a rough
equality of representation between the different groups that make
up society."[74]

From a feminist perspective, the problems in liberal conceptions of
neutrality and fair political representation are at once like and unlike
the problems described by liberal thinkers who have tried to rethink
the commitment to individual freedom through the lived reality of
people in cultural groups. Will Kymlicka (1989) and Joseph Raz
(1994), to take two well-known examples, have argued that individual
freedom cannot be conceptualized outside the rights of group difference.[75] Membership in a cultural group, in other words, is seen as the
contextual condition for "individual freedom and prosperity."[76] On
the one hand, feminist critics of liberalism would say something
similar, arguing that sexual difference and one's embodied existence
as a member of the group called women is the necessary starting point
for claims to autonomy and freedom. On the other hand, feminists are
critical of the idea that all women have the same or even similar
interest *qua* women. Would this move not amount to the very
attempt "to reduce plurality to unity" that Young characterizes as
the essence of liberal neutrality and impartial reasoning?[77] If we do
not hold "that all women have identical interests," writes Phillips,
"in what sense are we more fairly represented when we see our
representatives more like ourselves?"[78] In other words, whatever
problems may exist with liberalism's politics of ideas, which tends
to treat ideas as independent from those who hold them, what is to be
gained from switching to the politics of presence, which holds that
the diversity of an electorate cannot be properly accounted for unless
the diversity of ideas is represented by a diversity of groups? Can't
male elected representatives with feminist ideas substitute for the
presence of women as elected representatives?

In key respects, the problems raised by the idea of a politics of
presence stem from thinking, with liberalism, that politics is primarily an activity concerned with the legitimate exercise of state power
over individuals and restrictions on their freedom. For liberals,

individuals have a right to freedom *from* politics. I am free precisely there where the laws are silent, to paraphrase Hobbes. And isn't there something true in this claim? We need look no further than the rise of totalitarianism, which "subordinated all spheres of life to the demands of politics and its consistent nonrecognition of civil rights" to suspect that "freedom begins where politics ends," as Hannah Arendt puts it.[79] "Was not the liberal credo, 'The less politics, the more freedom,' right after all? Is it not true that the smaller the space occupied by the political, the larger the domain left to freedom?" she asks.[80]

This conception of freedom, which sees freedom as something to be protected by politics but not as the activity of politics itself, argues Arendt, is based on the idea of sovereignty or free will. Within this will-centered conception, freedom becomes the "*liberum arbitrium*, a freedom of choice that arbitrates and decides between two given things."[81] The idea of freedom as free will, writes Arendt, is both illusory and dangerous.

Politically, this identification of freedom with sovereignty is perhaps the most pernicious and dangerous consequence of the philosophical equation of freedom and free will. For it leads either to a denial of human freedom – namely, if it is realized that whatever men may be, they are never sovereign – or to the insight that the freedom of one man, or a group, can be purchased only at the price of the freedom, i.e., sovereignty, of all others ... If men wish to be free, it is precisely sovereignty they must renounce.[82]

In Arendt's critique, then, freedom as sovereignty is the hallmark of liberalism's highly antipolitical character. Politics is there to protect individual interests and rights, and individual freedom is there where politics is not. The identification of freedom with free will conflates the "I-will" with the "I-can," that is, it does not recognize that one needs be able to do what one wills, and that this ability depends on the presence of others. This ability to do, the I-can, is itself experienced in acting and in associating with others, not simply in willing and in the intercourse with oneself.

With Arendt's understanding of non-sovereign freedom as political action in mind, we can now return to the question raised by the politics of presence, namely, does it matter whether women are themselves elected members of government, or does it suffice to have men represent women's interests who are sympathetic to those interests? Focus on interests, which tend to be thought of in liberal political thought as pre-given and attached to groups, leads almost necessarily to the understandable worry that individuals may not be represented by the groups that claim to speak in their name. It can also lead to the worry that a politics of presence, whereby women represent women, must assume "that such representatives pursue homogenous or static group interest," as Phillips observes.[83] We can now suggest that at stake are not simply interests and their representation or misrepresentation, but women and their political participation in liberal democratic institutions. "The politics of presence is not about locking people into pre-given, essentialized identities," writes Phillips. "The point, rather, is to enable those now excluded from politics to engage more directly in political debate and political decision."[84]

LIBERALISM AND "CHOICE FEMINISM"

Although liberals recognize political participation as important, the right to be a participator in government is far from the center of liberal political thought. Instead, it is the right not to be governed by arbitrary power, the right to be governed by representatives of one's own choosing. It is the job of those representatives to ensure that the state protects the rights of individuals. These familiar ideas are, of course, central to feminist appropriations of liberalism, for feminism has always been concerned with securing and protecting women's rights. The question, however, is whether the liberal idea of freely choosing individuals should be considered to be a descriptive category or a norm. Though feminists, including those who are deeply critical of liberalism, embrace the normative idea of women's ability to choose a life course for themselves, to engage in activities on a voluntary basis, and so on, we have seen that most are deeply critical of the ways in which the very idea of choice in liberal theory conceals relations of power.

Liberal feminists such as Okin and McClain are also critical of the idea of choice. As we saw in the discussion of Rawls, the very idea of voluntariness hides the relations of power that sustain the sexual division of labor. Nevertheless, liberal feminists tend to see the problems associated with the language of choice exclusively in terms of the removal of obstacles to women's self-development. They more or less take for granted that what holds women back is not what women themselves desire but what men have put in women's way whenever they seek to escape the confines of the traditional family. Liberal feminists thus focus on the material reality of low wages, inefficient child-care options, a sex-segregated work force, etc. as that which stands in the way of women choosing a life of liberty. And they are in many respects clearly right to do so. These obstacles are real.

But what if the truly pernicious effect of male power turns out to be that stereotypical images of women are "most deeply injurious at the point at which they are empirically real," as MacKinnon puts it.[85] A woman may very well choose to stay at home and raise a family, to not pursue a career of her own, to not be involved in politics, and so on. This is the point at which liberal thought gets stuck, so to speak, for if the choice was not compelled, then it becomes hard to argue against it. That is why Rawls could not bring himself to advocate for state intervention in the family when women can be said to choose to be stay-at-home mothers. The more empirically real the stereotype of proper femininity, the harder it is to argue that it can or should be changed. The exercise of individual choice defines here the whole scope of freedom.

Liberals and liberal feminists, argues MacKinnon, cannot see the true nature of male power because they cling to the idea of choice. "Where liberal feminism sees sexism primarily as an illusion or myth to be corrected, true feminism sees the male point of view as fundamental to the male power to create the world in its own image, the image of its own desires, not just as its delusory end product," she writes.[86] If we accept the notion that individuals are more or less potent and potential makers of meaning who face obstacles that need to be removed, then we may well fail to see the very nature of the constraint that the laws, custom, and rules of a male-dominated society place on women. We will fail to see that many women have become what a male-centered society has allowed them to be. Consequently, their conventionally feminine choices will appear to be free. As Nancy Hirschmann explains:

This construction of social behaviors and rules comes to constitute not only what women are allowed to do, however, but also what they are allowed to be: how women are allowed to think and conceive of themselves, what they can and should desire, what their preferences are, their epistemology, their language ... [T]hese rules and norms of patriarchy are not simply external restrictions on women's otherwise natural desires; rather, they create an entire cultural context that makes women seem to choose what they are in fact restricted to.[87]

According to Linda Hirschman, the notion that individual freedom is wholly defined by exercising choice has found its way into contemporary feminist thinking in advanced liberal democracies. She calls it "choice feminism."[88] The idea here is that the feminist movement has removed most of the obstacles that have held women back and that they are now free to choose. As Michaele Ferguson has written, choice feminism "understands freedom as the capacity to make individual choices, and oppression as the inability to choose. Consequently, as long as a woman can say that she has chosen something [e.g., to stay at home, to wear makeup, to defer to her husband's opinion], it is considered by choice feminists to be an expression of her liberation."[89] Since choice is the only criterion according to which to determine whether a woman is free, "we should abstain from judging the content of the choices women make." A woman could not "choose her own oppression."[90]

The challenge for feminists working within liberal political democracies is how to consider two things at once: both the tenacity of structures of male power that continue to limit women's capacity to choose freely and the illusory character of choices that are made under those conditions. Feminists need to focus on external mechanisms that set the parameters of what choices a woman can make and the internal mechanisms that keep women tied to making choices that undermine their liberty. This is a tall task indeed.

NOTES

1. Mill, *Principles of Political Economy*, p. 952.
2. Okin, *Gender, Justice, and the Family*, p. 9.
3. For example, see Brown, *States of Injury*; Di Stefano, *Configurations of Masculinity*; Pateman, *The Sexual Contract*; Phillips, *Engendering Democracy*; and Eisenstein, *The Radical Future of Liberal Feminism*.
4. For example, see Okin, *Gender, Justice, and the Family*; Nussbaum, *Sex and Social Justice*; McClain, "'Atomistic Man' Revisited"; Shanley, *Feminism, Marriage, and the Law in Victorian England*; and Schaeffer, "Feminism and Liberalism Reconsidered."
5. Okin, "Gender, Justice and Gender," p. 1546.
6. Wollstonecraft, *A Vindication of the Rights of Woman*, p. 3.

7. On this point see Eisenstein, *The Radical Future of Liberal Feminism*; Landes, *Women and the Public Sphere*; and Gatens, "'The Oppressed State of My Sex'."

8. Taylor, *Mary Wollstonecraft and the Feminist Imagination*.

9. Maoine, "Revolutionary Rhetoric."

10. *Ibid.*, p. 3.

11. Mill, *The Subjection of Women*, p. 486.

12. Mill, *Principles of Political Economy*, p. 354.

13. *Ibid.*, p. 352. On Mill's obsessive concern with the procreative habits of the poor and its influence on his feminist thought, see Linda M. G. Zerilli, *Signifying Woman*.

14. Mill, *Principles of Political Economy*, pp. 368, 367.

15. Elshtain, *Public Man, Private Woman*, p. 144. For a sympathetic reading of Mill on the gendered division of labor, see Shanley, "Marital Slavery and Friendship."

16. Pateman, *The Disorder of Women*, p. 18.

17. Pateman, "'God Hath Ordained to Man a Helper'," p. 56.

18. Fraser, "Beyond the Subject/Master Model," p. 174.

19. Brown, *States of Injury*, p. 137.

20. Fraser, "Beyond the Subject/Master Model," p. 175.

21. For an excellent historical overview of the limitations associated with pursuing legal equality for women without taking proper account of extra-legal sources of women's oppression, see Shanley, *Feminism, Marriage, and the Law in Victorian England*.

22. For an account of how emerging seventeenth- and eighteenth-century liberal ideas about what counts as public, what private, influenced the access of women to public life, see Landes, *Women and the Public Sphere*.

23. Elshtain, *Public Man, Private Woman*, p. 6.

24. Higgins, "Gender, Why Feminists Can't (or Shouldn't) Be Liberals," p. 1630.

25. Tronto, *Moral Boundaries*.

26. Brown, *States of Injury*, p. 157.

27. Elshtain, *Public Man, Private Woman*, p. 123.

28. Hirschmann, *Rethinking Obligation*, p. 8.

29. See, for example, Di Stefano, *Configurations of Masculinity*; Pateman, *The Sexual Contract*; Elshtain, *Public Man, Private Woman*; Eisenstein, *The Female Body and the Law*; Jaggar, *Feminist Politics and Human Nature*; and Hartsock, *Money, Sex, and Power*.

30. McClain, "'Atomistic Man' Revisited," p. 1174. See Minow, *Making All the Difference*; Rhode, *Justice and Gender*; and West, "Jurisprudence and Gender."

31. McClain, "'Atomistic Man' Revisited," p. 1174.
32. *Ibid.* Here the work of Carol Gilligan on women's moral development and Sara Ruddick on mothering as a practice of care have been very influential. See Gilligan, *In a Different Voice* and Ruddick, *Maternal Thinking.*
33. McClain, "'Atomistic Man' Revisited," p. 1183.
34. *Ibid.,* p. 1204.
35. Young, *Justice and the Politics of Difference,* p. 100.
36. *Ibid.,* p. 101.
37. Young, *Justice and the Politics of Difference,* 101.
38. McClain, "'Atomistic Man' Revisited," p. 1175.
39. Rawls, *A Theory of Justice,* p. 148. Such feminist critics of Rawls include Hirschmann, *The Subject of Liberty;* Young, *Justice and the Politics of Difference;* and Benhabib, *Situating the Self.*
40. Okin, *Gender, Justice, and the Family,* p. 244.
41. McClain, "'Atomistic Man' Revisited," p. 1207.
42. *Ibid.,* p. 1176.
43. Rawls, "The Idea of Public Reason Revisited," p. 791.
44. *Ibid.,* p. 789; quoted in Okin, "Gender, Justice and Gender," p. 1565.
45. Rawls, "The Idea of Public Reason Revisited," pp. 790–91.
46. *Ibid.,* p. 790; quoted in Okin, "Gender, Justice and Gender," p. 1565.
47. Rawls, *A Theory of Justice,* §2; quoted in Okin, "Gender, Justice and Gender," p. 1563.
48. Rawls, "The Idea of Public Reason Revisited," p. 792; quoted in Okin, "Gender, Justice, and Gender," p. 1565.
49. Okin, "Gender, Justice and Gender," p. 1563.
50. On this point see Okin, "Gender, Justice and Gender."
51. Higgins, "Gender, Why Feminists Can't (or Shouldn't) Be Liberals," pp. 1639–40.
52. Okin, "Gender, Justice and Gender," p. 1567.
53. *Ibid.,* pp. 1566–67. Okin believes that the state can and should be proactive in reducing gender inequality. Measures such as state subsidized daycare, parental leave, and flextime are a few of the measures that would make it possible for women and men to share parenting and housekeeping responsibilities and thus for women to work outside the home. But Okin thinks the state should do more than compensate women for their disadvantage. It should also promote an ideal view of the family. In this way she puts forward a comprehensive liberal view of the good that is rejected by Rawls in *Political Liberalism.* She tells us that the state should "encourage and facilitate the equal sharing by men and women of paid and unpaid work, or productive and reproductive labor" (Okin, *Gender, Justice, and the Family,* p. 171). Although her end goal is

to create genuine non-sexist options that women will freely choose, she does not see choice as the ultimate arbiter in what the state ought to promote.

54. See Zerilli, *Feminism and the Abyss of Freedom*.
55. Eisenstein, *The Female Body and the Law*, p. 57.
56. *Ibid.*, p. 3.
57. *Ibid.*
58. *Ibid.*, p. 2.
59. Thornton, "Sex Equality Is Not Enough for Feminism," p. 77.
60. MacKinnon, "Feminism, Marxism, Method, and the State," p. 645.
61. *Ibid.*
62. MacKinnon, *Toward a Feminist Theory of the State*, pp. 215–16.
63. Schaeffer, "Feminism and Liberalism Reconsidered," p. 701.
64. Gerhard, *Debating Women's Equality*, p. 9.
65. *Ibid.*, p. 7.
66. *Ibid.*, p. 8.
67. *Ibid.*
68. *Ibid.*
69. *Ibid.*, p. 9.
70. Phillips, *The Politics of Presence*, p. 6.
71. *Ibid.*
72. *Ibid.*
73. Rawls, *Political Liberalism*.
74. Phillips, *Politics of Presence*, p. 19.
75. For a critical response to the idea of group or cultural rights, see Kukathas, "Are There Any Cultural Rights?" Kukathas argues that liberalism's emphasis on individual rights gives members of groups all they need to defend members of minority cultures. Okin argues that arguments for cultural rights do not take adequate account of the sexist character of many minority cultures, which make it difficult if not impossible for women to flourish as individuals and which underestimate the great difficulty that women would have should they wish to exit. Okin, "Is Multiculturalism Bad for Women?".
76. Raz, "Multiculturalism," p. 72.
77. Young, *Justice and the Politics of Difference*, p. 101.
78. Phillips, *The Politics of Presence*, 24.
79. Arendt, "What is Freedom?", p. 149.
80. *Ibid.*
81. *Ibid.*, p. 151.
82. *Ibid.*, p. 165.
83. Phillips, *The Politics of Presence*, p. 167.
84. *Ibid.*

85. MacKinnon, *Toward a Feminist Theory of the State*, p. 230.
86. Quoted in Schaeffer, "Feminism and Liberalism Reconsidered," p. 701.
87. Hirschmann, *The Subject of Liberty*, p. 11.
88. Hirschman, *Get to Work*.
89. Ferguson, "Choice Feminism and the Fear of Politics," p. 248.
90. *Ibid*. Okin and McClain would surely disagree with the basic tenet of choice feminism, namely the claim that the obstacles to women's self-development have fallen in the face of feminist challenges, so women can now make real choices that express their freedom. But even as they would insist that there is much work left to be done to realize the aspirations of feminism, Okin and McClain would also say that choice must remain a key – if not the key – criterion in our understanding of freedom.

16 The republican critique of liberalism

Liberalism is, notoriously, a protean political doctrine. Obviously, this presents a challenge for any discussion of the civic republican critique of liberalism. To be sure, there are political doctrines, some of which have been described by various authors as "republican," that simply cannot be reconciled with any plausible account of liberalism: here we might think of the perfectionist civic humanism associated with Hannah Arendt, or the brand of communitarianism associated with Michael Sandel.[1] When it comes to mainstream contemporary civic republicanism, however – the sort generally associated with the work of Philip Pettit, Quentin Skinner, Cass Sunstein, and others – there is no necessary incompatibility with liberalism. That is to say, there exist plausible versions of liberalism that can accommodate each of the central commitments held by contemporary civic republicans.

Accordingly, it is better to think of the republican critique of liberalism as a set of critiques of particular strands or tendencies in the liberal tradition – tendencies that, perhaps, are not essential to the latter doctrine, but which nevertheless are relatively common and thus worth attacking. The main purpose of this essay will be to review and assess the republican critique of these tendencies as they emerged historically. In the process, it will be suggested that a "liberal republicanism" shorn of such problematic tendencies might stand as a more robust and coherent political doctrine than any of the more popular varieties of contemporary liberalism.

The discussion will proceed as follows: in the first section, the central or defining commitments of republicanism and liberalism will be characterized in relation to the historical origins of the two traditions; in the next three sections, three particular strands of liberalism will be considered as they emerged and led to an increasing

381

separation between the two traditions; finally, the prospects for reintegrating liberalism and republicanism will be discussed in the conclusion.

I

Contemporary civic republicanism represents an attempt to revive and recast for modern purposes the classical republican tradition in Western political thought. The classical republicans were a loose family of writers beginning roughly with Machiavelli and his fifteenth-century Italian predecessors, running through the English commonwealthsmen such as Milton, Harrington, and Sidney to many Americans of the revolutionary and founding era such as Jefferson and Madison. Drawing inspiration from ancient sources – Polybius, Cicero, and the Latin historians especially – these writers shared many common ideas and concerns, such as the importance of civic virtue and political participation, the dangers of corruption, the benefits of a mixed constitution and the rule of law, and so forth. Most importantly, however, they were centrally committed to the value of political liberty or freedom, where this was understood as a sort of independence from arbitrary power or domination.[2] In the ideal political community, they believed, no one citizen would be the master of any other: In James Harrington's famous expression, such a society would be an "empire of laws and not of men."[3]

The liberal tradition is of somewhat more recent origin than the republican. On one very plausible view, liberalism emerged from the unhappy experience of religious conflict following the Protestant Reformation.[4] For generations, it had been widely, if only implicitly, assumed that social order was not possible except on the basis of some shared comprehensive doctrine such as was supplied by medieval Christianity. Of course we may disagree about a great many lesser things, it was thought, but how can we possibly live together in peace and order unless we agree on the most fundamental and important ethical, moral, and theological questions? It was precisely this view, inherited by Protestants and Catholics alike, that made religious disagreement so fearsome, and its resolution by any available means so urgent. After more than a century of bloody armed conflict failed to produce victory for either side, however, the need for some sort of modus vivendi gradually became apparent. Beginning with the 1648 Treaty of Westphalia, grudging acceptance of religious disagreement evolved through the writings of John Locke and his Enlightenment successors into principled defense of religious toleration and, eventually, a positive affirmation of diversity.[5] This was the kernel that blossomed during the nineteenth century into the modern liberal ideals of individualism and a private sphere guaranteed by constitutional rights.[6]

Contemporary liberalism, such as we find in the influential writings of John Rawls, Ronald Dworkin, or Isaiah Berlin, builds more or less continuously on its own historical tradition. Contrastingly, classical republicanism died out in the nineteenth century and was largely forgotten until disaffection with the dominant liberal tradition led to a republican revival in the late twentieth century. This revival was initiated by historians such as J. G. A. Pocock and Gordon Wood, but it received its fullest expression in the works of Philip Pettit and Quentin Skinner, among others.[7] In order to get a better handle on the current debate, liberalism and republicanism should be characterized more precisely.

Let us say that a public philosophy or *political doctrine* is a reasonably coherent set of normative principles for assessing public policies and institutions as better or worse. Among these principles, presumably, would be principles of social justice, principles of political legitimacy, principles of economic efficiency, and so forth. To be reasonably coherent, of course, a political doctrine must somehow assign relative weights or ranks to its various principles: otherwise, it would provide no guidance in cases where the principles conflict. So how might we formally characterize republicanism and liberalism as political doctrines?

In both classical and contemporary republicanism, the value of political liberty or freedom serves as an organizing principle. Accordingly, let us say that republicanism is any political doctrine in which a principle promoting freedom from domination is given a central place. Call this the *non-domination principle:*

NDP Public policies and institutions ought to be designed with the aim of reducing domination, so far as this is feasible.[8]

Roughly speaking, we can here regard domination as a sort of dependence on arbitrary power: persons or groups experience domination to the extent that they are dependent on a social relationship in which some other person or group wields arbitrary power over them. Domination in this sense is paradigmatically experienced by slaves at the hands of their masters, wives at the hands of their husbands under traditional family law, unprotected workers at the hands of their employers in markets with structural unemployment, and citizens at the hands of tyrannical or despotic governments.[9] Different versions of contemporary republicanism will characterize the centrality of the NDP differently, of course. On some accounts, the NDP might be regarded as a more or less complete political doctrine by itself, other principles being admitted only to the extent that they do not conflict with, or else can be derived from, the NDP. On other accounts, the NDP might simply be one among several independent principles, though having a degree of priority in cases of conflict.[10] These differences will not be important for our discussion, however: the issues we will consider arise for any political doctrine in which the NDP is given some sort of clear priority.

It is less easy to characterize liberalism precisely. For the purposes of our discussion, however, we may regard toleration as the central commitment of both traditional and contemporary liberal theory. Accordingly, let us say that liberalism is any political doctrine in which a principle respecting reasonable pluralism is given a central place. Call this the *liberal toleration principle*:

LTP   Public policies and institutions ought be designed with the aim of protecting a private sphere within which some range of individual conceptions of the good and their associated life plans will be tolerated.

Different versions of contemporary liberalism will characterize the centrality or priority of the LTP differently, of course. Furthermore, on some accounts the LTP will be supplemented by even stronger neutrality principles, as we shall later see. However, it is safe to say that any plausibly liberal political doctrine must at least include some version of the LTP.

Now it should immediately be apparent that there is no inherent or necessary conflict between liberalism and republicanism, so characterized: acceptance of the LTP does not entail rejecting the NDP, nor does acceptance of the NDP entail rejecting the LTP. In other words, there is no reason a political doctrine could not include both a commitment to promoting freedom from domination and a commitment to principled toleration. This observation is crucially important for our discussion. It helps explain, for example, the confusion of the two historical traditions in the eighteenth century. Many early liberals such as Locke, Blackstone, and Montesquieu inherited from the republican tradition not only a commitment to freedom from domination but many other ideas besides. Concurrently, once the idea of toleration was introduced by early liberals, many republicans such as Thomas Paine, Jefferson, and Madison heartily embraced it as central to their own political doctrines. It was only gradually that liberals began to distance themselves from republicans, for reasons we shall discuss below.

All contemporary mainstream republicans accept some version of the LTP, and thus should be considered liberals in a broad sense of that term. From one point of view, then, we might regard the debate between republicanism and liberalism as a debate within the liberal tradition itself, concerning whether or not a sound liberal political doctrine should include the NDP. From a different point of view, however, this characterization is somewhat misleading. Republicanism was a freestanding and fully worked out political doctrine in its own right well before liberalism emerged on the scene. Contemporary republicans often argue that a fundamentally republican political doctrine which happens to include the LTP is more attractive and compelling than a fundamentally liberal political doctrine which happens to include the NDP. We shall return to this question in the final section.

II

The central republican commitment, as we have seen, is to the value of political liberty understood as non-domination, or freedom from arbitrary power. This sort of freedom, the classical republicans believed, was by its nature a *res publica* or public good – that is, something that could be realized only through collective effort and shared institutions. Most significantly, on their view, it could be enjoyed only in a healthy self-governing free state or republic: in no other political system could citizens be described as genuinely free. Call this the *self-government principle:*

SGP The best political system, and the only one fully consistent with freedom, is necessarily some form of self-government.

This connection between political liberty on the one side, and self-government on the other, was so strongly held that classical republican writers often treated the two ideas interchangeably. Thus, in reflecting on ancient Rome for instance, they would commonly write that the Romans "gained their freedom" when the Tarquins were expelled, meaning that self-government had been introduced; and that they "lost their freedom" in the civil wars, meaning that imperial despotism has supplanted republican self-government.[11] Indeed, intellectual historians often use a writer's endorsement of the SGP in some form as a litmus test for assigning them to the classical republican tradition.

On what grounds did the classical republicans believe the connection between the NDP and the SGP were so strong? Many were content simply to elaborate on Machiavelli's oracular remark that "if the populace be made the guardians of liberty" as in a republic, "it is reasonable to suppose that they will take more care of it."[12] Why might this be, however? One reason is that encroachments on freedom are much easier to guard against in a republic. This was one of the most common arguments given by the seventeenth-century English republicans, for example. Let us suppose first, that most people value freedom from domination, but second that there is a natural tendency of power to corrupt its holders. When power-holders begin to exercise their powers arbitrarily, what are the people to do? As John Milton observed, in autocratic regimes, the rulers are "not to be remov'd, not to be controul'd, much less accus'd or brought to punishment, without the danger of common ruin, without the shaking and almost subversion of the whole land." By contrast, "in a free Commonwealth, any governor or chief counselor offending, may be remov'd and punishd without the least commotion."[13] This obviously speaks to the advantage of self-government in preserving freedom. Another related line of reasoning begins with the observation that preserving freedom requires the widespread cultivation of civic-minded dispositions: our freedom from domination cannot be secure unless people generally respect public laws and institutions, exercise restraint in pressing their self-interested claims, and do their part in supervising public authorities. The most reliable method for cultivating such dispositions, however, is surely to involve people in the political process: as Algernon Sidney observed, "men can no otherwise be engaged to take care of the publick, than by having ... a part in it."[14] The value of democracy in nurturing civic-minded dispositions later became one of the main themes in Tocqueville's *Democracy in America*.[15] For these reasons and others, then, it was taken as an established truth in the tradition that political liberty could be found only in self-governing republics.

When we turn from the classical republican authors to the early liberals, however, we find a striking contrast. On the one hand, it is quite evident in the writings of Locke, Montesquieu, or Blackstone that they shared the republican conception of political liberty as non-domination. Freedom is not, as Locke clearly states, "a liberty for everyone to do what he lists, to live as he pleases," but rather "to have a standing rule to live by, common to every one of that society," and "not to be subject to the inconstant, uncertain, unknown, arbitrary will of another man."[16] Montesquieu expresses the same idea, albeit less precisely, when he avers that "political liberty does not consist in an unlimited freedom," but rather in "a tranquility of mind arising from the opinion each person has of his safety."[17] But on the other hand, these same authors seem surprisingly uninterested in extolling the benefits of republican self-government, and indeed more or less reconciled to limited or constitutional monarchy. What accounts for this remarkable contrast?

Two factors in combination may have been at work. The first was the earlier-discussed experience of religious disagreement stemming from the Reformation. Nearly a century and a half of bloody warfare had concluded in a tenuous modus vivendi which there were powerful reasons not to upset. The second was the experience of the English Civil War. When a victorious parliament issued the Act for the Abolishing of the Kingly Office in 1649, it declared in obviously republican terms that it had "been found by experience that the office of a king" is "burdensome and dangerous to the liberty, safety and public interest of the people," and thus only by "being governed by its own Representatives" is it possible to provide for "the lasting freedom and good of this Common-wealth."[18] Alas the experiment in self-government was a failure, and monarchy was restored to England a decade later. The reasons adduced, rightly or wrongly, by Montesquieu for this failure were that successful republican government required a robustly virtuous citizenry. It was "a very droll spectacle," he comments, "to behold the impotent efforts of the English towards the establishment of democracy." Lacking the requisite base in political culture, after "the country had undergone the most violent shocks, they were obliged to have recourse to the very government which they had so wantonly proscribed."[19] For better or for worse, it may have seemed to many observers that, at least for the foreseeable future, prospects were dim for the introduction of self-government to European peoples so long accustomed to monarchy.

Whatever their deeper political sentiments may have been, the early liberal writers would have seen that the most practicable path forward involved pivoting away from the self-government aspect of the classical republican program, and toward the constitutionalism and the rule of law aspect instead. The latter cause was, to begin with, much more feasible politically speaking: limiting the discretionary authority of the sovereign was something both economic and social elites could support, and the rule of law could be secured through the relatively modest reform of establishing an independent judiciary – which, not surprisingly, Locke, Montesquieu, and Blackstone all strongly advocated.

Moreover, constitutionalism and the rule of law were essential prerequisites to the entrenchment and protection of individual religious rights. Clearly there was very much real good to be achieved immediately if the tenuous modus vivendi of toleration established in the wake of the religious wars could be transformed into a core political principle, as the early liberal writers sought to do. And finally, it is possible that they hoped these more modest reforms might, in the long run, prove beneficial with respect to freedom from domination as well: even if the ultimate security provided by republican self-government must wait, a robust rule of law in itself constitutes no small degree of freedom. As Blackstone noted, "laws, when prudently framed, are by no means subversive but rather introductive of liberty; for (as Mr Locke has well observed) where there is no law, there is no freedom."[20] Constitutionalism and the rule of law, once successfully introduced, might gradually prepare citizens for self-government sometime in the future.

Whatever their intentions, the early liberal writers were eminently successful in advancing the cause of toleration. But their strategy had the consequence, unintended or not, of decoupling the nascent liberal political doctrine from a strong commitment to democracy. Unlike the NDP, it does not seem that the LTP necessarily requires self-government, insofar as a wide range of regimes might recognize the instrumental benefits of toleration. In fact, many liberal authors of the period explicitly endorsed the more or less tolerant so-called enlightened despotisms of Frederick of Prussia or Catherine of Russia. While contemporary liberals now support democracy, of course, their commitment is still often criticized as weak, instrumental, and provisional in character.[21] In contrast, while the classical republicans were perhaps not strict democrats in the modern sense, the central place of self-government in their political doctrine finds its natural extension in the emphatic commitment to democracy among their contemporary heirs.

III

Given the liberal move away from the SGP, it is not surprising that when the American and French revolutionaries and their allies renewed the attack on monarchical government toward the end of the eighteenth century, it was often from the classical republican, not the liberal, tradition that they drew intellectual ammunition. As yet, however, there was no real opposition between the two doctrines. The early liberals, as we have seen, shared the classical republican conception of political liberty as non-domination, even if they downplayed the importance of self-government. Republicans, for their part, shared the liberal enthusiasm for constitutionalism, the rule of law, and an independent judiciary; further, they could easily take on board the newly appreciated value of toleration. Many framers of the American political system, especially Jefferson and Madison, are thus best regarded as both liberals and republicans: in the technical sense we have described, they held political doctrines including the NDP, SGP, and LTP all together.

Within a generation or so, however, the political and social landscape had changed dramatically. Once again, two convergent factors were probably at work. The first was the tumultuous course of the French Revolution and the Napoleonic Wars that followed. When peace and order was finally restored to Europe, there was inevitably a conservative reaction against the republican ideals partly responsible for initiating the revolutionary movements. The second was the fact that a powerful constellation of cultural, social, and economic pressures was in the process of upsetting traditional hierarchies and widening the scope of public concern to include workers, servants, women, national and racial minorities, and so forth. The classical pre-revolutionary republicans, of course, had been in many ways victims of the prejudices of their own era: when they advocated political liberty understood as freedom from arbitrary power, it was unsurprisingly an unspoken assumption that the relevant category of concern was limited to propertied white males. Once the category of concern is broadened, however, the radical implications of the NDP are readily apparent. After all, what is the authority of husbands, masters, employers, and so on but another form of arbitrary power? Combining the NDP with a more inclusive political ethic would mean granting independence from mastery to women, to servants, and all the rest. And indeed, many socialists and feminists of the early nineteenth century explicitly drew on the traditional republican ideal of freedom from arbitrary power, castigating the "wage slavery" of the factory worker, and the "slavish bondage" suffered by women under traditional family law and custom.[22] "Would men but generously snap our chains," writes Mary Wollstonecraft in a classical republican vein, "and be content with rational fellowship instead of slavish obedience, they would find us more observant daughters, more affectionate sisters, more faithful wives, more reasonable mothers – in a word, better citizens."[23]

Once again, liberals found themselves in a bind, and once again a single theoretical move offered relief from both pressures – namely, jettisoning the NDP. Given the powerful rhetorical appeal of political liberty, this was not so simple as abandoning freedom as a political value altogether. Conveniently, however, an alternative conception of freedom had been proposed some time ago by none other than Thomas Hobbes.[24] Perhaps to a greater extent than any previous thinker, Hobbes recognized both the power, and also the mutability, of definitions. Writing during the English Civil War, and fervently believing absolutism alone could deliver an end to the conflicts of his day, Hobbes faced a peculiar challenge. Since on the classical republican view, political liberty and arbitrary power are flatly incompatible, the supporters of the commonwealth could lean heavily on the powerful rhetorical appeal of freedom in advancing their cause. Hobbes hoped to diffuse this rhetoric by redefining freedom in such a manner that, contrary to all previous understanding, it could be shown compatible with the arbitrary power of an absolute sovereign.

He found his answer in what is now widely called the "negative" conception of freedom.

On the negative conception of freedom, we are free simply to the extent that we are not interfered with by others. There have been many variations on this conception since Hobbes, depending on how exactly one chooses to define "interference" in the relevant sense, but they all have in common the basic intuition that to be free is, more or less, to be left alone to do what one pleases. Now of course the value in being left alone had long been recognized; contrary to popular opinion, even the ancients were perfectly well-attuned to it. Thus, Thucydides recounts that Pericles approvingly remarked of Athens that, "just as our political system is free and open, so is our day-to-day life in our relations with each other. We do not get into a state with our next-door neighbor if he enjoys himself in his own way."[25] But it was always recognized that to be left alone to do as one pleased – sometimes termed "license" – was not at all the same as freedom or liberty in the political sense. Indeed, it was often pointed out by Machiavelli and the other classical republicans that too much license can undermine freedom by eroding the rule of law.[26]

The distinction between the two conceptions arises from the fact that having a master might easily be consistent with enjoying a considerable degree of noninterference. An imperial power might, for example, refrain from interfering much with the local administration of its colonies, much as a kindly master might refrain from interfering much with the day-to-day activities of his servants. This is significant because it answers precisely to Hobbes's aims. On the negative conception, as he says, political freedom is merely the "silence of the laws," and there can be as many or as few laws under any one form of government as under any other.[27] Thus, he infers, there can be no logical grounds for objecting to absolute sovereignty on the basis of political freedom:

There is written on the turrets of the city of Lucca in great characters at this day, the word libertas; yet no man can thence infer, that a particular man has more liberty, or more immunity from the service of the commonwealth there, than in Constantinople. Whether a commonwealth be monarchical, or popular, the freedom is still the same.[28]

By redefining political freedom in this way, Hobbes hoped to defang the most potent objection to absolute sovereignty. At the time, however, few were fooled. Famously responding to Hobbes just a few years later, Harrington observes:

> The mountain hath brought forth, and we have a little equivocation! For to say that a Lucchese hath no more liberty or immunity *from the laws* ... than a Turk, and to say that a Lucchese hath no more liberty or immunity *by the laws* ... than a Turk ... are pretty different speeches. The first may be said of all governments alike, the second scarce of any two; much less of these, seeing it is known that whereas the greatest bashaw is a tenant, as well of his head as of his estate, at the will of his lord, the meanest Lucchese ... is a freeholder of both, and not to be controlled but by the law; and that framed by every private man unto no other end ... than to protect the liberty of every private man, which by that means comes to be the liberty of the commonwealth.[29]

Indeed, as we have seen, not only republicans but also most early liberals continued to hold the non-domination view. Defenders of the American Revolution such as Paine, for example, commonly observed that "we may be as effectually enslaved by the want of laws in America, as by submitting to laws made for us in England," a claim unintelligible on Hobbes's negative liberty view.[30]

But a century and a half later, in light of the tremendous upheavals of the late eighteenth and early nineteenth centuries, liberal writers discovered the utility of Hobbes's conception of liberty afresh. If adopted, the NDP could be replaced with a *noninterference principle:*

NIP Public policies and institutions ought to be designed with the aim of reducing interference, so far as this is feasible.

The NIP was much more congenial to the political climate liberals now faced. It lacked the radical implications of the NDP: since non-interference is perfectly consistent with mastery so long as that master lets one alone, the NIP was far less disruptive to social order. Indeed, some liberal writers, such as William Paley, were perfectly candid about this advantage:

> those definitions of liberty ought to be rejected, which, by making that essential to civil freedom which is unattainable in experience, inflame expectations that can never be gratified, and disturb the public content with complaints, which no wisdom or benevolence of government can remove.[31]

Thus, the negative conception of liberty was enthusiastically adopted and promoted by Bentham and Constant, for example, and it quickly became the generally accepted view among liberals. Merely a generation later, John Stuart Mill could simply write without pausing for debate that "the only freedom which deserves the name, is that of pursuing our own good in our own way, so long as we do not attempt to deprive others of theirs."[32]

In the wake of these changes, the traditional republican view of liberty – and indeed the republican tradition along with it – was promptly either forgotten, or else confused with the dangerous sort of "positive liberty" (the so-called "liberty of the ancients") associated with Rousseau and the French Revolutionaries and accordingly dismissed. Contemporary liberals such as Berlin, Rawls, and Dworkin have inherited this tendency to define liberty as noninterference, even though doing so is not required by their commitment to toleration.[33]

IV

So far, we have seen how the liberal tradition, in response to various historical pressures, evolved from an initial commitment to toleration that was largely compatible with republicanism, to a political doctrine that explicitly rejected the central republican value of freedom from domination. This section will consider a third tendency in the liberal tradition that emerged only in the late twentieth century – specifically, the tendency to supplement the LTP with stronger principles of neutrality.[34]

Recall that liberal toleration as originally conceived requires only that we aim to protect a private sphere within which individuals have the opportunity to pursue a diverse range of conceptions of the good and associated life plans. It was not necessarily a part of this view that liberals must avoid controversial claims about the good for human beings altogether. Locke's account of the natural law, for example, is explicitly based on theological premises, and Mill's utilitarian argument for individual liberty depends partly on the assumption that experiments in living will help reveal which sorts of human experiences are objectively better than others. Over the course of the twentieth century, however, there developed a tendency among political theorists and philosophers to shy away from substantive arguments about the good. Unlike the two shifts discussed previously, this third shift cannot so easily be attributed to specific historical causes, though the increasing diversity of modern societies and an enhanced sensitivity to cultural difference, among other factors, may have played a role.

When John Rawls published his hugely influential A Theory of Justice in 1971, this move toward neutrality was clearly apparent, though imperfectly articulated. Rawls argued that the correct conception of social justice is the one reasonable people would select in an original position from behind a veil of ignorance. In addition to hiding information regarding our social or economic position, Rawls assumed that the veil of ignorance would also hide any knowledge of our particular conception of the good. The principles of social justice emerging from the original position could thus be described as "neutral" in the sense that their derivation does not hinge on the truth or falsity of any one conception of the good in particular. This seems to give the independent principles of social justice a sort of superiority over particular conceptions of the good. For example, while it seems wrong to enforce public policies supported merely by a controversial conception of the good that not all citizens share, public policies supported by a universal conception of the right (the purportedly neutral principles of social justice) seems more acceptable. This idea is often summed up in a slogan, derived from various passages in Rawls, regarding the "priority of the right over the good."[35]

In the years immediately following the publication of A Theory of Justice, many political theorists and philosophers began to strongly emphasize the thought expressed in that slogan. Several quite diverse examples illustrate this tendency. Here we might first consider Robert Nozick's Anarchy, State, and Utopia, published in 1974. This work directly challenged Rawls's theory of justice as fairness from a broadly libertarian point of view. Nozick elevated individual rights against any sort of unwanted interference to the role of an absolute standard against which all other moral and political considerations were considered trivial. On his view, the state has no business involving itself in any sorts of collective projects at all: its only job is to enforce our rights. To the extent that citizens hold personal conceptions of the good, it is entirely up to them to try to realize those conceptions through their own activities in the private sphere, provided of course that they do not violate the rights of others in the process.[36]

Two other books, written by legal scholars, further illustrate this tendency: Ronald Dworkin's *Taking Rights Seriously*, published in 1977; and Bruce Ackerman's *Social Justice in the Liberal State*, published in 1980. Interestingly, both these authors are liberal egalitarians like Rawls, and thus reject the harsher libertarian views expressed in Nozick's work. Nevertheless, both demonstrate the same tendency to emphasize the priority of the right over the good. Dworkin elevates the role of individual rights in political discourse, arguing that they should be understood as absolute "trumps" on public policies whose aims stem from controversial conceptions of the good.[37] Similarly, Ackerman argues that any arguments depending in any way on controversial conceptions of the good should be excluded from the political sphere: only strictly neutral arguments are admissible grounds for public policy.[38] Influenced by these and other writers, many (though notably, not all) liberals now embrace some version of what we might call the *liberal neutrality principle:*

LNP Public policies and institutions should not treat some conceptions of the good or their associated life plans more favorably than others.

Despite its popularity among liberals, the LNP has been widely criticized. Especially when combined with a commitment to negative liberty, it seems to rule out any political doctrine in which the common or public good plays an active role. Dissatisfaction with the LNP may partly explain the contemporaneous reemergence of civic republicanism: while many were unhappy with the new liberal doctrine of strict neutrality, not all were ready to embrace the usual communitarian or perfectionist alternatives, which arguably pose as many difficulties as they solve. Perhaps, some have thought, republicanism offers a path in between.

On the one hand, republicans must reject the LNP, for two reasons. The first is that the NDP itself probably relies on certain substantive claims about the nature of the good for human beings. The reason we should care so much about minimizing domination, republicans generally argue, is because enjoying freedom from non-domination is a necessary condition for human flourishing rightly understood.[39] In making out an argument along these lines, republicans cannot avoid referring to at least some controversial assumptions about the good – for instance, the assumption (denied by many thinkers, past and present) that human beings cannot succeed in leading flourishing lives when subject to domination.[40] Substantive arguments of this sort would presumably be blocked by the LNP.

The second reason republicans must reject the LNP is that they are committed to promoting civic virtue. The importance of civic virtue was among the most salient themes in the classical republican tradition, of course. Critics of republicanism often fear that this implies extensive self-sacrifice and frugality, a renunciation of individuality, and self-identification with the community.[41] Contemporary republicans have been at pains to show, on the contrary, that the possession and exercise of civic virtue is simply useful in establishing and maintaining the shared public good of freedom from domination, and not as something valued its own sake.[42] Roughly speaking, its value stems from the observation that the NDP will most likely be realized in a community where the citizens are committed to that principle, and each is willing to do his or her part in supporting it. For example, through collective political action, citizens can bring instances of domination to public attention; they can support laws and policies that expand freedom; and they can do their part in defending republican institutions when called upon to do so. Far from calling for the subjection of individual to collective aims, republican freedom is desirable precisely because it enables citizens to pursue their own private aims with assurances of real security.[43] Promoting this sort of commitment to republican ideals, however, may require a fairly robust program of civics education, together with a culture that rewards virtue with public esteem – both of which would fall afoul strong liberal neutrality and require some measure of interference.[44]

On the other hand, unlike communitarians or perfectionists, republicans need not swing so far the other way as to elevate a particular conception of the good above all others. On the contrary, as we have seen in our discussion of the origins of liberalism, the republican NDP is perfectly compatible with the LTP. Indeed, the NDP itself can generate several arguments for toleration. First, if our aim is to reduce domination in all its forms, then we must be careful not to introduce new forms in our efforts to combat old forms. It is not enough, for example, that some public policies or institutions will reduce domination in private or economic spheres, if in doing so they expand the arbitrary powers of the state so far as to introduce more domination than they remove. It follows that the NDP will rule out any policies that generate extensive political domination. Second, if we encourage some forms of life too enthusiastically at the expense of others, individuals who are not inclined to accept the favored conception of the good might find themselves socially anathema. This, in turn, may render them vulnerable to private or economic domination. So again it follows that the NDP will rule out any variety of policy creating such vulnerabilities.

Now it is difficult to imagine how we might succeed in discouraging all conceptions of the good to the exclusion of our favored one without greatly expanding the scope and intrusiveness of state authority. Similarly, it is likely that in such a state, individuals not well suited to the favored conception will find themselves social outcasts, and thus vulnerable to domination. It follows that the NDP gives us strong reasons to support the LTP, even if it cannot be reconciled with the LNP.

V

Republicanism, as we have seen, is not necessarily incompatible with liberalism. Not only is it possible for a coherent political doctrine to comprehend both the NDP and the LTP – as indeed Paine, Jefferson, Madison, and others did historically – but also there are indeed good reasons to think that the NDP itself gives solid theoretical support to the LTP. It is thus best to think of the republican critique of liberalism as a critique of certain strands or tendencies often manifest in the liberal tradition. The first is the tendency to relegate the value of democratic self-government to secondary importance; the second is the tendency to substitute freedom from interference for freedom from domination; and the third is the tendency to supplement toleration with a strong neutrality principle.

Now, of course, it is open to liberals to incorporate republicanism if they are willing to drop the LN and NI principles and embrace the ND and SG principles as supplementary to their central commitment to the LTP. The result might be a plausible sort of "republican liberalism."[45] Republicans, however, would argue that the better strategy is the reverse of this one: we should retain the NDP as our central commitment and emphasize the LTP as one of its entailments alongside the SGP.

The curious thing about liberalism historically is that, for all its appeal and resilience, it has had difficulty settling on a standard overarching doctrine. Early liberals such as Locke relied on arguments from natural right that no longer find favor today. In the nineteenth century, comprehensive liberals such as Mill relied on perfectionist accounts of the human good that accommodated imperialist notions about the superiority of European civilization. In the twentieth century, liberal minimalists such as Hayek and Berlin aimed to drain liberalism of nearly any substantive commitments at all, while political liberals such as Rawls aimed to square the circle by defending neutrality substantively through a revival of contractualism. The difficulty liberalism has had in finding a secure theoretical basis betrays, republicans might argue, an underlying limitation in the doctrine itself: while certainly an important political value, perhaps toleration is not well suited to the role of foundational commitment. In contrast, classical republicanism constituted a robust and coherent political doctrine in its own right, solidly grounded in a foundational commitment to freedom from domination. It is perhaps better to improve on this doctrine by embracing toleration – by becoming "liberal republicans" – than to abandon it for less certain theoretical waters.

NOTES

1. See esp. Arendt, *On Revolution* and Sandel, *Democracy's Discontent.* On the distinction between these approaches on the one hand, and the civic republican tradition (which will be the focus of discussion here) on the other, see Lovett, "Republicanism."
2. On the classical republican tradition in general, and the centrality of political liberty to that tradition, see Pettit, "The Freedom of the City"; Pettit, *Republicanism*; Skinner, "The Paradoxes of Political Liberty"; Skinner, *Liberty Before Liberalism*; and Viroli, *Republicanism.*
3. Harrington, *The Commonwealth of Oceana*, p. 8.
4. This account of the origins of liberalism is famously sketched in Rawls, *Political Liberalism*, pp. xxiii–xxviii. For a somewhat different view, see Kalyvas and Katznelson, *Liberal Beginnings.*
5. Here see esp. Locke, *A Letter Concerning Toleration* and Voltaire, *Treatise* on *Tolerance and Other Writings.*
6. As, for example, in Mill, On *Liberty*; or von Humboldt, *Limits of State Action.*

7. Pocock, The *Machiavellian Moment*; Wood, *The Creation* of the *American Republic*; Sunstein, "Beyond the Republican Revival"; Pettit, "The Freedom of the City"; Pettit, *Republicanism*; Pettit, *On the* People's *Terms*; Skinner, "The Paradoxes of Political Liberty"; and Skinner, *Liberty Before Liberalism*. See also the papers in Laborde and Maynor (eds.), *Republicanism and Political Theory*; and for a general review, Lovett and Pettit, "Neorepublicanism."

8. Here "reducing domination" could be taken as meaning either minimizing the sum total domination, minimizing equal domination, or some other such formula; republicans are not necessarily agreed on which version of the principle is best.

9. On the arbitrary power conception of domination, see Pettit, *Republicanism*, ch. 2; Pettit, *On the People's Terms*, ch. 1; or Lovett, *A General Theory of Domination and Justice*, chs. 2–4.

10. As an example of the former, see Pettit, *Republicanism*; as an example of the latter, Lovett, *A General Theory of Domination and Justice*.

11. See, for example, Machiavelli, *The Discourses*, esp. bk. I, chs. 2–5; or Sidney, *Discourses Concerning Government*, esp. ch. 2, §§ 11–12.

12. Machiavelli, *The Discourses*, p. 116.

13. Milton, "The Readie and Easie Way to Establish a Free Commonwealth," p. 413.

14. Sidney, *Discourses Concerning Government*, p. 196.

15. Tocqueville, *Democracy in America*, esp. vol. I, part 1, ch. 5.

16. Locke, *Second Treatise* of *Government*, ed. Macpherson, p. 17.

17. Montesquieu, *The Spirit of the Laws*, pp. 150–51.

18. Excerpted in Wootton (ed.), *Divine Right and Democracy*, pp. 356–57.

19. Montesquieu, *The Spirit of the Laws*, p. 20.

20. Blackstone, *Commentaries on the Laws of England*, vol. I, p. 122.

21. For a classic example of this sort of critique not by a civic republican, see Barber, *Strong Democracy*. For an example among the civic republicans, see Pettit, *On the People's Terms*, ch. 3.

22. Sandel, *Democracy's Discontent*, pp. 153, 172–74; Pateman, The *Sexual Contract*, p. 123. For further discussion, see Pettit, *Republicanism*, pp. 45–50.

23. Wollstonecraft, *A Vindication* of the *Rights of Men and a Vindication of the Rights* of *Women*, p. 240. For a more detailed republican reading of Wollstonecraft, see Coffee, "Mary Wollstonecraft, Freedom, and the Enduring Power of Social Domination," pp. 116–35.

24. The following discussion draws heavily on the especially detailed treatment in Skinner, *Hobbes and Republican Liberty*.

25. Thucydides, *History* of the *Peloponnesian War*, p. 145.

26. Machiavelli, *The Discourses*, pp. 112–13.

27. Hobbes, *Leviathan*, ed. Gaskin, p. 146.
28. *Ibid.*, p. 143.
29. Harrington, *The Commonwealth of Oceana*, p. 20, emphasis added.
30. Paine, "Common Sense," p. 29.
31. Paley, *The Principles of Moral and Political Philosophy*, p. 315.
32. Mill, *On Liberty*, p. 12.
33. Liberal perfectionists such as Joseph Raz are of course a complicated exception to this tendency, as they are to the tendency toward neutrality discussed next as well; theirs remains a minority view within contemporary liberalism, however.
34. For an overview of the emergence of liberal neutrality, see Wall and Klosko (eds.), *Perfectionism and Neutrality*, pp. 1–13.
35. Rawls, *A Theory of Justice*, esp. pp. 31–32, 446–52.
36. Nozick, *Anarchy, State, and Utopia*, esp. ch. 10.
37. Dworkin, *Taking Rights Seriously*, esp. ch. 7. It is worth noting that in his later work, Dworkin has moved away from this view and advanced a distinctive version of what is now sometimes referred to as "ethical liberalism."
38. Ackerman, *Social Justice and the Liberal State*, esp. ch. 1.
39. See, for example, Pettit, *Republicanism*, pp. 85–89; Lovett, *A General Theory of Domination and Justice*, pp. 130–34.
40. Both Plato and Aristotle, in contrast, held that many people can flourish only when dominated by a benevolent master.
41. Goodin, "Folie républicaine," pp. 55–76.
42. The latter view was held, of course, by perfectionist civic humanists such as Arendt, but it is explicitly rejected by mainstream contemporary republicans: see Sunstein, "Beyond the Republican Revival," pp. 1550–51; Skinner, "The Paradoxes of Political Liberty," p. 202; or Pettit, *On the People's Terms*, pp. 227–28.
43. Skinner, "The Paradoxes of Political Liberty," pp. 194–201; Viroli, *Republicanism*, ch. 5.
44. See Pettit, *Republicanism*, ch. 8; Dagger, *Civic Virtues*; Brennan and Pettit, *The Economy of Esteem*.
45. This position is adopted by Dagger, *Civic Virtues*.

17 The conservative critique of liberalism

PHILOSOPHICAL LIBERALISM AND LIBERAL ORDER

There is a philosophical critique of liberalism that hangs together, can properly be said to be conservative, has a considerable tradition behind it, and is interesting and important. But it takes some effort, historical and philosophical, to locate it.

A first task is to dispel some terminological haze. "Liberalism" has come to mean many, often incompatible, things. American critics of "liberalism" and French critics of "(neo-)liberalism," for example, have quite different things in mind. Critics of "liberalism" in one sense may themselves be "liberals" in another. Likewise with the word "conservatism." It can denote (1) a tough-minded version of liberalism that places emphasis on free exchange, a small but strong state, private initiative, and individual responsibility. This, or something in this area, is what people mean by "neo-liberalism." Then (2) there is a practical, down-to-earth attitude which we can call practical conservatism. Practical conservatives see virtue in keeping the show on the road – conserving and when necessary refreshing institutions and habits that work, whatever they are. They know that sometimes "If we want things to stay as they are, things will have to change."[1] But they may well take pride in having no philosophical view, unless it be an anti-abstract one. Importantly, they make no universal claims; what works is what works *here*. Finally (3) there is conservatism in the sense of an attitude that sees continuity, community, tradition, and hierarchy as organic elements of a good society and gives broad philosophical grounds for doing so. In this chapter we

Thanks to Andy Hamilton and Dudley Knowles for helpful discussion and advice.

shall be interested mainly in (3), but also in (2) insofar as it incorpo-
rates an anti-universalistic attitude.

Distinguished from these two conservative views is another outlook, viscerally hostile to liberalism, but which it is misleading to
think of as either "conservative," or "left" – it is too out of sorts with
modernity, or the "Enlightenment," to be either. I shall come back to
it in the fifth section.

What then is liberalism? We should distinguish two levels. At an
intellectual level liberalism is a set of ideas that hang together as a
moral and political philosophy; at the political level it is a political
ethos that provides a framework for policy. At both levels it is a broad
church with left and right wings. Our concern is with conservative
criticisms from outside the broad church, not the debates of left and
right within it; and our focus will be on the underlying philosophical
issues, that is, on philosophical liberalism.

I shall refer to the policy-framing level of liberalism as the *liberal
order*. It comprises (i) equal liberty for all citizens, of which an essential element is the right to act as one chooses subject to a law that
protects the equal rights of others; (ii) a distinctive and special protection of liberty of thought and discussion, and (iii) the *entrenchment* of these principles, either in an effective legal framework that
codifies them in basic laws or constitutional safeguards guaranteeing
equality of every citizen under law, or (perhaps) in a common law
tradition that effectively does the same.

Behind the liberal order have stood ideas that flow from a long
philosophical tradition. They can be traced back to natural law theorists, and philosophers such as Locke or Montesquieu. However,
while important elements of liberalism were present in early modern
Europe they came together in the specific unified form, which I shall
describe as *philosophical liberalism*,[2] only after the French
Revolution. One important feature of this new outlook is that liberals
came to recognize dangers on the left as well as on the right, and to
seek principled grounds on which to distinguish themselves from
both. Another is that they took on board philosophical and
Romantic critiques of the Enlightenment. By the same token, it was
also in the nineteenth century that significant criticisms of philosophical liberalism emerged on the left as well as on the right.

With this context in mind we can set out the philosophical liberalism that conservatives reject. Think of it as comprising three

principal tenets, intertwined and all contested by one or another kind of philosophical conservative:

- Individualism in ethics. This is the view that all value and right reduces to value of or for individuals, or to the rights of individuals.
- A doctrine of equal respect for all human beings based on the belief that all are equally capable of self-governance.
- A doctrine of liberty of thought and discussion based on belief in the unrestricted autonomy of reason – that is, the rational capacities of individual people – as the sole and sufficient canon of objective truth.

It is easy to pay lip service to these theses; taken seriously they are strong doctrine. Their shape and strength will become clearer as we consider criticisms. However, before coming to them let me note some other limits that I am placing on the liberalism that critics target.

First, I have not included the right to democratic participation as a defining part of liberal political order. We may think that democratic rights of participation in collective self-government follow from the basic philosophical outlook of liberalism that I have just described; alternatively, that if they do not then they should simply be added to the liberal order on good grounds of their own. Either way we tend to think of "liberal democracy" as a package deal. However the idea that liberalism and democracy are necessarily linked is quite a recent development. It is not obvious that liberalism entails democracy or indeed that democracy entails liberalism.[3] Many liberals have worried that democracy might turn out to be incompatible with liberal order, and if it is, they have been ready to prefer liberalism to unrestricted democracy. The view that democracy could be inimical to liberty was influential at least to the end of World War II, deriving, earlier, from the *Federalist Papers*, then Tocqueville's account of democracy in America and, later and more dramatically, from the experience of political cataclysm in interwar Europe.

To highlight the conceptual distinction between democracy and liberal order, imagine a meritocracy in which the ruling class is selected on a self-perpetuating basis by open examination, with no discrimination by class, gender, race etc. It nonetheless runs a liberal state. It honors the tenet of equal liberty by placing no restriction on entry to the examination and promoting strictly according to talent, and it entrenches negative liberty and liberty of thought and discussion. Hegel's conception of the role of the civil servant estate within his ideal constitution is not so far from this. He was highly critical of the philosophical liberal's first tenet – liberal individualism – and of democracy; but he was nonetheless a proponent of liberal order, though a conservative one. An interestingly similar standpoint seems to be evolving in some intellectual circles in China.[4] So conservatives may approve liberal order without approving either philosophical liberalism or democracy; philosophical liberals may reject democracy in whole or part; and democrats may reject liberalism.

True, one can argue that the liberal's philosophical thesis of equal respect creates at least a prima facie case for unconditional equal rights of political participation. And at the empirical level one can argue – contrary to evidence brought up by those who disagree – that once the right social conditions have been reached, democracy is not only a stable long-term setting for liberal order but also a reliable one. I myself find both these arguments quite plausible. Here, however, we are focusing on the conservative critique of philosophical liberalism itself, and this will not require us to examine its relationship to democracy, except at the very end.[5]

Turning to a second point: I take philosophical liberalism to hold that the three normative theses outlined above are quite simply *correct*, and hence in principle universally applicable – relevant to all societies at least in respect of setting goals for social development. Importantly, this epistemological claim is quite compatible with empirical recognition that the historical and social conditions for liberal order must be right. Still the historicism of a liberal like Mill in this regard, however striking, is very different from the standpoint of a practical conservative, who endorses and works to maintain the liberal political order only as "what works here." For a philosophical liberal, liberal order is universally the ideally best order; it's just that a process of development must take place for a civil society that can maintain it successfully to emerge. In contrast, a practical conservative may well simply regard the three liberal theses as what *we* have come to accept, *our* historically-arrived-at consensus, the tenets that have come to form the cementing allegiances of *our* society. This anti-universalistic stance will reject or at least eschew the third thesis in its unrestricted liberal version. It is skeptical or agnostic about the claims of natural reason as a canon of truth. Insofar as it defends liberal order, it will endorse freedom of thought, but not the epistemological underpinnings a philosophical liberal provides for it. Practical conservatism can defend established and continuous liberal traditions; it just does not make any universal claims for them. This is likely to make a difference at the level of policy: a practical conservative might well be against liberal intervention, for example, in cases where even a historically minded liberal favors it.

We could make objectivism about the truth of the three tenets explicit as a fourth tenet of philosophical liberalism; however, as just noted, it is implicit in the third. Note also that on this account of philosophical liberalism the rather popular idea that liberalism is based on rejection of the objectivity of values is misguided. A better picture is that non-objectivist forms of liberalism are a strategic retreat from classical liberalism. Many critics from both right and left have attacked the objectivity of liberal values in skeptical, subjectivist, or voluntarist terms, and many liberals, bending to the strength of these epistemological gales, have tried to adapt by finding ways of defending their liberal convictions without committing themselves to their objectivity. We shall come back to this.

Finally, something should be said at this point about the influential "political liberalism" of John Rawls. Seen from the standpoint of the classical liberal tradition, Rawls's liberalism is something of an outlier. In part this is a matter of its content, focused as it is on a strongly redistributive theory of justice. Rawls fits into the liberal broad church by the priority he gives to liberty in his two principles of justice;[6] however, insofar as his influence has contributed to the impression that a particular theory of justice is a *constituent* of liberal order as such, that impression should be corrected. Beyond the debateable minima already implied by the entrenchment of negative liberty, no further, more committal, theory of justice is *constitutive* of liberal order: indeed this is clearer than the analogous claim that democracy is not *constitutive* of liberal order.

It is also interesting that insofar as Rawls defends his account of justice on the grounds that it makes explicit the overlapping consensus to be found in Western societies, he adopts the methodology of practical conservatives.[7] Practically conservative, too, is his claim that the very question of whether philosophical (in Rawls's terms "comprehensive") liberalism is objectively true should be set aside, that is, not appealed to in the derivation of "political liberalism." Both these moves distance him from the philosophical liberal.

Two further elements of Rawls's political liberalism are likely to trouble a philosophical liberal: the doctrine that the state should not support any comprehensive conception of the good, and, even more, the doctrine of "public reason," according to which citizens and their representatives, when engaged in political deliberation and decision (including voting), should not appeal to ethical ideas with which other citizens cannot reasonably be expected to agree. Both these stances seem unnecessarily limiting from a classical-liberal standpoint, and in the second case, potentially illiberal. At any rate they are not constitutive of liberalism as discussed here, and their plausibility is beyond our remit, since our assessment of the conservative critique of liberalism concerns the powerful criticisms it makes of *philosophical* liberalism, which Rawls's political liberalism explicitly eschews.

THE CRITIQUE OF PHILOSOPHICAL LIBERALISM: (I) INDIVIDUALISM

So let us turn to liberal individualism. This is the doctrine that attracts the greatest and most widely shared hostility, on the left as well as the right – in both cases on behalf of an alternative conception which has come to be labelled "communitarianism." In its conservative version it is more precisely described as the rejection of liberals' ethical individualism in favor of an ethics of conservative holism.

To get to the core of this debate, we must eliminate some red herrings. The first of these identifies ethical individualism with egoism and perhaps an egoistically based contractarianism about the state, or about morality. Well, holding this kind of view does not disqualify you as a liberal, but as a matter of fact no notable philosopher of liberalism has held it. Hobbes, who did hold this view of the state, is sometimes described as a liberal, but it is unclear why. Locke, in contrast, can surely be described as at least a liberal ancestor, or proto-liberal; however, his version of the social contract does not rest on egoistic foundations but on a substantial theory of natural rights. True, some liberal philosophers, such as T. H Green, have founded their liberalism on a kind of ethical egoism, in the formal sense of the word "egoism," but their conception of the true interests of the self is very far from the picture of selfish self-interest – and their

metaphysics has been hostile to contractarianism. In fact, contractarianism was treated on all sides with a good deal of hostility in
liberalism's nineteenth-century heyday.

Another red herring is the idea that liberalism favors "negative" as
against "positive" liberty. Two points here. In the first place, though
negative liberty is unquestionably crucial to liberal order, the negative liberty that a liberal order institutes is not a liberty to do as one
likes, without any external constraint. To appeal again to Locke:

> Freedom is not, as we are told, *A Liberty for every Man to do what he lists* ...
> But a *Liberty* to dispose, and order, as he lists, his Person, Actions,
> Possessions, and his whole Property, within the Allowance of those Laws
> under which he is; and therein not to be subject to the arbitrary Will of
> another, but freely follow his own.[8]

This Lockean, as against Hobbesian, conception of negative liberty is
the very essence of liberal law.

But second, it is a mistake to think that liberal individualism is
necessarily concerned with negative *rather than* positive liberty.
Classically, it is concerned with both. In Kant's original formulation
of this contrast,[9] "positive liberty" refers to autonomy – where by
autonomy Kant means acting from recognition of how reason
requires one to act. Some subsequent liberal philosophers, starting
with Schiller and going on through Mill, wanted to enrich or supplement Kantian autonomy in their ideal of a fully developed individual,
but they didn't want to give it up. Autonomy in Kant's sense is central
to the classical liberal ideal of the person. If a conflict emerges within
liberalism between negative and positive liberty, the former understood as a property of liberal order, the latter as an ideal of the person,
it centers on the idea that negative liberty may legitimately be constrained by law in order to foster the development of the capacity for
autonomy – as argued against Mill by T. H. Green.

We arrive at the real issue when we turn to the characteristic holist
claim that individuals abstracted from community are *mere* abstractions. This claim can be "metaphysical,"[10] but its core is normative
and psychological. It is at this point that conservative criticism of
liberal individualism demands to be taken seriously.

Human beings are social animals. They gain their actuality and
satisfaction from social identities which confer obligation, standing,
and fullness of life. Communal obligations arise from the collectivities

to which a human being belongs – family, church, corporation, "platoon" – certainly nation and state. Crucially, they are inherently and essentially *agent-relative* – you have obligations to your family, or your state; I have obligations to mine. So to know what communal obligations you have, you need to know who you are, in the sense of where and how you belong.

These are the obligations Hegel has in mind when he asserts that "The individual ... finds his liberation in duty."[11] If we unpack this we find first the Kantian point about morality and positive freedom: You are free when you act from reason, and obligations are requirements of reason. Liberals can and should agree, since they can and should accept the Kantian connections between morality, reason, and positive freedom. But now comes a difference. Unlike Kant, Hegel does not think that the abstract reason of individuals can deliver duty. Rationality consists in understanding an immanent critique of a particular social morality; to achieve freedom is to be at home in a community with whose structure of obligations you can be rationally at one. Furthermore, those obligations remain *irreducibly* communal, hence, agent-relative. There is no agent-neutral, impartial, universal ethical standpoint from which they can be derived.

In contrast, such agent-neutral, impartial, universal ethical individualism is what the philosophical liberal posits as the only foundation for ethics. It is well stated by Green:

Our ultimate standard of worth is an ideal of *personal* worth. All other values are relative to value for, of, or in a person.[12]

That is a nice disjunction: Various ethical bases of liberalism – natural law, Kantianism, utilitarianism, perfectionism (of a certain kind) – can all agree with it. It is an agent-neutral standard of worth: absolute value resides in individuals, or their excellence, or their well-being, and it resides in all individuals alike, irrespective of their group membership.

So can liberals, as ethical individualists, accept that there are community-relative obligations? They can attempt to do so in various ways, depending on their wider ethical position. If they are consequentialists, they can do so in the manner of indirect consequentialism (people in general are better off if people in general act according to agent-relative rules), if rights theorists, by basing communal obligations on implicit agreement.

From the liberal standpoint, the remaining debate is psychological rather than ethical. It is a question of what satisfies human beings. Human beings are social animals in that they get great satisfactions from various forms of bonding. A liberal can agree with that – while arguing that human beings are also territorial animals that value individual property rights, and animals that like to walk alone as well as bond. At this level the dispute between conservative and liberal is an empirical dispute about human nature that does not raise an underlying purely ethical disagreement.

Many forms of conservatism could agree that the psychological question about human nature is what is essentially at stake.

However, this analysis of the issue is not likely to satisfy the more ethically minded conservative anti-individualist. The important thing to reject, from that point of view, is individualism as a *purely ethical* doctrine. Agent-relative communal obligation arises from the value of the collectivities to which the individual belongs. The important thing to see is that their value is both agent-relative *and* unconditional, irreducible, non-instrumental. The demands placed on me by my membership of a family are agent-relative – yet at the same time they are unconditional (they do not arise from a promise on my part, for example) and non-instrumental (they do not arise, for example, because if everyone fulfills such duties general well-being will be served).

It is this combination of unconditionality and agent-relativity that is crucial. It cannot be reconciled with ethical individualism; it is one of the conservative's strongest ethical convictions, whether or not made explicit. From this point of view value is *not* all "relative to value for, of, or in a person." There are collectivities – church, family, nation, state – that have intrinsic and non-instrumental value relative to their members; "value for, of, or in a person" is relative to *them*.[13]

Ethical holism, as against individualism, does not deny the ethical significance of individual *eudaimonia* (well-being, individual self-realization). But it holds that individuals achieve *eudaimonia* through playing their part in these agent-relatively valuable collectivities, and only do so because they rightly see them as *unconditionally* good. If liberal individualism is correct, they are laboring under an illusion. In this way, for the ethical holist, liberal individualism undermines or ironizes even when it tries to preserve.

Conservatives are thus likely to see the efforts of liberal individualists to take account of the importance of community as unstable:
The natural tendency of liberalism is toward cosmopolitanism. To be
clear: It is not that conservatives must regard *all* obligation as communal and thus agent-relative. They can recognize that obligations of
justice are non-communal, agent-neutral obligations. If you reck-
lessly harm the legitimate interests of another, then you have an
obligation to give just compensation, irrespective of whether that
person is a fellow member of any collectivity to which you belong,
including the state. Moreover these agent-neutral duties of justice
trump communal obligations.

But what a conservative may say is that because liberal individualism cannot recognize the unconditional and non-instrumental
basis of communal obligation, it inevitably concludes that duties of
agent-neutral justice are not just trumps in those specific contexts in
which they do obtain, but that they are the *only* fundamental duties.
And there will then be a tendency to fill the vacuum by producing
ever stronger cosmopolitan theories of justice (for example, ever
stronger theories of human rights). This is the high road from liberal
individualism to cosmopolitanism. A conservative who takes this
view is likely to be particularly dismissive of left-liberal communitarianism: He will see it as a feeble and wishful politics that tries to
combine recognition of the importance of community with an egalitarian cosmopolitanism that undermines the irreducibly agent-
relative moral values to which true community gives rise. As to
attempts to develop a liberal outlook with a less inflamed theory of
justice, and a better psychological sense of the importance of belonging, such a conservative will hold that within a liberal individualist
framework these are bound to be overwhelmed by a pure cosmopolitan egalitarianism.

THE CRITIQUE OF PHILOSOPHICAL LIBERALISM: (II) EQUAL RESPECT AND FREE THOUGHT

The issue of individualism in ethics focuses the difference between
philosophical liberals and conservative holists in a particularly sharp
way. In contrast, the other two tenets of philosophical liberalism
have been troubling not just to conservatives but to liberals

themselves. Many people in today's liberal democracies think and act as happy-go-lucky unreflective ethical individualists. Like Molière's *bourgeois gentilhomme* they speak the prose of ethical individualism without knowing it. The doctrine of equal respect is not so happily placed. It has assumed a neuralgic kind of importance. It is constantly affirmed, yet there is uneasy awareness that it is open to obvious objection. As to belief in the normative authority of autonomous reason: that has virtually collapsed across large parts of the intellectual and political world. The ideal of free speech remains, but if defended it is defended as a kind of individual right of self-expression, rather than as the fundamental public good, like free air, that it is on a classical liberal's conception of free thought. These two points, about respect and objectivity, are connected.

We must distinguish between equal concern and equal respect. As already noted, in contexts of justice a requirement of equal concern, that is, impartial consideration of the claims of any and every affected person, is incontestable on any reasonable view. Of course this leaves open what the contexts, and how strong the requirements, of justice are. But whatever the answer, in those contexts your children and mine (say) are equally "important," even though they are not equally important to me or to you – in those contexts their claims must be given equal and impartial consideration by everyone, including me and you.

It is also in the context of justice that the liberal doctrine of equal respect historically arose. It amounted, first and foremost, to rejection of any presumed authority, privilege, or discrimination that was based on class or status – then on gender, then race, then sexual orientation. It was and is a negative doctrine of the irrelevance of such distinctions, with some underlying conception of justice determining the contexts in which they are irrelevant. However, classical liberalism also harbored the liberal disposition to a more far-reaching, positive doctrine of equal respect, founded on the claim that all human beings have an equal potential for autonomy. This more far-reaching doctrine is impossible to defend without either going metaphysical or making very implausible psychological assumptions about nature and nurture. Kant took the first route; Mill took the second. Kant appeals to the idea that reason is equally, though transcendentally, present in every human being; Mill appeals to an associationist psychology that gives everyone equal rational potential.

However, if these assumptions seem heroically optimistic, then a way to guarantee equal respect a priori is to deny the objectivity of the normative, and to subjectivize the ideal of autonomy. Individuals deserve equal respect because there are no grounds for giving them unequal respect. Since there is no objective hierarchy of ends or values, the ultimate ends and values of individuals are unappraisable and incomparable. Liberals who go this way put in question the idea of objective reason, and thus the third tenet of philosophical liberalism. As a matter of logic, their standpoint gives no basis for the positive doctrine that everyone deserves equal respect, as against the negative conclusion that no one deserves any more respect than anyone else. Nonetheless, as a matter of powerful psychological fact, or need, the negative doctrine somehow transmutes into a positive one. The twentieth century saw a liberal stampede in this direction, to the point that subjectivism (nihilism, relativism, etc.) is thought of by some critics as nothing less than a constitutive liberal tenet. It is not. It is, rather, a historically fateful concession to populism.

Some account of what I take to be the true liberal doctrine of free thought is appropriate here. Thought that is genuinely free, that is, autonomous, is both spontaneous and open to dialogue. It is ruled by its own norms: by reason relations that it discovers through reflection on its own spontaneous activity. Furthermore, free thought is the only canon of truth. Equally important, for philosophical liberalism, is that first-person insight into truth requires unconstrained discussion with other seekers for truth, people who are responding not out of dogma but out of their own spontaneous normative dispositions. Of course, it is possible for one person to be right and all others wrong. Equally, however, no one can know that they are right without engaging in dialogue with others and reflecting on the others' responses. Thus, while the doctrine says that you should decide *for* yourself what is true, it does not say that you should or in any way could decide *by* yourself.[14]

Especially in ultimate questions of value, free debate that is thoroughly non-exclusive is essential – as a matter of the epistemology of the normative, not just of the ethics of democratic respect. Unsurprisingly, therefore, robust open-mindedness, as against dogmatic and stubborn, or weak and credulous, assessment of the responses of others is a prime liberal virtue. But it is at best a liberal illusion to think that everyone has it equally. Not every voice carries equal weight: In free and inclusive debate more and less authoritative voices inevitably emerge. It is *important* that they should – that authoritative voices should not be muffled, or hesitant in taking the lead. Putting it the other way round, one's personal independence or dignity is not diminished by free recognition of genuine authority in the common pursuit of truth, wherever one finds it. On the contrary, to recognize it is a mark of inward freedom.

This, one may say, is the elitism in liberalism.[15] Its epistemological rationale is that warrant ("for human beings") is dialogical and defeasible. Furthermore, just because warrant is dialogical, ancestral voices that have maintained authority over time still count. Dialogue inherently involves tradition and immanent critique.

Now there is a conservative critique of liberal elitism that agrees with its dialogical epistemology, as just summarized, but regards its historical sociology as naïve. This is the position of Hegelian or Thomist conservatives, at least insofar as their epistemological view is in line with that of their philosophical masters. To take the case of Hegel, the doctrine that reason is active in history is the doctrine that free thought is history's endogeneous causal factor, through the thinking of individuals. Likewise, the epistemology of Aquinas is that natural human reason is capable of reaching truth by its own exercise. Natural reason arrives at ethical and spiritual truths which revelation reworks and transforms. Both these doctrines, whatever else they involve, accept that freely exercised natural reason leads to truth (at least some truth).

Call conservatives of this kind "rational conservatives." What they emphasize, against liberals, is that if free thought, or natural reason, is to have its due influence among the people, it must be mediated by tradition and authority: for Aquinas, that of the church, for Hegel, that of a tradition of communal ethical life.[16] This, such conservatives say, is what mere liberal elitism lacks; in its absence it cannot help collapsing into arbitrariness and endless controversy, or domination by charismatic populists and charlatans, or utter anarchy.

This is a moderate conservatism. It says that without entrenched institutions of intellectual and spiritual authority, free thought simply leads to normative crisis ("anomie"). It does not deny the autonomy of human reason, it just denies that a liberal elitism of Mill's kind can be sufficiently effective to enable and ensure the role reason has to play in a good society (in Hegel's terms, make it "actual"). It was a debate that Mill well knew – in which he grasped the force of the conservative side, without acceding to it. Witness his carefully modulated sympathy with Coleridge, Comte, the Oxford Tractarians.

But, as already noted, to defend the underlying epistemology of reason as free thought is to put pressure on the liberal doctrine of equal respect, since it seems altogether evident that people differ as much in their sensitivity to reason as in any other competence. The fact that Kant and Mill resorted to implausible doctrines in defending the liberal conception of equal respect that they did so much to form is grist to the mill of rational conservatives. Just because they agree with the underlying epistemology, they fear that combining it with an unrealistic conception of equal respect and an outright liberal individualism is socially toxic.

THE CRITIQUE OF PHILOSOPHICAL LIBERALISM: (III) THE AUTONOMY OF REASON

What then of the other liberal response noted above – the denial, contrary to classical liberals and rational conservatives, that free thought can attain and be guided by objective norms of reason? We should at once note that there is a conservative version of that thought too. This kind of conservative thinks that the notion that free thought crystallizes a naturally authoritative human reason is nothing but arrogant self-delusion. Human thinking cannot have a self-authorizing normative objectivity; it cannot pull itself up by its bootstraps. If, therefore, it is to avoid skepticism it must find rest in some non-rational stabilization of belief. Options here are various. They include the Humean or Burkean[17] appeal to stabilization by habit or "prejudice," and Newman's appeal to the pre-rational authority of Christian doctrine. However, if we are most concerned with conservative attitudes after the emergence of classical liberalism in the nineteenth century, then various kinds of *voluntarism* – divine, collectivist, charismatic – are particularly relevant.[18]

What we must grasp, in order to appreciate the increasing cultural weakness of philosophical liberalism as it moved into the twentieth century, is that from about the time of Nietzsche (though by no means just because of him) the denial of rational objectivity in favor of various mixes of nihilism and voluntarism has grown into a cultural tsunami. Liberals can either resist it or try to flow with it without sinking. For those who flow with it, there have been – during the heyday of modernism – some not very coherent elite-existentialist options on offer; but in the end the biggest flow by far has been toward market-driven populism, which at least offers a kind of "equal respect" and "freedom of choice" – though to a classical liberal the words "respect," 'freedom," and "choice" can only be sad caricatures here.

In the first half of the twentieth century, populism did not work the liberal's way. Its ideal, rather, was the triumph of the will of the people, identified with the charismatic will of the leader. But in the century's second half, both liberal order and democracy, powered by capitalism, made a stunning comeback. And that, in turn, has come to allow for defenses of liberal democracy that are practical-conservative in their rejection of foundations and reliance on the stability of opinion. Richard Rorty's "post-modernist bourgeois liberalism" is a philosophically sophisticated (or over-sophisticated) version of this kind of defense.[19]

Both rational conservatives and classical liberals will object that these tactics are unhistorical and complacent. Yes, we have the good fortune to live in a prosperous liberal order that has seen off totalitarian challenges. But can we rely on that? If affluence, freedom from pain, and consumer "choice" came to seem better guaranteed by an illiberal brave new world, would anything be wrong with that? And if so, what and why? It is interesting that post-modern bourgeois liberalism came to the fore only at the apparent apogee of Western affluence and power. It is tempting to see it as a symptom of decline – the vehicle runs on because its previous momentum hasn't yet encountered a sufficiently adverse slope.

But before we step back to a final comparison of the less enervating positions of rational conservatives and philosophical liberals, there is a very striking historical phenomenon we should take into account: anti-liberal rage.

SOURCES OF ANTI-LIBERAL RAGE

Confining attention to cool and rational discussion between philosophical conservatives and philosophical liberals would ignore a social fact of first importance: namely, that liberalism in all its aspects has given rise not only to sober criticism but also to lava flows of hatred and disgust, from its first philosophical formulations in the nineteenth century.[20]

Rage distorts – we have touched on some of the distortions. Liberalism is neither a charter for selfishness nor a recipe for unlimited, arbitrary, or terroristic freedom. It is not a reductionist or instrumentalist view of reason. None of these criticisms can be fairly made of philosophical liberalism. Yet even when fully understood, philosophical liberalism has the power to provoke a reaction of existential outrage. The outrage is directed in part at the doctrine itself – at the dimensions of life it closes off or denies – and in part at complacent obtuseness or denial, on the part of liberals, as to what it closes off or denies.

The force and depth of these anti-liberal reactions cannot be conveyed in a couple of pages. Still, some points in the indictment recur in many versions and places. They are: irreverence, glib rationalism, anomie, self-delusion. Further, it will help to keep in mind two kinds of outrage – the heroic and the religious. Nietzsche and Dostoevsky, respectively, provide examples. In each case the attitude of rejection is radical: an existential insurrection against the liberal iron cage.[21]

Irreverence is the first and foremost thing that causes anti-liberals pain. It is implicit in the liberal humanist combination of individualism and equal "respect." Not merely is this combination tinny and banal; it is transgressive. For heroic anti-liberalism in the Nietzschean mould, it is a slave revolt against everything truly great, a denial and mockery of the "pathos of distance" that great things should inspire. For religious anti-liberalism it is blasphemy against the sacred. In this respect the two can come curiously close to each other, even though the first is aristocratic and naturalistic, while the second is religious and mystical.

The aristocratic attitude is nauseated by liberal destruction of an order of rank and a social structure of authority that true ordering of values demands. In their absence, immense spiritual distances between the great and the mediocre disappear from view: "The honourable term for *mediocre* is, of course, the word 'liberal'."[22] Religious criticism of equal respect is different: it is that liberal equality of respect is hubristic, that it elbows out the Christian virtues of humility and love, that it makes individual humans into lonely gods, cut off from God and nature.

Connected to irreverence is glib rationalism (or "humanism"). This criticism goes further than the criticism of the Enlightenment which its conservative and liberal critics shared. That criticism – Tocqueville on the French Revolution, Mill on Bentham and Coleridge – did not deny the objectivity and authority of reason. The outrage of anti-liberals is more extreme. It is outrage at the very idea that mere humans can achieve any kind of objectivity, any kind of detached superior standpoint, just by their own thinking: that there exists or could exist anything like the liberal's false idol of objective free thought.

On this view the liberal conception of free thought and reason can achieve only its own destruction in nihilism – bleak normlessness. The anti-liberal response is in one way or another voluntaristic. For Nietzsche, the path out of nihilism requires the imposition of value by strong spirits. For religious anti-liberals the guiding idea is that meaning, moral depth, normativity itself depend on divine will and require on the part of human beings an existential choice or leap of faith.[23]

The sheer *difficulty* of achieving meaning in the modern world is implicit in either view. Modernity and liberalism fuse: the difficulty lies in the arduousness of achieving an affirmative attitude to life and world in the face of liberal modernity – of finding any greatness in it that can give meaning to life, or achieving in it a redemptive affirmation of the sacredness of the world.

It is this sense of difficulty that leads to the picture of glib liberal self-delusion. Liberals who think at all delude themselves about the tenability of their own doctrines, about the consequences of their general acceptance, and not least about the realities of human nature. From the heroic standpoint these realities require the harsh aristocratic imposition of order. From the religious side what they call for is sorrow at the fallenness of humanity, yet pure joy that it is redeemable – a spiritual insight that is indispensable for true love of one's neighbor, but that "facile humanist cosmopolitanism," "the restless concerns of secular and instrumentalist thinking,"[24] cannot conceive.

In short, even if liberal *order* overcomes, by venal economic means, the worst dangers of totalitarianism, liberal *philosophy* can never give meaning. It contains no cause or object that justifies heroic virtue, and it closes any path toward redemption from fallenness. At most it entrenches the excruciating mediocrity of populist consumerism, the economist's ignoble calculations of benefit and cost, and interminable, self-indulgent debate about "values."

TOWARD AN ASSESSMENT

Our object has been to examine conservative critiques of liberalism rather than liberal responses to them. However, to measure the force of these critiques we should at least consider how answers might go. Philosophical liberals, it would seem, face challenges from three directions: there is the threat of a transmutation of liberalism into populism, there is the existential rejection, heroic or religious, of their most basic convictions as meaningless, and there is the rational conservative's critique of liberal individualism and the ideal of universal autonomy, discussed in the second and third sections.

It is striking how much turns out to hang on the liberal conception of rational objectivity, that is, the idea that truth is attainable, and best attainable (not least on normative questions) by unrestricted free debate. What may seem an abstruse topic in epistemology is really the heart of liberalism.[25]

On the one hand, it is because existential lines of thought take this conception of rational objectivity to be bankrupt that they predict the collapse of liberalism into populism. But an act of will or leap of faith toward heroic or redemptive values is a criticism of modernity itself, and a desperate one. Those values depend on pre-modern social forms that no longer exist.

On the other hand, rational conservatives agree with philosophical liberals about natural reason's potential for objectivity. This puts the debate on more tractable ground. Their disagreement is about what social conditions must be in place for reason to be actualized. If natural reason is to have its necessary social and not merely philosophical authority, these conservatives say, there must be institutions and moral and intellectual hierarchies that stabilize it.

Rational conservatives who take that view, against the liberal model of unrestricted free debate, take it because they consider the philosophical liberal's belief in the equal potential autonomy of all human beings to be grossly optimistic, even delusional. This (if not short-circuited by metaphysics or terminology) is a question of evidence and interpretation. Nonetheless, a realistic liberal should consider a strategic retreat. It is not a good idea to base liberal principles of liberty and civic equality on the doctrine that all human beings have an equal potential for autonomy. Such a claim may be rhetorically effective, but it is also widely misleading. It distorts what people really think about each other and provides a false foundation for concern for others and for justice and rights. (Consider, for example, the rights of people with mental disabilities, and the bases of our concern for them.)

What is really basic to liberal order is juridical equality, and beyond that a crucial civic, not metaphysical, ethos of respect. The latter is expressed in part by an attitude that presumes – even though defeasibly – that the other person's opinions and attitudes are freely and honestly formed, and should be heeded as such – further, that one's opinions and choices should be formed in the same way, and expressed as such.

This attitude ramifies in wide and subtle ways that have a deep effect on politics and society. It becomes stable, of course, only if it is not constantly defeated, and hence it depends on the active reasonableness and common sense of most citizens. It is this stability, however, established by experience, that provides the empirical anchor for the liberal model of free discussion – not the dogma of equal potential autonomy.

The liberal response can also note that in practice modern liberal democracies already have strong structures of moral and epistemic authority in place. For example, modern universities in liberal democracies are in part functional equivalents of medieval monasteries (for good and ill). True, they do not replace the central authority and powers of excommunication of the medieval church. But few rational conservatives take their analysis to the extreme of arguing for a guardian council of philosopher-scientists (in the manner of Auguste Comte) let alone of clerics (as in the Iranian constitution) – however much they reprobate the moral uncertainties and conflicts of liberal democracy.

Nineteenth-century liberals feared populist authoritarianism, but took it to be a danger of democracy, not of liberalism. Conceptually, as noted earlier, a liberal order can be combined with a pure political meritocracy. But if, as I believe, liberal premises lead from a combination of practical and philosophical reasons to some form of democracy, the question is what kind? Representative forms of democracy as they currently exist in the West mediate the popular vote through the activity of moral and intellectual elites. This may be objectionable to radical democrats, but it need not be objectionable to liberals, even to liberals who are well aware of the danger of vested interests and the need to take precautions against these.

There is, finally, an important ethical issue at stake: that of individualism, as discussed in the second section. An ethical holist says that communal obligations have their source in the unconditional, agent-relative worth of supra-individual social entities to which any individual belongs (if he or she is lucky): family, neighborhood, corporation, nation. This complex of overlapping social wholes, taken itself as a whole, is the "common good." It is irreducible to any function of individual goods – yet it is communal obligation that actualizes the individual. So individual good depends on the common good, not vice versa.

Liberals, it seems to me, must deny this doctrine of ethical holism. Their individualism is not negotiable. Against the conservative argument that liberal individualism collapses into thin, merely abstract, cosmopolitanism, they can appeal to powerful human sentiments of allegiance, solidarity and identity (though they may also fear them). True, that raises a significant question: How do these sentiments translate into practical reasons and ethical commitments? Must a liberal hold that they do so only by sophisticated derivation from an abstract, agent-neutral and individualist standpoint? Contrary to the conservative line of argument considered in the second section, liberals can accept that they are immediate – but not in the holist way. Human sentiments of solidarity toward other people who stand in various relations to oneself are the firm base of agent-relative commitments toward them, commitments which are immediately reasonable. They constitute a normative source that is *neither* based on any agent-neutral principle, *nor* dependent on the intrinsic agent-relative value of any supra-individual collectivity.

This response raises further questions which cannot be pursued here. But, finally, we should also note that, on the positive side, liberals can set the great liberation of ordinary people that liberal democracy has produced, and the space for stable and truthful communal life opened up by liberal institutions. To be sure, institutions can only "open it up" – maintaining a truly liberal ethical vision, as against a populist surrogate, requires continuing effort, both in politics and in civil society.

NOTES

1. Tancredi's remark to the Prince, in *The Leopard*, p. 27. More sententiously: "A state without the means of some change is without the means of its conservation" (Burke, *Reflections on the Revolution in France*, p. 19).

2. Or "classical" liberalism – where by the word "classical" I refer to the philosophical liberalism that emerged at this time, not to an economic theory of free markets. (See, for example, the distinction Mill makes, in *On Liberty*, ch. 5, para. 4, between the liberty principle which he there argues for, and the doctrine of free trade which, as he says, rests on different grounds; compare his nuanced discussion of laissez-faire in the *Principles of Political Economy*, bk. v, ch. 11.)

3. In the 1920s Carl Schmitt's aim was to "rescue democracy from its overlay of liberal elements" (quoted in Holmes, *The Anatomy of Antiliberalism*, p. 49).

4. See Bell and Chenyang (eds.), *The Idea of Political Meritocracy*. A number of papers in this volume make the case for varying degrees of liberal meritocracy.

5. I consider what arguments for and against democracy can be made from a liberal standpoint in Skorupski, "The Liberal Critique of Democracy."

6. Rawls, *A Theory of Justice*, §§39, p. 82.

7. However, some question how much justificatory weight he places on that defense. See Mulhall and Swift, "Rawls and Communitarianism," pp. 478–81.

8. Locke, *Second Treatise of Government*, §57.

9. Kant, *Groundwork of the Metaphysics of Morals*, pp. 446–47.

10. As it was for both idealist and positivist critics of liberal individualism. See Skorupski, "Ethics and the Social Good."

11. Hegel, *Philosophy of Right*, §149.

12. Green, *Prolegomena to Ethics*, p. 210.

13. One can take Hegel's view of marriage on the one hand, and Harriet and John Mill's view on the other, as exemplifying the difference between a holist and an individualist view.

14. Defence of this underlying epistemology leads into basic questions of philosophy. My own view of how to defend it is set out in Skorupski, *The Domain of Reasons*, part IV.

15. It is elitist, as against the populism of subjectivist liberalism; it is liberal, as against the illiberal idea that any doctrine can legitimately be imposed

on people by authority (of state, church or party). For further discussion see Skorupski, "Liberal Elitism."

16. This is not to ignore Hegel's affirmation that "the right of the subjective will," the freedom of the moral subject, is an inherent aspect of modern ethical life (for discussion of this see, e.g., Knowles, *Hegel and the Philosophy of Right* and Neuhouser, "Hegel's Social Philosophy"). It signals Hegel's acceptance of the epistemic grounding of reason in free thought, but does not cancel the conservative holism implicit in his overall treatment of ethical life.

17. As Hampsher-Monk nicely puts it (*A History of Modern Political Thought*, p. 304), "Although he in some ways anticipates the far more rationalist Hegel, Burke's fear of the inadequacies of individual reason has only an obscure counterpart in his belief in collective wisdom."

18. Voluntarism, the view that normativity is founded on will (of God, or of the individual or collective subject) is an ancient tradition in philosophy and theology. Irwin (*The Development of Ethics*) traces the conflict of voluntarism and naturalism (the appeal to natural reason) from the medieval period.

19. Rorty, "Post-Modernist Bourgeois Liberalism."

20. Holmes, *The Anatomy of Antiliberalism* is a very good review of a range of anti-liberals, from de Maistre to Roberto Unger.

21. Not that Nietzsche and Dostoevsky are on a par. Nietzsche is an example, Dostoevsky provides examples. The former's assault on liberalism is all-out and direct; the latter's treatment of secular rationalism, and religious faith or trust, is that of a great novelist: it is dialectical and proceeds by indirection, particularly impressively in *The Brothers Karamozov*. (Ansell-Pearson, *An Introduction to Nietzsche as Political Thinker* is a fine treatment of the political aspects of Nietzsche, though it rather underplays the inherent extremism of his view. Williams, *Dostoevsky: Language, Faith, and Fiction* captures the Dostoevskian dialectical relation to faith with subtlety, yet strongly presents him as on the side of faith.)

22. Nietzsche, *The Will to Power*, §864.

23. These two points are separate and can each be refined. Williams gives a convincing picture of how in Dostoevsky the "choice" of faith is not a matter of "mere" will. However, the idea that if God is dead everything is permitted, or less dramatically, all value is instrumentalized, seems to be assumed by both author and commentator.

24. The phrases are from Williams, *Dostoevsky*, pp. 181, 238.

25. A critique of liberalism which insightfully focuses on it is MacIntyre, *Whose Justice, Which Rationality?* (although it does not seem to me to give a fair-minded picture of what liberalism is).

BIBLIOGRAPHY

Ackerman, Bruce A. *Social Justice and the Liberal State*. New Haven: Yale University Press, 1980.

Acton, J. E. E. Dalberg. "The History of Freedom in Antiquity" and "The History of Freedom in Christianity," in *Selected Writings of Lord Acton*, vol. I, *Essays in the History of Liberty*, ed. J. Rufus Fears. Indianapolis: Liberty Fund, 1986, 5–28.

"Nationality," in *The History of Freedom and Other Essays*, ed. J. N. Figgis and R. V. Laurence. London: Macmillan, 1907, 270–300.

Adams, John. *The Revolutionary Writings of John Adams*, ed. C. Bradley Thompson. Indianapolis: Liberty Fund, 2000.

Ahmadi, Fereshteh. "Islamic Feminism in Iran: Feminism in a New Islamic Context," *Journal of Feminist Studies in Religion* 22, 2 (2006): 33–53.

Alonso, Facundo M. "Shared Intention, Reliance, and Interpersonal Obligations,"*Ethics* 119, 3 (2009): 444–75.

Amar, Akhill Reed. "The Bill of Rights as a Constitution," *Yale Law Journal* 100, 5 (1991): 1131–210.

Anderson, Benedict. *Imagined Communities*. London: Verso, 1991.

Anderson, Elizabeth. "The Fundamental Disagreement between Luck Egalitarians and Relational Egalitarians," *Canadian Journal of Philosophy* 36 (2010): 1–23.

"What Is the Point of Equality?", *Ethics* 109 (1999): 287–337.

Anderson, Joel and Honneth, Axel. "Autonomy, Vulnerability, Recognition, and Justice," in *Autonomy and the Challenges to Liberalism: New Essays*, ed. John Christman and Joel Anderson. Cambridge University Press, 2005, 127–49.

Ansell-Pearson, Keith. *An Introduction to Nietzsche as Political Thinker*. Cambridge University Press, 1994.

The Anti-Federalist Papers and the Constitutional Convention Debates, ed. Ralph Ketcham. New York: Mentor, 1986.

Appiah, Kwame Anthony. *The Ethics of Identity*. Princeton University Press, 2005.

Appleby, Joyce. *Liberalism and Republicanism in the Historical Imagination*. Cambridge, MA: Harvard University Press, 1992.

423

Arendt, Hannah. *On Revolution*. New York: Penguin Books, 1980.

The Origins of Totalitarianism. New York: Harcourt, Brace and World, 1951.

"What Is Freedom?", in Arendt, *Between Past and Future*. New York: Penguin, 1993, 143–71.

Arneson, Richard. "Democracy at National and Workplace Levels," in *The Idea of Democracy*, ed. David Copp, Jean Hampton, and John Roemer. Cambridge University Press, 1993, 118–48.

"Democracy Is Not Intrinsically Just," in *Justice and Democracy: Essays for Brian Barry*, ed. Keith Dowding, Robert Goodin, and Carole Pateman. Cambridge University Press, 2004, 40–58.

"Equality and Equal Opportunity for Welfare," *Philosophical Studies* 56 (1989): 77–93.

"The Supposed Right to an Equal Say," in *Contemporary Debates in Political Philosophy*, ed. Thomas Christiano and John Christman. Oxford: Wiley-Blackwell, 2009, 197–212.

Bailyn, Bernard. *The Ideological Origins of the American Revolution*. Cambridge, MA: Belknap Press, 1967.

Ball, Terence and Bellamy, Richard (eds.). *The Cambridge History of Twentieth-Century Political Thought*. Cambridge University Press, 2003.

Banning, Lance. "Jeffersonian Ideology Revisited," *The William and Mary Quarterly* 43 (1987): 3–19.

Banting, Keith and Kymlicka, Will (eds.). *Multiculturalism and the Welfare State: Recognition and Redistribution in Contemporary Democracies*. Oxford University Press, 2006.

Barber, Benjamin. *Strong Democracy: Participatory Politics for a New Age*. Berkeley: University of California Press, 1984.

Barry, Brian. *Culture and Equality*. Cambridge, MA: Harvard University Press, 2001.

"John Rawls and the Search for Stability," *Ethics* 105 (1995): 874–915.

Justice as Impartiality. Oxford University Press, 1995.

Bayle, Pierre [1688]. *A Philosophical Commentary on These Words of the Gospel, Luke 14:23, "Compel Them to Come In, That My House May Be Full."* Indianapolis: Liberty Fund, 2005.

Bell, Daniel. *The Cultural Contradictions of Capitalism*. New York: Basic Books, 1976.

Bell, Daniel and Li Chenyang. *The Idea of Political Meritocracy*. New York: Cambridge University Press, 2013.

Bellamy, Richard. "'Da Metafisico a Mercatante': Antonio Gevesi and the Development of a New Language of Commerce in Eighteenth-Century Naples," in *The Languages of Political Theory in Early-Modern Europe*, ed. Anthony Pagden. Cambridge University Press, 1987, 77–302.

Liberalism and Modern Society. College Park, PA: Penn State University Press, 1992.

Benhabib, Seyla. *The Claims of Culture: Equality and Diversity in the Global Era.* Princeton University Press, 2002.

Situating the Self: Gender, Community and Postmodernism in Contemporary Ethics. New York: Routledge, 1992.

Bercovitch, Sacvan. *The American Jeremiad.* Madison: University of Wisconsin Press, 1978.

Berkowitz, Peter. *Virtue and the Making of Modern Liberalism.* Princeton University Press, 2000.

Berlin, Isaiah. "The Counter-Enlightenment," in Berlin, *Against the Current: Essays in the History of Ideas,* ed. Henry Hardy. New York: Viking Press, 1979, 1–24.

The Crooked Timber of Humanity. London: John Murray, 1990.

The Magus of the North. London: Farrar, Straus and Giroux, 1994.

"Nationalism: Past Neglect and Present Power," in Berlin, *The Proper Study of Mankind: An Anthology of Essays,* ed. Henry Hardy and Roger Hausheer. London: Farrar, Straus and Giroux, 1998, 581–604.

"Two Concepts of Liberty," in Berlin, *Four Essays on Liberty,* ed. Henry Hardy. Oxford University Press, 2003, 166–217.

Berman, Paul. "The Philosopher of Islamic Terror," in *The New York Times Magazine* (March 23, 2003).

Binmore, Ken. *Just Playing.* London: MIT Press, 1998.

Blackstone, William. *Commentaries on the Laws of England,* vol. I. University of Chicago Press, 1979.

Boucher, David (ed.). *The British Idealists.* Cambridge University Press, 1997.

Bratman, Michael. *Faces of Intention.* Cambridge University Press, 1999.

"Shared Intention," *Ethics* 104, 1 (1993): 97–113.

Breen, T. H. *American Insurgents, American Patriots.* New York: Hill and Wang, 2010.

Brennan, Geoffrey and Pettit, Philip. *The Economy of Esteem.* Oxford University Press, 2003.

Breuilly, J. "On the Principle of Nationality," in *The Cambridge History of Nineteenth Century Thought,* ed. G. Stedman Jones and Gregory Claeys. Cambridge University Press, 2011, 77–109.

Brighouse, Harry. "Egalitarianism and Equal Availability of Political Influence," *Journal of Political Philosophy* 4, 2 (1996): 118–42.

School Choice and Social Justice. Oxford University Press, 2000.

Brown, Wendy. *States of Injury: Power and Freedom in Late Modernity.* Princeton University Press, 1995.

Brownson, Orestes A. *Orestes A. Brownson: Selected Writings* (Sources of American Spirituality), ed. Patrick W. Carey. New York: Paulist Press, 1991.

Burke, Edmund. *Reflections on the Revolution in France* [1790], Everyman's Library. London: J. M. Dent & Sons, 1967.

Bushman, Richard L. *From Puritan to Yankee: Character and the Social Order in Connecticut, 1690–1765*. Cambridge, MA: Harvard University Press, 1967.

Buss, Sarah. "Personal Autonomy," in *The Stanford Encyclopedia of Philosophy* (http://plato.stanford.edu/entries/liberalism/).

Butterfill, Stephen. "Joint Action and Development," *The Philosophical Quarterly* 62, 246 (2012): 23–47.

Button, Mark. *Contract, Culture and Citizenship: Transformative Liberalism from Hobbes to Rawls*. University Park: Pennsylvania State University Press, 2008.

Calhoun, C. *Nations Matter: Culture, History and the Cosmopolitan Dream*. London: Taylor & Francis, 2006.

Calhoun, John. *Union and Liberty: The Political Philosophy of John C. Calhoun*, ed. Ross Lence. Indianapolis: Liberty Fund, 1992.

Calvin, John. *Institutes of the Christian Religion*, trans. Ford Lewis Battles. Philadelphia: Westminster Press, 1960.

Caney, Simon. *Justice Beyond Borders*. Oxford University Press, 2006.

Carens, Joseph. "Liberalism and Culture," *Constellations* 4, 1 (1997): 35–47.

Cherniss, Joshua L. *A Mind in Its Time: The Development of Isaiah Berlin's Political Thought*. Oxford University Press, 2013.

Christiano, Thomas. *The Constitution of Equality: Democratic Authority and Its Limits*. Oxford University Press, 2008.

"Estlund on Democratic Authority," *Journal of Political Philosophy* 17 (2009): 228–40.

"An Instrumental Argument for A Human Right to Democracy," *Philosophy and Public Affairs* 39, 2 (2011): 142–76.

"Must Democracy Be Reasonable?", *Canadian Journal of Philosophy* 39, 1 (2009): 1–34.

"Rational Deliberation among Citizens and Experts," in *Deliberative Systems: Deliberative Democracy at the Large Scale*, ed. John Parkinson and Jane Mansbridge. Cambridge University Press, 2012, 27–52.

The Rule of the Many. Boulder, CO: Westview Press, 1996.

Christman, John. "Autonomy in Moral and Political Philosophy," in *The Stanford Encyclopedia of Philosophy* (http://plato.stanford.edu/entries/liberalism/).

"Freedom, Autonomy, and Social Selves," in *Isaiah Berlin and the Politics of Freedom: "Two Concepts of Liberty" 50 Years Later*, ed. Bruce Baum and Robert Nichols. London: Routledge, 2013, 87–101.

The Politics of Persons: Individual Autonomy and Socio-historical Selves. Cambridge University Press, 2009.

Social and Political Philosophy: A Contemporary Introduction. London: Routledge, 2002.

Cobden, Richard, *Speeches on Questions of Public Policy by Richard Cobden,* ed. John Bright and J. E. Thorold Rogers. London: Macmillan, 1903.

Coffee, Alan M. S. J. "Mary Wollstonecraft, Freedom, and the Enduring Power of Social Domination," *European Journal of Political Theory* 12 (2012): 116–35.

Cohen, Andrew Jason. "Toleration," in *The International Encyclopedia of Ethics,* ed. Hugh LaFollette. Oxford: Blackwell, 2013.

"What the Liberal State Should Tolerate Within Its Borders," *Canadian Journal of Philosophy* 37 (2007): 479–513.

What Toleration Is." *Ethics* Volume 115, 2004: 68–95.

Cohen, G. A. "Expensive Taste Rides Again," in *Dworkin and His Critics,* ed. J. Burley. Oxford: Blackwell, 2004, 3–29.

"Freedom and Money," in *On the Currency of Egalitarian Justice, and Other Essays in Political Philosophy,* ed. M. Otsuka. Princeton University Press, 2011, 166–92.

If You're an Egalitarian, How Come You're So Rich? Cambridge, MA: Harvard University Press, 2000.

"On the Currency of Egalitarian Justice," *Ethics* 99 (1989): 906–44.

Rescuing Justice and Equality. Cambridge, MA: Harvard University Press, 2008.

Cohen, Joshua. *The Arc of the Moral Universe.* Cambridge, MA: Harvard University Press, 2010.

"Deliberation and Democratic Legitimacy," in *Deliberative Democracy,* ed. James Bohman and William Rehg. Cambridge, MA: MIT Press, 2002, 67–92.

Philosophy, Politics, Democracy. Cambridge, MA: Harvard University Press, 2009.

"Procedure and Substance in Deliberative Democracy," repr. in *Philosophy and Democracy: An Anthology,* ed. Thomas Christiano. Oxford University Press, 2002, 17–38.

"Reflections on Habermas on Democracy," *Ratio Juris* 12, 2 (2002): 385–416.

Rousseau: A Free Community of Equals. Oxford University Press, 2010.

"Truth and Public Reason," *Philosophy & Public Affairs* 37, 1 (2009): 2–42.

Colburn, Ben. "Forbidden Ways of Life," *The Philosophical Quarterly* 58, 233 (2008): 618–29.

Connolly, William. *The Ethos of Pluralization.* Minneapolis: University of Minnesota Press, 1995.

Constant, Benjamin. *Political Writings,* ed. B. Fontana. Cambridge University Press, 1988.

Copp, David. "Reasonable Acceptability and Democratic Legitimacy: Estlund's Qualified Acceptability Requirement," *Ethics* 121, 2 (2011): 239–69.

Croly, Herbert. *The Promise of American Life* [1909]. New York: Capricorn Press, 1964.

Progressive Democracy. New Brunswick, NJ: Transaction Books, 1998 [1914].

Crowder, George. *Isaiah Berlin.* Cambridge University Press, 2004.

"Two Concepts of Liberal Pluralism," *Political Theory* 35 (2007): 121–46.

Cudd, Ann. *Analysing Oppression.* New York: Oxford University Press, 2006.

Cuypers, Stefan. *Moral Responsibility, Authenticity, and Education.* New York: Routledge, 2008.

D'Agostino, Fred. *Free Public Reason: Making it Up as We Go.* Oxford University Press, 1996.

Dagger, Richard. *Civic Virtues: Rights, Citizenship, and Republican Liberalism.* Oxford University Press, 1997.

Dahl, Robert. *Democracy and Its Critics.* New Haven: Yale University Press, 1989.

Darwall, Stephen. "Introduction," in *Contractarianism/Contractualism*, ed. Stephen Darwall. Oxford: Wiley-Blackwell, 2003, 1–8.

Davis, Gordon and Neufeld, Blain. "Political Liberalism, Civic Education, and Educational Choice," *Social Theory and Practice* 33 (2007): 47–74.

Delbanco, Andrew. *The Portable Abraham Lincoln.* New York: Penguin Books, 1992.

De Tracey, Antoine Louis Claude Destutt. *A Treatise on Political Economy.* Indianapolis: Liberty Fund, 2011.

Dewey, John. "From Absolutism to Experimentalism," in *John Dewey: The Later Works*, ed. Jo Ann Boydston, vol. V. Carbondale: Southern Illinois University Press, 1984.

"Individualism Old and New" [1930], in *John Dewey: The Later Works*, ed. Jo Ann Boydston, vol. VI. Carbondale: Southern Illinois University Press, 1984, 411–44.

"Liberalism and Social Action" [1936], in *John Dewey: Later Works*, ed. Jo Ann Boydston, vol. XI. Carbondale: Southern Illinois University Press, 1991, 1–66.

Di Stefano, Christine. *Configurations of Masculinity: A Feminist Perspective on Modern Political Theory.* Ithaca, NY: Cornell University Press, 1991.

Dickinson, John. "Letters from a Farmer in Pennsylvania" [1768], in *Classics of American Political and Constitutional Thought*, vol. I: *Origins Through the Civil War*, ed. Scott J. Hammond. Indianapolis: Hackett Publishing, 2007, 200–13.

Diggins, John Patrick. *The Lost Soul of American Politics.* New York: Basic Books, 1984.

Douglass, Frederick. "The Meaning of July Fourth for the Negro," in *Frederick Douglass: Selected Speeches and Writings*, ed. Phillip S. Foner. Chicago: Lawrence Hill, 1999, 188–205.

Dreben, Burton. "On Rawls on Political Liberalism," in *The Cambridge Companion to Rawls*, ed. Samuel Freeman. Cambridge University Press, 2003, 316–46.

Drolet, Michael. *Tocqueville: Democracy and Social Reform*. London: Palgrave, 2003.

Du Bois, W. E. B. *The Suppression of the African Slave Trade to the United States of America 1638–1870* [1897], repr. in *W. E. B. Du Bois: Writings*, ed. Nathan I. Huggins. New York: The Library of America, 1986.

Dubnov, Arie. *Isaiah Berlin: The Journey of a Jewish Liberal*. New York: Palgrave Macmillan, 2012.

Dunn, John. *The Political Thought of John Locke*. Cambridge University Press, 1969.

Dunoyer, Charles. "Notice historique sur l'industrialisme," in *Œuvres de Charles Dunoyer* (II). Paris: Ulan Press, 1870, 173–99.

Durkheim, Emile. *Professional Ethics and Civic Morals*. London: Routledge and Kegan Paul, 1957.

Dworkin, Gerald. *The Theory and Practice of Autonomy*. Cambridge University Press, 1990.

Dworkin, Ronald. "Liberalism," in *Public and Private Morality*, ed. S. Hampshire. Cambridge University Press, 1978, 113–41.

"Rights as Trumps," in *Theories of Rights*, ed. Jeremy Waldron. Oxford University Press, 1984, 153–67.

Sovereign Virtue: The Theory and Practice of Equality. Cambridge, MA: Harvard University Press, 2000.

Taking Rights Seriously. Cambridge, MA: Harvard University Press, 1977.

Ehler, Sidney Z. *Twenty Centuries of Church and State*. Charlotte, NC: Newman Press, 1957.

Ehler, Sidney Z. and Morall, John B. *Church and State Through the Centuries*. New York: Biblio-Moser, 1988.

Eisenberg, A. and Spinner-Halev, J. (eds.). *Minorities within Minorities: Equality, Rights and Diversity*. Cambridge University Press, 2005.

Eisenstein, Zillah. *The Female Body and the Law*. Berkeley: University of California Press, 1988.

The Radical Future of Liberal Feminism. New York: Longman, 1981.

Elkins, Stanley and McKitrick, Eric. *The Age of Federalism*. New York: Oxford University Press, 1993.

Elshtain, Jean Bethke. *Public Man, Private Woman: Women in Social and Political Thought*. Princeton University Press, 1981.

Engels, F. "Anti-Dühring," in *The Marx-Engels Reader*, 2nd edn., ed. R. C. Tucker. New York: W.W. Norton and Co., 1978, 725–27.

Epstein, Richard. *Principles for a Free Society: Reconciling Individual Liberty with the Common Good*. New York: Basic Books, 1998.

Ericson, David F. *The Shaping of American Liberalism*. University of Chicago Press, 1993.

Estlund, David M. *Democratic Authority: A Philosophical Framework*. Princeton University Press, 2008.

Ewin, R. E. *Virtue and Rights: The Moral Philosophy of Thomas Hobbes*. Boulder, CO: Westview, 1991.

Feinberg, Joel. "The Child's Right to an Open Future," repr. in Feinberg, *Freedom and Fulfillment: Philosophical Essays*. Princeton University Press, 1992, 76–97.

Harm to Others. New York: Oxford University Press, 1984.

Ferguson, Michaele L. "Choice Feminism and the Fear of Politics," *Perspectives on Politics* 8, 1 (March 2010): 247–53.

Fitzhugh, George. *Cannibals All!: or Slaves Without Masters*. Cambridge, MA: Harvard University Press, 1988.

Foner, Eric. *Free Soil, Free Labor, Free Men: The Ideology of the Republican Party Before the Civil War*. New York: Oxford University Press, 1970.

Politics and Ideology in the Age of the Civil War. New York: Oxford University Press, 1980.

Force, Pierre. *Self-Interest Before Adam Smith: A Genealogy of Economic Science*. Cambridge University Press, 2003.

Forcey, Charles. *Crossroads of Liberalism*. New York: Oxford University Press, 1961.

Forman-Barzilai, Fonna. *Adam Smith and the Circles of Sympathy: Cosmopolitanism and Moral Theory*. Cambridge University Press, 2010.

Frankfurt, Harry. "The Faintest Passion," *Proceedings and Addresses of the Aristotelian Society* 49 (1992): 113–45.

"Freedom of the Will and the Concept of the Person," in Frankfurt, *The Importance of What We Care About: Philosophical Essays*. Cambridge University Press, 1987, 11–25.

Fraser, Nancy. "Beyond the Subject/Master Model: Reflections on Carole Pateman's Sexual Contract," *Social Text* 37 (Winter 1993): 173–81.

Freeman, Samuel. "The Burdens of Public Justification: Constructivism, Contractualism, and Publicity,"*Politics, Philosophy & Economics* 6, 1 (2007): 5–43.

"Can Economic Liberties be Basic Liberties?" (http://bleedingheartlibertarians.com/2012/06/can-economic-liberties-be-basic-liberties/).

"Capitalism in the Classical and High Liberal Traditions," *Social Philosophy & Policy*, 28 (2011): 19–55.

"Illiberal Libertarians: Why Libertarianism Is Not a Liberal View," *Philosophy and Public Affairs*, 30, 2 (2001): 105–15.

Justice and the Social Contract: Essays on Rawlsian Political Philosophy. New York: Oxford University Press, 2006.

"Public Reason and Political Justification," in Freeman, *Justice and the Social Contract: Essays on Rawlsian Political Philosophy*. Oxford University Press, 2006, 215–56.

"Social Contract Approaches," in *Oxford Handbook of Political Philosophy*, ed. David M. Estlund. Oxford University Press, 2012, 133–51.

Frey, Sylvia R. *Water from Rock: Black Resistance in a Revolutionary Age*. Princeton University Press, 1992.

Friedman, Marilyn. "John Rawls and the Political Coercion of Unreasonable People," in *The Idea of A Political Liberalism: Essays on Rawls*, ed. Victoria Davion and Clark Wolf. Lanham, MD: Rowman & Littlefield, 2000, 16–33.

Friedman, Milton. *Capitalism and Freedom*. University of Chicago Press, 2002.

Furet, François. "The French Revolution Is Over," in Furet, *Interpreting the French Revolution*. Cambridge University Press, 1981, 1–79.

Galloway, Joseph. "Candid Examination of the Mutual Claims of Great Britain and the Colonies" [1775], in *Tracts of the American Revolution*, ed. Merrill Jensen. Indianapolis: Hackett Publishing, 2003, 350–99.

Galston, William. *Liberal Pluralism: The Implications of Value Pluralism for Political Theory and Practice*. New York: Cambridge University Press, 2002.

"Two Concepts of Liberalism," *Ethics* 105, 3 (1995): 516–34.

Garston, Bryan. "Religion and the Case Against Ancient Liberty: Benjamin Constant's Other Lectures," *Political Theory* 20, 10 (2009): 1–30.

Gasset, Ortega y. *The Revolt of the Masses* [1930]. New York: W. W. Norton, 1957.

Gatens, Moira. "'The Oppressed State of My Sex': Wollstonecraft on Reason, Feeling, and Equality," in *Feminist Interpretations and Political Theory*, ed. Mary Lyndon Shanley and Carole Pateman. University Park: Pennsylvania State University Press, 1991, 112–28.

Gaus, Gerald. "Coercion, Ownership, and the Redistributive State: Justificatory Liberalism's Classical Tilt," *Social Philosophy & Policy* 27 (2010): 233–75.

Contemporary Theories of Liberalism: Public Reason as a Post-Enlightenment Project. London: Sage, 2003.

"Hobbes' Challenge to Public Reason Liberalism," in *Hobbes Today: Insights for the 21st Century*, ed. S. A. Lloyd. Cambridge University Press, 2013, 155–77.

"Hobbesian Contractarianism, Orthodox and Revisionist," in *The Continuum Companion to Hobbes*, ed. S. A. Lloyd. New York: Bloomsbury, 2013, 263–78.

Justificatory Liberalism. New York: Oxford University Press, 1996.

"On Justifying the Rights of the Moderns: A Case of Old Wine in New Bottles," *Social Philosophy & Policy* 24 (2007): 84–119.

"On the Appropriate Mode of Justifying a Public Moral Constitution," *Harvard Review of Philosophy* 19 (2013): 4–22.

The Order of Public Reason: Freedom and Morality in a Diverse and Bounded World. Cambridge University Press, 2011.

"The Place of Religious Belief in Public Reason Liberalism," in *Multiculturalism and Moral Conflict*, ed. Maria Dimovia-Cookson and P. M. R. Stirk. London: Routledge, 2009, 19–37.

"Property and Ownership," in *Oxford Handbook of Political Philosophy*, ed. David M. Estlund. Oxford University Press, 2012, 93–113.

"The Role of Conservatism in Securing and Maintaining Just Moral Constitutions," in *Nomos: Whither Conservatism?*, ed. Sanford Levinson and Melissa Williams. New York University Press, forthcoming.

"A Tale of Two Sets: Public Reason in Equilibrium," *Public Affairs Quarterly*, 25 (2011): 305–25.

"The Turn to a Political Liberalism," in *The Blackwell Companion to Rawls*, ed. David Reidy and Jon Mandle. New York: Wiley-Blackwell, 2014, 235–50.

Gaus, Gerald and Courtland, Shane. "Liberalism," in *The Stanford Encyclopedia of Philosophy* (http://plato.stanford.edu/entries/liberalism/).

Gauthier, David. *Morals by Agreement*. Oxford: Clarendon Press, 1986.

"Public Reason," *Social Philosophy & Policy*, vol. 12 (1995): 19–42.

"Twenty-Five On," *Ethics* 123, 4 (2013): 601–24.

"Why Contractarianism?" in *Contractarianism and Rational Choice: Essays on David Gauthier's Moral's by Agreement*, ed. Peter Vallentyne. Cambridge University Press, 1991, 15–30.

Gellner, Ernest. *Nations and Nationalism*. Oxford: Blackwell, 1983.

Gerhard, Ute. *Debating Women's Equality: Toward a Feminist Theory of Law from a European Perspective*, trans. Allison Brown and Belinda Cooper. New Brunswick, NJ: Rutgers University Press, 2001.

Gore, George and Hobhouse, L. T. (eds.). *Property, Its Rights and Duties*. London: Macmillan, 1913.

Gibson, Alan. "Ancients, Moderns and Americans: The Republicanism-Liberalism Debate Revisited," *History of Political Thought*, 21, 2 (2000): 261–307.

"Impartial Representation and the Extended Republic: Towards a Comprehensive and Balanced Interpretation of the Tenth Federalist," *History of Political Thought* 12 (1991), 263–304.

Gilbert, Margaret. *Sociality and Responsibility*. Lanham, MD: Rowman & Littlefield, 2000.

Gilligan, Carol. *In a Different Voice*. Cambridge, MA: Harvard University Press, 1982.

Goodin, Robert E. "Folie républicaine," *Annual Review of Political Science* 6 (2003): 55–76.

Gray, John. *Liberalism*. Milton Keynes: Open University Press, 1986.

Post-Liberalism: Studies in Political Thought. London: Routledge, 1993.

"Reply to Critics," *Critical Review of International Social and Political Philosophy* 9, 2 (2006): 323–47.

Green, T. H. *Prolegomena to Ethics*, 5th edn. Oxford: Clarendon Press, 1906.

Greenleaf, W. H. *The British Political Tradition: The Ideological Heritage*. London: Routledge, 1983.

Greenstone, J. David. *The Lincoln Persuasion: Remaking American Liberalism*. Princeton University Press, 1993.

Gutmann, Amy. "Civic Education and Social Diversity," *Ethics* 105, 3 (1985): 557–79.

Democratic Education. Princeton University Press, 1987.

Guyer, Paul. *Kant on Freedom, Law, and Happiness*. Cambridge University Press, 2000.

Habermas, Jurgen. *Between Facts and Norms*. Cambridge, MA: MIT Press, 1996.

Hampsher-Monk, Iain. *A History of Modern Political Thought*. Oxford: Blackwell, 1992.

Hampton, Jean. "The Common Faith of Liberalism," in *The Intrinsic Worth of Persons*, ed. Daniel Farnham. Cambridge University Press, 2006, 151–84.

"Should Political Philosophy Be Done without Metaphysics?", *Ethics* 99 (1989): 791–814.

"Two Faces of Contractarian Thought," in *Contractarianism and Rational Choice: Essays on David Gauthier's Morals by Agreement*, ed. Peter Vallentyne. Cambridge University Press, 1991, 31–55.

Hanley, Ryan Patrick. *Adam Smith and the Character of Virtue*. Cambridge University Press, 2009.

Harrington, James. *The Commonwealth of Oceana and A System of Politics*, ed. J. G. A. Pocock. Cambridge University Press, 1992.

Hart, H. L. A. "Rawls on Liberty and Its Priority," *University of Chicago Law Review* 40, 3 (1973): 534–55.

Hartley, Christie. "An Inclusive Contractualism: Obligations to the Mentally Disabled," in *Disability and Disadvantage*, ed. Kimberley Brownlee and Adam Cureton. Oxford University Press, 2009, 138–61.

"Justice for the Disabled: A Contractualist Approach," *Journal of Social Philosophy* 40, 1 (2009): 17–36.

Hartley, Christie and Watson, Lori. "Feminism, Religion, and Shared Reasons: A Defense of Exclusive Public Reason," *Law and Philosophy* 28 (2009): 493–536.

Hartsock, Nancy. *Money, Sex, and Power: Toward a Feminist Historical Materialism.* New York: Longman, 1983.

Hartz, Louis. *The Liberal Tradition in America.* New York: Harcourt, 1955.

Hayek, F. A. *The Constitution of Liberty.* University of Chicago Press, 1960.

"The Errors of Constructivism," in Hayek, *New Studies in Philosophy, Politics, Economics and the History of Ideas.* London: Routledge and Kegan Paul, 1978, 3–22.

Law, Legislation, and Liberty, vol. II: *The Mirage of Social Justice.* University of Chicago Press, 1978.

"The Pretence of Knowledge," in *New Studies in Philosophy, Politics, Economics and the History of Ideas.* London: Routledge and Kegan Paul, 1978, 23–34.

Head, B. W. *Ideology and Social Science: Destutt de Tracy and Liberalism.* Dordrecht: Martinus Nijhoff, 1985.

Hegel, G. W. F. *Elements of the Philosophy of Right.* Cambridge University Press, 1991.

Hick, John. *Interpretation of Religion.* London: Palgrave Macmillan, 2004.

Higgins, Tracy E. "Gender, Why Feminists Can't (or Shouldn't) Be Liberals," *Fordham Law Review* 72, 5 (2004): 1629–41.

Hirschman, Albert. *Exit, Voice and Loyalty.* Cambridge, MA: Harvard University Press, 1970.

The Passions and the Interests: Political Arguments for Capitalism before its Triumph. Princeton University Press, 1977.

Hirschman, Linda R. *Get to Work: A Manifesto for Women of the World.* New York: Viking Press, 2006.

Hirschmann, Nancy. *Rethinking Obligation: A Feminist Method for Political Theory.* Ithaca, NY: Cornell University Press, 1992.

The Subject of Liberty: Toward a Feminist Theory of Freedom. Princeton University Press, 2003.

Hobbes, Thomas. *Leviathan,* ed. Edwin Curley. Indianapolis: Hackett Publishing, 1994.

Leviathan, ed. J. C. A. Gaskin. Oxford University Press, 1996.

Hobhouse, L. T. *Liberalism.* London: Henry Holt, 1911.

The Rational Good. New York: Henry Holt, 1921.

Social Evolution and Political Theory. New York: Columbia University Press, 1913.

Hofstadter, Richard. *The American Political Tradition.* New York: Vintage Books, 1948.

Holmes, Stephen. *The Anatomy of Antiliberalism.* Cambridge, MA: Harvard University Press, 1993.

Holtug, Nils. *Persons, Interests, and Justice.* Oxford University Press, 2010.

Honneth, Axel. *The Struggle for Recognition.* Cambridge, MA: MIT Press, 1994.

Honoré, A. "Ownership," in *Oxford Essays in Jurisprudence*, ed. A. G. Guest. Oxford: Clarendon Press, 1961, 107–47.

Hont, Istvan. "The Early Enlightenment Debate on Commerce and Luxury," in *The Cambridge History of Eighteenth-Century Political Thought*, ed. Mark Goldie and Robert Wokler. Cambridge University Press, 2006, 379–418.

Hooker, Brad. *Ideal Code, Real World: A Rule-Consequentialist Theory of Morality*. Oxford University Press, 2000.

Hopkins, Stephen. "The Rights of the Colonies Examined" [1764], in *Classics of American Political and Constitutional Thought, vol. I: Origins Through the Civil War*, ed. Scott J. Hammond. Indianapolis: Hackett Publishing, 2007, 160–66.

Hume, David. *A History of England*, 6 vols. Indianapolis: Liberty Fund, 1754–62. "Of the Original Contract," in *Hume: Political Writings*, ed. Stuart D. Warner and Donald W. Livingston. Indianapolis: Hackett Publishing, 1994, 164–81. *Political Essays*, ed. Knud Haakonson. Cambridge University Press, 1994. *A Treatise of Human Nature*, ed. L. A. Selby-Bigge, 3 vols. London: Clarendon Press, 1739–40.

Hundert, E. J. *The Enlightenment's Fable: Bernard Mandeville and the Discovery of Society*. Cambridge University Press, 2005.

Hurka, Thomas. *Perfectionism*. New York: Oxford University Press, 1993.

Huyler, Jerome. *Locke in America: The Moral Philosophy of the Founding Era*. Lawrence: University Press of Kansas, 1995.

Hyneman, Charles and Lutz, Donald. *American Political Writings During the Founding Era, 1760–1805*, vol. I. Indianapolis: Liberty Fund, 1983.

Irwin, T. *The Development of Ethics: A Historical and Critical Study*. Oxford University Press, 2007–2009.

Jaggar, Alison. *Feminist Politics and Human Nature*. Totowa, NJ: Rowman and Allanheld, 1983.

Jaume, Lucien. *Tocqueville: The Aristocratic Sources of Liberty*. Princeton University Press, 2013.

Jefferson, Thomas. "A View of the Rights of British America," in *The Portable Thomas Jefferson*, ed. Merrill D. Peterson. New York: Penguin, 1975, 3–21

Kallen, Horace. "Dewey and Pragmatism," in *John Dewey, Philosopher of Science and Freedom*, ed. Sidney Hook. New York: Dial Press, 1950, 3–46. "Individuality, Individualism, and John Dewey," *Antioch Review*, 19, 3 (1959): 299–314.

Kalyvas, Andreas and Katznelson, Ira. *Liberal Beginnings: Making a Republic for the Moderns*. New York: Cambridge University Press, 2008.

Kant, Immanuel. *Groundwork of the Metaphysics of Morals*, trans. M. Gregor. Cambridge University Press, 1997.

The Metaphysical Elements of Justice, 2nd edn., ed. and trans. John Ladd. Indianapolis: Hackett Publishing, 1999.

"Metaphysical First Principles of the Doctrine of Right," in *The Metaphysics of Morals*. Cambridge University Press, 1996.

Religion Within the Bounds of Reason Alone, trans. T. M. Greene and H. H. Hudson. New York: Harper & Brothers, 1960.

Kelly, Duncan. *The Propriety of Liberty: Persons, Passions & Judgement in Modern Political Thought*. Princeton University Press, 2011.

Kelly, Paul. *Utilitarianism and Distributive Justice: Jeremy Bentham and the Civil Law*. Oxford: Clarendon Press, 1990.

Ketcham, Ralph. *Framed for Posterity: The Enduring Philosophy of the Constitution*. Lawrence: University of Kansas Press, 1993.

Knowles, Dudley. *Hegel and the Philosophy of Right*. London: Routledge, 2002.

Korsgaard, Christine. *The Sources of Normativity*. New York: Cambridge University Press, 1996.

Kukathas, Chandran. "Are There Any Cultural Rights?" *Political Theory* 20, 1 (1992): 105–39.

The Liberal Archipelago. New York: Oxford University Press, 2003.

Kymlicka, Will. *Contemporary Political Philosophy*. Oxford University Press, 1990.

Finding our Way. Rethinking Ethnocultural Relations in Canada. Oxford University Press, 2008.

Liberalism, Community and Culture. Oxford: Clarendon Press, 1989.

Multicultural Citizenship: A Liberal Theory of Minority Rights. Oxford: Clarendon Press, 1995.

Laborde, Cécile and Maynor, John (eds.). *Republicanism and Political Theory*. London: Blackwell, 2008.

Laden, Anthony Simon. "Negotiation, Deliberation and the Claims of Politics," in *Multiculturalism and Political Theory*, ed. A. S. Laden and D. Owen. Cambridge University Press, 2007, 1–22.

Lampedusa, Giuseppe di. *The Leopard*. London, Vintage Books, 1960.

Landes, Joan B. *Women and the Public Sphere in the Age of the French Revolution*. Ithaca, NY: Cornell University Press, 1988.

Larmore, Charles. *The Autonomy of Morality*. Cambridge University Press, 2008.

"The Moral Basis of Political Liberalism," *The Journal of Philosophy* 96, 12 (1999): 599–625.

Patterns of Moral Complexity. Cambridge University Press, 1987.

"Political Liberalism," in Larmore, *The Morals of Modernity*. Cambridge University Press, 1996, 121–51.

Laski, H. J. *Political Thought in England From Locke to Bentham*. Ann Arbor: University of Michigan Press, 1920.

Lincoln, Abraham. "Address at Gettysburg, Pennsylvania, November 19, 1863," in *The Portable Abraham Lincoln*, ed. Andrew Delbanco. New York: Penguin Books, 1992, 295.

Locke, John. *Essays on the Law of Nature*, ed. W. V. Leyden. Oxford: Clarendon Press, 1988.

"A Letter Concerning Toleration," in the *Works of John Locke in Nine Volumes*, 12th edn., vol. v, London: Rivington, 1824, 1–58.

Persons, Rights, and the Moral Community. New York: Oxford University Press, 1987.

Second Treatise of Government, ed. C. B. Macpherson. Indianapolis: Hackett Publishing, 1980.

Second Treatise of Government, in *Locke: Two Treatises of Government*, ed. Peter Laslett. Cambridge University Press, 1960.

Lomasky, L. *Persons, Rights and the Moral Community*. Oxford University Press, 1990.

Lovett, Frank. *A General Theory of Domination and Justice*. Oxford University Press, 2010.

"Republicanism," in *Stanford Encyclopedia of Philosophy*, ed. Edward N. Zalta (http://plato.stanford.edu/archives/spr2013/entries/republicanism/).

Lovett, Frank and Pettit, Philip. "Neorepublicanism: A Normative and Institutional Research Program," *Annual Review of Political Science* 12 (2009): 11–29.

Macaulay, Thomas Babington. *Miscellaneous Writings and Speeches*. London: Longmans, Green and Co., 1889.

Macedo, Stephen. *Diversity and Distrust: Civic Education in a Multicultural Democracy*. Cambridge, MA: Harvard University Press, 2000.

Machiavelli, Niccolò. *The Discourses*, trans. L. J. Walker. New York: Penguin Books, 1983.

MacIntyre, Alasdair. *After Virtue*. Notre Dame: University of Notre Dame Press, 1981.

Whose Justice, Which Rationality? London: Duckworth, 1988.

Mack, Eric and Gaus, Gerald. "Classical Liberalism and Libertarianism: The Liberty Tradition," in *Handbook of Political Theory*, ed. Gerald Gaus and Chandran Kukathas. New York: Sage Publications, 2004, 115–30.

Mackenzie, Catriona and Stoljar, Nathalie. *Relational Autonomy: Feminist Perspectives on Autonomy, Agency, and the Social Self*. New York: Oxford University Press, 2000.

MacKinnon, Catharine. "Feminism, Marxism, Method, and the State: Toward a Feminist Jurisprudence," *Signs* 8, 4 (Summer 1983): 635–58.

Toward a Feminist Theory of the State. Cambridge, MA: Harvard University Press, 1989.

Macpherson, C. B. *The Political Theory of Possessive Individualism*. Oxford University Press, 2011.

Madison, James. *James Madison: Writings*, ed. Jack N. Rakove. New York: Library of America, 1999.

Mallet, Louis. *The Political Writings of Richard Cobden*. London: T. Fischer Unwin, 1903.

Mandeville, Bernard. *The Fable of the Bees or Private Vices, Publick Benefits*. Indianapolis: Liberty Fund, 1988.

Maoine, Angela. "Revolutionary Rhetoric: The Political Thought of Mary Wollstonecraft," Ph.D. dissertation, Northwestern University, 2012.

Margalit, Avashai and Halbertal, Moshe. "Liberalism and the Right to Culture," *Social Research* 61, 3 (1994): 491–510.

Margalit, Avashai and Raz, Joseph. "National Self-Determination," *Journal of Philosophy* 87 (1990): 439–61.

Marshall, John. *John Locke: Resistance, Religion and Responsibility*. Cambridge University Press, 1994.

Marx, Karl. "Critique of the Gotha Program," in *The Marx-Engels Reader*, 2nd edn., ed. R. Tucker. New York: W. W. Norton, 1978, 525–41.

May, Henry F. *The Enlightenment in America*. New York: Oxford University Press, 1978.

Mazower, Mark. *Dark Continent*. London: Penguin, 1998.

McClain, Linda C. "'Atomistic Man' Revisited: Liberalism, Connection, and Feminist Jurisprudence," *Southern California Law Review* 65 (March 1992): 1161–274.

McPherson, James M. *Abraham Lincoln and the Second American Revolution*. New York: Oxford University Press, 1990.

Medearis, Joseph A. *Schumpeter*. New York: Continuum, 2009.

Meisels, T. *Territorial Rights*. New York: Springer, 2009.

Mele, Alfred. *Autonomous Agents: From Self-Control to Autonomy*. New York: Oxford University Press, 1995.

Meyers, Diana. *Self, Society and Personal Choice*. New York: Columbia University Press, 1989.

Mill, J. S. "Bentham," in *Mill: Essays on Politics and Culture*, ed. Gertrude Himmelfarb. New York: Doubleday, 1963, 77–120.

Considerations on Representative Government. Amherst, NY: Prometheus Books, 1991.

"De Tocqueville on Democracy in America (Vol. I)," in *Mill: Essays on Politics and Culture*, ed. Gertrude Himmelfarb. New York: Doubleday, 1962, 187–229.

Liberty and The Subjection of Women. London: Penguin Books, 2006.

On Liberty, ed. Elizabeth Rapaport. Indianapolis: Hackett Publishing, 1978.

Principles of Political Economy. Harmondsworth: Penguin, 1970.

The Subjection of Women, in *On Liberty and Other Essays*, ed. John Gray. New York: Oxford University Press, 1991.

Utilitarianism, ed. George Sher. Indianapolis: Hackett Publishing, 2002.

Miller, David. *National Responsibility and Global Justice*. Oxford University Press, 2007.

On Nationality. Oxford University Press, 1999.

Miller, Perry. *Errand into the Wilderness*. Cambridge, MA: Belknap Press, 1956.

The New England Mind: From Colony to Province. Boston: Beacon Press, 1961.

Mills, Charles W. *The Racial Contract*. Ithaca, NY: Cornell University Press, 1997.

Mills, Claudia. "'Not a Mere Modus Vivendi': The Bases for Allegiance to the Just State," in *The Idea of A Political Liberalism: Essays on Rawls*, ed. Victoria Davion and Clark Wolf. Lanham, MD: Rowman & Littlefield, 2000, 190–203.

Milton, John. "The Readie and Easie Way to Establish a Free Commonwealth," in Milton, *Areopagitica and Other Political Writings*. Indianapolis: Liberty Fund, 1999, 414–49.

Minow, Martha. *Making All the Difference: Inclusion, Exclusion, and American Law*. Ithaca, NY: Cornell University Press, 1990.

Montesquieu, Charles de Secondat. *The Spirit of the Laws*, trans. Thomas Nugent. New York: Hafner Press, 1966.

The Spirit of the Laws. Cambridge University Press, 2002.

Moore, Margaret. *The Ethics of Nationalism*. Oxford University Press, 2001.

Morgan, Edmund. *American Freedom, American Slavery: The Ordeal of Colonial Virginia*. New York: Norton, 1975.

Morone, James. *Hellfire Nation: The Politics of Sin in American History*. New Haven: Yale University Press, 2003.

Morris, Christopher. "Justice, Reasons, and Moral Standing," in *Rational Commitment and Social Justice: Essays for Gregory Kavka*, ed. Jules L. Coleman and Christopher Morris. Cambridge University Press, 1998, 186–207.

"Moral Standing and Rational-Choice Contractarianism," in *Contractarianism and Rational Choice: Essays on David Gauthier's Morals by Agreement*, ed. Peter Vallentyne. Cambridge University Press, 1991, 76–95.

Mouffe, Chantal. *The Democratic Paradox*. London: Verso, 2000.

Mowry, George. *Theodore Roosevelt and the Progressive Movement.* Madison: University of Wisconsin Press, 1946.

Muldoon, Ryan, Lisciandra, C., Colvyan, M., Martini, C., Sillari, G., and Sprenger, J. "Disagreement Behind the Veil of Ignorance," *Philosophical Studies* 170 (2014): 377–94.

Mulhall, Stephen and Swift, Adam. "Rawls and Communitarianism," in *The Cambridge Companion to Rawls,* ed. Samuel Freeman. Cambridge University Press, 2003, 460–87.

Myrdal, Gunnar. *An American Dilemma: The Negro Problem and American Democracy.* New York: Harper and Row, 1944.

Nagel, Thomas. *Equality and Partiality.* Oxford University Press, 1991.

"Libertarianism Without Foundations," repr. in Nagel, *Other Minds.* New York: Oxford University Press, 1995, 137–49.

"Moral Conflict and Political Legitimacy," *Philosophy and Public Affairs* 16, 3 (1987): 214–40.

"The Problem of Global Justice," *Philosophy and Public Affairs* 33 (2005): 215–40.

Narveson, Jan. *The Libertarian Idea.* Philadelphia: Temple University Press, 1988.

Nash, Gary B. *Race and Revolution.* Madison: University of Wisconsin Press, 1990.

Nedelsky, Jennifer. *Private Property and the Limits of American Constitutionalism.* University of Chicago Press, 1990.

Neuhouser, Frederick. "Hegel's Social Philosophy," in *The Cambridge Companion to Hegel and Nineteenth Century Philosophy,* ed. Frederick Beiser. Cambridge University Press, 2008, 204–29.

Nickel, James. "Economic Liberties," in *The Idea of Political Liberalism: Essays on Rawls,* ed. V. Davion and C. Wolf. Lanham, MD: Rowman & Littlefield, 2000, 155–76.

Nietzsche, F. *The Will to Power,* trans. W. Kaufrman. New York: Random House, 1967.

Nozick, Robert. *Anarchy, State, and Utopia.* New York: Basic Books, 1974.

Nussbaum, Martha. *Frontiers of Justice: Disability, Nationality, Species Membership.* Cambridge, MA: Harvard University Press, 2007.

"Perfectionist Liberalism and Political Liberalism," *Philosophy and Public Affairs* 319, 1 (2011): 3–45.

Political Emotions. Cambridge, MA: Bellknap Press, 2013.

Sex and Social Justice. Oxford University Press, 1998.

Oakeshott, Michael. "Rationalism in Politics," in Oakeshott, *Rationalism in Politics and Other Essays.* London: Methuen, 1962, 3–36.

O'Donovan, Oliver and Lockwood, Joan. *From Irenaeus to Grotius: A Sourcebook in Christian Political Thought: 100–1625.* Grand Rapids, MI: Wm. B. Eerdmans Publ. Co., 1999.

Okin, Susan Moller. "Gender, Justice and Gender: An Unfinished Debate,"
    Fordham Law Review 72, 5 (2004): 1537–67.
    Gender, Justice, and the Family. New York: Basic Books, 1989.
    "Humanist Liberalism," in *Liberalism and Moral Life,* ed. Nancy
    L. Rosenblum. Cambridge, MA: Harvard University Press, 1989, 55–80.
    Is Multiculturalism Bad for Women? ed. Joshua Cohen, Matthew Howard,
    and Martha C. Nussbaum. Princeton University Press, 1999.
    "Is Multiculturalism Bad for Women?" in Okin, *Is Multiculturalism Bad
    for Women?,* ed. Joshua Cohen, Matthew Howard, and Martha
    C. Nussbaum. Princeton University Press, 1999, 9–24.
    "Multiculturalism and Feminism: No Simple Question, No Simple
    Answers," in *Minorities Within Minorities: Equality, Rights and
    Diversity,* ed. Avigail Eisenberg and Jeff Spinner-Halev. Cambridge
    University Press, 2005, 67–89.
Oshana, Marina. *Personal Autonomy in Society.* Aldershot, UK: Ashgate
    Publishing, 2006.
Otis, James. "Rights of the British Colonies Asserted and Proved" [1764], in
    Classics of American Political and Constitutional Thought, vol. I:
    Origins Through the Civil War, ed. Scott J. Hammond. Indianapolis:
    Hackett Publishing, 2007, 154–59.
Otsuka, M. *Libertarianism Without Inequality.* Oxford: Clarendon Press,
    2003.
Orwell, George. *Homage to Catalonia.* New York: Harcourt, Brace, and
    World, 1952.
Paine, Thomas. "Common Sense," in *Rights of Man, Common Sense, and
    Other Political Writings,* ed. Mark Philp. Oxford University Press, 1995,
    1–79.
Paley, William. *The Principles of Moral and Political Philosophy.*
    Indianapolis: Liberty Fund, 2002.
Parekh, Bhikhu. "Decolonising Liberalism," in *The End of 'Isms'? Reflections
    on the Fate of Ideological Politics after Communism's Collapse,* ed.
    A. Shtromos. Oxford University Press, 1994, 85–103.
    Rethinking Multiculturalism: Cultural Diversity and Political Theory.
    London: Macmillan, 2000.
Parfit, Derek. "Equality or Priority?", repr. in *The Ideal of Equality,* ed.
    Matthew Clayton and Andrew Williams. New York: Macmillan and
    St. Martin's Press, 2000, 81–125.
Parsons, Wayne. "Politics and Markets: Keynes and His Critics," in *The
    Cambridge History of Twentieth-Century Political Thought,* ed.
    Terence Ball and Richard Bellamy. Cambridge University Press, 2003,
    45–69.

Pateman, Carole. *The Disorder of Women: Democracy, Feminism, and Political Theory*. Stanford University Press, 1989.

"'God Hath Ordained to Man a Helper': Hobbes, Patriarchy, and Conjugal Right," in *Feminist Interpretations and Political Theory*, ed. Mary Lyndon Shanley and Carole Pateman. University Park: Pennsylvania State University Press, 1991, 53–73.

The Problem of Political Obligation. New York: John Wiley and Sons, 1978.

The Sexual Contract. Stanford University Press, 1988.

Pennington, Mark. *Robust Political Economy: Classical Liberalism and the Future of Public Policy*. Cheltenham: Edward Elgar, 2011.

Pettit, Philip. "Can Contract Theory Ground Morality?" in *Contemporary Debates in Moral Theory*, ed. James Dreier. Oxford: Blackwell, 2006, 77–96.

"The Freedom of the City: A Republican Ideal," in *The Good Polity*, ed. Alan Hamlin and Philip Pettit. London: Blackwell, 1989, 141–68.

On the People's Terms: A Republican Theory and Model of Democracy. Cambridge University Press, 2012.

Republicanism: A Theory of Freedom. New York: Oxford University Press, 1997.

Phillips, Anne. *Engendering Democracy*. University Park: Pennsylvania State University Press, 1991.

The Politics of Presence: The Political Representation of Gender, Ethnicity, and Race. New York: Oxford University Press, 1995.

Phillips, David. "Contractualism and Moral Status," *Social Theory and Practice* 24, 2 (1998): 183–204.

Phillipson, Nicholas. *Adam Smith: An Enlightened Life*. London: Penguin, 2010.

Pocock, J. G. A. *The Machiavellian Moment: Florentine Political Thought and the Atlantic Republican Tradition*. Princeton University Press, 1975.

Poole, J. R. *The Pursuit of Equality in American History*, rev. edn. Berkeley: University of California Press, 1993.

Popper, Karl. *The Open Society and Its Enemies*. Princeton University Press, 2012.

Putnam, Robert. *Bowling Alone: The Collapse and Revival of American Community*. New York: Simon and Schuster, 2001.

Quong, Jonathan. *Liberalism Without Perfection*. Oxford University Press, 2011.

Rahe, Paul. *Republics: Ancient and Modern: Classical Republicanism and the American Revolution*. Chapel Hill: University of North Carolina Press, 1992.

Rawls, John. "The Idea of Public Reason Revisited," *University of Chicago Law Review* 63, 3 (Summer 1997): 765–807.

"The Idea of Public Reason Revisited," in *John Rawls: Collected Papers,* 573–615

John Rawls: Collected Papers, ed. Samuel Freeman. Cambridge, MA: Harvard University Press, 1999.

"Justice as Fairness: Political Not Metaphysical," in *John Rawls: Collected Papers,* 47–72.

Justice as Fairness: A Restatement, ed. Erin Kelly. Cambridge, MA: Harvard University Press, 2001.

"Kantian Constructivism in Moral Theory," in *John Rawls: Collected Papers,* 303–58.

The Law of Peoples. Cambridge, MA: Harvard University Press, 1999.

"Outline of a Decision Procedure for Ethics," in *John Rawls: Collected Papers,* 1–19.

Political Liberalism. New York: Columbia University Press, 1993.

"The Priority of Right and Ideas of the Good," in *John Rawls: Collected Papers,* 49–72.

"Reply to Habermas," *Journal of Philosophy* 92, 3 (1995): 132–80.

"Social Unity and Primary Good," in *John Rawls: Collected Papers,* 359–87.

A Theory of Justice. Cambridge, MA: Harvard University Press, 1971.

A Theory of Justice, rev. edn. Oxford University Press, 1999.

Raz, Joseph. "Disagreement in Politics," *American Journal of Jurisprudence* 24 (1998): 25–52.

The Morality of Freedom. Oxford University Press, 1986.

"Multiculturalism," *Ratio Juris* 11, 3 (1998): 193–205.

"Multiculturalism: A Liberal Perspective," *Dissent* 41 (Winter 1994): 67–79.

Rhode, Deborah L. *Justice and Gender: Sex Discrimination and the Law.* Cambridge, MA: Harvard University Press, 1989.

Ridge, Michael. "Saving Scanlon: Contractualism and Agent-Relativity," *Journal of Political Philosophy* 9, 4 (2001): 472–81.

Ripstein, Arthur. *Force and Freedom: Kant's Legal and Political Philosophy.* Cambridge, MA: Harvard University Press, 2009.

Robin, Corey. *The Reactionary Mind.* New York: Oxford University Press, 2010.

Rorty, Richard. *Philosophy and Social Hope.* London: Penguin Books, 1999.

"Post-Modernist Bourgeois Liberalism," *Journal of Philosophy* 80 (1983): 583–89.

Rosenblatt, Helena. *Liberal Values: Benjamin Constant and the Politics of Religion.* Cambridge University Press, 2008.

"On the Need for a Protestant Reformation: Constant, Sismondi, Guizot and Laboulaye," in *French Liberalism: from Montesquieu to the Present*

Day, ed. Raf Geenens and Helena Rosenblatt. Cambridge University Press, 2012, 115–33.

Rothbard, Murray. *For a New Liberty: The Libertarian Manifesto*. Auburn, AL: Ludwig von Mises Institute, 2006.

Rousseau, Jean-Jacques. "Discourse on Political Economy," in *The Social Contract and Discourses*, trans. with an Introduction by G. D. H. Cole. London: J. M. Dent, 1973.

On the Social Contract. Indianapolis: Hackett Publishing, 1987.

Ruddick, Sara. *Maternal Thinking: Toward a Politics of Peace*. Boston: Beacon Press, 1989.

Ryan, Alan. "Liberalism," in Ryan, *The Making of Modern Liberalism*. Princeton University Press, 2012, 21–44.

The Making of Modern Liberalism. Princeton University Press, 2012.

Sabine, G. H. *A History of Political Theory*. New York: Henry Holt, 1937.

Sandel, Michael. *Liberalism and the Limits of Justice*. Cambridge University Press, 1982.

Sandel, Michael. *Democracy's Discontent: America in Search of a Public Philosophy*. Cambridge, MA: Belknap Press, 1998.

Scalet, Steve. "Legitimacy, Confrontation, Respect, and the Bind of Freestanding Liberalism," *Journal of Social Philosophy* 41, 1 (2010): 92–111.

Scanlon, Thomas. *What We Owe to Each Other*. Cambridge, MA: Harvard University Press, 1998.

Schachar, Ayalet. *Multicultural Jurisdictions*. Cambridge University Press, 2001.

Schaeffer, Denise. "Feminism and Liberalism Reconsidered: The Case of Catharine Mackinnon," *American Political Science Review* 95, 3 (2001): 699–708.

Scheffler, Samuel. "What Is Egalitarianism?" *Philosophy and Public Affairs* 31 (2003): 5–39.

Schlesinger, Jr., Arthur M. *Orestes A. Brownson: A Pilgrim's Progress*. Boston: Little, Brown, 1939.

Schumpeter, Joseph A. *Capitalism, Socialism and Democracy*. New York: Harper Brothers, 1942.

Scruton, Roger. *The Meaning of Conservatism*. London: Macmillan, 1980.

Sen, Amartya. "Equality of What?" repr. in Sen, *Choice, Welfare, and Measurement*. Cambridge, MA: MIT Press, 1982, 353–70.

The Idea of Justice. Cambridge, MA: Harvard University Press, 2009.

Identity and Violence. New York: Norton, 2006.

Inequality Reexamined. Cambridge, MA: Harvard University Press, 1992.

Shalpole, Robert. "Toward a Republican Synthesis: The Emergence of an Understanding of Republicanism in American Historiography," *William and Mary Quarterly* 29, 3 (1972): 49–80.

Shanley, Mary Lyndon. *Feminism, Marriage, and the Law in Victorian England, 1850–1895*. Princeton University Press, 1993.

"Marital Slavery and Friendship: John Stuart Mill's *The Subjection of Women*," in *Feminist Interpretations and Political Theory*, ed. Mary Lyndon Shanley and Carole Pateman. University Park: Pennsylvania State University Press, 1991, 164–80.

Sher, George. *Beyond Neutrality: Perfectionism and Politics*. Cambridge University Press, 1997.

Shklar, Judith. *American Citizenship: The Quest for Inclusion*. Cambridge, MA: Harvard University Press, 1991.

Redeeming American Political Thought, ed. Stanley Hoffmann and Dennis Thompson. University of Chicago Press, 1998.

Sidney, Algernon. *Discourses Concerning Government*, ed. Thomas G. West. Indianapolis: Liberty Fund, 1996.

Simmons, A. John. *Justification and Legitimacy: Essays on Rights and Obligations*. Princeton University Press, 2001.

The Lockean Theory of Rights. Princeton University Press, 1992.

Moral Principles and Political Obligations. Princeton University Press, 1981.

On the Edge of Anarchy: Locke, Consent, and the Limits of Society. Princeton University Press, 1993.

Simmons, A. John and Wellman, Christopher. *Is There a Duty to Obey the Law? (For and Against)*. Cambridge University Press, 2005.

Sinopoli, Richard. *The Foundations of American Citizenship*. New York: Oxford University Press, 1992.

Skinner, Quentin. *Hobbes and Republican Liberty*. Cambridge University Press, 2008.

Liberty Before Liberalism. Cambridge University Press, 1998.

"The Paradoxes of Political Liberty," repr. in *Liberty*, ed. David Miller. Oxford University Press, 1991, 243–54.

Skorupski, John. *The Domain of Reasons*. Oxford University Press, 2010.

"Ethics and the Social Good," in *The Cambridge History of Philosophy in the Nineteenth Century (1790–1870)*, ed. Allen W. Wood and Songsuk Susan Hahn. Cambridge University Press, 2012, 434–68.

"The Liberal Critique of Democracy," in *The Idea of Political Meritocracy*, ed. Daniel Bell and Li Chenyang. Cambridge University Press, 2013, 116–37.

"Liberal Elitism," in Skorupski, *Ethical Explorations*. Oxford University Press, 1999, 193–212.

Smith, Adam. *An Inquiry into the Nature and Causes of the Wealth of Nations*. Indianapolis: Liberty Fund, 1981.

Lectures on Jurisprudence. Indianapolis: Liberty Fund, 1982.

The Theory of Moral Sentiments. Indianapolis: Liberty Fund, 1982.

Smith, James K. A. "Determined Violence: Derrida's Structural Religion," *The Journal of Religion* 78, 2 (1998): 197–212.

Smith, Rogers M. *Civic Ideals: Conflicting Visions of Citizenship in U.S. History.* New Haven: Yale University Press, 1997.

"'One United People': Second-Class Female Citizenship and the American Quest for Community," *Yale Journal of Law and Humanities* 1 (1989): 229–93.

Sobel, David. "Backing Away from Libertarian Self-Ownership," *Ethics* 123, 1 (2012): 32–60.

Solum, Lawrence. "Constructing an Ideal of Public Reason," *San Diego Law Review* 30 (Fall 1993): 729–62.

Southwood, Nicholas. *Contractualism and the Foundations of Morality.* Oxford University Press, 2010.

Spinner-Halev, Jeff. *Surviving Diversity: Religion and Democratic Citizenship.* Baltimore: The Johns Hopkins Press, 2000.

Stark, Cynthia A. "Contractarianism and Cooperation," *Politics, Philosophy & Economics* 8, 1 (2009): 73–99.

"How to Include the Severely Disabled in a Contractarian Theory of Justice," *Journal of Political Philosophy* 15, 2 (2007): 127–45.

Storing, Herbert J. *What the Anti-Federalists Were For.* University of Chicago Press, 1981.

Sunstein, Cass. "Beyond the Republican Revival," *Yale Law Journal* 97 (1988): 1539–90.

Swedberg, Richard. *Tocqueville's Political Economy.* Princeton University Press, 2009.

Tamir, Yael. *Liberal Nationalism.* Princeton University Press, 1993.

Tan, Kok-Chor. *Toleration, Diversity, and Global Justice.* University Park: Pennsylvania State University Press, 2000.

Taylor, Barbara. *Mary Wollstonecraft and the Feminist Imagination.* Cambridge University Press, 2003.

Taylor, Charles. "Cross-Purposes: The Liberal Communitarian Debate," in *Liberalism and the Moral Life*, ed. N. Rosenblum. Cambridge, MA: Harvard University Press, 1989, 159–82.

Multiculturalism and the Politics of Recognition. Princeton University Press, 1992.

Sources of the Self. Princeton University Press, 1990.

Temkin, Larry. "Equality, Priority and the Leveling Down Objection," in *The Ideal of Equality*, ed. Matthew Clayton and Andrew Williams. New York: Macmillan and St. Martin's Press, 2000, 126–61.

Inequality. Oxford University Press, 1993.

Thaler, Richard and Sunstein, Cass. *Nudge: Improving Decisions about Health, Wealth and Happiness.* New York: Penguin Books, 2008.

The Federalist Papers, ed. Clinton Rossiter. New York: Mentor, 1961.

Thornton, Merle. "Sex Equality Is not Enough for Feminism," in *Feminist Challenges: Social and Political Theory*, ed. Carole Pateman and Elizabeth Gross. Boston: Northeastern University Press, 1986, 77–98.

Thrasher, John and Vallier, Kevin. "The Fragility of Consensus: Public Reason, Diversity, and Stability," *The European Journal of Philosophy*, forthcoming.

Thucydides. *History of the Peloponnesian War*, trans. Rex Warner. New York: Penguin Classics, 1964.

Tierney, Brian. *The Crisis of Church and State: 1050–1300*. Englewood Cliffs, NJ: Prentice Hall, 1964.

Tocqueville, Alexis de. *Alexis de Tocqueville: Letters from America*, ed. and trans. Frederic Brown. New Haven: Yale University Press, 2010.

Democracy in America, ed. J. P. Mayer. New York: Harper Perennial, 1969.

Democracy in America, trans. Henry Reeve, vol. 1. New York: Vintage Books, 1990.

Tomasi, John. "Democratic Legitimacy and Economic Liberty," *Social Philosophy and Policy* 29, 1 (2012): 50–80.

Free Market Fairness. Princeton University Press, 2012.

"Reply to Freeman: Thick Economic Liberty" (http://bleedingheartlibertarians. com/2012/06/reply-to-samuel-freeman/).

Tomasi, John and Brennan, Jason. "Classical Liberalism," in *The Oxford Handbook of Political Philosophy*, ed. David M. Estlund. Oxford University Press, 2012, 115–32.

Tronto, J. *Moral Boundaries: A Political Argument for an Ethic of Care*. New York: Routledge, 1993.

Turgot, Anne-Robert-Jacques. "In Praise of Gournay," in *Commerce, Culture and Liberty: Readings on Capitalism Before Adam Smith*, ed. Henry C. Clark. Indianapolis: Liberty Fund, 2003.

Turner, Piers and Gaus, Gerald (eds.). *The History of Public Reason in Political Philosophy*. New York: Routledge, forthcoming.

Unknown Author, *Discours sur la Permission de Liberté de Religion, Dicte Religions-Vrede au Pais-Bais* (1559), translation taken from *Texts Concerning the Revolt of the Netherlands*, ed. E. H. Krossman and A. F. Mellink. Cambridge University Press, 1974.

Vallentyne, Peter. "Libertarianism," in *The Stanford Encyclopedia of Philosophy*, Spring 2012 edn., ed. Edward N. Zalta (http://plato.stanford.edu/archives/spr2012/entries/libertarianism/).

Vallier, Kevin. *Beyond Separation: Uniting Liberal Politics and Public Faith*. New York: Routledge, 2014.

"Consensus and Convergence in Public Reason," *Public Affairs Quarterly* 25, 4 (2011): 261–79.

Vanderschraaf, Peter. "Justice as Mutual Advantage and the Vulnerable," *Politics, Philosophy & Economics* 10, 2 (2011), 119–47.

Varouxakis, G. *Mill on Nationality*. London: Routledge, 2002.

Velleman, J. David. *How We Get Along*. Cambridge University Press, 2009.

Vetterli, Richard and Bryner, Gary. *In Search of the Republic: Public Virtue and the Roots of American Government*. Totowa, NJ: Rowman & Littlefield, 1987.

Viroli, Maurizio. *Republicanism*, trans. Antony Shugaar. New York: Hill and Wang, 2002.

Voltaire, *Treatise on Tolerance and Other Writings*, ed. Simon Harvey. Cambridge University Press, 2000.

von Humboldt, Wilhelm. *The Limits of State Action*. Indianapolis: Liberty Fund, 1993.

von Platz, Jeppe. "Absolute Freedom of Contract: Grotian Lessons for Libertarians," *Critical Review* 25, 1 (2013): 107–10.

"Are Economic Liberties Basic Rights?" *Politics, Philosophy, and Economics.* Forthcoming.

Waldron, Jeremy. *God, Locke and Equality: Christian Foundations of Locke's Political Thought*. Cambridge University Press, 2002.

"John Locke: Social Contract versus Political Anthropology," in *The Social Contract From Hobbes to Rawls*, ed. D. Boucher and P. Kelly. London: Routledge, 1994, 51–72.

Law and Disagreement. Oxford University Press, 1999.

"Theoretical Foundations of Liberalism," *Philosophical Quarterly* 37, 147 (1987): 127–50. Repr. in Jeremy Waldron, *Liberal Rights: Collected Papers 1981–1991*. Cambridge University Press, 1993, 35–62.

Wall, Steven. "Democracy and Equality," *Philosophical Quarterly* 57 (2007): 416–38.

Liberalism, Perfectionism and Restraint. Cambridge University Press, 1998.

"Perfectionism in Politics: A Defense," in *Contemporary Debates in Political Philosophy*, ed. Thomas Christiano and John Christman. Oxford: Blackwell, 2009, 99–118.

"Perfectionism, Reasonableness and Respect," *Political Theory* 42 (2014): 468–89.

Wall, Steven and Klosko, George (eds.). *Perfectionism and Neutrality: Essays in Liberal Theory*. Lanham, MD: Rowman & Littlefield, 2003.

Walzer, Michael. *Spheres of Justice: A Defense of Pluralism and Equality*. New York: Basic Books, 1983.

Ward, Nathaniel. "The Massachusetts Body of Liberties, December 1641," in *Colonial Origins of the American Constitution: A*

Documentary History, ed. Donald S. Lutz. Indianapolis: Liberty Fund, 1998, 71–87.

The Simple Cobbler of Aggawam [1646], in *The Puritans in America*, ed. Alan Heimert and Andrew Delbanco. Cambridge, MA: Harvard University Press, 1985, 179–84.

Wapshott, Nicholas. *Keynes Hayek: The Clash That Defined Modern Economics*. New York: Norton, 2011.

Weber, Max. *The Protestant Ethic and the Spirit of Capitalism*. London: Routledge, 2001.

Weinstock, Daniel. "Immigration and Reciprocity," in *Nationalism and Multiculturalism in a World of Immigration*, ed. Nils Holtug, Kasper Lipper-Rasmussen, and Sune Laegaard. London: Palgrave Macmillan, 2009, 174–93.

"Le paradoxe du multiculturalisme libéral," in S. Guérard de la Tour (dir.), *Perspectives sur le multiculturalisme*. Paris: l'Harmattan, 2012.

"Value Pluralism, Toleration, and Autonomy," in *Nomos XLIX: Moral Universalism and Pluralism*, ed. Henry S. Richardson and Melissa S. Williams. New York University Press, 2009, 125–48.

Weithman, Paul. *Why Political Liberalism?* New York: Oxford University Press, 2010.

Welch, Cheryl. *Liberty and Utility: The French Idéologues and the Transformation of Liberalism*. New York: Columbia University Press, 1984.

Wenar, Leif. "Political Liberalism: An Internal Critique," *Ethics* 106 (1995): 32–62.

West, Robin. "Jurisprudence and Gender," *University of Chicago Law Review* 55, 1 (1988): 1–72.

White, Morton. *The Philosophy of the American Revolution*. New York: Oxford University Press, 1981.

Williams, Bernard. *Truth and Truthfulness*. Princeton University Press, 2002.

Williams, Rowan. *Dostoevsky: Language, Faith, and Fiction*. Waco, TX: Baylor University Press, 2000.

Winch, Donald. *Adam Smith's Politics*. Cambridge University Press, 1978.

Riches and Poverty: An Intellectual History of Political Economy in Britain, 1750–1834. Cambridge University Press, 1996.

Wealth and Life: Essays on the Intellectual History of Political Economy in Britain, 1848–1914. Cambridge University Press, 2009.

Winthrop, John. *Puritan Political Ideas*, ed. Edmund S. Morgan. Indianapolis: Bobbs-Merrill, 1965.

Wise, John. "A Vindication of New England Churches" [1717], in *Classics of American Political and Constitutional Thought*, vol. 1, *Origins Through* the Civil War, ed. Scott J. Hammond. Indianapolis: Hackett Publishing, 2007, 80–84.

Wollstonecraft, Mary. A Vindication of the Rights of Men and a Vindication of the Rights of Women, ed. Sylvana Tomaselli. Cambridge University Press, 1995.

A Vindication of the Rights of Woman. New York: Penguin, 2012.

Wood, Gordon. The Creation of the American Republic, 1776–1787. Chapel Hill: University of North Carolina Press, 1969.

The Radicalism of the American Revolution. New York: Vintage Books, 1993.

Wootton, David. Divine Right and Democracy: An Anthology of Political Writing in Stuart England. New York: Penguin Books, 1986.

Young, Iris Marion. Justice and the Politics of Difference. Princeton University Press, 1990.

"Structural Injustice and the Politics of Difference," in Multiculturalism and Political Theory, ed. A. Laden. Cambridge University Press, 2007, 60–88.

"Throwing Like a Girl," in Young, Throwing Like a Girl and Other Essays in Feminist Philosophy and Social Theory. Bloomington: Indiana University Press, 1990, 27–45.

Young, James P. Reconsidering American Liberalism. Boulder, CO: Westview Press, 1996.

Zerilli, Linda M. G. Feminism and the Abyss of Freedom. University of Chicago Press, 2005.

Signifying Woman: Culture and Chaos in Rousseau, Burke, and Mill. Ithaca, NY: Cornell University Press, 1994.

"Value Pluralism and the Problem of Judgment: Farewell to Public Reason," Political Theory 40, 1 (2012): 6–31.

Zuckert, Michael P. Natural Rights and the New Republicanism. Princeton University Press, 1994.

The Natural Rights Republic: Studies in the Foundation of the American Tradition. Notre Dame: University of Notre Dame Press, 1999.

Zwolinski, Matt. "Libertarianism," in The Internet Encyclopedia of Philosophy (www.iep.utm.edu/libertar/).

INDEX

Ackerman, Bruce, 395
Acton, H. B., 80
  on Mill, 339–40
Acton, Lord John, 338
Adams, John, 25, 27
Adichie, Chimamanda Ngozi, 148
agreement, 89–90
  by exclusion, 101–5
  fairness and justice, 90–93
  mutual advantage, 93–96
alienation, 149–50
American Civil War, 35–36
American liberalism, 21–22. *See also* United States
  Civil War and, 35–36
  core premises, 23
  diversity, 22–23
  freedom in, 27–28
  pre-revolutionary, 26–28
  racial, gender, and ethnic aspects, 33–35
  Revolution to Union, 29–33
American Revolution, 29, 389–90
Amery, Leo, 65
anarchism, 277
Appleby, Joyce, 28
Aquinas, Thomas, 42
Arendt, Hannah, 373
aristocracy, 218
Aristotelian Principle, 124, 370
armed forces, 31
atheism, 119
autonomy, 141–42. *See also* freedom; liberty
  children, 216–17
  comprehensive doctrine liberalism, 202–4
  conservative critique, 414–15, 418–19
  culture and, 152–55
  democratic institutions and, 156–58
    legitimacy, 157–58
  economic libertarianism and, 268
  equality and, 215

exit rights, 323–24
individuality and, 145–46
Kant on, 407
motives and, 146–47
necessity of, 216
personal
  comprehensive doctrine liberalism
    and, 191–92
  importance, 202
  state toleration and, 194
political, 164–69
  as non-domination, 387–88, 390–92
  aspirational values, 179–80
  authorization, 165
  collective authorization
    condition, 167
  constitutional vs. comprehensive, 168
  democracy and, 178
  desirability, 169–71, 181
  hypotheticalist view, 165–66
  justice and, 170
  modest vs. robust, 169
  moral requirements, 178–80
  normative status, 177–80
  participation condition, 167, 168–69
  pluralism and, 171–74
  public knowledge requirement, 177
  Rousseau on, 164–65, 178–80
  state toleration and, 196–97
  transmission, 169, 182
  weak vs. strong, 173–74, 181–82
protean concept, 145–52
religious, 156
resistance to, 142–45
right to exit, 152, 317–18
self-acceptance and, 148–49
self-control, 153
self-reflection and, 146–48
value invariance and, 150
autonomy liberalism, 319–20

Barry, Brian, 11
Bastiat, Frédéric, 48–49

451

Lightning Source UK Ltd.
Milton Keynes UK
UKHW020441060219
336813UK00020B/450/P